THE NIGHT IS YOUNG:
SEXUALITY IN MEXICO
IN THE TIME OF AIDS

Héctor Carrillo

THE UNIVERSITY OF CHICAGO PRESS
CHICAGO AND LONDON

Héctor Carrillo is a researcher at the Center for AIDS Prevention Studies, University of California, San Francisco, and the Center for Community Research of the Institute on Sexuality, Inequality, and Health at San Francisco State University.

The University of Chicago Press, Chicago 60637
The University of Chicago Press, Ltd., London
© 2002 by Héctor Carrillo
All rights reserved. Published 2002
Printed in the United States of America
11 10 09 08 07 06 05 04 03 02   5 4 3 2 1

ISBN (cloth): 0-226-09302-6
ISBN (paper): 0-226-09303-4

Library of Congress Cataloging-in-Publication Data

Carrillo, Héctor
    The night is young : sexuality in Mexico in the time of AIDS / Héctor Carrillo.

    p.   cm.— (Worlds of desire)
    Includes bibliographical references (p.   ) and index.
    ISBN 0-226-09303-6 (cloth)—ISBN 0-226-09303-4 (pbk.)
    1. Sex—Mexico—Guadalajara—Case studies. 2. Homosexuality—Mexico—
Guadalajara—Case studies.   3. AIDS (Disease)—Mexico—Guadalajara—Case
studies.   4. AIDS (Disease)—Mexico—Guadalajara—Prevention—Case studies.
    I. Title. II. Series.
    HQ18.M4 C37   2002
    306.7′0972′35—dc21

                                                    2001005010

The Night Is Young

WORLDS OF DESIRE:
THE CHICAGO SERIES ON SEXUALITY, GENDER, AND CULTURE
EDITED BY GILBERT HERDT

TO MY PARENTS AND SISTERS   TO STEVE

Contents

Preface

I arrived in Guadalajara in September 1993 to conduct research on sexuality and HIV prevention. My plan was to
study the connections between the social and cultural environment and decisions that Mexicans made about their
sexuality and sexual behavior. These topics seemed crucial because of the spreading HIV epidemic in Mexico.

I was returning to Mexico after many years of graduate
education and HIV prevention work in the United States.
I was being transplanted back into the soil of my own
roots and was leaving a social environment in California
that had very different rules of interaction—rules to which
I was now adapted. My situation was somewhat uncommon for the type of ethnographic research that I was about
to initiate, as I was both an insider and an outsider. I had
lived in Mexico long enough to understand the internal
logic driving Mexican society, the inner workings of local
social relations, including rules about the management of
sex and sexuality. Having grown up in Mexico City, where
I lived until my early adulthood, I had indeed been socialized into sexuality in Mexico. Yet, I was also an outsider,
as I now saw Mexico from a certain distance, particularly
with respect to the many changes that had taken place in
my eight-year absence.

As my interactions with Guadalajarans began to develop, people were somewhat confused by me, because they saw me as Mexican but also as coming from the United States. One of the areas in which my difference manifested itself was in my attitudes toward hanging out with people, especially at night, during the time of leisure and play. In San Francisco, I had become accustomed to not staying up past a certain hour of the night (my limit was usually midnight). I was also very used to what I had found to be a widespread attitude in the United States: a thorough respect for individualism and assertiveness. Even if my friends planned to stay up late, I had never experienced any pressure to keep going and join them in their reveling. Once I uttered the words "I'm going home," I was always free to do so, no questions asked.

Guadalajarans were quick to remind me that this strategy did not work in Mexico. Evening gatherings often took place with the assumption that participants should be willing to stay up and spend time together until the *altas horas de la noche,* the wee hours of the night. People thought me strange when I expressed my wish to go home at midnight. They thought me even stranger when I did, even after everyone present had pressured me to stay with them and continue partying. "The *gringo* in you is out," they said. "*La noche es joven* [the night is young]," they added, as compelling evidence of the absurdity of my decision. I soon understood that this phrase was shorthand for the expression of relevant cultural expectations.

The phrase *la noche es joven* helped establish the delimitation between the worlds of day and night. The night was constructed as the time of play and socialization, and thus the time of things sexual. It was a space of life quite distinct from the time of day. The rules were different, and there was an explicit acceptance of transgression of daytime rules and of exploration of the veiled prohibitions exerted in "normal," everyday life. The night was the time when sexuality made its full appearance, taking center stage and permeating all the interstices of social interaction, regardless of whether those interactions led to actual physical acts of sex. *La noche es joven* symbolized a separation between the space of everyday life and the space of sex. This is not to say that sexuality was absent from daytime life but only that at night it was allowed to be dominant and unapologetic. The association of sex and sexuality with darkness and night was symbolic of sex's transgressive nature.

The phrase *la noche es joven* expressed as well a strong expectation of participation in the collective project of nighttime play. Collectivity and participation were important ingredients to achieving a sense of belonging. And belonging was important. My wanting to retire early was interpreted, not as a desire to rest, but instead as a rejection of belonging and a tragic preference for isolation. "I want to rest" was never a good justification for leaving. People who did leave had to have a better reason: a horrible headache, sickness in the family, an important family gathering the next morning.

Needless to say, after a few weeks I had already begun to push my own limits. What started as midnight, was soon one, two, and three in the morning. I was motivated by the growing sense of comfort with the social networks that I was accessing, and the promises of belonging. Soon enough, such promises materialized. I knew I had been fully accepted the morning that I arrived home at six, in broad daylight, the birds singing, after a long night that had never stopped being young to the revelers. One of my neighbors, a woman in her late fifties, was already sweeping her sidewalk. With a noncommittal smile she said, *"Buenos días."* I knew that she knew that I had been out all night. But her greeting held no judgment.

As I walked up the four flights of stairs that led me to my apartment, to a morning of sleep, I remembered a story that my father had related to me many years earlier. When he and his brothers, the boys in the family, partied all night, they would stop at the market on the way home and buy breakfast foods. Their father would be awake and drinking coffee when they walked into their house through the kitchen door. "We got up early to buy breakfast, *Papá,*" they would tell him. My grandfather would look at their party suits, smile, and suggest that their walk to the market might have made them tired. This left the door wide open for them to justify going to bed. Although the family was well aware of what had really happened, they also understood that these were young men exploring their maleness and their sexuality, and appreciated their effort to cover their tracks and defer to the more respectable and explicit rules of family life. The breakfast foods seemed to be a symbolic transition from the world of the night to the world of the day—the ticket that guaranteed undamaged return. My grandfather's silent complicity was his way of telling them that "he had been there" and that it was okay for them to bend the rules so long as they made every effort to appear not to be doing so. I am sure his response would have been very different had the person returning after a night of partying been one of my aunts.

I begin with these anecdotes because I feel that they capture the book's overall essence. They provide an initial flavor of the place that sex and sexuality occupy in Mexicans' lives, as well as of how Mexicans manage and negotiate their sexual lives. From a different perspective, this book is nothing more than one glimpse of an aspect of life in Mexico that is not only very complex but also not well studied or empirically understood. I believe the metaphor also works in this regard: when it comes to the academic study of sexuality in Mexico, the night is also still young.

ACKNOWLEDGMENTS

First and foremost, I wish to thank the men and women in Mexico who participated in interviews and discussion groups, or who engaged with me in informal conversations about sex and sexuality. Without their participation, this book would not have been possible. I have made every effort to represent their personal stories fairly and accurately.

I am grateful to Carol D'Onofrio, my dissertation adviser at the University of California at Berkeley, for supervising the dissertation that led me to write this book. My thanks go, as well, to the other members of my dissertation committee: Denise Herd, Barbara Marin, and Kurt Organista. All of them gave me useful suggestions for planning and implementing the study in Guadalajara and provided thoughtful comments and observations. I also thank the faculty, staff, and students at the TAPS Postdoctoral Program, Center for AIDS Prevention Studies, University of California, San Francisco, for reading and discussing my manuscript: Dan Ciccarone, Katherine Fritz, Sonya Grant Arreola, Greg Greenwood, Rochelle Hartwig, Malcolm John, Susan Kegeles, Pam Ling, Janice Louie, Paula Lum, Dennis Osmond, Karen Seal, Sohini Sengupta, Pilgrim Spikes, Ron Stall, and Phyllis Tien. Those discussions helped me clarify my ideas and rethink some of my arguments.

For reading portions of the manuscript, or for stimulating my thinking in conversations about topics related to this work, I would like to thank Enrique Asís, Carlos Cáceres, Rafael Díaz, Richard Elovich, Kathleen Erwin, Gilbert Herdt, David Kirp, André Maiorana, Jesús Ramírez, Jorge Sánchez, Ruth Schwartz, Andrea Williams, and Dan Wohlfeiler. I also benefited greatly from comments by two outside reviewers chosen by the University of Chicago Press: Stephen O. Murray and Richard Parker. Both provided detailed suggestions that were extremely helpful in my final revisions of the manuscript. Finally, I am particularly indebted to Steven Epstein for investing so much time in reading drafts, pushing me to sharpen my analysis, providing suggestions for revisions, and sensitively helping me improve my writing skills in the English language. His efforts significantly enhanced the quality of this volume.

Doug Mitchell, my editor at the University of Chicago Press, took an interest in my manuscript at an early stage. His unflagging enthusiasm and commitment, expressed whenever and wherever in the world we happened to meet in the past few years, have been crucial to the successful completion of this project. I am also grateful to Pamela J. Bruton for her skillful work in copyediting the manuscript.

Many people along the way provided practical and logistical support. Lucía Avila and Miriam Canales opened their doors to me upon arrival in Guadalajara and oriented me in the practicalities of everyday life there. Rodolfo Ruíz, Patricia Campos, Juana Martínez, Aída de Luna, Francisco Alvarez, Alicia Yolanda Reyes, and Pedro Avalos gave me access to local AIDS organizations. Along with their volunteers, these HIV activists and educators allowed me to observe Guadalajaran HIV prevention work in action. Angeles Chapa conducted some interviews. Lucía Avila transcribed interview material. Naomi Porat, Dale Dombkowski, and Jeff Kilmer housed me when I traveled to the Bay Area to meet with my faculty and to conduct library research. Upon my return from Mexico, Dan Wohlfeiler, my colleague and supervisor at the STOP AIDS Project in San Francisco, helped me carve out time to begin writing this manuscript, and Andrea Scott-Greer, also at STOP AIDS, provided administrative assistance and offered many words of encouragement. I am grateful to all of these individuals.

The dissertation upon which this book is based was made possible by fellowships provided by The Inter-American Foundation, The Organization of American States, and the University of California MEXUS program. The writing of the book manuscript was conducted in part under the auspices of the TAPS Postdoctoral Program at the Center for AIDS Prevention Studies, University of California, San Francisco, with funding from the National Institutes of Health.

My deepest gratitude goes to my parents, who made a great personal sacrifice to educate me and who gave me the support that started me on this path, and to my partner, Steve, for being a source of happiness and a life force that sustains me.

Introduction

When I stepped out of the elevator in a downtown building in Guadalajara, Mexico, I found myself facing several fancy offices separated by glass walls. A few employees, returning to work after their midday lunch break, hurriedly walked by me. I was there to interview Antonio,* a young man whom I had met some days before through a common friend.

Antonio arrived more than twenty minutes later, motioning as he stepped out of the elevator as he apologized for his delay. He was dressed in formal office attire, wearing a suit and tie, and looked very different from the first time I had seen him, in jeans and T-shirt, a few days before. That time, a friend had introduced us when we stopped at Antonio's apartment to pick up some gay magazines that my friend was storing there (out of fear his parents would find them if he left them in his room). Antonio had spontaneously asked us to stay for a while and, before we could even respond, had proceeded to offer us *tequilas*[1] and to tell us about his dealings with an estranged male lover who had

---

*In order to protect identities, the names of those who participated in informal conversations, formal interviews, or discussion groups are pseudonyms. Identifying details about each interview participant can be found in appendix 1, "Descriptions of Interview Participants."

recently left him. In fact, the ease with which he involved me, a total stranger, in a conversation about very intimate matters had led me to ask him to participate in an interview. After thinking about it for a moment, he had accepted and requested that I come by his office.

As I pulled out my tape recorder, Antonio offered me coffee and called his secretary through the intercom while making eye contact with her through the glass. He treated her cordially but not without using certain inflections in his voice and selecting words that showed that he was a male boss talking to a female secretary. After the coffee arrived, and past the formality of the first few minutes, we began talking.

Antonio, much like other participants in my study, engaged with me in an in-depth discussion about his sexual life. We talked about his sexual identity, how he had learned about sex, his definition of sex and pleasure, his sexual experiences, and also specific sexual encounters—encounters during which he often had to consider how to avoid the risk of HIV (human immunodeficiency virus) infection.

It soon became apparent that interpreting Antonio's sexual life and sexual identity, as for many other participants in my study, was not a straightforward or simple task. Seated in his office and interacting with his female secretary, Antonio easily could have been taken to be a heterosexual, highly educated, middle-class, young, male Mexican executive. Instead, at the age of twenty-five, he openly identified as *gay* and chose this Spanish word to describe his sexual orientation. As part of this identity as *gay,* Antonio saw himself as a masculine and assertive man who was attractive to both men and women. He liked to seduce male coworkers whom he regarded as being heterosexual. Contrary to what might be expected, he was the one who anally penetrated them. He also emphasized having a strong and central role in his fatherless family and spoke of his ability to tell his mother and siblings bluntly about his homosexuality without any negative consequences.

Antonio had learned about sex when he was anally penetrated as a child, on separate occasions, by three of his eight older brothers. None of his brothers, however, had assumed a homosexual identity, and in fact, when he was sixteen, they had "baptized" him by taking him to have sex with a female prostitute. Other than this type of sexual socialization, he had not had access to any formal sex education.

But, despite the lack of sex education, Antonio had developed well-defined ideas about what he accepted and rejected regarding sex and sexual diversity. Besides regarding homosexuality to be normal, he supported the use of contraceptives, strongly opposed abortion, tolerated prostitution, saw adult masturbation as a sexual option, judged sexual promiscuity negatively, and felt that women should be supported if they decided to be single mothers or to get divorced. He thought of himself, ideologically speaking, as "moderate" and explained that some of his ideas were liberal, but his lifestyle and actions were very conservative and traditional. "Besides, I like Mexican tradition," he added. Antonio was well aware of a contrast between traditional Mexican ideas about sex and "newer" ideas that were being adopted, including his own ideas about homosexuality and gay identities.

At the time of the interview, Antonio was infatuated with a lover. In describing this relationship, he greatly emphasized the role of love and passion and how they contributed to a spontaneous flow in his sexual relations that he strongly valued. Although he was aware of his partner's potentially high previous risk for HIV infection, he had allowed his partner to take the insertive role during anal sex without condoms. Aware of his own previous risk, Antonio had taken an HIV test as a form of protection for his new partner, but the lover had not been willing to do the same out of fear of possibly obtaining a positive result. Antonio did not let other sexual partners penetrate him, including the heterosexual men whom he seduced, and saw this action, and his acceptance of potential risk for HIV infection, as the price he had to pay in the name of love and trust. Despite his being well informed about HIV transmission and motivated to be safe, and having a strong sense of power and control during sex, Antonio had not been capable of making the need for love compatible with the goal of HIV prevention. Like others in my study, he had experienced considerable dissonance between the methods that he learned regarding the negotiation of safe sex and the kind of sex that he favored in the context of a developing love relationship.

This account of Antonio's interview for my study encapsulates many of the specific topics of this book. The book is a study of the reciprocal relationship between Mexican sexual culture—the norms, values, and ideas about sex and sexuality[2] that prevail in Mexico—and Mexicans' individual sexual identities, desires, ideology, and behavior. My goal is to elucidate how individual sexual lives are affected by local sexual culture and in turn how this sexual culture is constructed as a result of the collective enactment of sexual behavior—including behaviors that involve HIV risk—and of debate regarding opposing ideas and values about sex and sexuality.

When I first set out to do the research upon which this book is based, my original motivation was to seek answers to questions about how to design public health interventions that would help reduce sexual HIV risk in Mexico. As in Antonio's account, there was anecdotal evidence that Mexicans were often not complying with the recommendations about communication, negotiation, and condom use that local HIV prevention messages promoted. I hypothesized that the reasons might be related to cultural factors. My initial interest was confined to a relatively narrow concern with finding ways to help individuals change their sexual behavior and adopt safety measures against HIV.

This interest has not changed, but it has become broader. I soon realized that the task was more complicated than I had originally envisioned, because Mexican HIV prevention work was itself inscribed in the larger history of contemporary Mexican sexuality. It constituted an important social force that, along with other equally important factors, was shaping the last phase of the history of sexuality in Mexico during the twentieth century. This history was characterized by rapid social change associated with modernization and globalization but also by strong resistance to change, in particular among those who saw these forces as a threat to Mexican traditions and culture. The study of HIV prevention, and of contemporary sex and sexuality in Mexico, *had* to be located within these larger debates about modernization and cultural change. The feasibility of the individual behavioral changes that HIV prevention educators advocated could not be adequately assessed without paying attention to the meanings attached to sexuality in the context of social change and modernization. As a result, analyzing the nature and mechanisms of social and cultural change associated with Mexican contemporary sexualities became a significant focus of my research.

This realization led to several sets of questions. At the broadest level, I consider questions about the historical evolution of sex and sexuality in Mexico and what the emergence of AIDS (acquired immunodeficiency syndrome) and HIV prevention have meant for this history, particularly in terms of the formation of sexual identities. I examine how ideas about sexuality were shaped in Mexico during the twentieth century and how their evolution relates to larger processes of modernization. What do Mexicans mean when they talk about traditional values, and how have these values changed as the country modernized? Do stereotypes that depict Mexico as a Catholic, conservative, and traditional country reflect the reality of people's lives? If not, how are Mexicans reinterpreting their sexual identities, desires, and behaviors to fit in a more contemporary Mexican world? I succinctly analyze this history in chapter 1, up to the arrival of AIDS in Mexico in the early 1980s. I then take up the subject again in chapter 9, in a discussion of the influence of the social responses to AIDS on the local history of sex and sexuality.

My specific goal in addressing these questions is to understand what cultural resources are available to Mexicans as they conduct individual and collective interpretations of their sexual desires, as well as make decisions about what kinds of sex they practice and with whom. A secondary goal is to analyze how modernization and globalization have affected views about sex and sexuality in Mexico and how Mexicans have gone about integrating new ideas into their repertoire of tools for interpretation. With these purposes in mind, I analyze in Part 1 the specifics of Guadalajarans'[3] acquisition of sexual identities, which I use to contrast traditional ideas and practices with more contemporary ones, as well as to illustrate the simultaneous use of both. Antonio's acquisition of an identity as *gay,* for instance, involved interpretations that were uniquely Mexican, as he envisioned his role as a masculine man in ways that suggested a view of himself as a Mexican *gay macho.* His stance contradicted cultural expectations of his role in sexual relations with men whom he regarded as being heterosexual. His adoption of this *macho* identity was also evident in how he related to women—for instance, in his interactions with his secretary—and his way of talking about them. In adopting his sexual identity, he had integrated new ideas about gay identities with older ideas about machismo.

A second set of questions concerns sexual socialization and the mechanisms through which culturally bound ideas are presented to, and integrated into, people's own personal sexual ideology. I undertake the analysis of these topics in chapters 6 and 7, the first two chapters in part 2, where I examine how and what Mexicans learn about sex, the nature of their sources of information, and how individuals and groups manage conflicting ideas about sexual topics. I pay attention to how individuals make sense of their own desires and behaviors and interpret them so that they are consistent with learned cultural expectations. I discuss, as well, their acquisition of culturally bound strategies to deal with sexual difference and to communicate about sex and sexuality in social settings.

The processes through which individuals, such as Antonio, integrate their sexual socialization into their sexual ideologies as adults, as well as how such sexual socialization helps them manage their adult sexual lives, are central to this discussion. This analysis is informed by two theoretical concepts that are particularly relevant to the study as a whole. One is Gagnon and Simon's concept of "cultural scripts," which refers to the collective guides—the syntax and understandings of roles and performance—

presented to individuals by their cultural group and which individuals assimilate, reinterpret, and internalize (Gagnon and Simon 1973; Gagnon 1986; Simon and Gagnon 1986; Simon 1973, 1989, 1996). The second is that of "strategies" as developed by Bourdieu (1994). "Strategies" here refers to individuals' understandings of the "rules of the game" (of the cultural scripts) and of how to best participate in the "game" of social relations. Their participation involves not only their knowledge of what to do in specific situations but also their agency to help change the rules of the game in the process—an awareness that their actions contribute to the reinterpretation and modification of the cultural scripts.

Related as well to questions about sexual socialization are questions regarding perceptions about the nature of sex, which are the focus of chapter 8, the last chapter in part 2. In this chapter I focus on Mexicans' expectations about how sex should be conducted, how it should be initiated and by whom, when it is appropriate and when it becomes a source of shame, how communication of sexual desires is achieved before and during sex, and what indicators demonstrate the achievement of pleasure and mutual surrender. Antonio, for example, had clear expectations about what kinds of sex took place in situations when he was seducing a masculine, non–homosexually identified man, in which surrender and passion involved his ability to dominate and seduce. His expectations were slightly different when he pursued sex in the context of love. My exploration of this set of issues seeks to establish a bridge between the broader sexual culture and the enactment of specific sexual encounters, and by extension between sexual culture and required measures for effective HIV prevention.

My last set of questions, which I discuss in part 3, concerns not only how to make HIV prevention efforts more effective but also the role that the AIDS epidemic and HIV prevention programs played in shaping sex and sexuality in Mexico in the last two decades of the century. In relation to the effectiveness of HIV prevention—the most practical and immediate goal of my study—I am interested in how individuals make decisions about protection against HIV during specific sexual encounters. How are those decisions influenced by their individual expectations and in turn by cultural expectations? When are expectations about sex consistent with the goal of prevention and when do they contradict it? Finally, what would help individuals enact their sexual desires as they wish, fulfilling their personal and cultural expectations, while also minimizing their risk for HIV infection?

Seeking answers to these questions implies an analysis of the correspondence, and contradictions, between current HIV prevention messages in

Mexico and cultural expectations about identities, sexual partners, relationships, and sexual encounters. Antonio, for instance, felt that condom use was incompatible with his desire to abandon himself to the whims of passion in the context of his love relationship. Condom use in his current relationship would translate into a loss of trust. What he had learned about condoms and safe sex—the presumption of planning, negotiation, and rationality—left him little room to consider how to make the goals of love and passion compatible with the goals of health and safety.

This issue raises, in turn, questions about the role of HIV prevention work in changing the social organization and expression of sex and sexuality in Mexico—the rules of the game. The AIDS epidemic put squarely on the table a perceived need for individuals to talk more openly about sex. As a social force, HIV prevention programs became a new source of ideas and expectations about sex that has influenced the history of sexuality in Mexico since the mid-1980s. In part 3 I analyze how the global HIV prevention discourse—which is tightly associated with public health, medicine, and psychology—is shaping sexuality in Mexico, as well as the apparent incompatibilities between the premises of HIV prevention models and local expectations about sex. Using HIV prevention work as an example, I also discuss the role of the professions in advocating broader social and cultural changes in Mexican sexuality.

The book ends with a more general analysis of the nature of social and cultural changes in sex and sexuality in Mexico, which is contained in the conclusion. I summarize the different filters through which cultural changes in sexuality can be observed, the diversity of social actors involved, and their roles in promoting, or preventing, greater social equality regarding sexuality and gender relations. I also consider how cultural change is being integrated into, and affected by, decisions made by individual people about their identities, lifestyles, desires, and behaviors, including sexual behaviors that prevent the transmission of HIV.

THE APPROACH

As in my analysis of Antonio's interview, I have approached the study of sexuality in Guadalajara from a perspective shaped by qualitative social science, combining anthropological approaches to the study of culture and sociological understandings of the social construction of sexuality. My choice of this combination reflects my academic interest in conceptualizing social reality through the filters provided by the anthropological tradition of ethnography and the sociological tradition of interpretive understanding.

My theoretical persuasion is one that emphasizes, as a fundamental aspect of the analysis, the consideration of meanings that individuals and groups attach to specific actions and practices (Gagnon and Simon 1973; Geertz 1973; Simon 1973; Herdt 1981; Ortner and Whitehead 1981; McIntosh 1981; Plummer 1982; Chauncey 1982–83; Cass 1983–84; Minton and McDonald 1983–84; Richardson 1983–84; Rubin 1984; Gagnon 1986; Escoffier 1985; Weeks 1985, 1995; Blackwood 1986; Marcus and Fischer 1986; Epstein 1987; Stein 1989; Parker 1991; Herdt and Stoller 1990; Herdt and Lindenbaum 1992; Lancaster 1992). This includes the study of meanings that individuals assimilate as they are exposed to socially prevalent guides of interpretation and performance, which they learn, internalize, and then later help transform as they apply them in their own lives. In this sense, my approach conceives of individuals not only as being influenced by their social environments but also as agents of change.

This book is based on two years of ethnographic participant observation within varied social settings and social networks in Guadalajara, Mexico. My study also included sixty-four semistructured, qualitative interviews with a variety of people aged eighteen to fifty-three, of different sexual orientations, and of lower-middle-class to upper-middle-class status, as well as three discussion groups conducted in a local public clinic. This research took place between September 1993 and August 1995.

My research design was influenced by the collective academic thinking at the time about the urgent need for ethnographic studies of HIV/AIDS that took into account the meanings associated with sex, sexuality, and interpersonal relationships (Aggleton, Davies, and Hart 1990; Parker and Carballo 1990; Prieur et al. 1990; Carrier and Magaña 1991; Herdt and Boxer 1991; Parker, Herdt, and Carballo 1991; Davies and Weatherburn 1991; Watney 1991; Abramson 1992; Bolton 1992; Herdt and Lindenbaum 1992; Levine 1992; Treichler 1992; Kippax and Crawford 1993). For details about my sample and my methods, please refer to appendix 2, "Methodology."

The work for this book builds upon and is generally consistent with other research about sexuality and AIDS conducted in Mexico and others parts of Latin America in recent decades, as well as with research conducted with Latino populations in the United States. This growing body of literature includes research on Mexico by Carrier (1972, 1976, 1985, 1989a, b, 1995); Taylor (1978, 1986); Gómezjara and Barrera (1982); Galván Díaz (1988); Bellinghausen (1990); Izazola et al. (1989, 1991); Döring (1990); González Rodríguez (1990); Lumsden (1991); Carrillo (1993–94, 1999); Ramírez et al. (1994); Gutmann (1996); Prieur (1998); LeVine

(1993); Rico, Bronfman, and del Río-Chiriboga (1995); Wilson (1995); Liguori, González Block, and Aggleton (1996); and Buffington (1997). My thinking has been influenced by work in other parts of Latin America, including that of Murray (1987, 1991, 1995), Balderston (1997), and Schifter (1998); in Brazil, Fry (1985), Parker (1991, 1993a, 1993b, 1999), Daniel and Parker (1993), Kulick (1998), Green (1999), Paiva (2000), and Terto (2000); in Nicaragua, Lancaster (1992); in Peru, Cáceres et al. (1991, 1994, 1997, 2000) and Cáceres and Rosasco (1997); in Costa Rica, Schifter (1989); and, in Argentina, Gogna and Ramos (2000). For research on sexuality in the United States, including the now vast literature on Latinos and HIV risk, I highlight here the work of only a few authors: Ramos (1987), Carballo-Diéguez (1989), De La Cancela (1989), Almaguer (1991), Carrier and Magaña (1991), Magaña and Carrier (1991), Marin and Marin (1990, 1992), and Díaz (1998, 2000). These lists are by no means exhaustive. They represent a sample of academic work that influenced me during the course of conducting my study in Guadalajara and then later in writing this book.

THE SETTING

I chose Guadalajara for my study for several reasons, including its size, location, and regional influence, and local culture regarding sex and sexuality. Compared to Mexico City, Guadalajara is more representative of Mexican urban environments. While Mexico City has a population of close to 20 million people and enjoys a status as a world-class city, Guadalajara, the capital of the Mexican state of Jalisco, is a more typical Mexican city. Despite its population of about 3.5 million, the city maintains a more provincial lifestyle and organization, which are somewhat reminiscent of those of other smaller cities throughout Mexico.

Guadalajara also has a unique position as a regional pole of influence. Located in the Mexican Altiplano (the central highlands) some three hundred miles northwest of Mexico City, it attracts immigrants from the large northwest region of Mexico, which extends from Michoacán to Sonora. Its culture and ideas influence, and are influenced by, a vast region of Mexico. The city and the region also have a unique relationship with California and the United States in general, because a large proportion of Mexican immigrants to California come from Jalisco, Michoacán, and other central and western states.

From a physical standpoint, Guadalajara is a city that is somewhat segregated by class. The city is shaped like an oval, crossed in the middle by an avenue that runs in the north-south direction and that divides the city roughly into two sections. The western part is more middle class and upper class. It is also regarded as being more conservative. The eastern side tends to be lower middle class and working class and contains some of the city's most marginalized areas. This information is relevant here, because most of my work took place in the western side of Guadalajara. During the two years of my study, I lived in a suburban neighborhood near Plaza del Sol, which was the first U.S.-style shopping mall in all of Mexico and which opened in 1972. A majority of the participants in my study lived or worked in middle-class neighborhoods in the western sector of the city, and their activities took place as well in the financial district and the historic downtown area. This means that my contacts were mostly with the broad sector of the population that is known as the Mexican urban middle class, and my sample did not include the very poor or the very rich.

Guadalajara has been a site of intense ideological clashes about sex and sexuality, and its image and current history in relation to these issues have been shaped by deep contrasts and are rich with contradictions. On the one hand, the city is considered to be one of the most conservative and traditional in Mexico. Nationally, it has been seen as the cradle of some of the quintessential icons of *mexicanidad* (Mexicanness) and of Mexican machismo. Guadalajara is in the region in Mexico where *mariachis, tequila,* and *charros* (cowboys) originated. The city is also famous for an idealized image of its beautiful women and their dark Moorish eyes, the *tapatías,* who are considered to represent Mexican women's most desirable characteristics in terms of decency and devotion to their husbands and families. These are all symbols that emerged in Guadalajara and that became central to Mexican culture and to what is recognized as Mexican worldwide. Yet, on the other hand, Guadalajara has for long also been regarded as being the most homosexual city in Mexico, somewhat like San Francisco in the United States, and many jokes about the city jointly invoke *machismo* and *homosexualidad* as part of the same context. Indeed, because of the visible presence of *homosexuales* in the city, Guadalajara has been the site of some of the most controversial clashes between conservative and progressive forces in the country.

In this tension between Guadalajara's two images, progressive Guadalajarans often invoke arguments about the obsolescence of old, Mexican traditional values about gender and sex and speak of the resistance among local conservatives to modernization, globalization, and cultural change. Conservative Guadalajarans argue, in response, that new ideas often corrupt the local population and make them vulnerable to the kind of negative influences that threaten morality. They claim that economic modernization does not need to imply sacrificing the inculcation and maintenance of true Mexican values and of a sound morality, and that it likewise does not mean that Mexicans need to accept all things modern. As a result of these debates, people in Guadalajara are engaged in reflection about what cultural change means and when it is to be desired or, instead, feared.

For my study, I generally had more access to individuals and groups who did not think of themselves as belonging to the most conservative factions of Guadalajaran society, although some of them had grown up in very conservative families and had rebelled against their families' way of thinking. Additionally, I had disproportionate access to the homosexual world in the city, but I did not solely study that world. Rather than considering this a limitation, I believe that it helped me write a book that is not just about heterosexuality or homosexuality in Guadalajara, about one of those two worlds studied in isolation from the other, but that considers the interactions between the two. It is in those interactions that ideological clashes between different groups of Guadalajarans are often enacted, and where social change, and the opposition to it, can be most readily observed.

Furthermore, in addition to the reflection that the presence of different local positions about sexuality produces, Guadalajarans constantly receive messages containing new ideas and images from other places—from other parts of Mexico and the world. In the context of expanding globalization, the radio and television airwaves expose them every day to news about worldwide events and popular culture from faraway places. They inundate them with U.S. television shows whose characters often depict sexual lives that differ considerably from those that are considered to be traditionally Mexican. But change is also emerging from inside, as the local population interprets and reinterprets the reality of their sexual lives, compares it with other options being enacted locally, and then participates in the search for new understandings and new strategies for interaction with others.

To put it differently, people in Guadalajara are confronted constantly with the need to decide between maintaining the past and the comfort that this may bring and trusting the promises of change and the acceptance of a somewhat amorphous, but hopefully better, future. The tension between these two options appears in the words of Guadalajaran people throughout this book and is an important ingredient flavoring my analysis.

1

AN INITIAL GLIMPSE
OF MEXICAN SEXUALITIES:
THE HISTORICAL CONTEXT

I first became interested in studying sexuality in Guadalajara in 1991, when I learned about the clashes that were taking place among gay and lesbian political groups, the local government, and conservative, influential groups and individuals. Such clashes had been motivated by the gay and lesbian groups' intent to hold the annual meeting of the International Lesbian and Gay Association (ILGA) in the city. The event had come about because the Grupo Orgullo Homosexual de Liberación (GOHL), which roughly translates as "Homosexual Pride Liberation Group," had become a member of ILGA some years before and had successfully lobbied within the international gay and lesbian political arena to bring the meeting to Mexico.

The idea of holding the ILGA meeting in Guadalajara was charged with symbolism for a number of different reasons and for a number of different players. In the eyes of the local gay and lesbian groups, it represented a victory. Guadalajara was about to host the annual meeting of the largest gay and lesbian association in the world, which meant that the city was mature enough to allow homosexual people to take a legitimate place in local social and political life. ILGA had been up to that point heavily focused on Europe and had never held its meeting in a de-

13

veloping country; by organizing the meeting, Mexico was leading the way toward the greater globalization of ILGA itself.

Open negotiations by GOHL's leaders with the local government to acquire permits and request police security were taken as an indication that *homosexuales*[1]—or what the leaders of the gay groups called *la comunidad gay*, "the gay community"—were not just a collection of people forced to conceal their same-sex attraction from public scrutiny. These negotiations meant that homosexual people could potentially form an increasingly proud and open community seeking to gain equality and civil rights in the city.

In the eyes of others the proposed ILGA meeting came to confirm that Guadalajara was, as is popularly believed throughout the country, the largest homosexual enclave in Mexico (a reputation that only the city of Veracruz rivaled). This image was particularly problematic for many Guadalajarans in light of Guadalajara's other, more prestigious reputation. As I mentioned before, Guadalajara is regarded as one of the most conservative cities in Mexico, and one that has produced some of the fundamental icons of *mexicanidad* (Mexicanness). Guadalajara has prided itself on maintaining those icons alive by resisting what local conservatives perceive as pervasive cultural changes that have invaded the rest of urban Mexico. For many, the city constituted a niche where true Mexican traditions were assumed to be safe from the effects of modernization.

The idea of disrupting the niche with an international gay conference was inconceivable among those who had the most investment in maintaining tradition: powerful conservatives who are prominent in Guadalajara's political and social elite and who openly and regularly react against anything that they perceive as a threat to the city's moral precepts (regardless of the fact that many in Guadalajara do not live by such moral precepts or necessarily agree with them). As soon as news about the ILGA meeting became public, local conservative forces lobbied the government against it and took direct actions using a full range of strategies. Officially, conservatives tried to prevent hotels from housing the meeting and meeting participants and asked the mayor to deny permits for the conference. More informally, openly known gay and lesbian leaders began receiving an increased number of anonymous death threats, and an underground graffiti campaign with the messages "Haz Patria. Mata a un Homosexual" (Be patriotic. Kill a homosexual) and "Muerte a Homosexuales" (Death to homosexuals) materialized around the city (González Ruiz 1994: 90).

The campaign against the conference also sought public support through the media. For instance, on May 21, 1991, the Asociación Católica de la Juventud Mexicana (Mexican Youth Catholic Association) placed the following ad in one of Guadalajara's prominent newspapers: "Mexico is a conservative country that has always been proud of the femininity of her women and the virility of her men. But in this country, and more precisely in Guadalajara, Jalisco, the scum of the world—homosexuals and lesbians—intend to have a congress of the followers of the *vicio nefando* [unspeakable vice]. . . . Give rights to the homosexual corrupters and the satanic worshipers will follow, asking for their right to put social evil on a throne, the drug addicts asking for the right to take drugs, et cetera" (Cortés Guardado 1997: 98).[2]

In the end, the mayor decided to allow the meeting but to deny police protection. Powerful conservative members of the Hotel and Motel Association, including its president, forced a resolution to expel any member that provided space for the meeting or rooms for its participants. Under direct threats and increasing opposition that endangered the safety of the participants, and facing multiple problems in housing the meeting, GOHL and ILGA decided at the last minute to move the conference to more liberal Acapulco. Unfortunately, due to the many logistical problems that the change in location entailed, as well as the justified fear among potential participants who had begun questioning whether they would be safe in Mexico, the meeting in Acapulco ended up being fairly poorly attended. GOHL's president, who was the main force among the Mexican organizers of the meeting, recognized in an interview that "he had made a serious error in trying to hold the conference in Guadalajara" (Carrier 1995: 186).

This example is illustrative of the contested social, political, and cultural setting in which Mexican (and Guadalajaran) sexuality is immersed. In an effort to further characterize this setting—the stage on which sex in Guadalajara is enacted—I provide in this chapter some historical background about the evolution of Mexican sexuality during the twentieth century. My analysis here is not exhaustive but instead focuses on the historical processes that explain the logics that individuals use today in making interpretations about sex and sexuality. My emphasis is on people's understanding of what they view as "traditional" and "modern." I also emphasize the emergence of a certain coexistence of the two, of "cultural hybridity" as García Canclini (1995) calls it.

The use of the terms "traditional" and "modern" requires some justification. It should be clear that my goal is not to insert the story of Mexico within a grand narrative of evolutionist progress—progress that follows a preestablished unilinear path from "inferior" to more "advanced" social forms.[3] Rather, the use of these terms in Mexico encompasses the tensions between "old" and "new," "Mexican" and "foreign." Most immediately, "traditional" should be seen as referring to actors' understandings of "how things used to be" (and perhaps still "ought" to be) and of ideas perceived to be prototypically Mexican. "Modern," in turn, refers to understandings of "new," emergent attitudes, norms, values, behaviors, or identities, including those perceived to arrive from outside Mexico. In other words, the terms "traditional" and "modern" are shorthand to separate perceptions of "what was in the past" and "what they inculcated in us," on the one hand, and "what is present or future" and (perhaps) "the change that we want to adopt," on the other. Generally speaking, in their own use of the terms, participants in my study had a clear sense of this separation. However, the location of the boundary between traditional and modern varied considerably from person to person. Where the traditional ended and the modern began was always subject to individual interpretation.

EXTERNAL INFLUENCE FROM EUROPE AND THE UNITED STATES

Mexico saw a substantial transformation in its social (and sexual) norms and traditions in the course of the twentieth century. Several authors have argued that such transformation was motivated considerably by external influence from Europe and the United States. They have also argued that such cultural influence was perhaps an unintended companion to the broader political and economic influence that supported Mexican economic development throughout the century (Monsiváis 1990, 1993, 1998; González Rodríguez 1990).

Monsiváis (1993), a distinguished Mexican essayist and social scientist, affirms that during the Porfirian regime—which lasted thirty years and ended abruptly with the beginning of the Mexican Revolution in 1910—the Mexican elite relied on French culture (and European culture in general) as the source of inspiration for the acquisition of refinement and, as a result, of new norms and values. European culture informed much of what the Porfirians viewed as worth pursuing in all areas of everyday life, including sexuality. Members of the aristocratic and educated Mexican elite, who had the opportunity to travel and live in Europe, were exposed to ideas that were influencing European thought about sexuality at the time and brought those ideas with them when they returned to Mexico.

Novo, writing in the 1930s, described the role played by the children of the elite in bringing to Mexico new sexual mores during the first two decades of the century. Referring to Antonio Adalid, heir of one of the most prominent Porfirian families, he observed: "Antonio had been sent to school in England. . . . Antonio returned from England in the full bloom of his youth and in the middle of the most opulent period of Porfirianism. That was the time when exquisite aristocrats threw lavish parties which, though private, no doubt made them wary of the small, placid city's thirst for gossip and scandal" (1979: 32). Novo also mentions a dance, "El baile de los 41 maricones," which was translated as "Dance of the 41 Faggots" in the U.S. publication of parts of Novo's memoir: "In short, that was the time of the famous Dance of the 41 Faggots. Antonio was the life of those parties—Toña the Fellatrix, as he was nicknamed because of his fondness for a form of lovemaking which must have been not at all current at the time, or which, perhaps, he performed according to the highest European standards of proficiency and dedication" (32).

Yet, in addition to a taste for more risqué and diverse sexual practices, Mexican travelers and students also brought to Mexico what Parker, writing about similar developments in Brazil, calls "a highly rationalized set of scientific and pseudo-scientific ideas about sexual life drawn largely from developments in European psychology, sexology, and sociology" (1991: 3). A medicalized version of sexuality arrived in Mexico together with positivism (the leading academic ideology during the Porfirian regime in Mexico, with its slogan of "Order and Progress") and its increasing reliance on science to conceptualize and justify social life (Paz 1985: 130).

I do not mean to imply, however, that Mexicans did not have their own local interpretations of alternative sexualities, as well as local strategies to enact them. For instance, there is evidence of the existence of clandestine homosexual subcultures in early-twentieth-century Mexico. According to Monsiváis, these subcultures were generally ignored by society at large during the nineteenth century. Monsiváis asks, "What is the explanation for the absence of laws and regulations about sexual minorities in the Mexican 19th century, or the absence of articles, books, literary characters, or even absurd representations of gay people?" (1998: 13). In his answer he theorizes that the prominence of silence in nineteenth-century Mexican society—"what is not named does not exist"—created a shift from the kinds of open condemnation of sodomites that took place during Spanish colonial times only a century before. To contrast this attitude with events happening in Europe, and in particular with the scandal surrounding Oscar Wilde and the labeling of homosexuality as "the love that dares not speak its name," Monsiváis wittily crafted the phrase "the hatred that dares not write the name of what it hates" (14).

Monsiváis (1998) estimates that the first public recognition of a homosexual subculture in Mexico took place when the police raided the "Dance of the 41" to which Novo alluded in the quotation above. This legendary dance took place on November 20, 1901. As the story goes, half the men were dressed as women, half as men, and Porfirio Díaz's son-in-law, Ignacio de la Torre, was in attendance. Taylor (1978) indicates that Ignacio was the missing forty-second participant, because the police protected his identity.[4] As the police burst into the place, some men were able to flee, others were arrested and forced to sweep streets, others bought their freedom, and still others were sent to do forced labor in Yucatán (Monsiváis 1998). The event was recorded in a now famous illustration by José Guadalupe Posada. This illustration was accompanied by verses that reveal social perceptions of male same-sex desire at the time, which were tightly connected to gender stereotypes:

Cuarenta y un lagartijos	Forty-one *lagartijos*,[5]
disfrazados la mitad	half of them dressed
de simpáticas muchachas,	as lovely girls,
bailaban como el que más.	danced joyfully.
La otra mitad con su traje,	The other half with their suits,
es decir de masculinos,	that is, like masculine men,
gozaban al estrechar	got pleasure from embracing
a los famosos *jotitos*.	the famous *jotitos*.[6]
(Monsiváis 1998: 15)	

Most interesting in these verses are the ambiguities and subtle distinctions made about the two groups of men. One group is made up of the *jotitos,* the men dressed as women, who were presumably effeminate. The other includes their dancing partners, who were dressed as men. The latter "get pleasure from embracing the famous *jotitos,*" which confirms that they are not *jotos* themselves. And yet, these men are also described as being dressed in suits "like masculine men," which implies that they are not quite the same as regular men. In some sense, they are considered to be located somewhere between men and *jotos.* I expand on these subtleties later in the book, in my discussion of the gender-based categories of sexual identity in Mexico.

González Rodríguez has referred to the availability of gathering places for men who participated in *el ambiente* at the turn of the century. *El ambiente,* meaning "the milieu" or "the environment," was a code to refer to the world of same-sex male desire throughout the century. His discussion includes a quotation from a text from the time, *Los inestables,* by Alberto Teruel:

This way, Alberto learned about, and became accustomed to, the gay and rowdy life of the city, which his friend showed him. But his friend was careful not to take him to places such as Leda, Los Eloines, Madreselvas, or many other places of *ambiente* that were in fashion, nor to places such as the popular *balnearios* [swimming pools], some busy streets, the lobbies of some aristocratic hotels. Nor to specific private parties, where the *crema y nata* [upper crust] of the capital's homosexuality gathered, and which he visited frequently when he was alone and looking for easy adventure—for someone to spend the night with, clearly behind Alberto's back. (González Rodríguez 1990: 55)

Taylor has reported on turn-of-the-century evidence of lesbian subcultures in Mexico City. He refers to an article that appeared in *Universal*, one of the capital's main and oldest newspapers:

In the town of Santa Maria, a big party of single women was raided. The motive given for the fiesta was "the baptism of a doll, which was given the name *Chilaquil*." The implication of the name is that the women were homosexual. After listing the names of fourteen women and stating that there were others, the article noted that the police were continuing to look for similar incidents throughout the land; that the women claimed that they had been having these parties every month without being molested; and that they did not invite men because it was the only way to avoid unpleasantness. (Taylor 1978: 28)

Mexico, during the time that these gatherings and police raids took place, was about to experience the complete destabilization of its social system. The second decade of the twentieth century brought tremendous social chaos during the Mexican Revolution, which began in 1910. In relation to sexuality, Monsiváis indicates that "the Revolution, with its temporary demolition of *pudor* [modesty], to some degree 'sexualized' the country" (1998: 18). This author provides several examples of new expressions of sexuality during this time of social upheaval: the emergence of highly erotic theater revues in which women and *maricones* (effeminate men) performed for "regular" men, the role of prostitution as release for the different armies involved in the civil war, and the emergence of single motherhood as a social phenomenon. In his opinion, the revolution brought about an overall questioning of the dignified silence about sexual matters and a generalized weakening of "moral prohibitions." Monsiváis also emphasizes the feeling of urgency—in the context of the armed confrontations, people began to think, "If they are going to kill me tomorrow, I had better sin right away" (1998: 18).

Monsiváis argues that the revolution simultaneously gave rise to a cult

of machismo that resulted in the persecution of those who did not conform to its expectations. Although sexuality had begun to step out into the
Mexican world, the military governments after the revolution undertook
to repress forms of desire that contradicted the project of reconstruction
of a nation ruled by machos. In this regard, Monsiváis (1998) discusses
unjustified arrests of effeminate men, particularly working-class men, and
even forced labor and deportation to the Islas Marías, a small archipelago
off the Mexican Pacific coast that served as a prison.

During the time of reconstruction, the 1920s, two large social and political developments were relevant to the evolution of sexuality in Mexico.
First, the external influence that had come from Europe during the Porfiriato gradually gave way to influence from the United States, as Mexico
increasingly opened up to North American culture and ideology. Second,
as the postrevolutionary governments engaged in the project of reconstructing the country, they placed special emphasis on the secularization
of social life.[7] Religious conservatism became one of the enemies of progress. The government sought to forge a new, heavily militarized (and by
extension macho) Mexico that would be set upon the path of modernization.

In terms of the shift in external influence, Monsiváis (1993) describes
how U.S. influence began to be felt in several aspects of social life such as
religion and fashion, as new postrevolutionary elites began to adopt the
so-called American way of life. The change implied an increasing social
sanction of an ideology of comfort, individualism and the idea of the "self-
made man," and a North American (Protestant) work ethic. Such values,
which were intrinsically associated with modernity, were most readily promoted by commerce and diffused through advertising.

This cultural transformation also differed from that of the Porfiriato in
that it was more democratic; U.S. values and ideas were not exclusively
adopted by the elite but slowly filtered through to members of the emerging urban middle class and even to the working class. Modernization-the-
American-way "redefined the aspirations of many and renewed the possibility of progress for all" (Monsiváis 1993: 507).

Yet, North American influence did not expand without opposition.
Groups on the right and left extremes of the political spectrum cam-
paigned against what they saw as the undermining of Mexican social values (Monsiváis 1993; González Rodríguez 1990). The result was the creation of new forms of Mexican nationalism that, in general, focused on the
exaltation of local cultural expressions and generated a new definition of
mexicanidad. One version of postrevolutionary *mexicanidad* was promoted

by the government and by leftist intellectuals. Another was advanced by conservative and religious sectors that saw secularization and other changes taking place in Mexico as a loss of morality. These forms of nationalism, especially the second, have played an important role in the evolution of Mexican interpretations of sexuality since the late 1920s. In the next section, I examine the role that conceptions of *mexicanidad* played in shaping contemporary Mexican culture, and in particular in consolidating machismo as a prominent characteristic central to the nation's overall culture.

THIS INVENTION CALLED *MEXICANIDAD*

Postrevolutionary notions of *mexicanidad* relied on two different sets of cultural symbols. One included symbols appropriated from Mexican pre-Columbian history, which came to represent the "original" or "true" culture. These symbols were used to create a discourse representing the search for equality, progress, and modernity that would result in reparations to those dispossessed by the old order. The other set included symbols of *criollo*[8] and *mestizo*[9] Mexican culture, which was founded upon the values of the well-to-do classes during the Porfiriato, with a strong emphasis on the *parte blanca,* the European side. Such symbols evoked the creation of a Mexican essence that had resulted from the four-century-long blending of European and indigenous cultures that followed the arrival of Hernán Cortés.

Both sets of cultural symbols were invoked separately, and by different groups, in the construction of a nationalist defense by those who opposed what they saw as a "North American cultural invasion." Government officials and leftist intellectuals—including figures of the caliber of Diego Rivera and Frida Kahlo—helped construct a romantic discourse that glorified the country's Indian past and inculcated a sense of national pride based on the original cultures that preceded the arrival of the foreign, symbolized by the Spanish invaders (Monsiváis 1993; Riding 1986). Spain, however, constituted less of a threat at the time that this discourse emerged; the real foreign cultural threat was the United States.

The other form of nationalism was advanced by conservatives (often members of the old provincial oligarchy in cities like Guadalajara) who undertook to protect what they saw as more immediate, "true" Mexican traditions. Such traditions were a reinterpretation of the values and ways of life of their parents and grandparents. The preservation of such traditions constituted the antidote against what was perceived to be a decline in moral values brought about by American-style modernization. The ideology of these groups materialized as a nationalistic form of traditionalism, which, as García Canclini puts it, "often appears as a resource for enduring the contradictions of contemporary life. In this epoch in which we doubt the benefits of modernity, temptations mount for a return to some past that we imagine to be more tolerable" (1995: 113).

This form of nationalism was most strongly promoted by the groups that opposed the secularization brought about by the postrevolutionary governments. In fact, the tension was such that the most conservative Catholics in central Mexico, including Jalisco and Guadalajara, rose up in arms and organized a movement that caused many headaches for the federal government. During the so-called Cristero War in the late 1920s, the military and the government were often labeled *matacuras,* priest-killers, and were constructed as enemies of Catholicism and of the Virgin of Guadalupe.

Although the conservative groups did not constitute a majority of Mexicans, what made their form of nationalism palatable for larger sectors of the population was its reliance on symbols that straightforwardly evoked the nation's pride in its people (largely of *mestizo* heritage), Catholic religion, and moral values. It glorified Mexican norms as *buenas costumbres* (good habits, good principles, solid standards), in contrast with the "looseness" of the customs arriving from the north. They believed that reconstructing Mexico did not require giving up good principles and being corrupted by new ideas. Ironically, the symbols of this second form of nationalism were "Mexican" cultural expressions that in many cases had a strong European flavor. It did not matter, for instance, that *mariachi* bands likely evolved from the French bands that played at weddings and that were popular in Jalisco during the second half of the nineteenth century (thus the linguistic connection between the Mexican word *mariachi* and the French word *mariage*) (Broughton et al. 1994: 544). It did not matter either that what was highlighted as most beautiful in women from Guadalajara were their *ojos tapatíos,* their dark, Moorish eyes, which symbolized southern Spanish heritage and, by extension, European blood in general. Many Guadalajarans today are also extremely proud of the light skin, blond hair, and green eyes characteristic of many people in the region. Jalisco, like other states north of Mexico City, attracted considerable immigration of Spaniards during the colonial period and of English, French, and other Europeans during the nineteenth century. The symbols emerging from Jalisco were those of Mexicans who were very different from the darker-skinned *mestizo* majority.[10]

Both forms of *mexicanidad* are relevant to an understanding of contemporary sex and sexuality in Mexico because, regardless of their differences, together they have helped construct what are perceived as Mexican traditions about family, gender relations, and sexuality. In regard to sexuality they are ultimately not incompatible. They are both, in fact, closely connected to ideas about Mexican machismo. The union of machismo and *mexicanidad* occurred, according to Monsiváis (1993: 478), between 1930 and 1950, when the waning effects of revolutionary violence were replaced with a "local adoration and adulation of machismo" in Mexican popular culture. The connections between machismo, *mexicanidad,* and tradition constituted a powerful ideology that justified the maintenance of patriarchal domination, women's subordination, and the traditional Mexican family (which included sexual freedom for the male outside monogamous marital relationships).

THE LEGACY OF MACHISMO

The characteristics of machismo have been described extensively in the literature about Mexican culture and society since the 1950s. In his 1950 book, *The Labyrinth of Solitude,* Octavio Paz described machismo as representing "the masculine pole of life" and suggested that "[one] word sums up the aggressiveness, insensitivity, invulnerability and other attributes of the macho: power. It is force without the discipline of any notion of order: arbitrary power, the will without the reins and without a set course." The macho's exertion of power is unpredictable and he is capable of committing "unforeseen acts that produce confusion, horror, and destruction" (1985: 81). Yet, Paz also presented what he regarded as more positive qualities of the macho. The macho is "hermetic" and "trustable." He is capable of confronting the "impact of the outside world" with stoicism, accepting defeat with dignity, being patient and long-suffering, and being resigned and strong "in the face of adversity" (31).

Therefore, Paz's conceptualization of the macho suggested two different faces of machismo, which Vicente Mendoza (quoted in Gutmann 1996) described as two types of machismo altogether. Gutmann refers to Mendoza's characterization in the following terms: "The first, authentic one is characterized by courage, generosity, and stoicism; the second, which is basically false, consists of appearances—cowardice hiding behind empty boasts" (1996: 223). In a similar vein, LeVine emphasizes that the macho may be "a man who is *formal y respetoso* [sic],[11] proud but not arrogant, reflective, authoritative, and hardworking" (1993: 80). In the background, however, the "unlimited" power of machos over their immediate world, and thus over women and their world, is a central aspect of machismo.

Women are in turn characterized as submissive to male desire. In Paz's view of machismo, women are seen as "an instrument, sometimes of masculine desires, sometimes of the ends assigned to [them] by morality, society and the law." Their role is dual: "When passive, she becomes a goddess, a beloved one, a being who embodies the ancient, stable elements of the universe: the earth, motherhood, virginity. When active, she is always function and means, a receptacle and a channel. Womanhood, unlike manhood, is never an end in itself" (1985: 35). According to Mexican machismo, women are divided into two groups: those who are good, decent, passive, and *abnegadas* (long-suffering and self-sacrificing); and those who are bad, immodest, active, impious, and independent.

Moreno, writing many years after Paz, described the dichotomy between "good" and "bad" women as being central to her personal experience of socialization:

> The world was already divided when we arrived: some girls are good. They demand respect. They are *pudorosas* [modest], discreet. They behave well. The others, the crazy ones, they offer themselves. They allow themselves to be touched. They go out with anyone. And they lose all. Because the most precious thing that a woman has is that [i.e., virginity and discretion]. . . . What is the line dividing the good ones from the crazy ones? One *desliz* [slippage]. One careless incident. It leaves you marked. But in the end, what did we want to be, good ones or crazy ones? (1990: 41)

The assumptions of machismo—the separation between a world of men and a world of women—were extended as well to sexualities regarded to be deviant. In a now classic study of male homosexuality in Mexico in the early 1970s, Carrier (1972) identified the existence among his working-class informants of strong differences between the *pasivo* (assumed to be effeminate and the receptive partner during anal penetration) and the *activo* (assumed to be masculine and the insertive partner during anal penetration) in male homosexual sex. In the context of machismo, and the unbridled power given to those men considered to be regular or normal, stigma was applied only to the *pasivo*, because of his effeminacy, which denoted that he was less of a man—a *maricón* or *joto*—and, by extension, "like a woman." The *activo*, on the contrary, could maintain his status due to his masculinity (Carrier 1995, 1989a, 1972). Within the dominance of machismo, sex between women was largely ignored by Mexican society, and the *machorra* or *tortillera*, the masculinized woman, was by no means accorded the kind of power or status given to men.

When Paz conducted his analysis in the 1950s, *machista* values seemed to dominate Mexican life. Between 1930 and 1950, the notion that Mexican society was solidly founded on a patriarchal system became institutionalized, with the nation as a whole becoming *machista* by definition. In Gutmann's words: "beginning especially in the 1940s, the male accent itself came to mean machismo and machismo to mean Mexico" (1996: 223).

Anyone who has closely experienced contemporary Mexican culture, however, would observe that the traditional description of machismo offered here does no justice to the enormous cultural changes that have taken place in Mexico in recent decades. As Gutmann (1996), LeVine (1993), Prieur (1998), and others have demonstrated, a considerable destabilization of the traditional roles and identities associated with Mexican machismo and a constant reshaping of the definitions of masculinity and femininity have occurred. Contemporary Mexicans have increasingly developed negative judgments about machismo and engaged in reflection about the tensions implied in a number of dichotomies: male versus female, active versus passive, heterosexual versus homosexual, domination versus submission, good women versus bad women, old values versus new values, and the mainstream versus the social margins.

HIGH AND LOW

An additional implication of machismo is the separation between family life (the world of "good" women) and a more secretive world where men could partake in what González Rodríguez (1990) has called "prohibited sexualities." This author argues that the latter were enacted in Mexican urban environments via the availability of *antros*, underground dives that "respectable" men could attend in order to establish contact with "bad" women and with *maricones*. Included were bordellos, cantinas, and certain cafés, which were assumed to operate during the night and only in certain neighborhoods where they were tolerated. I would expand this list to include other public places—such as certain streets, parks, public baths— as well as private places such as homes where social networks of homosexually active men gathered. The *antros* constituted what González Rodríguez calls *"los bajos fondos"* (the low ends), a nocturnal world that stood in opposition to a "high world" of collective, daytime life.

Although González Rodríguez's depiction of the separation between these worlds is somewhat simplistic, I find it useful for a number of reasons. First, it provides an interesting explanation for the social sanctioning of spaces where transgression was permitted. The *antros* fit well in Mexico, since machismo operated with the premise that men required a space to enact sex outside the realm of marriage. Such a premise is founded upon the notion that male sexuality is uncontrollable and needs to be expressed in ways more diverse than sex with a wife. Therefore, the *antros* not only supported men's sexual freedom but also helped protect "good" women by providing the escape valve for male sexual energy that would otherwise be directed at unmarried virgins, at widows, or at other men's wives.

Second, a common assumption in old Mexico was that men needed to learn about sex through experience, in preparation for their role as husbands. The *antros* were the training grounds for young men who received no formal sex education. In this sense, the *antros* provided an important social function.

Finally, because the *antros* stood apart, the Mexican mainstream could ignore their existence. By looking the other way, Mexican society avoided having to crack down on them, so long as the world of the low ends did not attempt to question its marginality or claim spaces considered part of the realm of the high world. The people in this world were, however, not just marginal. The *antros* also provided the space for their inhabitants to push the boundaries between the two worlds, especially as modernization began to take hold. In this sense they constituted breeding grounds for the reinterpretation of prohibited sexualities and for attempts to bring those sexualities into the open, into the sphere of the high world. They were, at least initially, the places where nonconformist women and *homosexuales* could attempt to change the rules. In this regard, González Rodríguez argues that cultural changes initiated in the world of the low ends have been influenced by ideas and values arriving from the United States and by local social processes associated with modernization. He claims that the separation is still valid but that the definition of what constitutes part of the low ends and what belongs to the high world is constantly shifting. In this sense, his conclusion is consistent with the idea of cultural hybridity, which is the topic of the next section.

CULTURAL HYBRIDITY

During the course of the twentieth century, the tension between *mexicanidad* and modernity has not been necessarily evident to most Mexicans. In fact, and perhaps ironically, since the consolidation of postrevolutionary Mexico in the 1920s, both a nationalistic view of *mexicanidad* and the "American way of life" were strongly disseminated through the very same media: radio, films, and, later, television. They were promoted side by side and integrated into a worldview that allowed both of them to "make sense," with little apparent contradiction between the ideas of staying

Mexican and of becoming modern. Mexicans of all classes became increasingly exposed to both an exalted nationalism that promoted *mexicanidad* and tradition, and a "foreign," yet increasingly popular, cultural ideology that brought with it a whole new set of evolving values about gender, family, and sexuality. The result is cultural hybridity, although people might not recognize it as such and would likely see themselves plainly as modern or "somewhat modern, somewhat traditional."

García Canclini (1995) has argued that cultural hybridity consists of a superimposition of ideas and values that makes both tradition and modernity available options for the formation of contemporary Mexican culture. However, not everyone agrees with this perspective. Other authors claim that, in the battle between tradition and modernity, modernity is ultimately winning (and displacing Mexican traditions). For instance, Monsiváis has concluded that the influence of the values of modernity began to prevail over a nationalistic view of *mexicanidad* during the 1940s:

> The Second World War was a great catalyst of Mexican life. [Mexico] had no choice but to realize that the international horizon for the country was the Free World, in its North American version. . . . The desire to live "like everywhere else" (that is, like in the United States) spread, and visible nationalism was transformed—its chauvinism becoming circus-like and its exhibitionism a mythomania seeking to be recognized as such. . . . Traditionalism responds with decreasing energy, institutionalizing the complaints for the customs that disappear. . . . Nothing is the same. Degradation coming from the north envelops us and the values that guided our parents become unrecognizable. (1993: 483)

Especially since the 1950s, the large urban centers in Mexico have witnessed the emergence of expressions of sexuality and changes in gender relations that have often resembled those occurring in countries such as the United States. Mexican essayists have described Mexican versions of the sexual revolution, the emergence of, and challenges posed by, a local "gay democracy," and the questioning raised by feminist perspectives.[12]

Monsiváis suggests that since the late 1950s, there has been a transition from silence about sexual matters, prudery, and guilt to a much more relaxed and modern society:

> the country known in 1958 is barely recognizable. In relation to sex, information abounds; psychoanalysis is not just a social fad . . . ; sexology advances, with the relative boom of Masters and Johnson; Freudian vocabulary was nationalized . . . ; the expression *¡adúltera!* [adulterous woman] has stopped being

the utmost melodramatic scream; . . . economic disaster helps promote birth control over the pope's decrees; . . . bordellos are an endangered species; neither divorce nor infidelity is a formal cause of scandal . . . ; the fight to legalize abortion is broad; the participation of women in all fields is almost irreversible (the last strongholds of machismo being politics and corporation control); "to make love" is no longer a synonym of *coger* [to fuck], but of a "significant relation between two human beings"; there are no more than 10 surviving "bad words" . . . ; the UNAM [Universidad Nacional Autónoma de México] has instituted Gay Cultural Week; the fight against AIDS rehabilitated two words that were mostly extinct ("chastity" and "condom"). Depending on the generation to which one belongs, everything is now preceded by nostalgia for the feelings of guilt or by the lack of comprehension of any nostalgia at all. (1990: 167)

Ultimately, Monsiváis also argues, although there has been resistance to adopting modernity and North American–style values, in the end such adoption has readily taken place: "Any 'liberal' or 'freed' conduct in the U.S. is surrounded first by alarm, then by joking, and then by imitation. . . . When the Latin American middle classes ask themselves 'how contemporary am I?' they are also asking 'how close or far am I from what is happening in the U.S.?' That's how colonized [Latin America is] and how inevitable [the process is]" (1990: 171). Common to these and other views about sexual modernization in Mexico is the notion that, although traditional values survive, Mexican sexual mores are in frank transition to a form of modernity that is not dissimilar to that found in the United States.[13]

I tend to side with García Canclini in arguing that the adoption of modern ideas is not as simple as a struggle between tradition and modernity that ultimately is being won by the latter. Many of the examples contained in this book suggest that the very same expressions of contemporary Mexican sexuality listed by Bellinghausen (1990) and Monsiváis (1990, 1993) are only to some degree comparable to their counterparts in places like the United States, and that there are marked differences caused by local interpretations. My research supports the notion that "cultural hybridity," and related concepts such as "cultural fluidity" or "cultural overlapping," are effective theoretical tools for the analysis of contemporary Latin American sexualities. This conclusion is consistent with findings in other parts of Latin America—such as in Parker's work (1991, 1999) in Brazil and Lancaster's work (1992) in Nicaragua.

Finally, more generally, I would argue that contemporary cultural hybridity respects the logic that has dominated in Mexico since colonial times—a logic that requires a seamless blending (at least in appearance) of cultures that are often incompatible. Otherwise, what we know as the Mexican nation would make no sense.

(

The history and concepts that I have discussed in this chapter provide a stage for my analysis in the rest of the book. The interplay between tradition and modernity features prominently in Mexicans' negotiations about their sexual lives and provides much of the flavor for the sexual culture that prevails in Mexico today.

I will return to a historical account again in the third part of the book, where I discuss the arrival of AIDS and the initiation of HIV prevention work in Mexico, as well as the changes that they caused. As we will see, the disease and the efforts geared toward combating it cannot be understood without paying attention to the issues and historical processes discussed here.

PART 1   SEXUAL IDENTITIES

THE QUESTION OF SEXUAL IDENTITIES

The concept of sexual identities has been central to the social scientific study of sexuality for several decades. Epstein (1987) notes that the term began to appear in the social science literature in the 1950s but became more standard as an analytical framework in sociology sometime in the 1970s. Sexual identities are understood to be interpretations made by individuals in response to questions about who they are, sexually speaking, and where they fit in their society. Important assumptions are that these interpretations are historically and temporally bound and that they are a "human invention" that has no automatic or direct correspondence with biological characteristics. Furthermore, although this latter characteristic of identities creates a certain flexibility of interpretation, such flexibility is, paradoxically, also limiting. As Epstein puts it, based on an interpretation by Berger and Luckman, "it is important to recognize that such identities are, at the same time, both human self-creations and constraining structures" (1987: 30). Identities create new options for self-definition—they expand the criteria and make room for new interpretations—but simultaneously limit the number of options deemed to be socially acceptable.

31

In a similar vein, Weeks refers to what he sees as other paradoxes created by the acquisition of sexual identities: "Identities are troubling because they embody so many paradoxes: about what we have in common, about what separates us, about our sense of self and our recognition of others, about conflicting belongings in a changing history and a complex modern world, and about the possibility of social action in and through our identities" (1995: 36). Included here is the idea that sexual identities contribute simultaneously to a sense of uniformity and to a sense of difference, as well as the perception that common identities may constitute a core point of reference for organizing and social action.

An additional important feature in the notion of "sexual identity" is the dialectical processes of their acquisition, as well as the "reflexivity," to borrow the concept advanced by Giddens (1990, 1991), implied in their adoption. The dialogue between individuals and society is characterized, using a view advanced by Habermas, as a "socialized sense of individuality, an internal organization of self-perceptions concerning one's relationship to social categories, that also incorporates views of the self perceived to be held by others" (Epstein 1987: 29). In this sense, identities are conceptualized, not as being permanent or fixed, but instead as able to undergo periods when they are "in flux" and to change as they link different aspects of a person's life and as personal biographies are reinterpreted "to conform with present self-understandings and achieve a consistent sense of self" (1994: 192). The dynamic nature of identities is what Barbara Ponse summarizes in the phrase "identity work" (quoted in Epstein 1987: 32).

The acquisition of a sense of identity is particularly needed as modern societies have become increasingly complex. The logic here is that with the breakdown of more traditional forms of community, individuals engage in a "quest for identity" and seek to resolve "identity crisis" and "find themselves" (Epstein 1987: 30). In Giddens's view (1990, 1991), modernity implies a constant examination and reform of social practices, and because this examination creates considerable uncertainty,[1] identities in such contexts provide reassurance.

The formation of identities, however, does not take place in a vacuum. Plummer (1981: 69) suggests that an essential part of identity formation is the personal interpretation of lived sexual experience—an interpretation that uses the relational aspects of sex and sexuality ("the significant encounters") as raw material. Dowsett (1996: 97) has taken this idea further by emphasizing what he calls the "performative" aspects of sexual identities and the role that they have in shaping individual and collective interpretations.

Not unlike Epstein, Weeks, and Plummer, Dowsett is critical of views that conceive of identities as immutable categories that are based on the assumption of "an existential function representing a psychic state, or a resolution of an individuated coming to the self" (1996: 95). He argues that assuming immutability leads to the incorrect notion that everyone easily fits in widely recognized categories, such as homosexuality or heterosexuality, and to the inaccurate assessment that members of communities defined around a specific sexual identity, such as gay communities, all share a uniform experience and a uniform identity.

By emphasizing the performative, Dowsett also pays special attention to what he calls a type of "skilling" that results from the practice of sex and that contributes considerably to the interpretation of identity. In this regard, he challenges the view that people acquire a sexual identity and then perform the sexual behaviors expected of that identity. Instead, he suggests that sexual desire and performance precede and inform the adoption of a sexual identity, as well as the adoption of a particular label for sexual self-definition. In this sense, he assigns sexual practice a central role in an individual's overall self-definition and conceives of a "sexual construction of society" which is a counterpart to the more common view of the "social construction of sexuality" (Connell and Dowsett 1992; Dowsett 1996).

These concepts are all quite useful for the purposes of my study and have guided my analysis in the four chapters that follow. Asking individuals about their sexual identities proved helpful in understanding not only their interpretations about themselves and others—in terms of sexual desires, personae, and behavior—but also the sexual world in Guadalajara and Mexico. In this sense, participants' ideas and interpretations, seen as representations of social views that are prevalent in the current historical moment in Guadalajara, provided snapshots of the landscape of sexuality in the city. A more general image of this landscape emerged from the patterns of interpretations offered and from the expression of apparent contradictions—contradictions both within individual narratives and among individuals.

ASSIGNING NAMES: SEXUAL IDENTITY LABELS

Most participants in my study in Mexico were capable of providing interpretations of their own sexual identity or the sexual identities of others. In my interviews, and during informal conversations, I asked them what they would call different types of people depending on their sexual attractions and desires. I also asked them what term they chose to describe their own sexual identity, sexual orientation, or sexual preference (terms that were used almost as synonyms by those familiar with the general concept). As they responded to these questions, participants used a variety of labels and were usually able to determine where different groups of people fit (or did not fit) in Mexican society, as well as to explain the logic that informed their interpretations. This happened in almost every case, even among those who requested some explanation of the terms "identity," "orientation," and "preference" as they applied to the arena of sexuality.

Participants' reflections provided eloquent views of their understanding of the Mexican field of social relations concerned with gender and sexuality. By the end of most of my conversations about this topic, participants had presented what constituted their own "grand vision" of the organization of categories of sexual identity—the separation of people into distinct groups—in Mexican society.

In explaining the logic of their interpretations of sexual identities, participants also pointed to what they perceived to be the accepted rules of categorization. Such rules were diffuse, in the sense that they were not written anywhere, and no one seemed to be imposing them or enforcing them. The locus of definition of the rules appeared to be society as a whole—or the amorphous entity that people described as *"la sociedad mexicana."* In this sense, participants' perception of rules of categorization was consistent with what Bourdieu (1994) called "strategies," which he associated with people's understanding of a "practical sense of things" or "a sense of the game." He used the metaphor of games and players to explain the role that individuals have in applying, maintaining, and changing the rules of social relations—in this case the rules of categorization of sexual identities. This distinction is relevant here, because it will help us understand how individuals develop the perception that certain rules of categorization exist as a given, as well as what kinds of "moves" would be advantageous, and which ones would be disadvantageous because they would be dissonant with the socially accepted rules of the game.

In general terms, participants were aware of two sets of categories that informed the understanding of sexual identities in Mexico. These were recognized as distinct from each other and as simultaneously available (and often simultaneously valid, despite their differences). One set included categories of classification that were based on gender/sex roles,[2] which were strongly flavored by notions of normality and deviance defined by demeanor; and the other included categories of identity based on object choice, a classification founded on the separation between homosexuals, bisexuals, and heterosexuals. These two distinct sets were used not only to assign labels to different types of individuals but also to judge the currency or obsolescence of the ideas and values of other people. Often, the boundaries between the two sets were blurred, and people used categories from one to interpret some identities, and categories from the other to interpret others. Sometimes, they even created definitions that resulted from a combination of categories from the two sets, blended into a new one.

The chapters that follow will show how different participants used these two separate forms of classification. It will be important to pay attention to differences in tone and ideas depending on whether individuals thought of their rules of classification as being universally shared and applicable, and also whether they experienced some discomfort with the socially accepted rules and presented a view that they regarded as more personal and adequate. This distinction was also, to some degree, an indication of a separation between individuals who were content with the status quo and individuals who emphasized a need for social change (and thus for changes in categorization or interpretation of specific identities). I now turn to a discussion of the first form of classification, which was based on gender/sex roles.

I AM *NORMAL*:
GENDER-BASED CATEGORIES
OF SEXUAL IDENTITY

Almost without exception, participants in my study were aware of categories of sexual identity that are defined in terms of two dominant criteria: biological sex and gender-based expectations of demeanor (masculine and feminine). These criteria define the four quadrants of the model of sexual categorization that I have represented in figure 1.

The categories and labels included in this model have been well studied and were identified in academic writing beginning in the 1950s. Paz (1985) provided what is perhaps the first organized depiction of the traditional system of classification of identities and sexual roles in Mexico. Since then, a number of scholars have further defined the interpretations associated with this classification.[1] Carrier (1972) should be credited for his careful identification of the taxonomy of classification prevalent within the subcultures of men with same-sex attraction, as well as Taylor (1978) and Murray (1995) for additional work and refinement of the analysis on this same topic.[2]

In this categorization, "normality" is usually and automatically assumed when there is concordance between a person's biological sex and the demeanor considered appropriate to that sex. Women are expected to act "feminine" and men to act "masculine." People who conform

Biological Sex: Male	Biological Sex: Female
QUADRANT 1 *Hombres/Hombres Normales* (Men/Normal Men) Men who are masculine and exclusively attracted to women. Men who are masculine and attracted to men and women or only to men. Assumed to be inserters in sex with men. Labeled *activos* in the milieu of sex between men.	**QUADRANT 2** *Machorras* Women who are masculine. Assumed to reject men and to be attracted to women. Labeled derogatorily by society as *machorras, manfloras, tortilleras,* or *chancleras.*
Internacionales Men assumed to take both *activo* and *pasivo* roles in sex with men.	
QUADRANT 3 *Maricones* Men who are effeminate. Assumed to be exclusively attracted to other men and to be the receptive partner in sex between men. Labeled derogatorily by society as *maricones, jotos,* or *putos.* Regarded as *pasivos* or *locas* in the milieu of sex between men.	**QUADRANT 4** *Mujeres/Mujeres Normales* (Women/Normal Women) Women who are feminine and exclusively attracted to men. Women who are feminine and attracted to men and women or only to women.

(Left margin: Demeanor: Masculine (top), Demeanor: Feminine (bottom))

Figure 1 Sex/Gender model of sexual identity categorization in Guadalajara

to these two criteria are simply given the labels of *hombre* (man) or *hombre normal* (normal man) and *mujer* (woman) or *mujer normal* (normal woman). These categories occupy quadrants 1 and 4 in figure 1. People who do not meet these criteria acquire a status that places them at the margins of society and are assigned labels that indicate their "abnormal" or "deviant" character. This dichotomy makes identities in two of the quadrants of this gender-based model "normal," while the identities in the other two are considered "abnormal."

In this model, the criteria used to define the categories, as well as to decide who falls in the realm of "normality," do not require knowledge about the sex of a person's sexual partners. It is merely assumed that masculine men are attracted to women, and that feminine women are attracted to men. It is also assumed that men play a more dominant role (as penetrators) and that women have a passive role (as sexually receptive partners) during sex. This second assumption also validates the notion, often associated with machismo, that the realm of the masculine dominates over the feminine (and by extension that men are superior to women).

The labels used in this classification to refer to men and women who exhibit demeanors considered to be of the opposite sex—effeminate men and masculine women—are all derogatory. The terminology includes the words *maricón, joto,* and *puto* for men; and *machorra, manflora, tortillera,* and *chanclera* for women. As reported by Carrier and Taylor in the 1970s, men who are effeminate (and assumed to be penetrated during anal sex) were traditionally labeled *pasivos* within the homosexual milieu *(ambiente),* and their masculine partners (assumed to be the insertive partners in anal sex) were labeled *activos.*[3] The latter are also assumed to be capable of retaining their status as "normal" men. Absent from this model is the notion of "bisexuality" as a separate category, because individuals considered *normal* are given some latitude to transgress and have sex with members of their own sex without losing their status, as well as to continue engaging in sexual interaction with members of the opposite sex.[4]

NORMAL AS A CONTEMPORARY SEXUAL IDENTITY

In strict terms, *normal* is not a label that people applied to themselves in their everyday lives. Their sexual self-identification was as *hombres* or *mujeres,* men or women, which not only indicated their biological sex but also denoted their "normality" in terms of demeanor and sexual attraction (meaning exclusive attraction to the opposite sex). *Normal* became a label of choice when individuals wanted to distance themselves from those whom they considered deviant or abnormal. The use of the term provided clarification about a person's sexual attraction and confirmed an essentialist perception of manhood and womanhood.

For instance, Dalia, a young college student, responded to a question about her sexual orientation by saying that she was "attracted to guys." I followed up with a request for clarification: "I asked you what your sexual orientation is and you said you like guys. Would you use any word to describe yourself if someone asked you about such attraction?" Dalia's succinct response was, "I am normal." Similarly, I asked María, a twenty-three-year-old woman, "Are you attracted to men, women, or both?" She responded, laughing, "I like men."

"How would you describe yourself given that you like men?"

"As a normal person."

Ramiro, a young factory worker, used the terms *puñal* ("dagger," a variation of the word *puto*) and *joto* to refer to men who have sex with other men. He had previously indicated that he had never had sex with men, only with women. "I am not attracted to that," he emphasized. I asked him whether he was familiar with the term *homosexual*.

"That he likes men?" he stated hesitantly, as if asking for confirmation or clarification.

I also asked him how he defined his sexual identity. "I would say I am a normal man," he responded. Later in the interview, I asked him whether he had ever heard the word *heterosexual*. He simply responded, "No."

For some of these participants, the use of the label *normal* indicated their belief that the concepts of sexual orientation, identity, or preference (which are used alternatively in Mexico to refer to the same idea) did not apply to people like them. They saw no need to seek a term that denoted sexual orientation when they assessed correspondence between a person's biological sex and his or her demeanor. The absence of such correspondence indicated "abnormality" and, thus, the need to apply a label that suggested "deviance." Others, however, had begun to understand that there was more to the classification than biological sex and demeanor and were applying the concept of sexual orientation to people with same-sex attraction by using labels such as *homosexual*. For them, *normal* was becoming the label with which they referred to opposite-sex attraction in terms of sexual orientation. For instance, talking about sexual orientation with Alicia, a twenty-five-year-old woman, I said: "You used the terms *homosexual* and *lesbiana*. What term would you use for a man who only likes women?" She responded with silence and a puzzled look on her face. I insisted, "And a woman who only likes men?"

"Well, I don't know how but, well, *normal*," responded Alicia.

This kind of response, which was not uncommon, also suggested that some of the people who used terms such as *homosexual* and *bisexual* were not aware of the term *heterosexual*.

Normal was not strictly a category of sexual identity, because the generalized use of the label commonly lacked the kind of reflection that is assumed to accompany the formation of sexual identities. However, in its use as an antonym to the words *homosexual* and *bisexual*, it did constitute the equivalent to a category of identity. At the time of my research, Mexicans were increasingly using the label *normal* to further specify the social adequacy of someone who would otherwise be plainly called *hombre* (man) or *mujer* (woman). In calling someone *normal,* people were often making a leap of faith and assuming that a person whose appearance and demeanor correspond to social expectations is also "naturally" attracted to the opposite sex.

In the environment where these perceptions were prevalent, people sometimes viewed any questions about their sexual orientation as reflecting a suspicion that they were not "normal." They felt threatened if they believed that the only ones needing a label are those who are "abnormal." In my study, several participants seemed surprised to be asked what their sexual orientation was or to explain what the causes of their "normality" were.

I expected that those regarded as abnormal in this classification would question their exclusion from the realm of normality or the use of the label *normal* to refer to heterosexual people. However, not all of them did. Some men who had adopted an identity as *homosexual* or *gay,* for instance, applied the label *normal* to heterosexual people who were close to them and who they saw as having "no defect." This was the case with Pedro, who identified as *homosexual* and who responded to the question, "How would you call a man who only likes women?" with the statement, "Ah, a normal man."

"And a woman who only likes men?"

"The same."

"What does it mean, *normal?*"

"That they are normal. I was born to them. I am talking of my mother and father."

It is poignant that Pedro reported being anally penetrated by close male relatives beginning at the age of three or four, first by an uncle and later by his grandfather. Although he did not explicitly say that he thought of these relatives as *normal,* in his comments he implied that these men were macho, and he never made any comments that suggested that he thought of them as *homosexuales.* Comments that he made about himself suggested that he had internalized a sense of shame about being *homosexual*—his use of the term *normal* seemed to indicate as well a perception of his own "abnormality."

In another example, Gabriela, who used the term *gay* to describe her sexual identity, used the word *buga* to refer to women who are attracted to men. *Buga*[5] is a term commonly used among Mexican homosexual people, sometimes derogatorily, to refer to *heterosexuales.*

"What does it mean that a woman is *buga?*"

"She is normal. She is the prototype of a woman," was her conclusion.

Finally, all the quotations in this section are from individuals who were born after 1960, which indicates that the adoption of *normal* as an identity that complements that of *hombre* and *mujer* is prevalent among younger Mexicans. I later contrast this perception with that of people who chose the word *heterosexual* to define the sexual identity of individuals who are exclusively attracted to the opposite sex.

A WORLD DIVIDED BY GENDER ROLES: SEX

Within the gender-based categorization of identities that I describe here, it is fairly common for Mexican men and women to assume the dominance of men in all spheres of everyday life, including sex and sexuality. The traditional sexual roles of men and women in Mexican society have been, in fact, thoroughly depicted in the literature on the topic, ever since Paz's influential account in his 1950 book, *The Labyrinth of Solitude.*

Awareness of a traditional cultural script that prescribes gender roles is so widespread that participants in my study easily summarized the overall social expectation for both sexes. They stated that men are assumed to have less control over their sexual energy; need, and should be allowed, more sexual exploration; and are the ones to establish the rules about sexual interaction. Women, by contrast, continued to be seen as having a lesser need for sex; as depending on the male's sexual prerogatives to define their sexual behavior; and as having the choice to be either "virtuous," "self-sacrificing," and thus "good" (the wife, the mother, the fiancée) or "common" and "bad" (the lover, the prostitute).

In either case, women lose. In the most traditional or stereotypical expression of the categories of "good" and "bad" women, the perception was that if they decide to remain virtuous, women should stay virgins and not have sex before marriage. They were also supposed to become completely devoted and faithful to their husbands and be understanding and tolerant of the husband's extramarital sexual behaviors (Döring 1990: 41). Having sex should not be a woman's prerogative, except when the husband so desired and often with the goal of bearing children, not for pleasure. And, given the expectation that a woman was to have only one man in her life, there was no guarantee that her sex life after marriage would be fulfilling.

If women decided to break these rules, they could cross the boundary of "decency" and become "common" or "bad." They would gain with this change an opportunity to have more sexual liberty and to explore their sexual desires more readily, but they would possibly have to live with the stigma of being ineligible for a long-term stable relationship or for marriage. They would be typically sought by men for fun, to be a temporary lover, but not for anything more formal (Lamas 1990; Moreno 1990; Döring 1990).

As I mentioned in the previous chapter, regardless of the strong social judgment against "common" women, historically they have been assumed to play an important social role. They are supposed to "teach" young men about sex and act as an escape valve for desires that men cannot fulfill with more "virtuous" women. In this sense, they have helped "good" women retain their role by becoming the recipients of the unbridled sexual energy of men. So long as men were capable of realizing their fantasies and releasing their energy with some women, they could keep other women pure and unexposed to the "darker" side of sex.

The description of the gender roles that I have offered in the previous paragraphs was recognized by many in my study, but most participants did not see them as remaining fully valid in contemporary Mexico. However, expectations about the roles taken by men and women *during sexual relationships* seemed to still inform contemporary perceptions, as participants often used them to justify their beliefs about specific partners or sexual situations. For instance, Alicia talked about the expectations of an older boyfriend with whom she had had sexual relations and had lived out of wedlock. The man was her father's thirty-year-old *compadre*. She was seventeen when their relationship started and was a virgin until the first time that they had sex, which occurred in a motel. Although they did not get married, they stayed together for four years. During those years she had sex with no one else. Alicia said that because of the way they met and how their relationship started, he treated her wonderfully and thought of her as "pure." In her comments, she implied that he measured her purity by her compliance to his will and that he was concerned that such purity could be tainted by her exposure to sex or to talk about sex. Alicia said: "He would say, 'it's white,' and I would say, 'it's white' [regardless of how I saw it]. But I never spoke out. . . . He watched porn films and he didn't want me to watch them. He said I was the purest, the cleanest, the prettiest, and he didn't want me to watch those kinds of films or have conversations [about sex] with other people."

Men in my study who separated their female sexual partners into "good" and "bad" also felt the need to engage in only the more conventional sexual practices with those women whom they placed in the category of "good." They reserved what they thought of as more daring, erotic practices for their encounters with more "common" or "bad" women—with prostitutes, casual sexual partners, and lovers.[6]

This was the case for Javier, a thirty-five-year-old married man. Javier said that he felt lucky because women often made sexual advances toward him in his work as a singer at a bar. He considered this a reversal of the more typical role: men attending bars and making sexual advances at the women who worked there. "They sent me drinks. Just the opposite [of what is expected]. It was like I was the prostitute and I was *fichando* [seeking to be paid for drinks or sex]." The result was that he had multiple opportunities to have sex with women. Such ample availability had made him become selective. His preference was for women who were not too aggressive, who demonstrated interest but allowed him to take the lead and fulfill his role as a man.

He had met his wife at the bar, where she was a patron. She had made her attraction evident but had been reserved in her approach to him. This led him to court her. During that time, he wanted to have sexual intercourse with her, but she rejected his advances. "Maybe that is what I liked," he said, grinning. "That she was different from the rest." The farthest he got with her before marriage was to touch her genitals and make her have orgasms through masturbation. She never saw or touched his genitals before marriage. "Nice, it was nice," he said as he described the sexual tension and repressed desire, as well as the fact that she did not let him go all the way.

When we talked about the kind of sex that he had with his wife, he indicated that "one doesn't treat his wife as a prostitute or a lover, although, deep inside, women like that. Even when they are very decent, in a certain way they would like to be prostitutes. Deep inside I realized that, at least in my wife."

"Tell me if there are differences in terms of sex behaviors with a wife or with a prostitute or lover," I requested.

"Yes," responded Javier. "For instance, the wife must be treated gently, with affection. And you would not use certain positions."

"Such as?"

"For instance, what is classic in marriage: men on top, both horizontal, and that's it, the story is over.[7] But opening their legs wide, doing it doggie style, having her sit on top of you, doing it standing or against the wall—those are things that happen in your imagination and that are easy to do with a lover or prostitute because you don't care if she feels used, manipulated. And if she has an orgasm, fine, but if she doesn't, fine too. You are there to get your own satisfaction." The diversification of sexual positions was, in Javier's mind, a sign that a woman was "common" and granted men permission to use her, manipulate her, and treat her with disdain.[8]

Javier complained that, in comparison to other lovers, his wife was not very good at sex. Yet, he had also found that with the proper motivation his wife was quite willing to experience her sexuality more freely. Javier showed a mix of puzzlement and pleasure at his realization of this transformation in his wife. "In fact, I began treating my wife that way [as a lover or prostitute] and she liked it. . . . When we are hanging out, we go to a hotel, and then she does initiate [sex]. It is great because when she is already drunk she dances and strips for me."

In this particular case, Javier seemed to feel in charge of how much the rules about his wife's sexuality changed. I never met his wife, so I do not know who she felt was truly in control. I have no way of telling whether she saw Javier as the agent of this change, whether she herself felt responsible, or both. This kind of change, however, would not be seen as acceptable within the constraints of the traditional good/bad dichotomy—it represents a blurring of the boundaries between the two possible female roles.

In another example, Esteban made comments throughout his interview that denoted that his ideas about sexuality were not traditional. Yet, his way of distinguishing different types of women and treating them differently conformed to the traditional gender roles discussed here. He had had sex with several woman friends and casual partners and had explicitly chosen not to have sex with his current girlfriend because he saw her as a good candidate for marriage. "Do you plan to marry her?" I asked him.

"I am seeing her with marriage in mind . . . formally, seriously. I try for *lo nuestro* [literally 'what is ours'] to be conventional and it's what I've dreamed of: a marriage with a honeymoon and the beauty that a moment like that may entail." Motivated by this goal, Esteban greatly appreciated his girlfriend's conservatism and saw it as a quality that made him "respect" her.

Not having sex with her was a conscious decision on his part in order to favor the process of their getting married. Esteban constructed his girlfriend as the type of woman who was pure and decent. He assumed that she was a virgin, but he had no way of telling because he had never asked her. Yet, having considered the possibility that she might not be a virgin, he expressed the opinion that virginity was not crucial. In this sense, Esteban departed considerably from traditional views. He added, however: "If she told me that she is not a virgin, it might not be bad for us to have a conversation, to learn why she lost her virginity. If she lost it for love, I would have to accept it, because she gave her feelings and love [to someone]. That he did not reciprocate is a different issue. What she will do with me is what matters, not what she did with the other one. It's that simple." Esteban invoked in this comment the notion that the only good reason for a "good" woman to have sex is as a demonstration of her love.

Esteban seemed to become somewhat disturbed when I suggested the possibility that, should his girlfriend confess to not being a virgin, she might have had sex just for sexual pleasure. But he managed to maintain his composure.

"If she put it in those terms, we would have to—the interesting part is that she must tell me before getting married. If she told me after being married, as a confession, I would be grateful to her for telling me, and I would still see her with the same eyes. That simple. But it would be very important to have a conversation prior to marriage." It was unclear what he would do, or whether the timing of conversation could change the outcome, but in responding to this question Esteban seemed to be confronting some level of discomfort. By contrast, Esteban never suggested that there would be a need for him to tell his girlfriend about his sexual exploration prior to meeting her and whether he had had sex for love or for pleasure.

Elsewhere in the interview, Esteban said that many women in Guadalajara were conservative, which severely limited the opportunities for a young man like him to have sex. He also described how he managed to seduce traditional, conservative women. He gave them a few drinks to encourage them to acknowledge their desire for sex—to help them overcome their repression. But, interestingly, he did not think of his girlfriend as belonging in this group of potentially seducible women.

This case suggests what seemed to be a very complicated understanding of women's sexual roles, which contrasted strikingly with the simplicity with which Esteban perceived the roles of men. For instance, discussing his views on people who have multiple sexual partners, Esteban stated, "I think the situation of men and women is very different. A man is by nature a hunter. He encounters all kinds of situations on the street. I am seeing this from a *machista* viewpoint. A woman has much to lose in the eyes of society, as much is said about a woman [if she has sex], and [society] cares about whether a woman is pure, chaste, and has respect for her partner." The implication was that a man could be sexual with little consequence.

In Esteban's account, the pool of Guadalajaran women comprised three distinct groups. One included emancipated women willing to have sex for the sake of sex itself. A second group included women who were to be viewed with respect and as potential wives. These were women with whom a man should consider having sex only after marriage. The third group included women who were traditional but could be convinced to have sex. A man could tell that they wanted it and help them overcome their resistance through seduction.

Consistent with the sexual role that he saw his future wife having, Esteban also envisioned her becoming a housewife with no desire to develop professionally. He wanted to talk with her before marriage and make sure they agreed that she would not work but instead be a dedicated housewife and raise their children. However, he was not fully closed to considering changes should his wife want to put them up for discussion. Esteban said, "If there are children, I feel it is the obligation of the man to take responsibility, to work and bring up his family successfully. . . . I do not intend to let my wife work once we have children. . . . I think it is important for the woman to develop . . . but ultimately the responsibility [of work and support] is the man's."

"And what would happen if you have children and your wife says that her work is important to her and that she wants to continue working?"

"I'll be honest with you," emphasized Esteban. "One of my main plans before marrying is to talk; to inform her about my policy, my way of thinking, and how I feel and manage certain situations. There must be a common agreement and the agreement should be respected. If my wife had such a desire, we would need to talk about it, put it up for discussion." Esteban believed in negotiation but ultimately would find it unacceptable for his wife to impose her will over his. He thought it his obligation to initiate a dialogue to ensure clarity—a move toward equity, in his own mind—but also had the goal of imposing his desire in the process.

I will refer to Esteban again, because his ideas about sex and sexuality often mixed perceptions that reflected traditional values with perceptions that are regarded to be much more contemporary. In fact, this was the case even in relation to the sexual role that he saw his future wife taking. I asked him, "Would you prefer for her to be sexually experienced when you and she start a sexual life, or would you prefer her to know very little about sex, or something in between?"

"I have no preference. Simply that she loves and respects me and tries to experience with me what we will experience together. I don't care whether she is [sexually] experienced or not. If she is experienced, our sexual relationship will be one way. If not, [I would] try at that point to treat her more calmly, censoring my fantasies."

Ultimately, Esteban envisioned that his wife should fully participate in the search for new sexual sensations and that both partners should be capable of taking the initiative in such a search. In this sense he departed considerably from the traditional notions that the initiative to have sex or to decide what to do during sex is a male prerogative and that women who take sexual initiative are also saying that they are "easy" or "common."

This perception that initiative indicates "looseness" in women was also addressed by Lola, a twenty-four-year-old single mother who had lived her sexuality fairly freely since the age of fourteen. Lola said, "It was surprising to men . . . the fact that I took the initiative, as if they thought, 'Why are you so experienced?' And in fact many women are inhibited . . . we are inhibited in a first relationship due to the reactions of men. 'Oh! *Tienes mucho mundo*' [you are a woman of the world]. . . . The reaction is that you are *muy correteadita* [have been around the block]." *Tienes mucho mundo* was a reference to being emancipated, and thus loose.[9]

In other comments, Lola implied that women ought to be careful about how they present themselves to men in order to avoid being automatically placed in the category of "common" or "bad" women. She was aware that even when she had a freer sexuality, she had to pretend to be somewhat submissive and inexperienced in order to be accepted as a more stable, potentially marriageable sexual partner.

The inequalities in sexual roles described here were not restricted to male-female couples and were sometimes also replicated in same-sex relations. This seemed to be especially true for men who had fully adopted a role as *mujeres* or *pasivos* and who embraced, as part of their identity, a traditional and stereotypical feminine role—a role that may be more extreme than that of many women. I expand on this topic later in this chapter.

The roles described above have an enormous effect on the lack of power that many women and *pasivos* experience in terms of self-determination and control over decisions that might affect their personal interests. Men— "masculine," "normal"—in Mexico still have much higher levels of income, education, opportunity, independence, and cultural and financial capital.

EMA AND GREGORIO: INEQUALITIES OF POWER

In the political economy of male-female relations, "traditional" gender roles in Mexico were enormously pervasive. Among other things, they formalize the strong inequality between men and women, which is manifested in all spheres of social life. Although the proportion of women who are not exclusively housewives has consistently increased in the past decades, many men still view their female partners' jobs as secondary, and many working women must do a second shift of housework to justify having a job outside the home.[10]

In this study, I observed the evolution of several relationships between men and women in which the power differences between the partners were immense. Perhaps the most eloquent example is that of Ema and Gregorio, who separated in 1994 after a twelve-year relationship.

Ema had been raised in Mexico City, where she had been independent and sexually free until she met Gregorio. He came from a traditional background and had grown up in a rural town. Because Gregorio perceived Ema as being sexually experienced, he never considered her a potential marital partner. He had nonetheless proceeded to have a child with her. Over the course of their relationship, there was constant tension between Ema's desire for more equality and freedom and Gregorio's desire for a more conventional arrangement (but without marriage).

The couple shared an apartment in a lower-middle-class suburb of Guadalajara. She was a clerical worker and he was employed as a professional in a corporation. Although his salary was three times hers, his interpretation of equality was that household expenses were to be split evenly. He also expected that Ema would take care of the housework (in effect, doing a second shift after work).[11] Although he had total freedom to decide what to do with his leisure time, he was extremely jealous about Ema doing things alone or with friends during the little free time that she had left.

In terms of the expenses, Gregorio invested a good proportion of his contribution to the household in the mortgage for their apartment and in the payments for a new car, appliances, and other material goods. He mostly invested in hard assets, which he considered his personal property, as opposed to family property. Ema's salary was spent on food and general household expenses.

The relationship took a turn when Gregorio lost his job in 1993. To survive, Ema took a second job and paid for most of the household expenses for a period of eight months. During that time, she managed to achieve greater equality, to negotiate Gregorio's participation in housework, and to have more freedom to do things with her friends. However, when Gregorio started a new job, he requested that they return to the old pattern. He suggested that Ema should continue working at her regular job and be a housewife after work. In exchange, he would again contribute money to the household. His hope was that, as things returned to normal, he would also stop being expected to do his share of the housework or to be lenient in his demand for Ema's full attention to his needs.

Ema found this offer to be unacceptable and decided to leave him.

The decision was very hard for her. She went through a traumatic period, knowing what she wanted but feeling enormous remorse about what Gregorio would think of her actions, as well as concern for the possible consequences that their child would face. Fearing that Gregorio would act violently or try to "sweet-talk" her into staying, she made all the arrangements for her move in secret, when Gregorio was not at home. She also decided to tell Gregorio at the last minute and to leave all the packing for the few hours between the moment when she planned to break the news to him and the arrival of the movers she had hired.

She told Gregorio she was leaving the evening before her move, without saying that the movers were coming the following morning. He was too stunned to respond. The next day he left for work furious but still unable to respond. Ema had recruited a few friends, mostly homosexual men, to come help her pack and get things ready for the move. A small army of people descended on her house that morning and worked determinedly. Unfortunately, the movers showed up early, and many things were not ready. Ema had a momentary emotional breakdown and felt that her decision was wrong. Sitting on a box, in tears, she mourned the extent of her oppression and how, even now, she was in a difficult situation because of the accommodations she had to make in order to avoid having more problems with Gregorio.[12]

In the end, Ema was successful in implementing the change that she greatly needed. Yet, even then, the inequality in her relationship with Gregorio was pervasive: she left with her son to rent an apartment and begin a new life from scratch, with no capital. Gregorio retained the apartment and all the appliances, of which he was the sole owner (the car had been repossessed due to his inability to pay while he was unemployed).

During the years that they were together, Ema strove for change and for the achievement of more equality in their relationship. She was able to take some steps toward her goal when Gregorio found himself jobless and in a more vulnerable and less powerful position. But as soon as he regained his financial independence, he immediately reverted to what he saw as logical roles for him and Ema. In his determination, there was little room for negotiation.

In 1998, Ema told me that she had finally regained most of the material stability that she had before she met Gregorio. Carefully managing her limited salary, she had been playing the primary role in supporting her son, had managed to buy most of the appliances that she needed for her apartment, and had managed to obtain a government loan to buy the apartment itself. She was now paying a mortgage instead of rent and felt that the next thing on her list was to buy a car. She also commented with pride that she had been able to achieve all this by herself, without relying on a man. She regretted that during the time that she lived with Gregorio, her salary had been considered by him to be a subsidy.

The kinds of assumptions about gender roles that men like Gregorio make, as well as the ways in which women internalize them, seem to limit Mexican men's and women's abilities to create more egalitarian relationships. As for sex itself, power differentials validate and preserve the double standard described in the previous section. Based on their greater power, men not only manage to maintain a dominant role but also justify having a freer sexuality while, at the same time, limiting the sexuality of their primary sexual partners—of the women whom they regard as "good," "virtuous," or "pure."

Javier, whom I quoted in the previous section, had several extramarital relations with women, which his wife eventually discovered. He reported that when he told her that her suspicions were true, she accepted the situation and just said, "Now I understand." Javier felt lucky about his wife's understanding and said that now she would not see his infidelity as a terrible thing (although he had pledged not to do it again). On the other hand, should his wife be unfaithful, "I would feel very angry," Javier said. "I told her, 'If you want to do it, I will understand that,' because she never had sex with anyone else, she didn't even masturbate. . . . I [also] told her, 'If you ever want to know how it feels with someone else, tell me, because if you do it without telling me, that's the end of our marriage.' Actually, what is really bothersome is if they [women] hide things from you." Javier's comments suggested that he ultimately saw her role as different from his and her status as lower. In his opinion, his wife should seek his permission before making any decisions about her own sexuality.

Discussing this topic in his analysis of attitudes about extramarital sex in his sample of men in Mexico City, Gutmann concluded that men who justified male adventures had

a more difficult time sifting through the layers of meaning when a question of women's delinquencies arises. Juan came into the kitchen of his home one day as Angela and I were talking about adulterous friends and neighbors. Angela looked up and said to Juan, "Now, tell Mateo whether a man would forgive a women for such an offence. Would you forgive her?" . . . "Men almost never forgive such woman, and when they do it's because they really love them—" Juan started to respond. . . . "Or 'because he's an ass!' That's Juan's expression," Angela shot back. (1996: 137)

Although in these two sections I have referred exclusively to relationships between men and women, the inequalities and roles extended to some same-sex relations as well. I describe this phenomenon in the next section.

THE CORNER IN THE PLAZA

I met Raúl, who was young and effeminate, when I was out for a drink at a gay bar and disco with a group of friends. I noticed that he was flirting with us. He stood close by, or walked by us with his friends, looking insistently at my group but with a coy expression in his eyes. He would smile but not talk to any of us. He would make his intention apparent and then disappear into the crowd, only to reemerge a few minutes later.

One of my friends said that he was a *loquita* (a little crazy woman), suggesting that he was the type of homosexual man who acts like a woman and who is blatantly effeminate, and added that Raúl and his friends were all working class *(de clase baja)*.[13] My friend also indicated that if I wanted to talk to Raúl I would probably have to be the one to approach him. Later in the evening, Raúl's group and mine ended up standing right next to each other at the bar. We began to talk and joke around. I told him that I wanted to interview him, but not in the bar. We made a plan to meet the next afternoon, in front of the Degollado Theater, in downtown Guadalajara.

Our meeting place was one of Guadalajara's four main downtown plazas. I knew that he had chosen a spot that was right across from a gathering point for working-class, effeminate men. Every afternoon, there was a group of around thirty young, feminine men in this corner of the plaza. Overt, sometimes extreme, effeminacy seemed to be more prevalent among these working-class *homosexuales* than among their middle-class counterparts.

I was impressed by the availability of this location to these men because the plaza was next to the municipal palace and behind Guadalajara's cathedral and was always very crowded with passersby and families. On several occasions, I had sat close to where the men gathered. As each man arrived, he made his round of social kissing. The men constantly joked and seemed to gossip about each other and about people passing by. They made no attempt to hide their feminine demeanors, and their interactions made them boldly noticeable. One time I saw them hold an impromptu *pasarela,* a street version of a fashion show, without the women's clothes but with all the right attitudes. They also whistled playfully or shouted *piropos* (compliments) at men whom they found attractive. This last action was socially risky, given that *piropos* have traditionally been directed by men to women passing by them as an expression of power, flirtation, innuendo, and plain harassment. Prieur (1998: 219) summarized these social functions of *piropos* as a kind of "labeling power." For the effeminate men in Guadalajara's plaza, *piropos* certainly seemed to give them some power and, in my few observations of this activity, I did not see a single person respond or confront the group.[14]

Neither the parents sitting nearby watching over their children playing in the plaza, nor the businessmen getting a shoe shine, nor the street vendors selling candy or cheap toys seemed to pay much attention or be disturbed by the effeminate behaviors of these men. There were also a few masculine-looking women sitting by themselves or interacting with the effeminate men. These women would traditionally be labeled derogatorily as *machorras* (tomboys), *tortilleras* (tortilla patters), or *chancleras* (sandal tappers), the last two terms suggesting the idea of sex without a penis. A few steps away, the guards at the municipal palace performed their everyday duties without having any visible interaction with the effeminate men or concern for their presence in the plaza.

The men in this corner of the plaza belonged to the category of men who have publicly given up their masculinity, either by fully dressing as women or by being overtly effeminate in public. Their femininity transferred them from the category of *hombre* or *normal* into the category of *maricón, joto,* or *puto.*[15] Not surprisingly, these street terms were strongly derogatory (and evoked sentiments similar to those conveyed by the English words "faggot," "sissy," and "queer").[16] These men were, in essence, the ones who incarnate deviance, the ones who are subject to rejection and scorn, the ones who confirm the masculinity of others and allow them to establish distance.

When I arrived that afternoon at the plaza, Raúl was already there. He asked whether I wanted to go for a walk and pointed out a friend to whom he wanted to say hello. His friend was Juan, a young man who worked as a cook in a downtown restaurant. Juan was feminine and outspoken and had been with Raúl the night before at the *disco gay.*

Juan said that he was sad because his partner had just left him, after being together for a week. He said that "as a woman," he had done everything he could to keep him, and he felt betrayed. I asked him, in light of his self-identification as a woman, whether that was how he thought about his sexual orientation.

"I don't know, what do you mean by that?" Juan replied.

"If you wanted to tell someone that you like men, what term would you use to describe yourself?"

"I would tell him that I am *gay*."

"So you describe yourselves as *gay?*" I asked, looking at them.

"Of course," Juan said. Raúl nodded as well.

I then asked Juan whether there was any connection between being a woman, being *gay*, and being either *pasivo* or *activo*. Juan took this question as an opportunity to lecture me about his role as a gay man who was also a woman. "That is important to say when you are planning to have a partner. They must know what you expect. We are the women for you, we are more affectionate, we have nice gestures for you, we take care of our partner, we look after them."

"Wait a second," I said in reaction to his statement. "Why are you placing me in a different category?"

"I can tell."

"What can you tell?"

"I don't know, what a question!" Juan said coyly and playfully.

I asked again how he would know how to place me in the category of men, instead of women. Juan retorted, "The truth, because of your gaze. You have a strong gaze. We have a more submissive gaze, we never look directly. But men do."

Raúl interjected at this point. "There is another reason; it's because he knows that you come with me and he knows that I am *pasiva* [feminine of *pasivo*, which further emphasizes the feminine role] and he imagines that you must be *activo* because otherwise you would not come with me."

"So, he is assuming that I am your partner or that I am interested in you?"

At this point, Raúl looked away and slowly twisted his body in a way that indicated his desire to appear coy and shy. "I see," was my reply. For Juan, this was Raúl's way of telling me that he was a woman. Given that I did not adopt the same behavior, he concluded that I did not act as a woman, and thus that I was a man.

Juan added that their expectation was that men respect them and love them. He said that men could expect many nice gestures in return. He believed in enacting a role of complete submission and self-sacrifice toward a partner. I asked him whether he expected reciprocation. Juan responded that he loved to receive flowers or stuffed animals from a partner. The partner who had just left him had bought him a bracelet engraved with the date of their first date, which he showed me as proof of their relationship.

In talking about their behavior at the disco the night before, Juan and Raúl said that if one of them is attracted to someone, he would make it evident with his eyes but would never speak to the man. He would patiently wait for the other to make the first move. By enacting a coy gaze, Juan or Raúl would also indicate to the potential partner that he was a woman. If the man did not approach, Juan or Raúl would interpret his dismissal as a sign that he was not interested, that he was not really a man, or that he was dumb. But if the man approached, they would immediately respond.

Later in our conversation, another man walked by who was the cashier in the *disco gay* where I met Juan and Raúl. He was masculine looking and had a moustache, but his demeanor was not macho. Juan called to him and asked that he join us, and immediately adopted a seductive pose. Juan also proceeded to tell the cashier that he never expected to see him in this part of town (meaning, at this corner of the plaza) and that it was a nice surprise. I asked the newcomer about his work at the disco and whether he was often propositioned by clients. He said that it happened sometimes and that he was always polite because "the client is always right," but he did not encourage further interaction. The exception was when there was mutual attraction, when the man was a *cuero* (literally "a pelt," meaning a hunk), because then it was nice to interact with him and the night went by faster. He clarified that for him a *cuero* would be a good-looking, masculine man. I asked whether this meant that they were *activo*, and he said that he believed more in the gay model—meaning reciprocal relationships among masculine men—and that whether they were *pasivo* or *activo* was not important.

When he left, Juan and Raúl said that the cashier was *pasivo*. I asked why they believed that and they said that he gave himself away by his gaze, that he was too sweet. They had also decided, without the man ever saying it, that he liked to be anally penetrated *(le gusta que se la metan)*. Juan seemed disappointed about this realization. He was also disappointed to find out that the cashier was involved in a ten-year-old relationship. He said this confirmed that the cashier was *pasivo*, because otherwise his relationship would not have lasted so long. His assumption seemed to be that, as *pasivo*, it was up to him to look after his more masculine partner and maintain the relationship.

When we were alone, Raúl told me more about his preferences during sex. He felt that he ought to do anything his partner wanted and follow his lead. He could not conceive of taking the initiative. He would only lay down, stay stiff, and let his partner do everything. This seemed to be a learned role, because he said there were times when he found himself betraying his desire to be a woman and "acting like a man during sex." This meant that he was the one taking the initiative and guiding the interaction. He also talked about a time when, in the middle of the night, he woke up from a dream and realized that he was trying to penetrate the man with whom he was sleeping.

In Raúl's case, there was a strong contrast between his image of himself as a woman and the way his body was built. His features and body type were such that he could easily pass as a "regular" masculine man. Although he criticized people who were *locas* (literally "crazy women") and who could not pass as men, he also emphasized his desire to look like a woman. On a later occasion, Raúl reported that he had been working on his walking and on how to better show the curves of his body. He then walked away from me and asked me whether he could be taken to be a woman when he walked. He also asked whether I would invite him home and let him clean my house as a way for him to taste what it would be like to adopt a woman's role. His preoccupation was more strongly focused on developing the ability to enact a feminine identity than on enacting a specific role during sex. The middle-class friend who had been with me at the gay disco the night that I met Raúl, and who labeled him *loquita,* not without judgment, was present when Raúl expressed interest in cleaning my house. He said to me later, "that was so weird, I told you he was a *loquita.*"

PASSING AS *NORMAL*

By adopting roles as *pasivos* and women, men like Juan and Raúl give up their status as *normales,* their status as "real men." The gender-based classificatory system, however, does not require that all men who engage in sex with other men renounce their masculinity or stop thinking of themselves as regular men. In fact, one of the most interesting features of this system is that the label *normal* does not automatically preclude individuals from having an interest in, or sexual involvement with, members of their own sex. The absence of object choice as a defining criterion makes it possible for individuals to be sexually involved with members of their own sex without necessarily breaking the rules—without having to cross the boundary between normality and abnormality and without having to give up an interest in, or sexual behavior with, members of the opposite sex.

In this classification, men who are attracted to men can easily remain "normal" by choosing to respect, at least publicly, social expectations of masculinity. They most likely have to conceal their sexual behaviors with men in order to maintain their status, but in some instances they might still be able to maintain their status even when others know about their same-sex attraction. They might also find a few spaces and social networks—those made up mostly of other men "who understand" and whose discretion can be trusted—where they can more readily admit that they are interested in men and where this interest would not automatically label them as deviant. And, in any case, they would need to take some steps to protect their masculinity. There is some evidence that some of these men might even need to conceal their male-male sexual behaviors from themselves, through elaborate psychological mechanisms that help them avoid being fully aware that their sexual partners are men.[17] In this sense, they conform to the old-fashioned statement "Que no me entere yo mismo de lo que hago en las noches" (May I not realize what I do at night), which Monsiváis (1998: 19) quotes in his discussion of traditional conventions about sexuality.

Should their same-sex behavior become publicly known, people around these men could assume, at least initially, that there must have been special circumstances—"he was drunk" or "he was too *caliente* [horny]"—and that they were the insertive, or dominant, partners in the sexual interaction. But the information would nonetheless create some kind of scandal and gossip. These men might be able to convince themselves and others that their behavior was just a *desliz* (a slippage, a mistake) and continue to conceal future sexual involvement with men. In response to rumors about his sexual behavior with men, a masculine man could also simply deny that they are true. His identity as a "normal," masculine man might also be further enhanced by his having female sexual partners, perhaps even a wife, as well as children of his own, regardless of whether he is sexually attracted to women or not. His ability to have sex with women might prove to himself and to others that "he functions" as a man.

However, the risk is that people might also begin to think of such men as *anormales* (abnormal) and link them to those men who are effeminate. There is some historical evidence that even in this situation people made a distinction between these "abnormal," not obviously effeminate men and those who were overtly effeminate (who would also be assumed to be their receptive sexual partners). Their *maricón* or *joto* sexual partners would most certainly have labels to distinguish them from men who are not interested in sex with men, words such as *mayate* and *jalador* (Prieur 1998; Taylor 1978). Having sex with effeminate men, or men who act and dress as women, might be the only strategy that simultaneously provides access to the enactment of same-sex desire and protection of masculinity.

The ability of these men to retain their status as *normales* is in stark contrast to the full transferring of the *maricones* into the realm of deviance. For the latter, the acquisition of a label denoting deviance can be forced, sometimes from an early age, due to the perceptions and judgments of those around them. However, it could also happen by the men's own choice, as a way to fully reject the social expectations of attraction to women, avoid the burden of secrecy, and make their availability clear to potential masculine partners.[18] In this case, a man in this category would exercise agency—he could emphasize his "femininity" and adopt a look and demeanor that place him fully and unequivocally outside the realm of masculinity and men as a conscious strategy. He would likely pay a large social price for this decision. But his existence would also be seen as "logical" (in the sense of "fitting within the rules of the game"), and he might be able to achieve a certain level of acceptance (or at least tolerance) within certain social networks and within the constraints imposed by an "abnormal" status. This is to say, as well, that when the use of gender-based categories predominates, the existence of effeminate men who adopt "deviant" identities makes sense and is perhaps less threatening than the idea that two masculine men would have sex with each other.

It is important to note that the gender-based classification leaves little room for the consideration of lifestyles other than the two that I have described. Men who desire sex with other men have the option either of giving up their status as men and demonstrating effeminacy or of hiding from society that they are attracted to men and passing as *normales*. The former are assumed to be interested in "normal" men; the latter, in effeminate men. This means that, within the traditional system, it is hard to classify men who are masculine and attracted to other masculine men. Their lives and identities remain hidden in the silent overlaps between normality and deviance. Monsiváis makes indirect reference to their historical invisibility when he states: "according to rigid classifications, until recently there were in Mexico only two types of homosexuals: the *joto* in a *tortería*[19] or bordello and the *maricón de sociedad* [with social position]. The rest are fleeting shades that, without a pigeonhole, develop a halo of malicious rumor or are always treated in a condescending manner or with the diminutive ('Juanito/Robertito') that underlines the eternal infantilism of those alien to the maturity of marriage" (1998: 21). As we will see in the following chapter, this invisibility is changing as more contemporary homosexual identities are making the attraction between masculine men a more valid option.

The invisibility of masculine men who are attracted to each other in the gender-based classification also prevents the consideration that men might choose to take both the insertive and the receptive roles during anal sex—to seek to be both *activo* and *pasivo*, with one or with different sexual partners. In strict terms, the idea of such behavior in this classification would be somewhat of an oxymoron. The closest to describing such behavior would be a term identified by Carrier (1972) and Taylor (1978): *internacional* (international). As a separate category, *internacional* is a departure from the gender-based classification because it represents a break from the rules of gender roles. The use of the term *internacional* thus denotes the belief that indulging in both penetrating and being penetrated is foreign and exotic.[20] However, the category may be regarded as belonging in this model insofar as it defines behavior in terms of gender roles and not object choice.

I now turn to analyzing a different model of sexual identities, which are based on object choice and are considered more modern interpretations. I am referring to the categories of homosexual, bisexual, and heterosexual, which, in places such as the United States, serve as the dominant categories for sexual identity classification. As we will see, however, their application in Mexico is not completely straightforward.

NEW FREEDOMS, NEW BOUNDARIES: BECOMING *HOMOSEXUALES,* *BISEXUALES,* AND *HETEROSEXUALES*

Over the course of the twentieth century, an understanding of categories of sexual identity that are based on object choice increasingly filtered to a considerable proportion of Mexicans, particularly the categories of *homosexual* and *bisexual.* These categories arrived in Mexico soon after their development in Europe, brought by books and wealthy Mexicans who participated in the European academic world at the time. Their terminology began to be used in Mexico in the more formal, often medicalized discourse on sexuality early in the century and had become institutionalized in a number of fields by the 1930s.[1] Referring to the field of criminology, for instance, Buffington wrote:

In a 1934 article on, "The Anti-Social Character of Homosexuals," written for *Criminalia,* the newly inaugurated professional journal for Mexican criminologists, Dr. Alfonso Millán buttressed Lombroso's old argument about atavistic homosexuals with up-to-date references to Freudian psychology and recent discoveries in endocrinology (the study of hormones). Extrapolating from these prestigious "scientific" sources, he concluded that male homosexuals took on the negative traits of both sexes: "from the man [*macho*] he has a somewhat aggressive, hostile, and vain spirit, while from the woman, the gossipy scheming, the subtle intrigue of the eighteenth-century salon, and traitorous coquetry." . . . And, although he distinguished between active and passive homosexual types, he added . . . that active partners were "as or more dangerous" than their passive counterparts because they were more aggressive and difficult to identify. (1997: 123)

In this quotation, we see a significant departure from the notion that the only partner in a same-sex relationship who is deviant or abnormal is the one who is effeminate or "passive." In this kind of discourse, which at the time appeared to be limited to an educated minority who read, we see the adoption of a notion of deviance that is based on sexual attraction. The masculine, active sexual partner is fully included in the category of homosexual—and different from men who are exclusively attracted to the opposite sex—and constitutes an even greater threat because of his ability to pass as a "regular" man.

In my study these categories were more readily accepted and understood by Mexicans who were younger and by those who were more educated. They were also more prevalent among those who had engaged in personal reflections about their sexuality, which most often included *homosexuales* and people who identified openly as *bisexuales* and who were seeking explanations or acceptance of their attraction. Yet, self-identification with the identity of *heterosexual* was also somewhat prevalent, especially when participants wanted to remark or emphasize that they were not *homosexual* or *bisexual*.

Awareness about homosexuality—defined by sexual attraction—was sometimes present even among heterosexual people who thought of themselves more regularly as *normal* or who did not fully understand the concept of *orientación sexual*. In fact, a great majority of participants readily used the term *homosexual* to refer to people who are attracted to their own sex. A smaller proportion used the Spanish word *gay*. Most participants often were also able to recognize that men did not have to be effeminate, or women to be masculine, to be homosexual. They also understood that the main criterion used to place an individual in one of the categories of identity was sexual attraction, although they often saw this as intrinsically tied to, or blurred with, what they conceived to be "abnormalities" in gender roles or demeanor. Finally, most participants had some degree of understanding about the fact that the object choice categories had stricter boundaries than categories based on gender roles, and identified each category as describing a distinct group of people.

Figure 2 describes the categories included in an object choice model

	Biological Sex: Male	Biological Sex: Female
Attraction to Women	**QUADRANT 1** *Hombres Heterosexuales* **(Heterosexual Men)** Men who are exclusively attracted to women and who are assumed to be masculine and not homosexual.	**QUADRANT 2** *Lesbianas* Women who are attracted exclusively to other women, regardless of whether they or their partners are masculine or feminine in demeanor. Women adopting identities as *lesbianas, mujeres homosexuales,* or *mujeres gay.*
	Bisexuales Men who are attracted to women and to other men.	*Bisexuales* Women who are attracted to men and to other women.
Attraction to Men	**QUADRANT 3** *Homosexuales/Gays* Men who are exclusively attracted to other men, regardless of whether they or their partners are masculine or feminine in demeanor. Men adopting identities as *homosexuales* or *gays.*	**QUADRANT 4** *Mujeres Heterosexuales* **(Heterosexual Women)** Women who are exclusively attracted to men and who are assumed to be feminine and not homosexual.

Figure 2 Object choice model of sexual identity categorization in Guadalajara

of sexual categorization in Guadalajara. In this case, one criterion is biological sex; the other is sexual attraction. Demeanor and gender roles disappear as dominant criteria and become secondary. Biological men can be either *homosexual, bisexual,* or *heterosexual,* regardless of whether they are masculine or feminine, *pasivo* or *activo.* For women, the situation is fairly similar: lesbians are identified as such regardless of their femininity or masculinity, so long as they assume an open lesbian identity.

The category of *bisexual* comprises men and women who openly assert their liking for both sexes as central to a separate identity and to their life-style. As we will see in the next chapter, this category is different from the hybrid category of *heterosexuales* who exhibit occasional homosexual be-haviors. The category is also conceived to be different from the identities of men and women who identify as "normal" but who have sex with both men and women. In this model it is more difficult for these self-described "normal" people to retain such an identity, however. This is due to a more widespread awareness that individuals who are attracted to their own sex are *homosexuales* or, at best, *bisexuales* if they have, or pretend to have, an attraction to the opposite sex. This shift is quite significant. In this model of categorization, public knowledge of homosexual behavior automatically transfers individuals from "normality" into a separate category altogether, even if they do not end up in the category of *bisexual.*

The most evident difference between this model and the gender-based model in figure 1 (above on p. 38) is the change in the conceptualization of male homosexuality. In contrast to *maricones* or *jotos,* who are assumed to be effeminate and the passive partners in a sexual relationship between men, *homosexuales* can be passive or active, as well as masculine or femi-nine. The category of *homosexual* or *gay* represents a certain normalizing of the *internacional,* a term which in fact is falling into disuse among *homo-sexuales* as they increasingly identify with object choice categories that im-ply less of a need for the category of *internacional.* In my study, although homosexual men in general knew the term, I only heard it once being used by someone to refer to his own role during sex.

In relation to homosexuality, the use of object choice categories among participants in my study was highly prevalent. Among fifty-five partici-pants with whom I discussed the topic of male homosexuality, fifty-three used the term *homosexual* to refer to a man who is attracted to men. Only two of them used the more traditional and derogatory term *joto.*[2] It is striking that many of these participants were the same who defined their own sexual orientation as *normal.* To refer to women who are attracted to women, forty out of forty-nine participants used the word *lesbiana* (les-bian). Among the other nine, one used the term *chanclera* (sandal tapper) and another used *manflora,*[3] which are both gender based and derogatory; two people did not know what to call these women; one woman called them *bisexual;* and four participants, including two women who identify with this category, used the terms *mujer gay* (gay woman) or *mujer homo-sexual* (homosexual woman). These last two terms were selected based on the perception that the term *lesbiana* can be derogatory.

Among participants who acknowledged being exclusively attracted to their own sex, all of them referred to themselves as *homosexual, lesbiana,* or *gay.* This was the case even among those whose identities were more consistent with the gender-based categories, as Juan's example in the previous chapter illustrates. No participants used the terms *activo* or *pasivo* or *internacional* to describe sexual orientation. These terms, along with others such as *loca* (crazy woman), *mayate,*[4] *mujer* (woman), *hombre* (man), and *hombre-hombre* (man-man), were used only as secondary descriptors, often as descriptors of roles during sex.

Several people in the study, most of them young, had fully assumed an identity as *heterosexuales,* which was based on an understanding of their attraction to the opposite sex, as well as the absence of attraction to their own sex. I asked Francisco, who was a young student, "What is your sexual identity?" He responded, "My identity? I think of myself as a heterosexual person."

"What does it mean for someone to be *heterosexual?*"

"I am *heterosexual* because all in my mind, my fantasies, my behavior, is oriented toward the opposite sex, what gives me pleasure."

For some, there was a recognition that heterosexuality brings with it privilege. I asked Ernesto, who was eighteen years old, "How do you identify sexually speaking?"

He responded, "*Heterosexual.* Personally it means that I feel fine about myself, I am seen as a good person by society, I am sure of who I am, and I truly don't feel any regret to be like this. I am fine this way. A man has never caught my attention."

Among some, the term *heterosexual* was used mainly to emphasize "the opposite of homosexuality." This is reminiscent of Foucault's (1980) argument about the emergence of heterosexuality as a sexual identity, which he saw as a reaction to the invention of homosexuality. It also seems connected to Chauncey's argument about the central role of homosexuality in defining the contours of modern categorizations of sexual identity: "in mapping the boundaries of the gay world it necessarily maps the boundaries of the 'normal world' as well. . . . Not only did the 'queer folk' of the gay subculture define themselves by their differences from the dominant culture, but the 'normal people' of the dominant culture define *themselves* by their difference from the gay subculture: they constitute themselves as 'normal' only by eschewing anything that might mark them as 'queer'" (1994: 25, emphasis in the original).

When I asked Isabel, a thirty-two-year-old woman, "How would you call a person who has sex with members of the opposite sex?" she responded:

"Heterosexual."

"What does it mean to be *heterosexual?*"

"That it is not two men or two women. It is the couple, woman with man. Or man with woman."

In this case, there was not only a complete emphasis of object choice but also the premise that heterosexuality is "what is not homosexuality." The concept of "normality" filtered in only by her reference to the relationship between man and woman as "the couple" *(la pareja),* which subtly implies that two men or two women could not form a couple. That homosexuality is the pivot around which heterosexuality is defined is important because it illustrates a shift in emphasis from the gender-based categories. In my study, when people used object choice categories of identity, they often seemed to place homosexuality in the center and to use the label of heterosexuality only to create distance from this new core. Another important shift was the recognition that a *heterosexual* and a *homosexual* can look exactly the same, which is a complete break from the assumptions of the gender-based model, where appearance and demeanor were the primary criteria for location and placement.

One corollary to these ideas is that some participants described their sexual identity as *normal* until they were asked to confirm that they were not sexually interested in people of their own sex. They were *normales* (meaning regular masculine men and feminine women in the "natural majority") but they were also *heterosexuales* (meaning not homosexual).

THE ADVANTAGES OF BEING *HOMOSEXUAL*

The centrality of homosexuality in the creation of contemporary categories of sexual identity in Mexico is also reflected in the individual transformations experienced by those who openly called themselves *homosexual, gay,* or *lesbiana.* These identities allowed people who were attracted to their own sex to question their location in the realm of "abnormality" and were fostering a stronger sense of self-acceptance. For instance, I asked Mario, "What is your sexual orientation?"

"Homosexual," he responded directly.

"What does it mean to be *homosexual?*"

"To me . . . there are certain facets of one's life in which you don't know how to present yourself to society and you tend to pretend, but now I am myself."

For Mario, being *homosexual* implied a unified identity—being able to integrate his sexual desires with his image as a man, and to not pretend to be *heterosexual.* Mario also felt that being a *homosexual* had given him a different perspective in life that he greatly valued. "You are born this way, being *homosexual,* with this characteristic. . . . If I were to be born again, I would like to be the same. . . . I have enjoyed life."

"What advantages do you see in being *homosexual?*"

"You see life from a different viewpoint. You achieve greater development. . . . The fact that you are *homosexual* makes you try to give the best in you."

In another example, Eugenio, who was forty-eight years old, emphasized that there was no contradiction between homosexuality and masculinity and blamed effeminate men for the social rejection of homosexuality. When I asked him what his sexual orientation was, he replied, "I am *homosexual.*"

"What does that mean?"

"That I am a male, but my sexual preference is for other males. Because I feel completely male. I don't believe I am effeminate, neither my looks nor my manners, nothing. In fact, I reject people who are effeminate. . . . I understand them, because we are all in the same pot, but I have no direct relationship with them."

"Why do you feel like that toward effeminate people?"

"I think that to a great extent they are responsible for the marginalization of *homosexuales* because their behaviors make society believe that all *homosexuales* are like that, which is not true. I think they are [responsible] for the rejection."

In his own way, Eugenio attempted to tie homosexuality to normality. Other participants did not exclude people who did not conform with expectations of gender-based demeanors. I asked Carmen, "What would you call a woman who has sex with other women?"

"*Lesbiana.* A woman who loves other women."

"What are the causes of lesbianism?"

"There is no cause. I feel it is absurd when people talk about an absent father or other causes. . . . I think it is something natural, an alternative like any other, a sexual option. If there are women who select to be with men, there are also women who want to be with a woman, and that's it. I don't think it is a disease; on the contrary, it is very healthy to live what is born inside of you. It is wonderful to be able to feel it, to live it."

For some, the complete normalization of homosexuality was achieved by the label *gay.* In response to the question "How do you describe your sexual preference?" Gabriela said:

"*Gay.* I don't like to use *lesbiana.*"

"What is your reaction to the term *lesbiana?*"

"Aggression. I know where the word comes from and its meaning, but I still feel that words such as *lesbiana* or *joto* are an attack."

"What does the word *gay* represent?"

"It is another milieu; it is more subtle, more refined."

The use of *gay* had several different implications. The word provided a sense that a homosexual lifestyle is more than just an attraction or a sexual behavior. For some, the emphasis was on a more confrontational, in-your-face attitude that led to self-acceptance. For instance, Antonio said in relation to his identity as *gay,* "I am conscious of my attitudes, of my sexual preferences, of my psychological needs. The fact that I like to do it one way and you like it in another way is your problem if you don't accept it, because I accept myself."

For some, adopting an identity as *gay* meant not having to comply with social expectations about marriage (a strategy that was common in the past among *homosexuales* leading double lives). I asked Arturo, "Is there a difference between being *gay* and being *homosexual?*"

"Of course. . . . [A gay person] structures his life around his sexual preference. If he is *bisexual,* he can plan to marry [a woman] and also have a gay partner. If he is *gay* and not interested in women, he makes no plans to marry. He does not evade his condition as *homosexual.*"

Arturo strongly emphasized his opposition to leading a double life, which he defined as marrying a woman in order to sustain the pretense of being *heterosexual.* Similarly, Gabriel said that his definition of *gay* was "simply not hiding or leading double lives for the sake of society. I am not going to become *bisexual* as a result of hiding, so I defined myself recently as *gay.*"

Note that these men's definition of "double lives" did not include their careful avoidance of disclosure of their sexual orientation outside the homosexual milieu. Osvaldo, a twenty-one-year-old man, commented: "Now I am *homosexual,* I am *gay,* but I don't think of myself as a *maricón.* My behavior in society continues to be normal, as a man, but in my personal life it is going to be different. I am part of a different world. I have my world in which I relate to normal people (well, not 'normal,' because we are all normal), with people who are not of *el medio* [the gay milieu], and then I have my world with people in *el medio.*"

"Do you keep those worlds separated?" I asked.

"Yes, I try to keep them like that, a little separated. In fact, I feel that sometimes they collapse." Despite his discretion, Osvaldo had been forced by a brother to disclose his homosexuality to all his family and had suffered many negative consequences that drove him to attempt suicide. Another of Osvaldo's brothers was a homosexual who was married to a woman. When he realized that the family now knew about Osvaldo's homosexuality, and worrying about his own reputation, instead of supporting Osvaldo he threatened him.

The fear of being found to be homosexual in the heterosexual world seemed to be well justified. Although most nonhomosexual people in the study identified *homosexuales* as a separate group, their identification by no means guaranteed their acceptance. *La homofobia,* as people had begun to call negative attitudes toward *homosexuales,* was extremely prevalent in Guadalajara and varied along a wide range of possibilities: from mild tolerance, to indifference, to outright rejection and even physical violence. The fear of rejection was seen as the reason some people who could not hide their same-sex attraction chose to say they were *bisexuales,* as a desperate attempt to avoid the stigma of homosexuality. Bisexuality, however, was already being seen by others as a legitimate and separate sexual identity and one that they believed was even more stigmatized than homosexuality.

BISEXUALITY AS A CHOSEN SEXUAL IDENTITY

Only two men in the study identified as *bisexuales* in ways that resembled the definition of bisexuality in an object choice system. In one case, Adrián had fully adopted a bisexual identity in his early twenties. He became aware of his bisexuality when he started noticing that he was looking at men and not only thinking, *"está bien guapo"* (he is quite handsome), but also experiencing stronger feelings that were sexual. He had felt attracted to women much earlier, and this attraction continued. I asked him: "In terms of attraction, what happened first, women or men; what was your process?"

"Look, women first, but I am not from here; I am from a small town."

I found it significant that he would emphasize his rural origin as a corollary, or a justification, for why he had been attracted to women before realizing his attraction to men. He moved to Guadalajara when he was sixteen years old to go to school and "to see new things, diverse customs, different ways of thinking. You know, [I was only exposed to] traditional customs in terms of morality; principles taught at home that are closer to a *machista* way of thinking. You get here and see very different things; you see [homosexuals] who are more masculine, and this gives you an emotional charge. You start experiencing an emotional undressing." His choice of the word "undressing" seemed charged with symbolism. Accepting that he was also attracted to men was not simple for him. "I resisted and told myself, 'this can't be.' Especially because of the values that I had from before."

Adrián felt quite guilty after his first sexual experiences with men. He said he felt this way in part because the encounters were purely sexual, without mutual feelings of love. As time passed, however, he realized that he could also have an emotional connection with a man, as well as with a woman. At the time of the interview, he was more interested in having a relationship with a man. He explained that he found this endeavor more interesting and challenging. He felt women pursued him for his good looks and that women were in general more available. This meant for him that sex with a woman was less exciting.

Adrián was open about his sexual orientation with homosexual friends, with whom he felt he could be bolder, and he accepted their criticism of his bisexuality. He was concerned that most people seemed to have very negative reactions toward bisexuality. He believed people in Guadalajara had developed a view that was accepting of heterosexuality, tolerated homosexuality, and strongly rejected bisexuality, which was never considered an option. People questioned him: "How can you do that? Do you deceive people?" His response to that was "I don't deceive anyone."

Adrián, however, was extremely careful about disclosing his bisexuality. He did not like to mix his homosexual and heterosexual networks, which allowed him to avoid telling women about his interest in men. He felt that women's "mentality" would prevent them from understanding the situation. In this sense, he imagined women as more "fragile" than men and said, "with women you have to be more delicate, pay more attention to what you say," which is reminiscent of comments about women made by heterosexual male participants.

But, in addition, Adrián was careful about not being unfaithful to his sexual partners, regardless of their sex. He said to me, "With women I have plenty of opportunities . . . but I feel [it would be] somewhat selfish to deceive someone, it can't be. If I have a relationship with a woman . . . nothing happens with a man. If I am with a man, nothing happens with a woman." His homosexual friends did not believe this and told him "not to be a fool . . . that I am bad in the head, and 'poor girl.'" Adrián seemed to believe that, in his homosexual friends' minds, he was just a repressed homosexual deceiving women and trying to pass as *heterosexual*.

Adrián clarified that he did not seek effeminate men or "an imitation of a woman." He had no attraction to effeminate men whatsoever. In this sense, he firmly accepted his attraction to masculine men and to feminine women. He talked about the different sensations he had touching a man in comparison to a woman—men were more *tosco* (rough) and he found that to be exciting. He also said that when it came to having a sexual role, he was always *activo*.

Toward the end of the interview, Adrián said that he was "*bisexual* permanently" but also that he had a bit more of an orientation toward men. He added that he was quite demanding in a relationship with a woman and that he found sex with women to be much more reciprocal. This also meant to him that reaching orgasm with a woman was a bit harder. So far, he had had two significant relationships that lasted about one year each— one with a woman and one with a man. In the future, he contemplated getting married and settling down with a woman. Part of his motivation was that he wanted to have "a child of my own blood."

The other self-identified *bisexual* in my sample was Angel, who explained how he had arrived at a self-definition as a *bisexual*. "I have analyzed this; I don't know why, but for a while I have been curious and have read about the topic [of bisexuality]. I have cataloged myself with that term, although maybe it is just temporary. We cannot say [identity] is definite, and life has many changes." To him, everyone is born *bisexual,* and some people later become exclusively *homosexual* or *heterosexual.* But some people are more versatile and retain their attraction to both sexes. He felt that there are many people in this situation, but that they do not assume a bisexual identity due to the fear of stigma. A person's final definition was "based on one's own lived experiences."

Angel realized his attraction toward men early in his life. He grew up hearing messages of heterosexual normativity. "I saw that society stipulated characteristics that said: 'you have to have a girlfriend.' [As a child] I know that I wanted to have a girlfriend, or did have a girlfriend, but at the same time I told myself, 'I like that boy.' I said, 'I have an attraction,' not just being pleased, but what was already an attraction."

He had his first sexual interaction with a woman at age fourteen. His first sexual experience with a man was with a male cousin at age seventeen. Later he established a significant relationship with a male high school teacher. He moved to Guadalajara at age eighteen and got involved with a girlfriend. During the same time, he started seeing a man who was in his late forties. When I interviewed Angel, he was sexual almost exclusively with men, but he did not discard the idea of having a relationship with a woman. He said, "I look at pretty women and recognize that I do like women. I would like to have children. I am very fatherly, very sentimental . . . but it has been a while since I had sex with women; it has been more with men. That doesn't mean that I might not, in the future, have a relationship with a woman. . . . Currently, I feel [equal satisfaction] with a man and with a woman. . . . It is great."

"Where do you see yourself in five years?"

"I see myself being single . . . but with plans to marry, and without ruling out the possibility of having sex with men."

Angel reported that he did not know how he would handle communication about his bisexuality in such a context. He was concerned that society in general might not understand the arrangement. So, he would consider keeping the two parts of his sexual life separated as a form of protection. "I would prefer to keep both worlds separated because, unfortunately, not everyone would understand. . . . I don't care if they don't understand but they could harm the people I love."

Like Adrián, Angel kept his two worlds separated and felt that living a double life was an intrinsic aspect of being *bisexual*. Also, as in Adrián's case, Angel's homosexual friends knew about his bisexuality because he felt he did not have to keep it secret from them, regardless of their negative reactions. Angel was aware, though, of the stigma attached to bisexuality and felt that this stigma had been boosted by fear of HIV. "I have read that . . . part of the stigma is that we would be considered a high-risk group . . . for infection with the AIDS virus. [The assumption is that we] infect both men and women. But I defend myself by saying that it doesn't matter with whom you do it but how you do it." This last comment seemed to be a direct repetition of a message that was commonly voiced by HIV educators in Guadalajara. Angel was a volunteer at an AIDS organization.

Living a double life was frustrating for Angel. "They tell you that it is not normal, that it should not be, that it is bad. Then you opt for keeping it quiet. It is difficult to not be able to tell people what you want the most and what you like and what you feel. It is hard when you want to divulge it. [Say] 'I am in love' or 'I like such and such.' It is painful because one would really like his family to know what one is doing." Note that he avoided using the first person in making these comments, which I interpreted as a need to create some distance.

I ran into Angel during a visit to Guadalajara in 1999, five years after his interview. He said that his father was trying to establish communication with him about the fact that he was *gay*. They were at his father's doctor's office, just before his father had surgery, and his father said, "You have to know that your mother and I accept you as you are." Angel, shocked, said in response, "So, you know?" The father nodded. Angel told his father that it was not the right time or place to talk about that topic, that they would talk later.

I noticed that Angel was now using the word *gay* to refer to himself. I asked him whether he did not identify as a *bisexual* anymore. He looked surprised by my question, thought for a moment, and stated, smiling, "Oh no, I changed that a couple of years ago." I interpreted his surprise as an indication that he did not remember that he had self-identified as a *bisexual* in his interview. His assessment during the interview that his bisexual identity might be temporary and not fixed had proven to be correct. Additionally, five years after the interview he did not seem to be contemplating marriage to a woman as he had predicted before.

HETEROSEXUALITY AND REFLEXIVITY

The examples in the previous sections suggest that these individuals engaged in some level of analysis and reflection about their sexual desires before adopting a sexual identity based on object choice. This was also the case among some of the people who explicitly identified as *heterosexual*.

One particularly interesting example involved Francisco, a twenty-two-year-old psychology student. Francisco believed that heterosexuality is hereditary, that it is encoded in a person's genetic information, and that it creates a certain predisposition toward being attracted to the opposite sex. In talking about his own sexual orientation, he said that he assumed he had been born with a heterosexual preference, and that this preference had been confirmed as part of his learning *(aprendizaje)*. He felt that homosexuality developed in a similar way.

He also believed that a person's innate sexual orientation could be changed by environmental events that could create pathologies. This meant that a child who was born heterosexual or with heterosexual tendencies could become a homosexual. However, in discussing the situation of a friend of his that seemed consistent with this scenario, he wavered and shifted back to claiming that his friend had probably been born a homosexual. Francisco was talking about a man who had been induced by a brother to have sex with him when he was a child. His friend was now openly homosexual as an adult.

Francisco assumed that his friend must have been born with a predisposition to homosexuality that became fully manifest after his brother had sex with him. He felt that it would be impossible for him to accept his homosexuality otherwise. Had he been born heterosexual and turned homosexual, he could not have assumed the identity so readily.

I asked Francisco to analyze the following scenario: "A man is born with a homosexual predisposition and is induced into having sex at age seven by a female cousin. They have vaginal intercourse. What happens to his identity?"

"I believe that the experience can satisfy him physically, but not to the degree that he would make it a part of him, as a heterosexual person would. The relationship would not be complete; he would not be realized by it."

"So he would continue to be homosexual?"

"Yes, he could probably have a girlfriend, but if a guy shows up in his life, he would get much more pleasure."

Francisco concluded that a man born with homosexual tendencies could probably "perform" with a woman but would always continue to be strongly attracted to men, and to that extent he would never stop being a homosexual. Francisco did not consider that the man in question could turn out to be *bisexual*. However, his conclusion was quite different when he analyzed the reverse scenario. I asked him, "Let's think of the opposite situation. A boy born with heterosexual tendencies is induced into sex at age seven by his male cousin. What would be the result in this case?"

"I think he would stay the same, or perhaps become *bisexual*. Truthfully I am not sure. He would probably have internal conflicts about it for a long time, deciding between one [heterosexuality] and the other [bisexuality]." Francisco did not go as far as suggesting that he could become homosexual.

In this second scenario, Francisco concluded that the event would create considerable conflict in the boy—who would be forced to decide between sticking to his innate tendency (heterosexuality) and pursuing the option that had been opened to him by his same-sex sexual contact (bisexuality). In his interpretation, Francisco seemed to be mixing two different, contradictory, viewpoints. He saw homosexuality as innate, like heterosexuality, and resilient (seduction by a woman would not make a homosexual boy heterosexual). But he also felt that environmental influence could change a person's orientation—when the person was *heterosexual,* that is. While homosexuality was resilient, heterosexuality was vulnerable. In this sense, Francisco gave homosexuality considerable power.

Later in the interview, Francisco described how he had handled a situation in which a homosexual friend attempted to seduce him. He was sleeping and his friend, who was sleeping next to him, started caressing his back. He told him, "I respect you, but I don't share this." He felt that the experience had strongly confirmed his heterosexuality and his lack of temptation to try out homosexual behaviors.

Francisco also talked about feeling the need to explore whether there were any traces of attraction to men in him. He purposely engaged in an exercise in which he tried to visualize what it would be like to have sex with a man. He saw taking such "psychological risk" as a way to better understand himself. He tried to imagine a handsome man, who emerged as an abstract image of someone younger than him. In the fantasy, he approached this man and started caressing him and kissing him. He was able to imagine physical contact of this kind but not the man's genitals or any activity involving penetration. Francisco felt that his ability to do this was related to his need to have physical contact with his male friends as a form of camaraderie. But once he went beyond that, the person in his fantasy immediately turned into a woman, which was further evidence for him of his lack of interest in having sex with men. This was a confirmation of his heterosexuality.

The depth of Francisco's reflections about the topic of sexual orientation was somewhat atypical among heterosexuals in my sample; most participants were not able to articulate their ideas and thoughts about sexual orientation and causality with such elaboration. During the interview, Francisco worked hard to apply consistent criteria and expressed the feeling that the interview provided him with an opportunity to test and demonstrate what he had learned in his professional training. But, in broader terms, his account illustrates how difficult it was for participants to explain to themselves the logic of competing conceptualizations of object choice sexual identities, as well as the intricacies of the reflexive processes associated with self-identification. It must be granted that this was a psychology student, so he probably thought about these issues more than other people, but I believe that, in one way or another, all people who adopted object choice categories engaged in some, perhaps simpler, version of Francisco's analysis.

THE TENUOUS LINE BETWEEN REJECTION, TOLERANCE, AND ACCEPTANCE OF DIFFERENCE

Like Francisco, most nonhomosexual people in my sample were capable of offering a personal theory of the etiology of homosexuality. This meant that they had engaged in reflection about the topic. They had attempted to understand why some people differ from what they thought to be the norm.

Their conclusions about the causes of homosexuality roughly separated them into three groups. Some believed that homosexuals are born homosexual. A second group argued that homosexuals are born "normal" and become homosexuals because of environmental influences. A third group felt that some people are born homosexual and others become so.

Their agreement with any one of these theories seemed not to be motivated by their attitudes about homosexuality. In each case, there were individuals who used their theory as justification for either accepting or rejecting homosexuals. For instance, people who thought homosexuals are born homosexual sometimes also argued that, as a result, *"ellos no tienen la culpa"* (it's not their fault) and thus they should be accepted. Because they did not choose their sexual orientation, homosexuals should be treated like everybody else. Others, instead, suggested that homosexuals were born sick or defective and alluded to problems with genes and hormones. They argued that homosexuals ought not to be blamed for their sexual orientation but also that they should recognize "their problem." They condemned homosexuality and could only envision tolerance of those homosexuals who do something to control their impulses and who hide their sexual orientation.

Similarly, some people who believed that homosexuals become homosexual felt that they should be rejected for making the wrong choice and for not attempting to reverse the environmental influences that turned them homosexual in the first place. Others argued that if homosexuals had no control of the events that turned them homosexual, they should not be blamed for desires that were now fixed and could not be reversed. In discussing the possible environmental causes of homosexuality, people talked about the consequences of allowing boys to play with dolls or girls with trucks, as well as about sexual abuse of a boy or rape of a girl by an older man. Interestingly, explanations of homosexuality that pointed to the behavior of parents—a weak father, a dominant mother—were mostly absent in the discourse about environmental influence.

Another interesting contrast with these theories of homosexuality is provided by people's opinions about heterosexuality. Perhaps not surprisingly, given widespread ideas about "normality," a majority of these participants believed that attraction to the opposite sex was innate. Nonhomosexual participants rarely reflected on this premise and often felt that considering the idea that heterosexuality is not inherent to human nature was ridiculous. The only instance in which they acknowledged that heterosexuality could result from environmental influence was when they argued that a homosexual—or a person with "homosexual tendencies"—could be taught to become heterosexual. From that perspective, homosexuality must necessarily be viewed as deviant.

Despite these ideas, when I asked nonhomosexual participants whether they would accept a homosexual son or daughter, most said that they would. They assumed that kinship and parental love had to be greater than the feelings of rejection or disappointment that they would experience. They often added that homosexuality could be prevented by providing the right kind of education to children and by protecting them from bad influences. If a child showed signs of homosexuality at an early age— which basically meant demeanors of the opposite sex—people believed they would have the responsibility to try to "fix" them through medical or psychological intervention. These ideas, along with the theories of causation, contributed to a very widespread perception of *homosexuales* and *bisexuales* as second-class citizens and to the notion that they should not acquire the same status or rights as "normal people."

The extent to which intolerance and rejection of homosexuals existed is most graphically expressed in the collection of adjectives that participants used to describe homosexuals and their lifestyle. When talking about homosexuals, they used expressions such as *sucios* (dirty), *raros* (strange), *viciosos* (with many vices), *envidiosos* (envious), *degenerados* (degenerate), *desviados* (deviate), *anormales* (abnormal), and *no naturales* (unnatural). In some cases, people expressed *temor* (fear), *asco* (revulsion), or *repugnancia* (repugnance) when discussing the idea of being around homosexual people.

Among those who expressed acceptance of homosexuals, few saw such acceptance as unconditional. More commonly, they proposed a strict separation between the homosexual milieu and the rest of the world. Ernesto voiced his tolerance of homosexuals in the following terms: "To me, as long as they are in their world and not affecting third parties, welcome. . . . As long as they don't interfere with the lives of others, or my life, I see them as anybody else, with the same rights. In Mexico we have freedom and they are not living in a repressive country; they are normal people as long as they don't affect third parties." This notion of "not affecting third parties" was common among people who were not against homosexuality and meant everything from keeping homosexual behaviors secret or separate to not saying anything that could be interpreted as a flirtation or advance and that would be threatening to *heterosexuales*.

In a similar vein, Olga said, "In the same way that I respect their point of view, [homosexuals] must respect ours. I know people of that kind who are really disrespectful . . . they know they are wrong (well, I don't know if they know it), but they don't care and they want to make it public in ways that are disrespectful. They don't control themselves around people who aren't like them. . . . I cannot say that they are bad. I think there is an infinite variety of sexual modalities, so I should not say whether it is good or bad, but they must be respectful." The message to homosexuals here, again, was that acceptance would be subject to homosexuals' willingness to stay out of sight.

In the case of self-accepted *bisexuales,* the situation was even worse. Both heterosexual and homosexual people were strongly judgmental toward bisexuality. *Bisexuales* were seen as *desubicados* (out of place, disoriented, and being neither here nor there), *indefinidos* (undefined), *promiscuos* (promiscuous), *degenerados* (degenerate), *descontrolados* (those who cannot control themselves), and *sucios* (dirty). People also associated bisexuality with *engaño* (deceit), regardless of whether the sexual partners were aware or not, and felt that *bisexuales* "don't know what they want."

It is fascinating that although the view of bisexuality as a chosen sexual identity was overwhelmingly negative, people did not judge as harshly the situation of "normal" people who had occasional same-sex sexual relations. In this case, there was a sense that those individuals "made mistakes" or "had a slip" but not a sense of their "permanent ambiguity." What strongly bothered Mexicans about self-professed bisexuality was this perception of their permanent ambiguity and the notion that *bisexuales* were opportunistic, oversexed, and deceitful. In this sense, someone who confessed to a permanent bisexual identity was considered a person who could not be trusted—a wolf in sheep's clothing.

Furthermore, although participants understood in general that some people engaged in sex with both men and women, some also felt that everyone eventually selects a primary attraction for one sex or the other. This sense that equal, permanent attraction for both sexes is not feasible led them to believe that, ultimately, true bisexuality does not exist. They felt that all of those who call themselves *bisexuales,* or who have bisexual behaviors, really are repressed homosexuals who bend to the social pressure and the stigma. Although this is a stereotype, there are clearly some people who, like Angel, use bisexuality as a transitional identity before accepting their homosexuality. The opposite vision, however, that some of these *bisexuales* are repressed *heterosexuales* living their lives as *homosexuales* did not make it into this theory.

Finally, negative attitudes about homosexuality and bisexuality such as the ones described in this chapter created an environment in which non-heterosexuals strongly feared rejection, even from the more tolerant Mexicans. Leading a double life became perhaps the only alternative short of confronting the consequences of an open homosexual or bisexual life. As we will see in chapter 5, for Guadalajaran *homosexuales* and *bisexuales*, the fully open identities that they hear are possible in cities such as San Francisco and New York are often inconceivable.

(

Several of the examples that I discussed in this and the preceding chapter should begin to suggest the simultaneous use in contemporary Mexico of classifications of sexual identity based on gender/sex roles and on object choice. Participants engaged in such simultaneous use when they divided men into *normales* and *homosexuales;* when they thought of themselves at the same time as *gay* and as *pasivo* and a woman; and when they identified as *normales* but also as *heterosexuales*. In the chapter that follows, I explore this topic more fully and analyze the existence of hybrid categories of identity that result from the superimposition of both models of categorization. I also refer to some of the more subtle ways in which cultural hybridity emerges in the narratives about sexual identities offered by study participants.

AMALGAMS AND CONVOLUTIONS: SUBTLETIES OF INTERPRETATION IN CONTEMPORARY SEXUAL IDENTITIES

Several of the examples that I have presented suggest that Mexicans' classifications of sexual identity are not always clear-cut. In explaining their interpretations of sexual identities, participants in my study sometimes combined criteria of the two maps that I outlined in the previous two chapters. At times they also resisted being placed, or placing someone else, in preestablished identity categories and came up with interpretations that provided nuance to the categorizations. They did this as they tried to make sense of competing understandings that they did not deem to be automatically contradictory.

This phenomenon is reminiscent of Chauncey's description of the transitions that took place in New York during the first half of the twentieth century. Chauncey argued that the transition from gender-based to object choice categories occurred between the 1930s and the 1950s. He also noted that this happened unevenly: "Multiple systems of sexual classification coexisted throughout the period in New York's divergent neighborhood cultures: men socialized into different class and ethnic systems of gender, family life, and sexual mores tended to understand and organize their homosexual practices in different ways. Most significantly, exclusive heterosexuality became a precondition for a man's identification as 'normal' in middle-class culture at least two generations before it did so in much of Euro-American and African-American working-class culture" (1994: 13). Such superimposition was not permanent. Chauncey explains, "Over the course of a generation, the lines had been drawn between the heterosexual and homosexual so sharply and publicly that men were no longer able to participate in a homosexual encounter without suspecting it meant (to the outside world, and to themselves) that they were gay" (22).[1]

It is somewhat unclear whether the mixed interpretations that I found in Mexico are transitional, or whether they belong to a contemporary Latin American conceptualization with greater staying power. In Mexico there were signs of both cultural transition and lasting coexistence between older and newer interpretations. This combination, which sounds perhaps paradoxical, is consistent with notions of "cultural hybridity" that have been used to explain the dynamics of Mexican culture as a whole (García Canclini 1995). In this context, some sexual identities seemed to be changing rapidly while others resisted change. Those that changed were sometimes shaped without discarding older ideas that were still deemed to be valid. Those that resisted change were often reinterpreted; they were adapted so that they continued making sense in the context of contemporary ideas and practices.

The cases included in this chapter illustrate these phenomena. The superimposition of different criteria of classification is readily evident in some of the interpretations that I discuss. Other cases exemplify subtleties of interpretation that questioned the existence of single definitions of the different categories. My discussion focuses on the logics that participants used to arrive at their definitions, as well as the varied interpretations of specific lifestyles or practices that resulted.

THE *HOMOSEXUAL* IS THE *PASIVO*

Participants who used the terms *homosexual, gay,* or *lesbiana* commonly included in these identities all individuals who were exclusively attracted to their own sex, regardless of whether these individuals appeared to be masculine or feminine. Nevertheless, some participants who recognized the existence of a separate category of men that they called *homosexuales* considered the *homosexual* to be exclusively the receptive partner in anal sex between two men—the one who performs a "feminine" role and is thus penetrated. For instance, Gerardo, a thirty-one-year-old man who identified as *heterosexual,* said that he had known several male *homosexuales* and had become friends with one who was his coworker. He mentioned that his friendship with this man was based on mutual respect and clarified that nothing ever happened between them that could be seen as being remotely sexual.

Like many other participants in my study, Gerardo had a theory of the etiology of homosexuality. He thought homosexuality could result from a lack of certain genes or from bad education and saw this sexual orientation as immutable once it took hold of someone's life: "The branches of a bent tree can never be straightened," he indicated. He added that homosexual men were somewhat repugnant, especially if he "[imagined] how they have sex, the penetration." He could respect *homosexuales* as long as he did not have to visualize what took place in their sexual interactions. Throughout this conversation, his comments suggested that he thought of both partners in sex between men as *homosexuales*.

Later, however, Gerardo's emphasis switched as he began to discuss male homosexual roles in more detail. He clarified that although the sexual relationship involved two men, only one was *homosexual*. Gerardo said: "To me, the *homosexual* is the one who receives, the one who seeks the relationship, the penetration. The other, well he is the *heterosexual,* even when he is penetrating a man, because he can have sexual relations with a woman or with a man."

In this interpretation, the male homosexual's sexual partner was defined as a heterosexual man, regardless of the fact that he might not have any interest in women. This is consistent with the gender-based view of *hombres normales* ("normal" men) who have sex with *maricones.* Yet, the interpretation is hybrid in that one partner, the one who enacts the receptive role during sex, is judged on the basis of his object choice, regardless of whether he is masculine or feminine in his demeanor. The other, the insertive partner, is assigned an identity label that is based on object choice *(heterosexual)* but using criteria based on gender roles (that he is the man).

Gerardo's view constituted a reinterpretation of the category of *homosexual* that was loosely based on a combination of two contradictory perceptions: (1) that all men who have sex with each other are *homosexual* and (2) that to be *homosexual* a man has to take the woman's role, which brings one of the homosexual partners into the realm of heterosexuality. Gerardo assumed that the insertive partner could potentially have sex with a woman, but if this partner was not interested in women, in effect we would have the paradoxical case of a heterosexual man who is not attracted to women. This would be a contradiction in terms in a classification that is purely based on object choice. In this hybrid interpretation, however, no such contradiction exists: the man is *heterosexual,* and he can also be exclusively attracted to men.

Gerardo did not make an explicit connection between the version of heterosexuality that he applied to himself and the one that he applied to the insertive partner in homosexual sex. However, he had considered the possibility that he could have been one of those men. When I asked him what he would call a man who is attracted to both men and women, he said, "He is supposed to be a *heterosexual,* but he has a psychological trauma." (It is noteworthy that Gerardo never used the term *bisexual* as a sexual identity.) He then talked about his own potential to become such a person. He said that his first sexual experience, involving a female prostitute, had been very traumatic. "Had I not overcome [the trauma] I might have developed an aberration concerning women . . . to feel that women would not give me pleasure, and I could have channeled my [attraction] to men." But if Gerardo had done so, he would have continued to be *heterosexual.*

Gerardo established distance from this identity by expressing feelings of repulsion at the idea of two men having sex together, which I interpreted as a need to reassure himself of his own status as a heterosexual man who is also *normal.* When I asked him what he was repulsed by, he said, "both [men] in this case, because they are seeking to obtain pleasure from another man." The heterosexual penetrator in sex between men repulsed him, but this did not compel Gerardo to place him in the category of *homosexual.*

Despite this negative attitude about homosexual sex, Gerardo felt that *homosexuales* were better friends than *heterosexuales.* "It is like you have more trust. It is like a *homosexual* would not disappoint you as much as a woman."

"And compared with another heterosexual man?"

"You can count more on a *homosexual,* I mean, as a friend. In many ways. I don't say that I have much experience with that, but you sometimes become so disappointed [with heterosexual male friends]! A *homosexual* does not try to hurt you . . . or give you trouble."

The friend whom Gerardo had in mind when he was making these remarks ended up becoming so intimate with him that he felt comfortable telling Gerardo about certain aspects of his homosexual life. When Gerardo announced to him that he was getting married, his homosexual friend gave him as a present a *show travesti* (a female impersonation show) as entertainment for the wedding.

Raúl and Juan, whose identities I described in chapter 2, were openly effeminate men who identified as *homosexual* or *gay*—in terms of their sexual identity—and as *pasivos, pasivas,* or *mujeres* (women) in terms of their sexual role and specific homosexual subculture. Note that although they could be seen as incarnating the traditional identities of *maricones* or *jotos,* they had a primary identification with the larger homosexual, or gay, culture.

Unlike the *jotas* in Prieur's (1998) study in a marginal suburb of Mexico City, these men did not attempt to pass as women. Even the Mexico City *jotas,* however, also thought of themselves as *homosexuales* and understood the implications of the label. Although they were aware of the distance separating them from the middle-class *homosexuales,* they were aware that their lives were in some sense connected to the larger development of a homosexual milieu that was defined by attraction between men. Their emphasis on becoming women was the strategy that seemed to make most sense within the particular set of social rules that prevailed in their working-class environment. I believe the same could be said about working-class, openly effeminate men in Guadalajara.

In my study, I did not have the opportunity to interview working-class *mayates,* who in Prieur's sample lived an identity as *normales* and were attracted to men who adopted identities as women. I find it fascinating, however, that the *mayates* interviewed by Prieur in Mexico City were beginning to understand that, in a different environment, they could be regarded as *homosexuales.* This realization is significant, because it means that their identities as *hombres normales* were being destabilized by an awareness that there are men in Mexico who are masculine, who are attracted exclusively to men, and who are not like the rest of *hombres normales* (normal men).

For the men who identified as *homosexuales* or *gay* in my study, and who emphasized their masculinity, the terms *activo* and *pasivo* continued to have some significance only in two types of situations. One involved the initiation of a sexual relationship when the men were concerned about the sexual roles that they and their partners would play. In such a context, they could ask each other questions such as *"¿Eres activo?"* (Are you active?) or *"¿Eres pasivo?"* (Are you passive?). This was especially relevant if one of the partners had a strong preference for anally penetrating or being penetrated. Finding out that both partners wanted to take the same sexual role could lead to an embarrassing situation or to sexual frustration. Men who felt they were incompatible for that reason explained their disappointment with expressions such as *"es como juntarse a hacer tortillas"* (it's like getting together to make tortillas). Friends who wanted to indicate that a particular pairing would not work out (presumably because they knew the role preferences of both parties) would playfully call them *tortilleras* (tortilla patters). Both are references to lesbian sex, or sex in which any possibility of penetration was assumed to be precluded.

The terms *pasivo* and *pasiva* were also used when homosexual men wanted to tease others by implying that they were effeminate. This reflected the strong value placed on masculinity, and the fear of losing it. It also suggested a strong rejection of male effeminacy. One implication was that feminine men are *obvias* ("obvious," but using the feminine form of the word) or *locas* (crazy women) and cannot pass as *normal,* which was a great concern among homosexual men who led double lives. A broader implication was that as *homosexuales* or *gays,* men felt they could emphasize their masculinity or choose a life of overt effeminacy, without many shades in between.

NORMAL BUT ALSO HETEROSEXUAL

I previously discussed heterosexual people's primary identification as *hombres* and *mujeres,* as *normales,* as well as their use of the label *heterosexual* as secondary descriptor indicating that they were not *homosexuales.* When they chose the label *heterosexual,* they were acknowledging that homosexuals might look exactly like them—that they could act like them and pass as *normal.* It is as if they said, "I am *normal,* but yes, I am also *heterosexual.*" This also meant "I am not the kind of normal person who is attracted to his [her] own sex." In the past, such an explanation was not needed. The availability of the word *heterosexual* and the dissemination of a definition of homosexuality in object choice terms have changed the tone of conversations about the identity of *normales* in ways that make the explanation relevant.

In a context in which this awareness did not exist, asking someone who identifies as *normal* what his or her sexual identity was could be taken in itself to be automatically offensive. The response would be: "What do you mean, do I look like a *maricón?*" or "Do I look like a *machorra?*" But in the current environment in which both *normal* and *heterosexual* coexist as labels of sexual identity, the need to use the latter is emerging, particularly when a reference to homosexuality or bisexuality is made.

This means as well a shift in the definition of boundaries. In a gender-based classification the boundaries are strict in terms of expectations about correspondence between biological sex and gender disposition, but there is considerable room to transgress in terms of sexual behavior and the sex of sexual partners. When categories of identity based on object choice are used, by contrast, the boundaries regarding attraction and the sex of sexual partners become more rigid. It becomes more difficult for individuals to transgress, and pursue same-sex desires, without permanently jeopardizing their membership in the category of heterosexuality. Having sex with a person of the same sex could automatically transfer the person to a new category (Foucault 1980). The only alternative would be a hybrid interpretation, such as Gerardo's view of a heterosexual man who is not attracted to women.

Yet, on the other hand, object choice classifications do provide more flexibility for men and women to adopt homosexual identities without being pushed to give up, respectively, their masculinity or their femininity. They also reduce the pressure to select same-sex sexual partners whose demeanor is opposite (in terms of masculinity or femininity) to one's own. Ultimately, they create room for individuals who are attracted to their own sex to develop a sense that they are also normal, and thus that they can question their being placed in the realm of deviance.

HETEROSEXUALS WITH A HOMOSEXUAL INTEREST

So far, I have referred to two sexual identities involving bisexual behaviors. One is the gender-based identity of *hombres normales* who engage in sexual behavior with men, some of whom also have sex with women (by desire or to fulfill social conventions). This identity has its equivalent among women who think of themselves as *normal* but have sex with both men and women. The second is the identity of *bisexuales* who think of themselves as distinct from both *homosexuales* and *heterosexuales*. This second sexual identity appears to be fully dominated by social meanings related to object choice—the notion that attraction to both sexes marks a legitimate identity that is distinct from both homosexuality and heterosexuality.

Now I focus on a third interpretation of the same desire, which resulted in the identity of individuals who thought of themselves as "heterosexuals with a homosexual interest." Three participants in the study, two women and one man, fit this description, which was based on a strongly assumed heterosexual identity that was flavored by occasional homosexual relations. These participants had an awareness of a greater interest in the opposite sex, yet recognized an additional desire to pursue occasional sexual relations with members of their own sex.

Although it would be tempting to think of this identity as being the same as that of *normales* who have occasional sex with members of their own sex, the difference is that these participants had fully adopted object choice categories of identity to make their interpretations. Yet, for different reasons, all felt that their occasional involvement with members of their own sex did not warrant their transferring into the category of bisexuality.

Both of the women had participated in lesbian organizing and felt identified with a lesbian/feminist agenda. However, from the point of view of their sexuality, they had realized that they strongly preferred male partners for sex. One of the women, Carmen, had at some point identified as *bisexual* but had recently changed her definition to *heterosexual*. "In this stage of my life I am preferably *heterosexual,* but in a previous moment I could have defined myself more as *bisexual,*" she stated. She had concluded this based on her interpretation of the Kinsey scale and her belief that sexual identity changes over time—that individuals can move along the scale as they go through different stages in their sexual lives.

Carmen started her sexual life at age twenty-two with a boyfriend. She began having sex with women later, mostly out of curiosity. Men, she found, gave her much more physical satisfaction. Women gave her more emotional satisfaction. She felt "tremendous respect" for lesbian love but ultimately knew that she could not have a relationship with a woman. She rationalized that "when I had fantasies . . . in the end I always visualized a man, never a woman." However, the fact that women did make it to some degree into her fantasies had prompted her to explore sex with women. "I told myself I could not miss trying that."

She felt fortunate that she had allowed herself to explore sex with women. "If I had allowed myself to conform to my family's ideals, I would now be a true *heterosexual,* and I would feel very guilty for having fantasies [about women]. I feel freer by having broken some family taboos that had been imposed on me since I was a child. And perhaps that has allowed me to enjoy sexuality more. I feel more inclined to be driven by my own nature."

Carmen saw lesbianism as "something natural, an alternative like any other, a sexual option." However, like bisexuality, it was not the choice for her because of her greater interest in men. She mourned the fact that she was not a true *bisexual:* "I believe that bisexuality is very enriching," she said. Carmen added, contradicting herself, that she would not like to have a relationship with a bisexual man. Her reasoning was that she would feel threatened by his desire for men. "Theoretically, it seems great. . . . But in my private life, imagining that my [male] partner has had sex with a man [would be difficult]. . . . I would imagine that when we were having sex he would not enjoy my body as much because he is also attracted to the body of a man, and men's and women's bodies are so different! I would think, 'well, maybe he is now thinking about a man with an erect penis, flat chest, chest hair, and so forth.' I would not want him to have such a fantasy. That is why I like heterosexual men. Then I can think that they like my body because I am a woman."

This would not be a problem with a bisexual woman because, although the relationship could be emotional, she would not see it as primary, or as a love relationship: " . . . a woman I cannot love passionately. I can be playful with her, I can fantasize, live some experiences with her. . . . [But] with a man, I can fall in love."

When I pointed out that there seemed to be a contradiction, she was quick to respond. "What happens is that when one theorizes, one can make an argument and defend many things. But when one is living something more personal, the theory you created might not be coherent with your own *vivencia* [lived experience]. I can say that, theoretically, I could have male bisexual friends, and love them and spend time with them fabulously. But . . . having a bisexual [male] partner, I would have to think twice. Because that would be my lived experience. And I don't think that I have to be coherent about that."

The second participant in this category was Marcela, who presented herself as a feisty woman who had grown up in a household of women, with her mother and four sisters. Marcela had been sexually active with women and had participated in lesbian organizing. She never identified as *lesbiana* or *bisexual,* and she resisted being pigeonholed in a specific identity, which suggested her degree of reflection on the topic of sexual identities and her agency in choosing a unique, nonconformist interpretation of her own.

Marcela felt that the hetero/homo/bisexual classification was very limiting. Instead, she thought of herself as a "human being who wants to love another person, nothing else." Marcela added: "I don't care if [the person] has a vagina or a penis. What matters is that I can live and feel, and give and receive. . . . people are really stuck, because if they don't wear a T-shirt that says, 'I am *buga*' [straight] or 'I am a *lesbiana*' or 'I am *bisexual*,' they are in conflict. I understand that it has to do with identity and that you need a name (for some reason we have names)."

"Why do you think identity is so important?" I asked.

"Because it gives you a place in the world . . . a space in society. It makes you different from others and then . . . you can understand who you are. . . . If you are a woman and a rebel, they say you are feminist. It is like you are something strange that does not fit in the model. 'What name will we give it? What T-shirt should we assign? Let's name her *feminista* so that she belongs in a little drawer.' . . . What is the least important to society is that people are free."

She believed that we are all born *bisexual* and that we learn, through experience, what path to follow. In her case, her interest in women had been sparked by her need to question her socialization as a heterosexual woman and by her desire to better understand one of her sisters, who had revealed to the family that she was a *lesbiana*. She added that as she became involved in a lesbian group, she found herself enjoying the flirtation and opportunities for casual sex.

Marcela had begun having sex with men at age fifteen. At the time of her interview, she was living with a boyfriend. Most of her sexual activity had taken place with men, and she made comments that suggested that she found sex with men to be fulfilling. Marcela could not imagine having an emotional sexual connection with a woman but was open to the possibility. So far, her sex with women involved only one-night stands. Some of her women partners had tried to engage her in a longer, more involved relationship and she had resisted. Although she strongly rejected being labeled as *heterosexual,* she seemed at ease with her role as a "regular" woman who wanted to live her sexuality freely, including the possibility of having sex with women. Her emotional and sexual life appeared to be fairly conventional: she had a monogamous and committed relationship with a man and did not see her exploration with women as defining.

I was struck by how much her identity resembled the situation of a more traditional, *mujer normal* (normal woman) who also has sex with women (an identity she would have also rejected). However, in her case, her rejection of identity categories seemed to be more "postmodern" than "premodern." She in fact used the term "postmodern" in describing how her sexual ideology compared with the dominant ideology in Mexican culture.

The third participant in this category was Eduardo. Eduardo differentiated between his identity as *heterosexual* and a bisexual identity in terms of proportion. I asked him: "You used the term 'heterosexual with some homosexual tendencies' to describe yourself. How did you arrive at that identity?"

He responded: "I lived fooling myself thinking that I was absolutely *heterosexual.* I thought the time I had sex with a guy was because I was drunk. . . . I have learned more and have eliminated some mental cobwebs that I had about homosexuality. . . . Definitely, that tells me, 'You are *heterosexual,* but don't fool yourself, you already had one or two homosexual relations.'"

"How is your identity different from a bisexual identity?"

"I feel that a *bisexual* has relationships with both [sexes] indiscriminately and without a single preference. Essentially that is the difference. I feel that my preference leans heavily toward women." Although he confessed sometimes noticing a handsome man, he added that this never had the intensity of his attraction to women.

In Eduardo's case, he had made a conscious calculation in order to place himself along a continuum of desire—the proportions of your attraction to men or women gave you a location in the spectrum. Bisexuality meant 50% attraction for either sex. The result of his calculation told him that he heavily leaned toward the heterosexual side of the spectrum and that he was not a true *bisexual* (Carmen did the same using the Kinsey scale). An additional indicator of his identity as a heterosexual man was his sense of how important it was for him to be in command—"being the one who holds the conductor's baton," he said. In this second component of his assessment, notions of masculinity, gender roles, and control filtered into the equation.

Eduardo's sexual encounters with men had not been very satisfactory and had usually involved the use of alcohol. He felt a desire to be penetrated, but this was complicated by his perception that being penetrated was equivalent to losing control. He felt that men had used him and had strongly objectified him. He, in fact, had to confront his own repulsion for homosexuality in order to deal with his desire. He had finally accepted that he had some "homosexual tendencies" by having candid conversations with openly gay men. In Eduardo's case, his choice of an identity and his confrontation of his homosexual desires seemed to be deeply intertwined with his emphasis on masculinity and with perceptions of a male role (having control, command, and leadership).

Common denominators among these three participants were their level of agency in defining their identities and the degree to which each one of them had engaged in analysis about sexual identity and how it related to their own lived experiences and sexual desires. Their reflections and ability to articulate their arguments might have been related to their education and their social environments. Eduardo belonged to a family that openly and regularly discussed the topic of sexuality. Marcela was a college student with a major in communications who had to confront and come to terms with her sister's lesbianism. Carmen was a psychologist with a specialty in family therapy. Although their situations were not representative, they were also not as uncommon as those who hold more traditionalist views of Mexico would assume. Their views are not typical, but they are indicative of the variety of views advanced by Mexicans who are questioning existing values about sexuality and reflecting on alternative definitions.

HOMBRES NORMALES WHO HAVE SEX WITH HOMOSEXUALES

Several male homosexual participants in this study reported having significant relations with men who regarded themselves as *normal* in terms of their sexual identity. Some of these partners were married or involved in steady relationships with women. Some also preferred to be penetrated by their homosexual partners. Overall, homosexual men described these sexual partners as having a strong need to maintain secrecy about their sexual behaviors with men.

None of these characteristics seem at all new or exceptional when compared to those of the more traditional *mayates*. What makes these partners of *homosexuales* appear distinct from the *mayates* is that they did not seek male sexual partners who looked like women. Instead, they engaged in sexual relationships with *homosexuales* who were often very masculine. For instance, Eugenio, who was quite masculine and identified as homosexual, spoke of his sequential long-term involvement with two different men who thought of themselves as *normales* and who were involved in primary relationships with women. These men had seen Eugenio on the side, as a lover whom they visited when they felt the need for having sex with a man. Eugenio had suffered in these relationships because he had fallen in love with the men in question, neither of whom had reciprocated his feelings.

In general terms, comments made by their sexual partners suggest that these *normales* often realized their attraction for men but repressed it for some time in order to maintain an identity as regular men. They might feel satisfied in their relations with women and develop significant relationships with them, in many cases marrying and forming a family. Yet, eventually they began to act out their sexual interest for other men.

The folk wisdom among many homosexual men is that there are many "regular" men in Guadalajara who participate in sexual activity with *homosexuales*. They felt that, in order to have sex with men, *hombres normales* just need the right kind of encouragement, sometimes through alcohol consumption. Rodrigo, a homosexual man, said it succinctly: "It is said that many times the difference between a *gay* and a non-*gay* is only a six-pack." But homosexual men like Antonio, whose sexual activity with *hombres normales* I described in the introduction, also talked seriously about more direct seduction.

Given that secrecy was an important factor, one option for these men was to cruise for sex in public places or attend locales that passively condone sexual activity among men, such as saunas and some cinemas. For example, Arturo, a very masculine man, reported a case in which a married man picked him up on the street and took him to his house. This man's wife and child were not at home, and he proceeded to initiate sex with Arturo in the bathroom. Arturo put a stop to the encounter when the man told Arturo that he did not want to use a condom for anal sex.

Sometimes, as in Eugenio's case, the *normales* established significant relations with other men provided that there was assurance that the relationship would remain secret (or veiled by an appearance of strong camaraderie or friendship). Even in such cases, however, they continued to have a primary identification as *normales* and regarded sex with men as something that must be clandestine. Socializing with openly homosexual men in public or having any connection with the homosexual world appeared to be extremely threatening to these men, so they often did not attend gay bars or discos. Eugenio had met his partners in union and leftist political groups that he attended.

One of the most interesting cases of this type was described by Miriam, a heterosexual woman in her forties who had been married for fifteen years to a man who would fit in this category. She realized his homosexual interest over time, as she slowly began to recognize the many indicators of his sexual and emotional interest in men. The first one was his lack on interest in having sex with her, which she first interpreted as a low motivation to have sex in general. Later she realized that he bonded easily with masculine male friends and students (he was a university professor) and that he always seemed to have one "special" male friend with whom he spent much of his free time. He would bring such male friends home and spend hours with them locked in his office. He would explicitly ask her not to disturb them, arguing that they needed to stay concentrated on whatever work they were supposed to be doing.

Miriam felt that she gained full awareness of the situation only after they divorced. Her ex-husband moved on to marry women twice more before he died. At some point, she confronted him with questions about his sexual activity with men, and he confirmed her suspicion.

Miriam said that life with him had been good, except for the sex. He was always loving and caring, and she appreciated that he encouraged her to study and develop as a woman (she is now a successful professional). As for the lack of communication about his desires, she only resented that he did not tell her, because she thought that they could have found an alternative arrangement in order to stay together as a family and continue living with their three children. After their divorce, she had not been shy about finding lovers, and she thought she could have pursued this while still having a connection with her husband.

When this man suffered a heart attack, his current wife, his two ex-wives, some of his children, and a close, long-time male friend showed up at the hospital. The doctor came out and told the group that Miriam's ex-husband had just passed away and that someone should come in to *amortajarlo* (perform a preparation ritual for the corpse that is common in Mexico). Everyone turned to look at Miriam as if suggesting that she should be the one to do that. At that point, the male friend said that it would be an honor for him to join her in the task. Miriam then realized that she was facing the man who had been her ex-husband's steady male partner for twenty-five years. They had in fact stayed together throughout the duration of her ex-husband's three marriages and the many affairs that he had with other men. Without the wives openly knowing it, her ex-husband's friend had been a silent member of their families for a long time.

Subsequently, this man, who revealed to Miriam that he was exclusively homosexual, became a part of her family, and she accepted him as having played an important role in her ex-husband's life. He then developed a friendship with her children, now young adults, and every year he was the one to organize a family visit to the cemetery on the anniversary of Miriam's ex-husband's death.

Although Miriam may have been unusually accepting of this complex arrangement, stories like hers were not uncommon in Guadalajara. In fact, the topic was often brought up in conversations, and people felt that this kind of situation was quite widespread. Ema and Gregorio, for example, had an upstairs neighbor whom they strongly suspected of having a very similar pattern of behavior. In confidence, this man's wife complained to Ema about how tired her husband seemed to be all the time and how little sexual attention she obtained from him—her interpretation was that his sexual energy was low because of his exhaustion. Every Saturday, the wife would leave the house to take the children to see their grandparents. The husband would leave as well to the soccer game (he played, and he was also the trainer and referee for a team). After the game, and before the wife returned, he would come back with one or two members of his team (who were masculine adolescents or young adults). He would lock the door and take showers with them. Ema said she could hear them talking and laughing in the shower and speaking to each other over the sound of running water.

One time, the wife showed up early. Ema was outside and joined her as she climbed the stairs. The wife was very puzzled about why the door was locked from inside. She could not open it and had to ring the bell. Ema reported that it took the husband a long time to open the door and that he emerged with a young man, both dressed in their soccer uniforms but soaking wet under their clothes. "If he was just taking a shower," Ema reflected, "why would they have to lock the doors and then dress hurriedly without drying themselves first?"

Ema was torn about whether to tell the woman, who was her friend, about her suspicion. In the end, she decided against it and commented: "she comes from a very traditional family, and she was taught that she should never pursue sex, that she should only have it when her husband wants it. I know she doesn't like that, but she is resigned to it. It is not my role to disrupt that. But I feel bad for her."

HOMBRES NORMALES WHO HAVE SEX WITH HOMBRES NORMALES

One young, married man described having had a long-term relationship with another married man. In this case, the connection was with a man whom he did not consider to be *homosexual*. Again, this is a subtle, yet significant distinction in terms of the identities of the actors involved, because it marked the availability of an interpretation that would allow two masculine men engaging in sex with each other to continue thinking of themselves, and one another, as *normal* and nonhomosexual men. Their sex with another masculine man did not turn them into *homosexuales* or *bisexuales* and did not seem to constitute a threat to their masculinity. In selecting a male partner and enacting their desire, they did not feel pushed to seek a man who was clearly effeminate or who fully attempted to pass as a woman. They did not feel compelled to seek someone who identified as a *homosexual* either.

The situation developed in the context of friendship between the two heterosexual couples. Soon after the couples' friendship started, my informant realized that he felt attraction to the other man and that the attraction was probably mutual. The two men managed to begin seeing each other socially without their wives, and their interactions eventually led them to initiate a sexual relationship. They remained lovers for four years.

Throughout the men's relationship as lovers, the two couples continued to be friends. Rafael, the man telling me this story, believed that his wife never suspected that he was having sex with their common male friend. However, the other wife did learn about their sexual activity and chose to remain silent about it.

My conversation with Rafael took place at a *disco gay*. I had been there with a friend, standing in the back, waiting for the female impersonation show to begin. Rafael and his friends had a table, and one member of his party was flirting with my friend. This got us an invitation to join them at the table to see the show. After the show ended, Rafael inquired about the kind of work I did and, upon learning about my research, had proceeded to tell me his story. He thought it would be worthwhile for me to consider it for my study.

Rafael was very keen on making sure that I understood that he accepted his interest in men but that he was also somewhat different from the rest of the men in the disco. After I learned some of the details of his four-year relationship, I asked him whether he was still married. He said that he was and that his wife had no idea where he went with his friends. He assumed that she thought he was out partying and even perhaps having sex with other women.

At this point we were interrupted, and the group conversation moved in a different direction. Yet, Rafael seemed to remain focused on the theme of our conversation. Later in the evening, my flirtatious friend asked him what size his shoes were. He said this seductively as a double entendre, which Rafael immediately picked up on. But instead of doing what would be more usual, to continue playing the game and somehow managing to brag about his penis size by talking about his shoes, Rafael was quite blunt. He opened his fly and pulled out his penis. "Is this what you wanted to know?" he asked my friend, who at this point looked at me pleased and awestruck but also embarrassed by Rafael's directness. I interpreted Rafael's action to be related to his desire to make his masculinity clear and to take a powerful stance in response to my friend's seductive approach.

Some of the men in this category seemed to convince themselves that their desire for men was something that happened to all men. This was the case with Miguel, a twenty-one-year-old man whom I met in one of Guadalajara's main plazas while he was looking for a man with whom to have a sexual encounter. I asked him whether he was *gay*. He responded, "No, I like women, but sometimes I also like men." I wanted to know what that meant. He said, "Nothing, it doesn't make me any different. It is normal, it happens to all men." In his opinion, everybody felt this. "It's just that they don't talk about it," he said. Miguel explained that he had only had sexual intercourse with women, never with men. His experiences with men were limited to encounters in the plaza that led to quick, nonpenetrative sex in public places, such as "the foyer of a dark building."

I asked Miguel about his vision of the future. He responded: "I plan to marry my girlfriend and have children. I really want to have a family. Then, if every once in a while I see a man whom I like [*que se me antoje,* literally 'whom I crave'], I do it and that's that." He then criticized the desire of some men to be openly homosexual, because "*gays* have no family or children." Miguel wanted to have a family. I commented that in some places men have both things: they are openly gay and live together with their partners as family, and they may have children as part of that family. He said that it would not be the same, to not have a wife, because of how society would view it. His expression made me think that he felt that I was making this up: he did not believe me when I said that a gay family could exist.

(

The collection of cases presented here should provide a good sense of the fine distinctions that people made in interpreting their own and others' sexual identities. Such distinctions resulted in a variety of meanings associated with a single form of sexual desire or behavior. A man who was sexually involved with another man and with a woman could choose to identify as bisexual, as a normal man who is also attracted to effeminate men, as a heterosexual who has some homosexual interest, as a regular man enacting what every man somehow desires, and so forth. The existence of this variation in interpretation is consistent with the theory of sexual scripting (Gagnon and Simon 1973). This theory accounts for the complicated mechanisms that lead to the multiplicity of meanings that a single sexual behavior can have, depending on the psychological characteristics, interpersonal relations, and contextual situations of the actors.

Although I have labeled the arrangements throughout the chapter with phrases such as "heterosexuals with a homosexual interest," I must clarify that those phrases do not generally constitute labels of identity. In other words, actors interpreting their identities and arrangements did not necessarily label themselves with such complicated phrases. Instead, they used the simple identity labels *normal, heterosexual, homosexual, lesbiana, gay,* and so forth. The thicker and more elaborate interpretations of what these labels meant for them in terms of their own sexual identities, and the identities of others, became clear only when they explained exactly what they meant by the use of each term. This also means that it would be a mistake to try to map out the different situations as new, fixed categories of identity, because they are not. What is significant about the variety of interpretations is not the labels but the logic behind them and the individual reasoning that defines them. This is especially true if we consider that in contemporary contexts of accelerated cultural change, the construction of new interpretations of sexual identities is dynamic and rarely stable. A map of these hybrid interpretations would depict the categories as static and frozen in one time period and would not represent the flexibility that hybridity generates.

Finally, people's varied interpretations point toward both their ability to reflect and analyze and their agency in crafting their own sexual identities. Participants in my study who had reflected about the topic of sexual identities had often asked themselves a number of profound questions: "Who am I, sexually speaking?" "Where do I fit?" "How do I make sense of my desires and make them fit?" Through their interpretations, they were not only selecting their own identifications but also contributing to the shaping of the sexual landscape itself.

Is it then justified to conclude that the resulting interpretations of sexual identities are hybrid, or is their existence just a sign of uneven modernization? In other words, are Mexicans really culturally hybrid, or are some Mexicans just a bit ahead of others in the appropriations of modern beliefs about sexuality? Giddens (1990, 1991) has argued that modernity dominates even in places that appear to be hybrid. Referring to the role of tradition in modern societies, Giddens contends that "this role is generally much less significant than it is supposed by authors who focus attention upon the integration of tradition and modernity in the contemporary world. For justified tradition is tradition in sham clothing and receives its identity only from the reflexivity of the modern" (1990: 38). I agree with Giddens's contention that modern reflexivity causes the reinterpretation of tradition, even among the most "traditionalist," but I would not go so far as to state that hybridity is a fiction caused by the presence of "tradition in sham clothing." For the Mexican case, I would not minimize the importance that the superimposition of the new on top of the old has for the creation of contemporary Mexican ideas and values.

As we will see, the logics and processes of interpretation that I have discussed here also have an effect in the negotiations that individuals make in order to pursue lives that are consistent with the identities that they have adopted. I now turn to a consideration of the diverse ways in which individuals, relying on these categories, go about the business of conducting their day-to-day lives.

FROM CATEGORIES TO ACTION:
NEGOTIATING EVERYDAY LIFE

**NEW MASCULINITIES AND FEMININITIES,
OLD MACHISMO**

Back in 1992, when I was proposing the research that eventually brought me to Guadalajara, faculty members in my doctoral program raised thoughtful questions about whether Mexican women would want to talk about sexuality, especially with a male researcher. My intuition was that women indeed would want to discuss the topic. I also felt that my being a man would generally not be an insurmountable barrier, but I recognized that it was important to provide options. Upon my arrival in Guadalajara, I recruited a young woman who was a social psychology student and trained her to conduct interviews. The goal was to be able to offer participants the opportunity to select whether they wanted to be interviewed by a woman or by a man.

My instinct proved to be correct in both cases. Not a single woman said she would not talk to a man about sexuality, although some did indicate their preference to be interviewed by a woman and took advantage of the option. Furthermore, generally it was not hard to recruit women to participate. The same applied to homosexual men. To my surprise, it was harder to recruit heterosexual men, who provided the largest number of refusals and excuses for not participating and required the most convincing on my part. It also took some effort to recruit lesbian women, mostly because of their greater invisibility.

It took me some time to understand that some Mexican middle-class heterosexual men were wary of openly discussing and analyzing sexuality because they were content with the status quo and feared that the interview would raise questions about their own privileged status. They felt no need to try to fix something that they perceived was not broken. For some of these men, acceptance of the status quo seemed to rest on a fragile foundation that required avoidance of reflection on the issue. It was perhaps threatening to engage in a serious conversation in which I, the researcher, was given carte blanche to ask questions that might disrupt the foundation of their beliefs.

For women and homosexual men, the situation was exactly opposite. Individuals from these groups seemed eager to share with me the results of their own analysis and reflections about aspects of Mexican social and sexual life that they felt needed to change. Their discomfort with the inequalities that they often experienced inclined them toward open discussion of what they considered to be difficult topics in Mexican society, with an assumption that breaking the silence about such topics contributed to challenging the status quo and promoting change. In short, women and *homosexuales* or *gays* had a vested interest in talking about sexuality and gender.

In his ethnographic study of masculinity and machismo in a Mexico City neighborhood, Gutmann arrived at a similar conclusion when he stated: "where changes in male identities and actions have occurred in Mexico City, women have often played an initiating role. Social groups that hold power, no matter how circumscribed, rarely give it up without a fight, much less out of a collective sense of fairness" (1996: 24). Change required that men become aware of the inequalities that support their status. I would argue that some of the refusal and suspicion that I confronted among heterosexual men in Guadalajara had to do with the existence of such awareness. Participating in an interview, and analyzing their position, might force them to confront their contradictions and to face the need for them to engage in deeper reflection. This in fact was a theme that emerged to some degree in my conversations with heterosexual men.

Despite this resistance, recent changes in perceptions of manhood and womanhood in Mexico are remarkable, especially among the younger urban generation. Gutmann (1996) found that younger married men refused to identify with the term *macho*, which they considered to be largely pejorative, and thought of themselves instead simply as *hombres* (men). The definition of *hombre* as "non-macho" implied a new perception of masculinity that provided room for men to treat women with more equality and to avoid negative attitudes commonly associated with Mexican machismo. Yet, on the other hand, these men were also careful to emphasize that they were not *mandilones* either. *Mandilón* means "a man with an apron," and it suggests that the man in question is dominated by his wife and has taken his wife's role in the household. This emphasis suggests that these men still felt a need to assert their status over that of women, to be heads of their households, and to be stronger than their wives and never dominated by them. Their interpretations also seemed somewhat hybrid, and Gutmann concluded that "these men are precisely betwixt and between assigned cultural positions" (1996: 222).

A similar phenomenon took place among young women interviewed by LeVine (1993) in her study of women and social change in Cuernavaca. These women had achieved improvements in their status through structural social changes—education, the ability to work—which also helped them find a socializing space away from their parental homes or their marriages. In Gutmann's opinion, social changes that were bringing women into the workforce, putting them through junior high school, helping them reduce the number of births, and exposing them to feminist ideas were contributing to "the fact that the ground is shifting under the feet of many men in Mexico" (1996: 24).

Despite the changes that this represented, however, the older roles of women were alive and still promoted. Mothers in LeVine's study felt that their daughters should prepare themselves to be self-sufficient if needed and that they should enjoy "a period of freedom before they undertook marriage and motherhood and the self-sacrifice those roles required" (1993: 78). As the last comment suggests, these mothers wanted their daughters to be self-sufficient but continued to envision that their path would lead to becoming wives and mothers and accepting self-sacrifice. These women took the responsibility, as their own mothers probably had, for regulating their daughters' freedom of movement in order to protect their virginity, modesty, and honor. That the daughters develop a reputation as "decent," in preparation for marriage and motherhood, continued to be emphasized and idealized.

LeVine is right to note that these mothers, through their own actions and the inculcation of traditional values in their children, also participated in the reproduction of machismo. They valued aspects of the "true macho"—such as a sense that "the fulfillment of family responsibilities is of primary importance; he drinks only in moderation and keeps his infidelities, if any, secret from his wife" (1993: 80). They valued as well that their macho husbands allowed them to reign, somewhat freely, in the realms of home and family, which they sometimes did in tyrannical fashion, imposing many of the same unquestioned rules that their husbands used to control them. LeVine remarked that the dominance of women in the home made them become *machas* when their husbands were not present. Their power ended, however, at the point where their husbands' began, particularly in decisions that were considered to be a male prerogative. In some fundamental way, the role of mothers as powerful over their children but submissive to their husbands (at least in appearance) was also a characteristic of machismo (97).

Women's complicity in the reproduction of unquestioned male power is seen as necessary to inculcate good values in the children. These mothers wanted their children, particularly their daughters, to not have to experience some of the oppression that they themselves had suffered, but at the same time they wanted them to conform to cultural expectations. In the case of the sons, this means making sure that they respect women but do not become *mandilones* or, even worse, *homosexuales*.

Although many of the women in LeVine's study had been forced by economic reality to supplement their husbands' limited incomes by working at home, the fact that the work was informal helped them "maintain the fiction that the husband's support is adequate" (1993: 83). They had realized that they often could not rely on their husbands and that, in fact, their husbands even undermined their efforts to keep their families "together and on track" (90). In this sense, the support of other women was perceived as being more reliable.

In Guadalajara, I witnessed this phenomenon, as well as the networks of solidarity established by women (relatives, neighbors, or friends) in order to confront the challenges of everyday life and the perceived ineffectiveness of male partners. They appreciated that their partners did not fully conform to the old values of machismo, but they seemed resigned to never achieving true equality with them. They had decided to rely on each other for strength and for support in enacting identities that were to some degree separate from, though still rooted in, their relations with men. They accepted the fact that they were changing faster than men and that they had to be patient and put up with the inequalities as best they could. This sentiment was well represented in María Novaro's popular 1990s film *Danzón* (featuring the experiences of women), where a character stated, "Men are all the same, but they are the only ones there are."

The emergence of new masculinities and femininities in Mexico marks the relaxation of constraints on more equitable gender relations imposed by the old machismo. But the new roles also reveal the desire of Mexican men and women to retain characteristics of the old system, at least those that they saw as positive or as reinforcing the foundations of Mexican family life. Men wanted to be non-macho, but without fully giving up their control of women. Women were striving for greater self-determination and independence and were confronting the assumption that they must be *sumisas* (submissive) to the whims of their male partners, but they rarely envisioned complete equality (LeVine 1993: 97). Even with all the changes and reductions in inequality, the assumption that the world of men is to some degree "naturally" superior to, and dominant over, the world of women continued to be hegemonic in contemporary Mexico. And yet, further change was also on the horizon. As with other aspects of contemporary life in Mexico, it would be inadvisable to offer a simple interpretation of the changes taking place as new conceptualizations and ideas are adopted.

ACCOMMODATIONS IN CONTEMPORARY HETEROSEXUAL LIFE

Men in Guadalajara who struggled not to be macho, but not submissive either, and women who were determined to change their submissive role, but without acquiring a reputation as emancipated, were often forced to work around all kinds of cultural expectations in order to achieve what they wanted. This required them to engage in the creation of carefully crafted personal strategies, seeking to negotiate their personal identities without facing negative consequences, as the examples that follow demonstrate.

Lola

Lola had grown up in a family environment where it was not a taboo to discuss sex. She had experienced sexual abuse by her father at age seven. Her father was also abusing her brother. The siblings eventually disclosed this information to their mother, which led the couple to divorce.

Lola had her first sexual experience with a boyfriend, under pressure from him, at age fourteen. He had told her that his doctor had suggested that sex would help his diabetes and that he did not want to be unfaithful to her—that is, he did not want to seek other women to obtain his "remedy." His sole emphasis on sex eventually made her break up with him. She expected more romance and did not want to have sex just for the sake of having it.

Sometime after this breakup, and no longer having the pressure of virginity, Lola began to have sex with other men. "I had a boyfriend who stayed with me for a year. What happened is that *me desaté* [I let loose]. The next man, who was twenty-seven, became the father of my child. I was with him for two years, living together with our daughter and all. There were many problems—I believe it was my immaturity. I was seventeen when the child was born, but it was impossible that I—I did want to have the relationship, the child, and everything."

Her pregnancy was unplanned, but this does not mean that Lola was unprepared for sex. She had an IUD in her body when she became pregnant. "You can't say that I did not know how to protect myself. My mother was always very attentive to that. [Upon becoming pregnant] I could have used a different option [abortion] but rejected it. I wanted to have my child. My mom was ready to drag me all the way to the doctor. And she indeed took me to one who ended up becoming my gynecologist. Then my mom accepted it. I don't regret it, but it was a very rapid change; I had to mature *a puros fregadazos* [blow after blow], but ultimately it is something that I decided [to not have the abortion]." Lola said later in the interview that she had had three abortions so far in her life, which indicates that her decision to have this child was not based on her opposition to abortion. Her having had three abortions also suggested that she may not have been as well prepared to use contraception as she claimed.

Lola tried to take control of her life after her child was born. She began to work and, at the same time, took care of her child. After her partner left her, she had to support herself and her daughter. At the time of the interview, she worked as a truck dealer. Lola said that she had crafted this role for herself in a place where women were assumed to always be secretaries. She added that women coworkers had to always maintain a mask of decency while, at the same time, putting up with the fact that all the men in the workplace assumed that they were available for sex. Lola talked extensively about the problems that she saw with Guadalajara's *doble moral* (double standards for men and women) and with the limitations put on women in their relationships with men.

As part of her identity, Lola had made an explicit decision to live her sexuality more freely and to be in control in the process. But this did not mean that she could be completely open with men about her acceptance of her sexual desire and her wanting to have sex for pleasure. She was capable of taking the initiative to seduce a man, begin a sexual encounter, and dominate in the relationship. But she had also realized that she had to veil her initiative in order for the man not to feel threatened and to prevent his thinking of her as a "loose" woman. I quoted Lola earlier in the book regarding these ideas. Lola had developed a way to get what she wanted while at the same time creating room for her partner to presume that he was in command and that she was posing resistance. This meant, in broader terms, that Lola accepted that her beliefs about woman's liberation and the need to adopt new roles could not be implemented through direct confrontation.

In a different aspect of her connections with men—her emotional and long-term relationships—Lola was fairly conventionally located in the category of emancipated, "loose" women. However, she was striving to recover her status as someone who would be eligible for marriage. At the time of the interview, she was involved in a relationship with a married man and was expecting his child. She said that they were very focused on finding a way for him to obtain a divorce from his wife, so that they could marry. At the age of twenty-four, Lola was now seeking the stability of a marriage with a man whom she loved and with whom she could raise her children. Although Lola believed that her partner was ready to make a commitment to her—to leave his wife and start a new marriage with Lola—comments made by men in my study made me wonder whether his promises were real or whether he was using them to maintain what he saw as a secondary relationship with an emancipated woman. Also, should the marriage take place, it was somewhat unclear whether she would manage to maintain the independence and decision-making power that she enjoyed as a single mother or whether he would ask her to assume a more traditional role as a mother and wife.

I now turn to another case, that of Elena, who was older than Lola and had experienced life circumstances that had led her to reject the idea of marriage altogether but without losing the goal of having a family.

Elena

Elena was a fifty-three-year-old woman who had lived a relatively free sexuality. She began her sexual life at age twenty-four, in 1965, with a man who had been her professor in law school. They stayed together as lovers for a couple of years, but their relationship did not flourish because he was married. She continued having affairs with classmates and friends and finally married at age twenty-nine. She had also had premarital sex with the man she married. Soon after her marriage, her husband died. Grieving, she left Guadalajara to return to her hometown seeking to obtain comfort from her parents. Some time later, she returned to Guadalajara to regain her independence and became sexually active again, but always having in mind that she wanted a stable relationship. Elena said, "I was searching for a permanent relationship but without marrying because I don't like to have *quién me mande* [someone who orders me]." But this relationship never occurred. As time passed, she realized that what she really needed was a family and decided that she was following the wrong path.

At the time of the interview, Elena, who was a high school teacher, had created what she called "her own small family," which consisted of students who had been in her classes and whom she brought into her household. Some of them lived with her permanently, and others stayed for a period of time, left, and later came back. To participate in this alternative family, they had to respect certain rules of cohabitation that she had created, including a system to share the expenses. These rules included as well a requirement that the young people who became part of this family be seeking affection and mutual support (both emotional and practical). The way she described this arrangement suggested that she had become a mother figure to young adults who saw her as being much more than just a landlady. "This to me constitutes a family," said Elena. "They are my adopted children and I am a kind of second mother, or godmother, or aunt. Whatever you want to call it, but I am shaping them into adults."

I asked Elena how it had been for her to have a freer sexuality during her youth. She responded: "Socially speaking, I had to be careful to hide it. Morally speaking, I had severe internal conflicts. I felt dirty, that I was doing wrong, [acting] against morality. In fact, my first relationship ended in part because I could not accept it or resolve the contradiction. I felt shame sometimes, but no one ever discovered it or [at least] said it to me to my face at that age. I know now that they [her male friends] did discover it. . . . And I scold them because they were in the same business [having casual sex with women]."

I also asked Elena how she felt about her sexual history today. She said, "I feel good. One of the things I learned in therapy is that I must forgive myself. . . . If I remember [my mistakes], they are not painful any longer. This, which I tell you, was so hard to tell my psychoanalyst, and now I state it so calmly." She seemed to have enjoyed her sexuality enormously and talked very passionately about what love and sex had given her.

Miriam

I referred to Miriam in the previous chapter, in her account of her realization that her husband engaged in homosexual activity. After attending high school in the United States and working for a few years in her hometown, a northern city, Miriam had immigrated to Guadalajara in order to attend college. Once in Guadalajara, she resumed an interrupted nonsexual relationship with a boyfriend from her hometown who was now living in Guadalajara as well. Because she was bilingual, she had many work opportunities, including a position in the American consulate. At age twenty, she had what she described as "a very good job" and was also a college student with a literature major. Although her boyfriend was a student and did not have the resources to support a family, he proposed marriage to Miriam. The idea was that her salary would provide them with enough money to survive. He would continue to be a student and she would be a student and work.

She was a virgin when they married. She had wanted to have sex with her boyfriend previously, but he had refused, indicating his emphasis on respect (for her and for her family). During their two-week honeymoon trip, they had sex only once. She was the one who had to propose it, because he would not initiate it. After that, their sexual contact was infrequent. When she asked for more sex, he would tell her that sex was not everything in married life and that she should focus on other things instead. He went on to become a university professor and fully supported her desire to continue working and studying. Miriam said that, other than sex, the rest of their marriage involved a very close, friendly, and loving relationship.

Some months into their marriage, she began protesting more loudly about the lack of sex, and he complied, making her pregnant. She eventually had two children with him, and her attention shifted to her professional development and her family life. Fifteen years into her marriage, she decided that "enough was enough" and confronted him, saying that she wanted to have a sex life, which she was not getting from him. They divorced and she found a new male partner, with whom, she said, the sex was great. Her ex-husband went on to marry a twenty-three-year-old woman. Years later Miriam confronted him about her suspicion that he had sex with men, and he confirmed that he did.

At the time of my conversation with Miriam, she had been in a relationship with a man for eleven years. Her partner was ten years younger than Miriam. They had recently paused the relationship because she could not stand his jealousy. Previously, she had left him for a year. This time, he told her that if she decided to leave, she should do it when he was not around because otherwise he would prevent it. Miriam got up one morning, packed her things once he left for work, and, with the help of two friends, moved to a new apartment. When he came back, she was gone, which Miriam felt was a great shock for him. This strategy is reminiscent of Ema's (described in chapter 2). This should not be surprising, as Ema and Miriam were now friends, after Miriam had done couple's counseling for Ema and Gregorio before their separation.

Miriam had followed a very traditional path: she had stayed a virgin until marriage and had remained faithful to her husband for fifteen years, even in the absence of a sexual life with him. But Miriam was also not conventional for her time in the sense that she had pursued an education and a professional career and that she felt entitled to have greater equality in her relationships with men. After her marriage ended, she had pursued the type of sex and relationships that she wanted and was working on maintaining a long-term relationship with her current lover. And all along she continued to emphasize her role as a respectable woman and mother. Miriam said that her current partner was the man she would always love, regardless of whether they ended up staying together; she was sure that they would return to being a couple again after a temporary period of separation. Miriam seemed to act with determination and security and saw her current separation as a step toward ensuring the continuity of her relationship.

(

Miriam, Elena, and Lola are examples of contemporary Guadalajaran women who had developed heterosexual identities that implied a shift from the traditional roles that were assigned to them and that their up-bringing had taught them. The three of them were explicitly interested in pursuing sex and sexuality for the fulfillment of their own personal development and pleasure. They broke with a cultural proscription that established that a decent woman's justification for sex should be love. These women were also seeking to assert themselves as individuals and to establish more egalitarian relations with men, even when, as in the case of Lola, this might mean having to veil their initiative and authority to allow the male partner to feel that he was in control. I now turn to examining the identities of some of the men who were, coming from the opposite direction, aiming to avoid adopting the cultural prescriptions of traditional machismo.

Francisco
Francisco had initiated his sexual life at age eighteen, just four years before the interview. When he was sixteen, his friends had tried to take him to a bordello to have sex with a prostitute. He had resisted because he did not want his first sexual experience to involve such an impersonal arrangement. However, by the time of his eighteenth birthday, he could resist

his friends' pressure no more. His friends said that he was now an adult and that he had to prove to himself—and it seems to the friends as well—that he was also a man. Francisco ended up having sex with a prostitute on his birthday while his friends were waiting for him outside. Francisco, who insisted on using a condom for this encounter, felt deeply disappointed. "This did not satisfy me even minimally," commented Francisco. "There was no expression [of affect]. She even said, 'no kisses.' It was quick and I did not like it. We ended up just talking afterward, in part because I was already becoming interested in psychology." Francisco also said that he did not like the encounter because "it was like doing it [sex] to an object."

Francisco added that because of the long time that he spent inside with the prostitute, mostly talking, his friends were outside thinking "this guy is awesome." The friends seemed to be fulfilling a need to confirm that they were doing a good deed. They were also participating in a collective—perhaps even homoerotic—ritual of confirmation of male sexual prowess. From Francisco's account of this encounter, it seems that his male friends enjoyed their fantasy about what Francisco was doing much more than Francisco enjoyed the sex. Francisco said that when he came out he had to brag, as was expected by his friends, thus adding validity to their fantasy.

Since then, Francisco had had nonpenetrative sex with several women. He emphasized that he did not want to have penetration because of his fear that he could make someone pregnant. In these encounters, he had engaged in caressing and mutual masturbation with different girlfriends, all older than him. "They were the ones who took the initiative," said Francisco. "My first *chava* [girlfriend] here in Guadalajara really inhibited me. She made me reach a point at which I was not very affectionate. Other *chavas* have made it clear that they took the initiative. I followed their lead and I then felt less inhibited." Most of his sexual interactions with these women had taken place in public spaces, "in a park, a Vocho [a VW car], even at a street corner that was dark. They have all happened in the *vía pública* [the streets], looking for empty dark places."

When I asked him how he felt about virginity, he said that he always assumed that these women were not virgins, "given how easily they managed this type of approach, of caressing. *Cuando yo iba, ellas ya venían* ['when I went, they were already coming back,' meaning that they were much more experienced]." He had only had one girlfriend who had explicitly said that she was a virgin and that she did not want more than making out.

Francisco strongly desired not to follow the path that had been presented to him, not to become a dominant macho. He enjoyed knowing that he could allow himself to follow the lead of women who took the initiative to have sex. It was unclear whether he viewed these women seriously, with marriage in mind. The frequency with which he changed girlfriends suggested that he did not. He did think of his relationships with them as being significant, however. Francisco believed in having sex only in the context of relationships, when there was love present, or at least affection. He did not want to pursue sex solely for pleasure. This attitude contradicted the pattern of most men in my study. Finally, Francisco aimed at establishing balanced relationships with women—relationships without the assumption of male dominance, which Fernando, my next case study, also strongly emphasized.

Fernando

Similarly to Francisco, Fernando's sexual encounters had occurred mostly with older women who were more experienced than he was. Fernando was a young, middle-class man who defined himself as sexually *pasivo,* a term that he used to indicate that he did not take the initiative during sexual relations. He said, "I am a very calm person, sometimes quite a dreamer who sees the world through rose-colored glasses [*ve todo color de rosa*]."

Fernando was well aware of Mexican society's double standards regarding men and women, and he was critical of social attitudes that forced women to be subordinate to men. But to some degree he also agreed with those attitudes. Such agreement showed as he attempted to describe what he considered to be a balanced male-female relationship. Fernando was critical of feminist ideas, particularly about women's bodies. He especially disliked the feminist view that a woman can do what she wants with her body. This meant, to him, that a woman might want to get an abortion if she became pregnant and the male partner did not want to have the child. This was for him an illustration of how a woman might wrongly want to use her body. Not only did he oppose a woman's making the personal decision to have an abortion, but he also assumed that abortion would not be an issue should the male partner accept fatherhood and state that he wanted the child. In this case, Fernando thought, the man's acceptance of his responsibility would mean that there is harmony in the relationship ("in all other aspects, economic, life, their family life—when a man is in unison with his woman") and that this harmony would result in common goals for both partners (in which case, the woman would not act on her own and "do what she wants with her own body"). In short, Fernando understood gender equality to mean that a man becomes more responsible and caring toward his female partner but not that a woman exercises her will or makes decisions on her own. Fernando added, later in the interview, that he did not see marriage as a personal goal and felt that he might never be prepared for it. This possibly reflected his own fear about whether he could be responsible and create the conditions leading him to be "in unison with his woman."

Fernando's ideas about who should take the initiative during sex were different. He felt that both men and women should be able to do so, and this idea reflected, as well, his personal experiences: "There is always the myth that men must be the one taking the initiative, but when I have had sex, it is always women who take the initiative." His first sexual experience took place at age fourteen, during a vacation. He met a woman who brought him home, where she lived with her aunt. She kissed him and caressed him and led him to having vaginal intercourse. She was sixteen. He added that she was a virgin. He had sex with two other women, and in both cases the women suggested having sex after he had been going out with them for a year. Of the three women with whom he had had sex, only one had not been a virgin when their encounter took place.

Fernando also said he valued virginity and a woman's desire to maintain it. He was surprised by, and mildly opposed to, what he thought was a changing social attitude about virginity. "*¡Me he llevado unos chascos bien buenos!* [I've been so shocked!]," he said. "One time I was talking to friends and one said, 'To me virginity is like drinking a glass of water.' I was hitting myself, 'What's wrong?' Girls now are so liberal! You go to a disco and you see the *chavas* who are so liberal. They meet a guy that night and go to bed with him." However, he also rejected women who were scared by sexuality, which he saw as the other extreme.

(

Both Fernando and Francisco were young heterosexual men who emphasized gender equality and who were not shy about their vulnerabilities during sex and their taking a nondominant role during sex with women. Both of them also valued women's initiative during sex and disagreed with some of the roles that they felt society imposed on them as men. And yet, both of them were also conventional in terms of their lack of questioning of the expectations that friends, and others, imposed. Francisco had never confronted his friends about the discomfort that they had caused him by pressuring him to have sex with a prostitute. Fernando had had casual sex with two virgin women, yet he also argued that virginity should be protected. He thoroughly enjoyed his sexual exploration with these "more liberal" women but seemed to be to some degree judgmental about the ease with which they had sex.

Overall, these five cases should illustrate the intricacies of contemporary heterosexual lifestyles in Mexico as well as the degree to which individuals need to circumvent cultural expectations in order to enact what they think of as more "modern" identities. I must clarify that these examples are not meant to be representative of the Mexican population as a whole. On the contrary, they should be read as representing those Mexicans who are questioning the traditional roles of machismo and attempting to create more egalitarian relationships between men and women.

I now turn to an analysis of the strategies used by *homosexuales* to enact their lifestyles in Guadalajara. Compared with the *heterosexuales* in this section, for the *homosexuales* the questioning of hegemonic gender relations was not a central issue. For them, a more pressing need was to live out their attraction for the same sex more openly, without increasing their stigma or becoming isolated from the mainstream in the process. Despite these differences, there are unifying similarities between *heterosexuales* and *homosexuales* in terms of the negotiation of their lifestyles. Both sought to effect change without disrupting fundamental aspects of Mexican traditional collective and family life. These daily struggles illustrate the practical aspects of the notion of cultural hybridity.

BEING A *HOMOSEXUAL* IN GUADALAJARA

Homosexuality has become one of the most debated and contested sexuality-related issues in contemporary Mexico. The topic was placed squarely on the table of national discussion in the mid-1980s as a result of the emergence of a local AIDS epidemic. The adoption of what we think of as modern homosexual lifestyles began much earlier, however. Mexican *homosexuales* were not oblivious to the developments that had been taking place in the large urban centers of Europe and the United States since the late 1960s. Men and women were already striving to live their homosexuality differently by the time AIDS arrived, but access to knowledge about the culture that they were forming was limited to other *homosexuales* and to the small number of heterosexual sympathizers who participated in that culture. AIDS changed that.

This section is about the enactment of contemporary homosexual identities in Guadalajara. My analysis here focuses on three aspects of homosexual life in the city. I first examine how homosexual socializing influences the organization of urban space. I then examine the personal strategies that allow individual people to live as *homosexuales, gays,* and *lesbianas.* I end by discussing whether the notion of a distinct gay community and identity politics have a role in shaping the lives of Guadalajaran *homosexuales.*

Homosexual Life and the Organization of Urban Space

During the time of my research in Guadalajara, homosexual identities and desires were enacted in a number of different places throughout the city. There is evidence of the existence of distinct homosexual spaces since the late 1960s, as was demonstrated in Carrier's groundbreaking research in Guadalajara between 1968 and 1972 (Carrier 1972, 1976, 1985, 1989a, 1995). In 1995, there were at least a dozen locales in Guadalajara that were identified as *discos gay* (gay dance clubs) or *bares gay* (gay bars). There were also several parks, plazas, cafés, and streets where *homosexuales* gathered, either to socialize or to seek each other for sexual or romantic encounters (an activity labeled *ligue,* the Mexican Spanish equivalent of "cruising"). There were also specific cinemas and steam baths that were not exclusively *gay* but where men found each other to have sex, as well as hotels that had a clientele of male couples seeking privacy. Homosexual men and women gathered in homes and sustained a number of tight social networks that constituted a source of support and solidarity. Finally, an interesting addition to the list of options were the AIDS groups that formed in the late 1980s, where *homosexuales, gays,* and *lesbianas* could socialize and do "community work," yet without having to make a public statement about homosexual rights or about their own sexual orientation.

The aggregate of these options constituted a kind of grid of homosexual spaces and social networks that was superimposed on the nonhomosexual city.[1] As they explored their same-sex desires, men and women eventually found their way into places and situations where their affinities with others like them could be expressed. On the streets, homosexuals, most often men, relied on specific codes of recognition that allowed them to identify each other while surrounded by unsuspecting nonhomosexuals. The extended grid of gay spaces and interactions remained mostly unnoticed by those who did not participate in it.

People with a variety of interpretations of their same-sex desire converged in the same spaces. Such confluence sometimes created marked differences in identity among acquaintances or between sexual partners. It also created sources of support for those who were most reserved and concerned about protecting their reputations or who were just beginning to explore their same-sex attraction. During my fieldwork, I witnessed how several men became increasingly open, sometimes even bold, about their attraction to other men as they gained confidence and received support from others who had already learned to negotiate a Guadalajaran homosexual, or gay, lifestyle.

I must note that, in general, lesbian women had fewer alternatives. During the time of my research, not a single public venue could be claimed to be exclusively lesbian. In 1995, only two of the gay venues allowed women to attend; the prevailing opinion was that some lesbians sought to enact a macho, violent trait and that they "commonly initiated fights over matters of love." "Lesbian machismo" was blamed for the exclusionary policy, although the real problem seemed to be the biases against women among the male club owners. In contrast to gay men, lesbians had not developed equivalent codes of recognition that facilitated *ligue* in public places. An important option for lesbian socializing was the existing social networks, to which women gained access through acquaintances or lovers, as well as participation in small political groups, such as Patlatonalli, which were organized around feminist and lesbian issues.

During the 1990s, several interesting shifts in the organization of the gay spaces in Guadalajara were under way. One had to do with increasing awareness among nonhomosexual people about the existence of gay bars and discos. By 1995, anyone could easily access information about the location and characteristics of the gay clubs in the section called "De ambiente" of a weekly entertainment supplement published by a local prominent newspaper. The section included matter-of-fact reviews of each homosexual gathering place. By 1999, the weekly entertainment supplement had been transferred to a new daily. In its new entertainment supplement, the homosexual gathering places appeared under the rubric "Fuera del closet" (Out of the closet).

The change in labels is significant. The phrase *de ambiente* is ambiguous and emphasizes respect for "homosexual tradition." *Fuera del closet* has a more modern, action-oriented tone, perhaps even political connotations. The listings themselves reflect an explicit effort to give more visibility to homosexuality and provide a taxonomy of the organized options for socializing that were available to homosexual people. Around the same time that this visibility was increasing, there were also growing numbers of sympathizing heterosexuals who were interested in attending gay venues in order to socialize with friends, to see female impersonation shows, to feel trendy and chic, or to experience certain freedoms that they felt were absent in heterosexual nightspots.

A second shift was related to the location of the more openly recognized gay gathering places. Before the mid-1990s, these places were relegated to areas of the city far from the middle-class, residential sections of Guadalajara, mostly to the working-class areas downtown and in the eastern neighborhoods. According to a local gay leader, Pedro Preciado, people in the eastern section were more tolerant of the gay places. The reason seems to be in part that people in those neighborhoods had less political power than their more conservative counterparts in the western side. When I arrived in 1993, only three places existed in the western side of the city, and all were somewhat inconspicuous.

Middle-class patrons participated in an interesting nocturnal migration during weekend nights, as two main roads led them to the larger discos in the eastern side. Cars full of homosexual men traveled on these roads. The men began to engage in the rituals of the night as they glanced at each other from car to car, gossiped about men in other cars, playfully joked around and initiated connections, and speculated about which disco a particular man or group was heading toward. The nature of this ritual, however, began to change when new places opened on the western side.

By 1997, two new places had opened just a block apart from each other in the heart of the financial district, in a neighborhood that is also residential and middle class. One of them, Angels, a large and trendy dance club, opened next to a prominent Catholic church, across from a luxury hotel. The other, Arizona, was a working-class stripper bar that attracted a middle-class clientele. The location of Angels is particularly interesting since, around the same time that it opened, the church's priest complained about the noise generated at a neighboring heterosexual nightclub and successfully lobbied the city to close it. Apparently, the priest was not disturbed by the presence of a gay disco. To prevent conflict with the priest or the neighborhood residents, the management of Angels had posted signs asking its clientele to keep the noise down outside the club and used its staff to rapidly disperse the crowd that gathered outside at closing time.

A third interesting shift was the increasing specialization—by social class, style, and subculture—of the different gay gathering places. Although many of the same people attended several of the bars and discos alternately, each place aimed to promote a slightly different subcultural identity. Furthermore, through their participation, patrons of the different places contributed to the formation of different perceptions of local gay identity, sometimes borrowing concepts that they felt were prevalent in other Mexican cities or in other countries, sometimes reaffirming a sense of local traditions. I illustrate some of these subcultural differences in the paragraphs that follow.

Mónica's and the encompassing of male diversity. Mónica's was the oldest and most established *disco gay* in the eastern side of Guadalajara. The venue's overall image was mainstream and middle class, with an emphasis on U.S. pop music, dancing, and discreet cruising. Like most *discos gay* in town, this place had a *show travesti* every night.

Most interesting in Mónica's was the diversity of the crowd that attended, as well as the formation of amorphous, yet identifiable subsections within the club that were defined by age, social class, interest, identity, and gender/sex roles. It was possible to observe a number of different subgroups simply by moving from section to section inside the club, as several shades of identity were clearly evident within the club's internal geography. For instance, the younger, middle-class gay men congregated in a section that one participant referred to as *el Kindergarten,* an allusion to the age of the crowd. The same participant referred, not without some disdain, to a more working-class, less urban section of the disco as *Siberia,* implying that this section was boring and "frozen." In *Siberia,* some men looked quite stereotypically macho—wearing Mexican cowboy boots and hats—while others appeared to be fairly effeminate. In *el Kindergarten,* differences based on gender roles were much less evident, and the men openly aimed to emulate behaviors and looks that they perceived to be "American," including the idea of having men in tight blue jeans take off their shirts to dance on raised platforms above the crowd.

Although the music was one and the same throughout the whole *disco gay,* the styles of the dancers and forms of interaction varied widely. Near *Siberia* was an area with tables and chairs closest to the stage where the nightly *show travesti* took place. The show began promptly at midnight and lasted about forty-five minutes. Some of the middle-class men moved toward the area to see the performance, while others complained about the interruption and about how dated the practice of female impersonation seemed to them. This latter group used the break in the music to talk and drink, waiting for the show to be over and for the dance music to start again. The show was also the only time in the night when the music shifted from the latest U.S. dance hits to Mexican songs (as all the lip sync was done in Spanish).

The geographical organization within the space of one club represented an interesting moment in homosexual life in Guadalajara: the creation of specific tastes and subcultures by social class and age, but without the more acute differentiation observed in cities like New York and San Francisco. In an unspoken but clearly evident manner, men in the club gravitated toward those who shared their interests and social characteristics, and yet they were also sharing a single common space. They subdivided the space in ways that made different sections recognizable to those who felt they belonged there, and to those who felt they did not. The *lugar gay*—the gay space—was one, but also many at once.

El Taller and the emulation of U.S. styles. The other large *disco gay* in the eastern side was called El Taller (the Auto Mechanic Shop). This place aimed to create a different image. The emphasis here was on a heightened gay masculinity, with strong advocacy for a more global gay-male style. El Taller did not have a *show travesti*, which was quite an anomaly for Guadalajara's homosexual places, and instead offered a male strip show. Its decor created a hypermasculine environment by co-opting industrial-looking objects that would be found in a factory (and, in fact, the space that it occupied had previously been a car mechanic shop). The club also actively promoted a sex-positive environment (in contrast to Mónica's, where references to sex were discouraged) and emulated some of the subcultures in the United States by organizing special leather, jeans and T-shirt, and skirt nights.

The construction of U.S.-like expressions of homosexual subcultures in this place was only partially successful. Every one of its special nights was announced to the audience in advance with the hope that people would choose to show up dressed in accordance with the specific theme of the night. Yet, once the message was out, every man interpreted the theme according to his own taste and persuasion. The result usually was an eclectic collection of reinterpretations of the original theme that suggested cultural hybridity much more than the adoption of a homogeneous U.S. style.

Take, for example, what happened when the club organized a "skirts night" in 1994. This was the time of the short-lived fad among subgroups of young gay men in U.S. cities who wore certain types of plaid skirts with boots and white T-shirts to go out or to attend specific parties. The club made an effort to introduce the concept into Guadalajara.

A group of my friends eagerly wanted to participate and asked me for advice on what to get for their outfits. Unlike their counterparts in U.S. large cities, they did not have the luxury of gay stores where such outfits could be assembled. Instead, we had to go to a store that sold school uniforms for girls and that was populated mostly by women. In the end only two of us were brave enough to select a skirt, but we did not have the courage to try them on, given the disapproval displayed by some of the women clients. As we paid for the skirts, the clerk seemed both puzzled and full of curiosity. One of my friends said to her, "We are buying them to wear at a *disco gay* that is having a *noche de faldas* [skirts night]." She smiled and seemed relieved to learn that there was an explanation for our actions. As we left, the group was jubilant about the transgression that it had just committed.

Upon arrival at the disco, we realized that the original theme had given rise to a multiplicity of interpretations. In U.S. gay mainstream communities, a party of this kind would have resulted in a fairly homogeneous look. The style would have been coded as belonging to a single subculture with a single form of membership. In Guadalajara, the more fluid interpretation resulted in men of all ages and social classes wearing all sorts of styles of skirts: from denim and leather miniskirts to South Asian batik skirts, to diaphanous white-lace skirts and even cocktail dresses. The men wearing these different skirts had considerably different perceptions of the practice, from those who saw wearing a skirt as a form of postmodern "gender-fuck," to those who were simply copying gay masculine models they had seen in magazines, to those who thought of wearing a skirt or dress as an expression of their femininity. The more effeminate men seized this opportunity to show up in women's clothes and break the club's rule that prevented any woman or transvestite from entering. The concept that ended up seeming most strange to people in the club was in fact the one that corresponded to the original theme: the highlighting of one's masculinity by wearing a T-shirt and boots while also wearing a feminine schoolgirl skirt created considerable confusion, as well as some cultural dissonance.

S.O.S. and the pioneering of mixed spaces.   S.O.S., in addition to being the only homosexual dance club located in the western side of Guadalajara before 1997, was also (aside from Gerardo's, a smaller bar) the only fully mixed place that could be attended by homosexual men, *lesbianas*, and *heterosexuales* alike. The club was located on the third floor of an office building, and many of the patrons came to watch the *show travesti*, which was the club's main attraction because it was led by a *vestida* (transvestite) who was also a good comedian. The place's popularity among homosexual men relied on its reputation for friendliness and lack of pretension. Yet, S.O.S. was not perceived to be a very exciting place either.

By virtue of being mixed, S.O.S. facilitated the attendance of *homosexuales* who were concerned about protecting their reputation. Anyone who did not want to be identified as *homosexual* or *lesbiana* and who ran into an acquaintance there could claim that they were liberal and tolerant *heterosexuales* enjoying the *show travesti*. For that reason, the dance club was also popular among men who came from the outskirts of Guadalajara for the night or weekend and who were wary of going to the gay-exclusive places, where they knew that everyone inside would automatically assume that they were *homosexuales*. The need for this kind of safety indicated as well the prevalence of homosexual people who enacted their identities just a shade away from complete secrecy. There was no question that S.O.S. was a homosexual gathering place, and yet it left a door open to deny one's homosexual identity if necessary.

The "More Mexican" drinking places: The contrast with things American. Besides the large dance clubs, the 1995 weekly listings of *lugares de ambiente* included several downtown bars and cantinas that catered to a more working-class, less homosexually identified, and often more rural crowd. Here, the emphasis on gender roles was much more present, and although some were openly known to be homosexual places, others were considered to be regular cantinas frequented by "regular" men and by effeminate men, without necessarily being *bares gay*. In these places, identities that reflected the gender-based separation between masculine and effeminate men were more readily enacted.

In one corner cantina near Guadalajara's main plaza, for instance, men gathered around tables talking, watching television, and drinking beer. An older Mexican woman patted tortillas and made *quesadillas* and *tacos* for the clients. Glances were exchanged between "the men" and the *afeminados*, but not overtly, as discretion seemed to dominate. The music playing in the background was not U.S. pop but Mexican *música ranchera* and *norteña*. This space was culturally quite distant from dance clubs such as Mónica's, El Taller, and S.O.S.

An interesting intersection between this world and the world of more gay-oriented men was a bar called El Botanero, a place that played only Spanish-language music and where men seemed to feel freer to engage in couples dancing because of the club's more Mexican flavor. El Botanero attracted a large crowd of men of all social classes every Sunday for the early evening dance. Many of the men attending considered this a first stop before continuing on to Mónica's. At El Botanero, television screens showed the most popular Sunday variety show. Every time a well-known romantic song played, many of the men in the bar not only sang along but also wept at the expressions of love, passion, loss, and deceit that characterize many *ranchero* songs and ballads in Mexico. El Botanero was also the only place where I saw men slow dance and kiss on the dance floor, as they swayed to the slow beat of *boleros* and other romantic music. El Botanero provided a space where middle-class men could experience, not without some nostalgia, a part of Guadalajaran culture that was absent in other *discos gay*.

Angels and rapid generational shifts.   Finally, although Angels opened after I concluded my research, I decided to include a short discussion about it because it adds an interesting element to the development of homosexual spaces in the city. My analysis here relies on three visits to the club—two in 1998 and one in May 1999—and on short conversations about the place with some of the original informants in my study.

Angels disrupted the previous dynamics of homosexual socializing in Guadalajara in two fundamental ways. First, by presenting itself as young, trendy, and sophisticated, the club initially drew away from Mónica's and El Taller many middle-class men. Second, the club opened its doors to heterosexuals and homosexuals alike, but without losing its identity as a *gay disco*.

In 1998, Angels had a central dance floor, surrounded by an area with tall tables where small groups of men congregated. Around this area was a corridor delineated by a short barrier constructed with pipes. On the other side of the corridor a mirrored wall extended on two sides of the rectangular locale. This wall had a small shelf on which people could put their drinks. Along this wall stood two kinds of men, mostly alone or in pairs, who were openly flirtatious. Among one of the groups, clothing styles and demeanors that denoted that the men were from surrounding rural areas or were more working class predominated. There were also middle-class men who split temporarily from their groups to have a drink while checking out the parade of men walking along the corridor. As in Mónica's, Angels had some level of stratification, although the main space did not lend itself so well to the creation of completely separate areas.

By 1999, the crowd at Angels seemed to be much younger. Now the middle-class older men tended to stand exclusively in the area next to the bar. The tall tables and the dance floor were dominated by the younger crowd, which included a considerable number of women. Heterosexual young men were also noticeable, as were groups of young *lesbianas*.

In a quieter separate bar, several young male teenage couples holding hands and kissing strolled by the tables. In 1994, such behavior was viewed by other men with contempt even inside the *discos gay*. At the time, couples who wanted to kiss and hold hands sought the darker corners of the clubs. One man in my group that night remarked that the new generation of homosexual men not only were much more open about their physicality in public but also were beginning to engage in those behaviors in non-gay public places and in broad daylight. I was not in Guadalajara long enough on that visit to confirm this observation.

When I asked about the presence of *heterosexuales* in the club, one of the men in this group said, "Isn't that great?" In his opinion the presence of *heterosexuales* symbolized the remarkable shift being achieved by a younger generation. Young gays were revealing their sexual orientation to heterosexual friends more readily, and in turn, it was fashionable for middle-class youths to have *gay* friends and attend *gay* places with them. The feeling in this group was that young heterosexuals were attracted to Angels in part because it was "the most fashionable place in Guadalajara" and in part because they found more freedom than in heterosexual nightspots. At Angels, heterosexual women did not have to stick to conventional gender roles that call for constant discretion. For the heterosexual men, Angels offered the opportunity to meet women who were more "liberal." In the opinion of these "older" gay men (all in their mid- to late twenties and early thirties), the new generations of middle-class people in Guadalajara were thriving on the achievements of the previous generations of *homosexuales* and attaining rapid transformations. I have to agree that the shift was rather striking.

(

These examples illustrate not only how the spaces available for homosexual socializing influence the construction of homosexual identities in Mexico but also how changes in individual homosexual identities are in turn reshaping the homosexual spaces themselves. I would argue as well that the increasing familiarity of many nonhomosexual people with the homosexual milieu in Guadalajara is influencing the overall perception of sexual identities, as some of the examples in previous chapters have also suggested.

In discussing the fate of the *antros*, or underground "dives," which provided a space for the enactment of prohibited sexualities in the past, González Rodríguez (1990) predicted that these places would not disappear as a cultural casualty of modernization. Instead, he argued that the "high world" and the world of the "low ends" increasingly overlap, which, rather than erasing the low ends, allows them greater visibility. Bautista has argued that this shifting of boundaries may transform many aspects of previously marginalized sexualities, destroying what he calls, referring to homosexuality, "the legendary fraternity of a minority forced to live in the underground" (1990: 125). These statements are complementary and, as we will see, apply as well to the individual strategies that *homosexuales* and *lesbianas* are using to negotiate their everyday lives in a heterosexual world.

Crafting Individual Gay Identities

Men and women who identified as *homosexual, gay,* or *lesbiana,* and who participated in Guadalajara's gay life, found considerable support and solidarity in the social networks that they established in and outside the gay clubs. Gay socializing relieved them from the pressures of having to pass as "regular" in the bulk of their everyday lives. Most of the homosexual people who participated in my study felt the need to live a double life, and no one trusted that they could disclose their sexual orientation freely everywhere without suffering negative consequences. This was the case even among those who were actively pursuing the unification of their personal identities by disclosing their same-sex attraction to friends, coworkers, and family. One interesting case is that of Enrique, who was twenty years old when I first met him in 1993.

Enrique had revealed his homosexuality to many of his heterosexual friends, whom he brought to gay discos. His parents had also become aware of his sexual orientation when Enrique's therapist assumed responsibility for telling them without Enrique's consent. When his parents confronted him, he denied being homosexual. He told them that he had revealed to the therapist exploration that verged on homosexual behavior but that her conclusion that he was therefore homosexual was wrong. At the time I met Enrique, he kept from his parents anything that had to do with his personal life, and his parents did not know about Enrique's forty-year-old partner. They were aware, however, that Enrique was a volunteer at an AIDS organization.

Three years later, Enrique's situation was quite different. He had broached the topic of homosexuality with his parents and had introduced to them a new partner. The parents now allowed Enrique and his partner to live together in a house owned by the family, welcomed the partner to family gatherings, and even intervened when the couple were having difficulties, as parents might typically do when the marriage of a child is in danger. The rest of Enrique's family was not explicitly told, and the parents were now complicit in ensuring that Enrique received silent tolerance from his relatives. Enrique had also disclosed his homosexuality to his boss and to many of his coworkers. He had been able to create for himself a fairly open gay life while maintaining strong ties with his extended family and with little fear about anyone finding out about his attraction to men. Nevertheless, he continued to be selective about whom he told and strongly emphasized passing as a regular, masculine man in society at large.

Others engaged in even more complicated arrangements in order to simultaneously lead a gay life and protect their reputations. Mario, for instance, had been in an eight-year relationship with a married man. After a short period of what Mario described as courtship, his partner had told him that he was homosexual and that he, the partner, would be "playing with fire" by proposing that they become lovers. In order to facilitate the relationship, both men asked at work to be relocated to Guadalajara. Mario's partner left his family behind and lived with Mario for ten months. His wife and two children then moved to Guadalajara, and Mario's partner moved back in with them. Two years into the relationship, the partner finally told his wife about Mario. He also told her he did not want to disrupt the relationship that he had with his children. The wife agreed to pretend nothing had happened. The only change was that they stopped having sex.

By the time I met him, Mario had a good connection with his partner's children. He also had many opportunities to spend the night with his partner because the wife was in the medical field and often worked at night. To everyone in his partner's circle, except the wife and a few of the couple's close friends, Mario was a good friend of his partner and nothing else. On Mario's side many of his close relatives, including his mother and some siblings and their partners, knew the nature of the arrangement.

With regard to identity, Mario said that he believed in role versatility and equality within a male-male relationship. His reality was different. His partner not only adopted a dominating role but also asserted his authority over Mario's life. He was extremely jealous and was threatened by any attempt by Mario to socialize with other gay men. Although Mario had a fairly integrated identity as *gay* and had disclosed his orientation to his family and to some of his friends and coworkers, he also felt compelled to make accommodations that helped his partner maintain discretion and feel reassured. This meant, in part, being forced into adopting a role as a submissive partner, which contradicted his belief in, and desire for, equality in a relationship with a man. In return, he enjoyed the stability of his relationship and feeling a sense of "gay family" when he spent time with his partner and his children.

Another interesting example was offered by Judith and Gabriela, ages thirty-four and thirty-five, who lived together as a *gay* couple. Both were independent professionals and each had her own child. Gabriela had married a man at age twenty-three, complying with social expectations. She later realized that for years she had been attracted to a woman with whom she had lost contact. That woman was Judith.

Judith had been raped by a boyfriend at age twenty-one and had realized later that she was attracted to women, especially to Gabriela. When they met again, the two women did not hesitate to initiate a relationship. Gabriela was separated from her husband by then, and Judith was single and living with her family. In order to make the relationship happen, they decided to stage a wedding so that Judith could leave her family home legitimately. They arranged for Judith to marry one of their gay male friends. Soon after, Judith underwent a divorce and moved in with Gabriela and her son.

Using artificial insemination, which Gabriela performed with a turkey baster and semen from a friend, Judith became pregnant and had a daughter. Her family knew that the insemination had happened, but not that Gabriela had done it. Nor did they know that Gabriela and Judith lived together with their two children. Judith's mother, upon becoming a widow, had requested that Judith's daughter come live with her to keep her company. In so doing, the mother did not consider the child as being related to Gabriela at all, nor did she seem to suspect that Judith and Gabriela were a couple.

Similarly, Gabriela had not told her family that she was a lesbian or that she lived with Judith. The official story in both families was that these were two single mothers who were close friends, who greatly supported each other, and who spent time together and with their children. It is unclear whether the families truly did not know about their relationship or whether they knew and chose to stay silent in order to avoid conflict or the need to cast a negative judgment.

Gabriela felt that Judith's and her ability to pass as regular women helped. In fact, like other homosexual participants, she was judgmental of women who were masculine, whom she labeled *machorrines*. "If *buga* [straight] people realized that we are truly normal people, that we lead double lives but have different feelings, I believe they would slowly accept us. But we don't need to pretend to be what we aren't, because no matter how macho you feel you don't stop being a woman." Gabriela concluded that hiding effeminacy in a man or masculinity in a woman was a necessity of life. "Everyone has their own double life."

Negotiating the Group: Gay Communities and Identity Politics

As a gay couple, Judith and Gabriela had achieved much of what their counterparts can have in places like San Francisco. They lived together in what appeared to be an egalitarian relationship, they had children whom they were raising together, and they planned on a future as a lesbian family. Yet, their arrangement and negotiations were heavily influenced by a need to conform to existing social rules about gender, normality, silence, and discretion. They managed to live as single, independent, divorced women who supported each other—identities that were in themselves not conventional or traditional for women but that were less threatening than being a lesbian couple with children. In choosing this public identity, they made no bold statement to society about their sexual orientation and avoided the social repercussions that they feared openness about the true nature of their relationship could bring.

They also envisioned their life project as a personal one, and they did not see it as part of any larger efforts to build a gay community or as a way to promote broader social and political change. In this sense they were similar to many other homosexual men and women in my study, who did not see the changes that they were enacting in their lives as belonging to the realm of identity politics or community formation. Indeed, most of them were strongly opposed to any organized efforts to change their status in Mexican society.

This detachment from the notion of organized change is perhaps what made Carrier suspicious of the effects of "gay liberation" in Guadalajara and of the existence of a local homosexual community. Carrier stated:

> insofar as I can determine, the gay liberation movement in Guadalajara has not brought about any significant changes in the size of the gay subculture. . . . [J]udging from the number of existing gay institutions in Guadalajara, the gay subculture is still quite small. There are only a few gay establishments and no exclusively gay bathhouses. Gay neighborhoods do not exist. And GOHL's [Grupo Orgullo Homosexual de Liberación] informative news magazines . . . and radio magazine . . . all folded some years ago; and their more recent and

ambitious "Gay Cultural Information Bulletin for Latin America," . . . had to be discontinued for lack of funds. (1995: 192)

Carrier measured the absence of a gay community in Guadalajara using indicators that denote the existence of gay communities in U.S. cities.

A more optimistic local view was offered by Bautista, who felt that we need to read the signs of community formation in the increased visibility of homosexuals and the greater public discourse about the topic:

> Perhaps most important is that during this decade [the 1980s] homosexuality left the basements and began to constitute a sexual option and to distance itself from the condemnation of the church and of "science," even when this phenomenon occurred only in cities such as Mexico City or Guadalajara, and only in the middle class. This is more important than it appears to be at first sight because it implies a change in values that is not limited to the gay community. The concept of "community" is in itself innovative, and regardless of whether it is justified or not, it shows the increasing will among homosexuals to come together as a group with particular interests and expectations, which was unimaginable during the era of repression. (1990: 126)

Bautista used as his measure of community the increasing ability of urban homosexuals in Mexico to gather and to shape their lives as individuals and as groups.

Homosexual participants in my study seemed to agree with a combination of these two perspectives. They were generally convinced that the kinds of institutions and organized efforts that they perceived to exist in cities such as San Francisco would never be feasible in Guadalajara. This view was partly based on stereotypical ideas about the more liberal character of U.S. society regarding sexual matters. It was also motivated by a critique of the undesirability of building what looked like a separate society. Taylor notes this attitude and explains the view in Mexico that "in the United States, the gay community tends to isolate homosexuals, to cut them off from the rest of life; while the system common in Mexico keeps homosexual people from becoming isolated from the mainstream of life" (1978: 144). The prospect of severing ties with the nonhomosexual aspects of their lives was simply too threatening.

The participants in my study were primarily concerned with finding strategies that allowed them to live a gay life, and only secondarily with participating in the community formation or the pursuit of social change. They tended to share the perspective that society as a whole would change as a result of people realizing that some among their loved ones are ho-mosexual and learning to accept them. They also strongly needed to main-tain a sense of belonging in the mainstream world. Ironically, in order to belong they were often willing to accept remaining silent about their sexual orientation and thus to respect what they perceived to be unchangeable social rules of interaction. Their reasoning was contradictory since they desired the kind of change that is achieved through personal efforts while also justifying their failure to disclose their homosexuality to those who had a significant role in their lives.

Whether the kind of normalization through individual disclosure that these middle-class people desired could be part of a strategy of homo-sexual organizing is an open question. The tactic is reminiscent, however, of a comment by Chauncey: "The history of gay resistance must be un-derstood to extend beyond formal political organizing to include strategies of everyday resistance that men devised in order to claim space for them-selves in the midst of a hostile society" (1994: 5). Those strategies include the creation of spaces where homosexuals can be open while at the same time protecting their identities in other places: "Many gay men, for in-stance, described negotiating their presence in an often hostile world as living a double life, or wearing a mask and taking it off. Each image has a valence different from 'closet,' for each suggests not gay men's isolation, but their ability—as well as their need—to move between different per-sonas and different lives, one straight, one gay" (Chauncey 1994: 6).

In this sense, I do not mean to minimize the efforts that these partici-pants made in order to live a semi-open homosexual identity under pre-carious conditions. In fact, for some of them, the solidarity that they ob-tained from their social networks, and the common struggle to be gay without becoming separated from the mainstream, gave them strength to be themselves at the risk of being found out, and even to disclose their homosexuality more openly. As several previous examples attest, some of them were beginning to question living a double life forever and were in-deed making changes that increase the overall visibility of homosexuality in Mexican society.

It must be recognized, however, that the constraints on disclosure that these participants experienced were often related to their middle-class status. For them, it was important to avoid the practical consequences of disclosure, which they thought could threaten their social status, their pro-fessional development, and their standing in their families.[2] Because most of them conformed to social expectations of demeanor, they were not au-tomatically marginalized and were not pressured to assume a status as "abnormal" unless they disclosed their homosexuality. In their opinion, this explained why participation in bolder, political efforts was limited to those who did not have a reputation to protect. By this they meant effeminate men and masculine women who they assumed to be marginal or working class and who they perceived to be the main supporters of the incipient gay organizing efforts in the city. In making this assessment they were not particularly envious or admiring of these men and women.

What was identified in Guadalajara as the "gay movement" included a small, outspoken cadre of activists. The movement had managed to organize a few small marches in response to police repression throughout the 1980s, and its leaders had some political clout that allowed them to negotiate with government officials for the continuity of the gay gathering places. The leaders had also learned to work with the media. They were often quoted in newspaper articles and were invited to debate the topic of homosexuality on radio and television shows. The movement had also provided a spark for the initiation of community-based AIDS-related efforts in the city.[3]

Despite the merits of this small movement, a majority of the middle-class *homosexuales* did not support its existence. Some felt that the efforts were justified but did not feel the need to participate. Others had outright negative opinions and felt that sexual orientation was meant to be private—that there was no need for *homosexuales* to advertise something so personal to the world. Ignacio, for example, put it in these terms: "I don't agree with the idea of going around proclaiming that I am gay and that I want rights for gays." He realized that this idea implied an intrinsic inequality with *heterosexuales*. "It is true that *heterosexuales* proclaim everywhere [their orientation] and that we should have the same right. But I also believe that sexual life is something that belongs strictly in the sphere of private life." Critiquing gay organizing strategies, he stated: "I believe it is not the most adequate path. Our society is very traditional and very moralist. Perhaps it is also hypocritical. But that's how it is and has been for centuries. So, to try to change it *de golpe y porrazo* [so abruptly] through aggression, to gather a bunch of *vestidas* [transvestites] and plant yourself in an area and ask for rights, is not best." His fear was that any outspoken demand for homosexual rights would constitute an affront to society, as well as a sign of immaturity on the part of homosexual people.

These attitudes implied, as well, social class judgments and shame about demeanors that did not conform to social expectations. Ignacio and others in my study who opposed the idea of a gay movement were bitterly judgmental of the overtly effeminate men and masculine women who participated in the gay marches. Like Eugenio, they felt that these individuals gave a bad name to homosexuality and legitimated social perceptions of abnormality (see also Carrier 1989a: 248). For instance, Gabriela said, referring to the women in Patlatonalli, the local lesbian group, "They are *puros machorrines* [only masculine, macho women]. . . . A woman, despite being gay, must be [a woman]. But to dress yourself as a man! No way. I believe these are people who discredit the *ambiente gay* [gay milieu]."

It makes sense that because of their marginal status, men and women who overtly transgressed social norms with their demeanors were also better positioned to openly question social attitudes about homosexuality and to make demands for gay rights. Yet they were also regarded as being more traditional, perhaps even old-fashioned. The irony is that, in effect, those who thought of themselves as more "modern" frequently also found themselves more constrained to be secretive about their sexual orientation. They were also less capable of envisioning organized or political efforts to promote change or of considering the fight for gay rights as part of their personal agendas. More than identity politics, they emphasized a kind of group solidarity in which the notion of community depended, not on having separate neighborhoods or institutions, but instead on supporting each other in the individual project of carving out a gay life in an otherwise heterosexual world. In this context, disclosure of one's sexual orientation ("coming out" as the action has been labeled in the United States) was not required—nor was the notion that becoming an organized group would help legitimize their status as a "different people," as a discriminated people in search of equal rights, within Mexican society.

With their survival strategies, these middle-class *homosexuales* did not question the structures that confined them in the first place. By trying to be gay while simultaneously maintaining their affiliation with the larger society without significantly changing it, they ended up perpetuating a second-class status for homosexual people. They felt they could not be unapologetically open because they had much to lose. And indeed they were right: they could severely jeopardize their relationships with their families, with whom most of them lived; they could be fired from their jobs; and they could experience stark discrimination. But, as a result, they ended up living the kind of double lives that gays and lesbians in some other countries would find unacceptable. And yet, they found comfort in being able to be open in some spaces, to participate in social networks that provided them with support and solidarity, and to find a niche for themselves as *homosexuales*, *gay*, or *lesbianas* in a world that seemed extremely hostile to their lifestyles.

(

This chapter has covered considerable ground regarding the implications of modern sexual identities in the lives of Guadalajaran men and women. The cases in these and the previous four chapters should provide evidence of the multiple layers of interpretation that accompany the formation of contemporary sexual identities in Mexico. They should also suggest that the formation of these identities is intricately intertwined with individuals' sexual, relational, and social needs—that in their interpretations Guadalajarans define their identities based on the simultaneous consideration of multiple needs and on the accumulation of events that are part of their personal histories. These interpretations appear to be informed not just by Mexican traditional ideas or exclusively by a more recently acquired modernity but simultaneously by both. Cultural hybridity, in this sense, constitutes an important force that makes the formation of Mexican sexual identities distinct from that of other places. Finally, the broader cultural values influencing the direction of Mexican sexual identities seem to be defined by perceptions of family, solidarity, and belonging, more than by identity politics of the form that exists in the United States and other countries.

I now move to the second part of the book, where I analyze the acquisition of ideas, norms, and values about sex and sexuality among Guadalajarans. Throughout the first part I have emphasized the role of cultural hybridity in shaping contemporary perceptions of sexual identity. In the chapters that follow, we will see that in their socialization, individuals are often exposed to contrasting ideas about sex and sexuality that stem from a variety of often disparate sources. I will pay attention not only to the mechanisms by which individuals are presented with norms and values about sex but also to how they engage in internal analysis about what to accept, what to reject, and what to reinterpret in forming their own ideas. As a result, my analysis will point once again to processes of self-reflection to which I often alluded in my discussion of sexual identities.

PART 2   SEXUAL SOCIALIZATION

Taken together, the three chapters in this second part
on sexual socialization attempt to answer several interre-
lated questions: How did individuals in Guadalajara learn
about sex and sexuality? How did they integrate what they
learned into their norms and values about sex, and thus
into their own personal ideologies regarding sexual matters? What did sex mean to these participants, and how
were their definitions influenced by the ideas and concepts to which they were exposed during their socialization? What did they emphasize during sex in order for any
given encounter to meet their expectations in terms of
pleasure and other desires?

This part of the book is a continuation of my analysis
in part 1, but I now use as a filter participants' recollection
of their upbringing and their acquisition of information
about sex and sexuality. The focus here is not on self-
definition and classification but rather on individuals' interpretations of their sexual desires in relation to the
norms and values that prevailed in their immediate families and social networks in Mexico. I will argue that such
interpretations helped individuals to develop expectations
about sex and to decide what is acceptable or unacceptable regarding sexual practices and sexual lifestyles. They
also learned what is pleasurable during sex and how to

manage a sexual encounter so that it is conducive toward the fulfillment of a variety of desires (pleasure, connection, love, dominance, and so forth) but with a minimum of negative social consequences.

My approach to analyzing this process of sexual socialization is consistent with the concepts of sexual scripts, as advanced by Gagnon and Simon (1973), and of the *habitus,* as proposed by Bourdieu (1994). A central claim resulting from the utilization of these concepts is that individuals not only are exposed to a variety of messages—explicit or implicit—about sexuality and gender from an early age but also internalize them and learn how to integrate them into their "view of the world." The internalized scripts, the *habitus,* become tools that help individuals "make sense" of the place of sexuality in their individual and social lives, give them a perspective on social expectations, and inform their interpretations and strategies as they are confronted with decisions about their own sexuality. This theme, as we will see, will be relevant throughout the rest of the book.

LO QUE ME INCULCARON:
LEARNING SEX,
MANAGING SEXUALITY

For most of the Mexicans with whom I talked about their sexual upbringing, sex had not been a topic of discussion at home as they grew up. Parents and children rarely discussed sexual matters formally. Conversations about sex in the context of family life were, in fact, commonly banned, in deference to a strong cultural value placed on "respect." Sex education in schools was extremely limited, if not completely absent. Children and adolescents often had no adults to whom they could turn in order to ask about the changes taking place in their bodies and their emerging sexual desires.

Despite these limitations, by the time they reached adulthood most of these Mexicans had managed to learn the basics about sex, even if not formally. They engaged in conversations with friends and peers. They learned from their own sexual explorations and sexual interactions with others who had more experience. They also accessed considerable amounts of information about sex in the popular media, including radio, television, magazines, and newspapers. Relying on these sources, they navigated through a learning process about sex that was often misguided by inaccurate information and by popular myths. They constantly had to evaluate what was true and what was not.

My discussion in this chapter, however, is not just about Mexicans' ways of learning about sex but also about a parallel process that seems just as important. As I engaged in conversations about their sexual upbringing with participants in my study, I soon realized that they were also talking about their acquisition of social norms concerning the management of sexuality. Besides maintaining silence about sex in the family, parents also used proscriptive messages to exert control and ensure that their children grew up to fit within the social core of "normality." In the process, the children also learned how to participate in the reproduction of "sexual silence"—a widespread method used to keep transgressive sexual behavior under wraps in order to maintain the appearance of normality. They indeed discovered how one can transgress and simultaneously comply with cultural expectations, how nonnormative behaviors can be carried out without triggering negative social consequences. This included, as well, learning that certain forms of sexual joking were allowed in order to refer to sexual matters in good company or to safely express interest or desire to potential sexual partners.

I HEARD IT FROM MY FRIENDS: SEX EDUCATION

A majority of the participants in this study felt that they received inadequate sexual education during their childhood and adolescence. Out of thirty-seven participants with whom I discussed the topic, twenty-nine never had a single conversation about sex with their parents. The overall sentiment among all participants was that there are few opportunities for children, adolescents, and young adults to have formal communication about the topics of sex and sexuality with the people in charge of their education, namely parents, teachers, and other adult figures.[1] Typically, parents ignored the topic of sexuality in their conversations with their children and assumed that they were too young to learn about sex-related topics. The pattern of silence was not rectified as the children grew older and began to discover sexual feelings and desires.[2]

Participants in my study regretted having grown up in an environment in which sex was an unmentionable topic. Carmen, a thirty-three-year-old woman, commented, "My family was very traditional, very conventional, like many Mexican families, with a rigid father and a mother who is *abnegada* [self-sacrificing]. Where both [parents] are predisposed to not discussing sex, to believing that it is a taboo, a forbidden topic. . . . If their parents didn't talk to them, why should they talk to their children? . . . I grew up in a very prejudiced family regarding sex." Similarly, Gonzalo, a young homosexual man, stated: "At home they have traditional ideas

[and] Catholic, apostolic, religious education. [Sex-related] topics were somewhat taboo. Now that we are older we can talk a little more [about sex] but still not much. When we touch a related topic, everybody turns tense and silent, and that's the end of it."

In the case of girls, the mother sometimes, though not always, explained the basics of menstruation and pregnancy. This information was often supplemented with an effort to inculcate in the girl moral values about the perils of sex and the need to wait until later in life (traditionally until marriage) to be sexually active.[3] The conversation was part of parental efforts to protect the virginity and honor of girls, and thus also of the family as a whole.[4]

Claudia, a twenty-three-year-old woman, had such a conversation with her mother. "Well, we only talked the first time that *me bajó* ['it came down on me,' referring to menstruation]. I had no idea. And my mom kind of explained but, well, just why [it was happening] and that's that." Claudia had at least obtained a biological explanation for the bleeding that she experienced and some limited information about the role that it would play later in her life. This, however, was insufficient for her to fully understand what sex was, and she did not really learn until later, when she talked to friends. "The truth is that I realized it from friends, because from my parents . . . they are *chapados a la antigua* [crafted in the old way] and they don't talk much. My mom [talks] a bit, but not too openly. I learned from talking to my friends, not from my parents . . . at age fifteen."

Like Claudia, other women in my study did not gain any comprehensive knowledge about sex until late in their teenage years. Alicia, who was twenty-five years old when I interviewed her, had learned about sex from a girlfriend at age seventeen, at a time when her friend was already having sex. "[S]he told me that she did it with her boyfriend. . . . She was older and had films . . . porn films." Martha said, in relation to the same topic, "I learned by talking with others at school. In my family there was never any opportunity to ask questions. . . . That's how I learned, listening, talking with girlfriends and classmates. . . . I was seventeen. How stupid, right? So old, to begin to listen at seventeen. I used to hear, 'I went with so and so and got laid.' But I had not the slightest idea about what that meant. I understood fully [only] when I turned twenty-two." This happened right around the time that Martha had sex for the first time with a boyfriend. It is striking that these women were all born around or after 1970—they belonged to the generation of Mexicans who were coming of age at the time of my study.

The other opportunity for formal exposure to information about sex came during sixth grade in biology class. This was the case only for those who attended sixth grade after 1972, when the policy was implemented nationally. Participants talked about this instruction, however, as being too basic and incomplete. They described it as a short, and frequently overlooked, class about the reproductive tract and the genitals, menstruation, and procreation, which was based purely on biological information. No one could recall any effort on the part of teachers to address the emotional or pleasurable aspects of sex and desire or even to describe the different steps involved in sex, from attraction, to arousal, to sexual interaction, to orgasm. Neither could participants recall any school-based discussion of masturbation or sexual fantasy, which were probably most relevant to them at that age. And most certainly there was no effort to cover sexual diversity and homosexuality.

Overall, these preadolescents had little opportunity to relate the biological information being presented in class with their own emerging sexual feelings, desires, fantasies, and attractions. In the best-case scenario, they obtained some information about the biology of the sexual tract, pregnancy, and reproduction. In the worst-case scenario, the teachers' own values about sexuality prevented any significant coverage even of those basic topics. One participant indicated that his school had decided to skip that chapter of the biology textbook altogether (defying the national mandate coming from Mexico City).

Mario provided a poignant example of the consequences of a sole focus on biological, heteronormative information. He learned about sex around the time that his own sexual desires were emerging. "[I learned] when I was eleven or twelve, in school, from teachers. I used to ask them because I was very interested in the topic. The teacher told me, 'It is contact between partners, the vagina, the penis enters and fertilizes [an egg].' But I couldn't ask anything beyond that. . . . My mother told me that it was an important topic but also told me basically what I knew already: 'It is when we have relations, your father and I, and the sperm fertilizes the egg.'"

"Did they ever talk to you about masturbation and other topics?" I inquired.

"No, absolutely not," responded Mario.

"How did you learn?"

"I heard it from my friends, *con morbo*." [5]

Mario had questions about sex because he had begun to feel attracted to other boys. However, nothing in the responses that he obtained opened the door for him to ask about this desire. In what he learned, sex was reduced to the mechanical insertion of a penis in a vagina to reproduce. Mario, like most *homosexuales* in my study, became aware of his "difference" completely alone. Yet, he might have been lucky, considering the kinds of attitudes toward homosexuality he might have encountered among adults and the potential for adults in his life to try to "fix" him and turn him *heterosexual* or to brand him as "deviant" at an early age.

In the absence of formal sex education, participants recalled most readily two sources of information about sex. One was conversations they had with friends, and the other was their personal exploration of their own bodies and fantasies, including sexual arousal and masturbation. "I began to discover, alone, empirically, my own sexuality through masturbation," Ignacio, a thirty-year-old man, said.

"Did someone tell you?" I asked.

"No, I did it alone, out of curiosity, touching myself a little, without knowing what it was. Then you begin to know it and I talked with my friends."

"Did you know about the existence of orgasm?"

"No, I experienced it."

Similarly, I asked René, a nineteen-year-old, working-class man, "Did your parents talk to you about sex?"

"No, we never talk that way; we don't have communication."

"How did you learn then? From school? Friends?"

"No, nothing, it came out of myself and I did it."

Masturbation, particularly among boys, provided a good excuse to talk about sex with friends. Some men reported being induced into masturbating by other boys or by older adolescents or adults. Arturo said that he had "heard [about] it from my friends when I had no idea about erections or anything like it. I was in fifth grade and that information was covered in sixth grade. My friends have always been older, and it came up in conversation. . . . I learned how to do it; they gave me the information about how to masturbate." [6]

In some cases, participants were forced by relatives to have sexual activity that went beyond masturbation. That was the case with Antonio, who was anally penetrated by three older siblings; with Lola, who was molested by her father; and with Pedro, who was anally penetrated by an uncle and by his grandfather. These three participants talked about such sexual activity in the context of my asking how they had learned about sex, but they clearly did not think of it as a source of information about sex. And yet, the activity seemed to profoundly affect their sexual lives as adults. Unfortunately, my study was not set to explore this issue in more depth, and I do not have a sense of how widespread the phenomenon of forced sex was in the rest of the sample.[7]

Friends played an important role by passing on information (or misinformation) about sex to others their own age or younger. The common complaint about this source was that the information being transmitted was loaded with *morbo* and provided in the context of joking and teasing. This imperfect communication left people dissatisfied in situations in which they were thirsty for information that they felt they could not obtain otherwise.[8]

The most common word used to describe the feelings associated with the acquisition of formal knowledge about sex and sexuality among participants was "loneliness." A majority in my sample resented having had to confront their attractions, their desires, and ultimately the initiation of their sexual lives without any substantial formal guidance. Among the ones who did not use this word were individuals who, like Esteban in the next section, had parents who provided sexual education in a trusting family environment.

Exception to the Rule: Esteban

One somewhat exceptional, although not unique, case in terms of home-based sex education involved Esteban, who was a twenty-three-year-old, heterosexual man. Esteban grew up in a family that, in his opinion, "had no taboos about sex." He remembered learning about sex gradually ever since he was five. "I learned about sexuality slowly, from my parents. Comments that they made. Important talks with my father. Conversations among men in which they explained step-by-step the woman's organs, the man's organs, the nature of women."

Esteban said his parents told him more as he grew older and his questions became more complex. "I was told what sex was, the game of sex; what were the steps to follow. . . . I was told about reproduction and about physical attraction . . . that I might find physical attraction that could be momentary, pleasurable, and casual. . . . I had been told about masturbation much earlier, about the games of a man and of a woman. Masturbation was not presented as a taboo but as a human physiological need . . . I was told to do it by myself and not in front of other people, and not in excess." When I asked him how he felt about his parents' talking with him about these issues, he plainly said, "grateful."

When Esteban was eleven, a seventeen-year-old male neighbor tried to seduce him. "Given the situation, and the kind of ground on which I stood at home—I had been told about that situation and I approached my father and told him. We had a conversation about what it meant if I had sex with this boy." Esteban decided he did not want to have that experience. "[My father] talked with him and explained, very respectfully, that he should keep his distance." When I asked him what his father had told him about homosexuality, Esteban said, "[M]y father had told me about sexual attraction among men. I could then overcome that . . . aggression— I guess you could call it—but I have to say that it was a situation that really helped me grow up, to be able to see things from his [the neighbor's] point of view."

Most striking is that the father was not alarmed by homosexuality but rather explored with Esteban the possibility of his desiring another boy. It is unclear, though, whether his explanation was balanced, or how he would have responded if Esteban had had sex with his neighbor. Esteban viewed his neighbor's advance as an "aggression." When asked about what he would do should a son of his be *homosexual,* Esteban said he would try to change him. "I would try to observe carefully his first years, see what his tendencies are. . . . I would try to educate him like they educated me and avoid some of the [negative] reactions that families sometimes have when a son turns out to be attracted to men. I would try to attack the problem from the medical and scientific perspectives, see what possibilities there are for the child to straighten out [*enderezarse*], for him to have a normal taste for women. But if that didn't happen, I would support him . . . try to support him morally and set him up for success. His being *homosexual* should not limit him or prevent him from being respected."

The education that Esteban received from his family was fairly open, although biased toward heterosexual normativity. In the case of homosexuality, Esteban had learned both to have tolerance and respect and to believe that it is best not to be *homosexual.* Similarly, he had acquired some traditional perspectives on women, which I described in chapter 2.

Nevertheless, Esteban had something that most participants mourned not having: sufficient trust in his parents to initiate conversations about sex to learn and obtain advice. In relation to the event with his neighbor, more commonly a child would have concealed it, having learned somehow that "sex between men is wrong." Had the parents found out, they probably would have felt threatened. If they were to discover sexual behavior between two male adolescents, or even interest in it, they would most likely seek to correct the situation through punishment or by preventing contact between the two boys, but without discussing the issue. The only comments that might be made would be simple statements such as "stay away from that boy" or "it is wrong," which are direct but can be said without inviting any additional discussion or providing an explanation.

Parental Prohibitions

The absence of formal sex education at home did not mean that parents were uninterested in their children's sexuality. But instead of offering information, parents typically attempted to shape their children's views through simple proscriptive messages intended to help the children differentiate between good and bad. In practice, this mostly meant telling them what not to do.

Parents thought it was their responsibility to counteract any potential "bad influences" by transmitting "good values." This preoccupation was evident among those who had children or were planning to have them. Participants commonly summarized the results of these efforts with the phrase *lo que me inculcaron*, "what they inculcated in me." This notion encapsulated people's exposure to ideas about sex and gender that were transmitted by the adult world as they grew up. *Lo que me inculcaron* was also a statement about the *habitus* of the previous generation, about social beliefs regarding the rules of the game and the strategies available to manage one's sexual desires and sexual life.[9]

In her discussion about the socialization of women, Moreno refers to the veiled character of such inculcation of ideas: "No one told us anything and we nevertheless knew that it [sex] was something essentially bad. That it was related to that dark and dirty world of masculinity. The bad words. The sins. Hidden and secretive, couples at the park at dusk. Who was not prohibited from having a boyfriend? Who was not prohibited at least from seeing him alone? Who was not warned, 'he will try to abuse you'?" (1990: 40). The emphasis in the messages was on prohibition.

Proscriptive messages, stated without elaboration, did not register in participants' minds as a primary source of formal sex education because their effect was more diffuse and abstract. Individuals placed them in a less concrete category of ideas that they internalized growing up—ideas that were somewhat magically "inculcated" in them, without being part of a lecture or formal conversation. It is perhaps precisely for this reason that these internalized, diffuse ideas have special relevance; they appeared to have more power in influencing participants than the actual, limited formal sex education that they received. Adults' reliance on proscriptive messages was convenient, because it substituted for the discomfort of sitting down with children, answering their questions, and conducting formal sex education. "Inculcation" can rely on more indirect messages, or on directive, unquestioned statements, such as "boys do not do that," "you should never touch there," or "good women don't let boyfriends touch their bodies." Saying those statements does not invite discussion or require an explanation. Asking "why?" would invite punishment.

The perceived need to say these proscriptive messages stemmed more from a concern with regulating children's sexuality—and their future adult sexuality—than from an interest in teaching them about sex. The use of the imperative form helped convey that sex is a topic that is not open for discussion. In this regard, the use of proscriptive messages is consistent with the concept of sexual silence. Sexual silence is, as we will see, a socially accepted strategy to deal with situations where the inculcation and control fail and individuals break the rules demanded for the maintenance of a status as "good" or "normal."

SEXUAL SILENCE

Mexican culture, and Latin culture in general, have been characterized as lacking open and formal verbal communication about things sexual. This phenomenon has been labeled "sexual silence," a term that summarizes the complicated strategies that allow individuals to avoid talking openly about sex while at the same time maintaining some veiled communication about the topic. In this regard, the pattern of silence should be understood not only in terms of sex education but also in relation to broader, socially accepted ways of "dealing" with sexual matters (Carrillo-Rosado 1995; Díaz 1998).

At first glimpse, it might seem that sexual silence in the Mexican context is exclusively an avoidance strategy denoting a desire to not deal openly with sexual matters. It could be seen solely as providing an easy way to evade the realities of sex by preventing verbal dialogue about the topic. This function is certainly present, but sexual silence seems to have an even broader role. Looking more closely, it becomes apparent that sexual silence is a foundation stone of the traditional management of sexuality in Mexico: it constitutes the only acceptable strategy to deal with sexual difference because it provides avenues for the tacit tolerance, and perhaps even acceptance, of sexual desires and behaviors that escape the narrow confines of the core of "normality." In a sexual system that relies on unspoken assessments of normality and deviance, which are based on correspondence between biological sex and demeanor, sexual silence is centrally located.

In such a system, discretion and silence facilitate individuals' ability to maintain the appearance of conformity with social rules in situations in which the rules are being broken. This is something of a paradox: the rule is that the rules can be broken if individuals, and those around them who are "in the know," are careful to keep the transgressive behavior secret. There may be a verbal agreement, both among the individuals who share such behavior and between them and others who become their accomplices, but quite often the agreement to maintain secrecy can be made without any verbal communication.

In the latter situation, the unspoken message sent by "those who know" is: "I tolerate you and your behavior so long as we never talk about it." The message in return is: "I know you know, and I also know that you don't want me to talk about it." A tacit agreement is established, one that can potentially be fraught with misinterpretations and wrong assumptions but that Mexicans often make work, as the examples that follow make evident.

Before delving into those examples, I must note that individuals in my study often had mastered the rules about how sexual silence ought to be enacted without ever receiving any explicit instruction about the topic. The rules about sexual silence as a strategy of veiled communication were themselves included in the indirect process of inculcation of ideas, norms, and values to which I referred in the previous section. As individuals learned norms about sex from their parents and other adults in the form of proscriptive messages, they were also learning how to address sexual matters indirectly, using sexual silence, often without having to make any reference to the nature of those sexual matters. They obtained the veiled messages but also learned the method used to convey them.

Ruth: The Family Perspective

Ruth was a forty-two-year-old woman who worked as a schoolteacher and participated as a volunteer in a local AIDS group. In her early twenties she began to suspect that her brother was *homosexual.* This happened after he introduced her to some of his friends who, to her, seemed clearly homosexual. "When I met the four friends that he wanted me to meet, I was shocked. And I asked myself, 'Well, what's going on here?'" Ruth said. Ruth added that she was confused by his openly talking about having girlfriends. Despite his comments about women, during the years after her first suspicion she concluded that her brother was *homosexual,* and she secretly accepted his sexual orientation as a given. She never talked with him about the issue and she passively tolerated his bragging about women.

When the issue came up in her therapy many years later (four years before her interview for my study), she decided to confront her brother with questions about his sexuality. They used to talk about many topics except for homosexuality, and in a conversation one thing led to another and they ended up broaching the topic. She was hesitant to engage in that conversation, but she had told herself that she would when she felt that he was ready to tell her. Her brother probably received a hint from her, which he took as permission to speak. He told her that he had sex with men but also with women. He also told her that most of his friends were *homosexuales*.

Although Ruth's brother implied that he was *bisexual,* Ruth was convinced that this was just part of the mask that he did not dare to completely take off in front of her. She felt that he had always been exclusively *homosexual* but could not take the extra step to tell her that.

After this disclosure, their relationship rapidly became tinged with sadness because of other life circumstances. Ruth's brother had been on a trip to Africa and had told her that he experienced many new things there, including smoking hashish. She took this opportunity to try to find out whether he had ever taken an HIV test. From her account, it is clear that this conversation was very awkward, indirect, and uncomfortable. She asked him whether, after trying out everything that he wanted, he had taken any lab tests (but without ever saying "HIV"). He said, "Yes." She asked again, "Are you sure?" And he said, "Yes." She then asked yet one more time, "All of them?" He said, "Yes." She finally asked, "There is no problem?" And he said, "No." That was the extent of the conversation.

Unfortunately, soon after having that conversation, the brother started feeling sick and had to be taken to the hospital. He was given an HIV test and the result was positive. The doctors told the family that the disease was in an advanced stage. While at the hospital, the brother told Ruth that he was HIV-positive. Ruth seemed to believe, or wished to believe, that he had not told her a lie a few weeks before, when he denied that anything was wrong. "I think [before that] he didn't know, or I don't know, I really don't know," Ruth concluded, not being sure about what to believe any longer.

Ruth felt that, somehow, she had always known that her brother was *homosexual.* "Since he was very young he had certain demeanors that were different." However, it took her many years to arrive at the point where the need to confirm her suspicion openly was stronger than her ability to keep it secret. The rest of the family continued to deal with her brother's sexual orientation and disease in silence, even after his death. "My family does not speak about it; they don't speak about my brother's homosexuality, even when they all know it."

The brother's partner, an older man who had lost a son the age of

Ruth's brother, had been brought into the family network as a friend. The family had in fact continued to see him after Ruth's brother had died. Ruth felt that they all knew what role this man played. Yet, they never acknowledged the type of relationship that he had with their son and sibling. Ruth's brother had been quite complicit in helping create the image of his partner as just a friend. "He introduced him to us by saying, 'This man is close to me because he had a son my age who died in an accident and he sees that son in me.'" They portrayed their relationship as that of two close friends united by an affection of a somewhat fatherly nature.

Ruth recalled one time when the two men expressed physical affection for each other in the presence of the family. Ruth said that family members immediately started looking at each other uncomfortably (*esas miradas*, or "those glances"). The rule of pretense was being broken, and the family did not know how to respond, but essentially no one took any explicit action in support of, or against, the men's behavior. As Taylor points out, the assumption in Mexico is that the polite thing to do in a situation like this is to "assume that no one present is homosexual and that all nice people are heterosexual. In essence, there is a social collusion in which homosexuals are expected to engage in various strategies of stigma management to conceal their homosexual orientation, and in which everyone is expected to ignore inadvertent homosexual cues" (1978: 39). Even when those cues are present, the expectation is that no one would react explicitly. Ruth added, "I don't know, perhaps I was a little shocked, but not so much. My love for him was much stronger than my aversion." That occasion marked Ruth's more complete entrance into the circle of those who "were fully in the know" about her brother's homosexuality, because afterward he opened up much more to her. Ruth said that he ended up telling her who else knew and relating details about how he had started having homosexual sex. Ruth felt that if her parents realized the specifics about how he started his homosexual life and with whom, "they would have a heart attack." Ruth did not go into more detail, but her comments suggested that there were others known to the family, or in the family, with whom her brother had initiated his homosexual life.

I told Ruth that I was interested in what I saw as a culture of silence, and she elaborated that, in the case of her brother, the silence also had to be used to deal with his disease and his death. "We constructed this whole scenography in order to tell people what was happening with him. Maybe people already knew it and weren't telling us. But, socially speaking—the moment when he went into the hospital I was told that he had hepatitis and that the hepatitis had caused cancer. I already knew what he really had. And yet, when I arrived, a friend of ours who was also his godfather told us: 'This is what is going to be said.'" Ruth said that her brother's godfather had oriented them. I told her it seemed more like he had created the "official story" for them. When the godfather sensed that Ruth might not comply, he pulled her aside and remarked that it would be very damaging to her brother's reputation to divulge the real situation.

Ruth's use of the word "scenography" is appropriate, because sexual silence is a strategy that involves what could be seen as the creation and staging of a play for the sake of respecting what people perceive to be the rules of society. It constitutes a kind of desirable fantasy world that reduces the potential for social conflict and stigma. It becomes "real" insofar as performers and audience manage to convince themselves that it represents the truth, or parts of the truth. Even when Ruth succeeded in twisting the rule of silence and confronted the issue of homosexuality openly with her brother, they both still remained involved in performing in agreement with the play's script for the sake of others. Ruth moved from the role of audience into that of actor, as she eventually became part of the inner group of people who knew about her brother's real story. She became an actor insofar as she then had responsibility for playing a role that helped maintain the illusion of her brother's "normality"—that is, insofar as she accepted her complicity.

In this sense, the need for silence was not just the family's (the immediate audience) but also the actors' (particularly Ruth's brother but also those who openly knew and kept the secret). Ruth's brother was quite involved in the creation of an alternative version of reality, which he accomplished by providing all kinds of justifications that veiled his true actions. This he did in order to protect himself and the rest of his family from having to talk about his difference. The "official story" would probably be told by the parents in the following terms: They had a son who never got married. He was a bit of a *mujeriego*[10] and had several girlfriends, but he was ultimately a good person. He also had a very close older male friend who thought of him as a son. He had unfortunately become sick with hepatitis and died of complications that turned the hepatitis into liver cancer. Because the family knew the real story, they were partly in the audience—silently observing their son's performance—and partly on stage performing the expected script for a larger audience of relatives, friends, and acquaintances.

This phenomenon was previously noted by Carrier, who indicated that parents continue to participate in the maintenance of silence even when the son has disclosed his homosexuality openly to the family. "When acceptance or accommodation occurs, which appears to be the case in most families when the youths' homosexual behavior is known, gay youth and their families often cope with the problem by using a conspiracy of silence. In social functions with relatives and neighbors, gay youth are frequently treated by their families as though they were straight" (1989a: 230). In reproducing the silence, they become active participants in the staging of the fantasy world that protects their child's, as well as their own, reputation.

Ruth's comments indicate that she suspected that some of the people in the family's larger social circle, who were being told the official story, did indeed know or imagine the truth. They too, along with the family members, would then be participants in the reproduction of the silence. They might also participate in gossip—use phrases such as *eso es lo que dicen* (that's what they say) after they repeat the official story, and add later *pero hay más* (but there's more) and proceed to state their own version or their suspicion. But by complying with the social expectation of silence, they would help all involved avoid direct confrontation with issues that are uncomfortable to discuss. Their complicity would also allow them to avoid stigmatizing someone who was close to them (which, to protect one's own reputation, would be the socially expected response) should a relative's or friend's transgressive behavior become publicly known.

The Individual's Perspective

For individuals such as Ruth's brother in the example above, sexual silence constituted a useful tool to meet social expectations of "normality" while, at the same time, enacting sexual behaviors and lifestyles that betray such expectations. Other individuals did the same, although not all used sexual silence in exactly the same manner. There was some variation in the role that sexual silence played in relations with family and friends.

Some participants felt that sexual silence was a permanent tool that prevented their families from ever realizing the true nature of their sexual lives. This was the case, for instance, of Martha and other young women like her who had been involved in premarital sex with men. Martha told me that very few people knew that she was not a virgin, and she trusted that her parents would never find out about her sexual exploration before marriage. She envisioned marrying a man who would be willing to keep the secret—for her and for his own sake—and continue pretending that he was the only man with whom Martha had ever had sex. The possibility that this might not happen as she planned concerned her. She did not know how she would handle the situation should she fall in love with a man who strongly valued virginity. She wondered whether he would be willing to accept the fact that she was not a virgin and move on, keeping her secret, or whether he would at some point feel compelled to reveal the secret to her family as a form of revenge against her.

Martha operated under the premise that her parents would never imagine that she would not stay virgin until marriage. However, assuming ignorance or lack of awareness on the part of the family was not a requirement for the use of sexual silence. Individuals often believed that their families and friends were probably well aware of their difference or transgression. They also believed that families and friends were complicit and willing to make their awareness evident through silence, in order to avoid direct communication or confrontation. Eugenio, for instance, like other homosexual men, felt that his parents knew about his homosexuality. He believed that the lack of confrontation was a sign of respect, and perhaps even of tacit acceptance. The assessment of many homosexual men was that tolerance and acceptance could be articulated only through silence and that such tolerance would vanish should they disclose their homosexuality verbally and explicitly. They assumed that verbal communication would leave the family with no choice other than to express rejection, in compliance with social expectations about how to react to "deviance."

Other individuals believed that both awareness and ignorance about sexual difference could be present simultaneously. For example, Judith and Gabriela had engaged in elaborate schemes and arrangements to be able to live as a lesbian couple while also pretending that they were divorced women supporting each other as close friends. They thought their families did not really know about the true nature of their relationship, but they were simultaneously aware that their families had some suspicion. In Judith's case, one of her cousins had verbalized this suspicion when he asked her about rumors that she was a *lesbiana.* And even then, Judith had chosen to continue using sexual silence and provide an ambiguous answer that neither confirmed nor refuted her cousin's suspicion. This ambiguity was important for the continuation of sexual silence. It denoted Judith's awareness that her family probably knew about her homosexuality and that she accepted her task in respecting the silence as a way to ensure continued tolerance. If she confirmed the rumor, the silence would be broken and the tolerance might be no longer available. Should she instead plainly deny the rumor, then those who were silently aware of her lesbianism could judge her negatively for lying. Ambiguity ensured that the silence was not broken but also that no lies were involved in its maintenance.

In another example, Julio, a twenty-five-year-old homosexual man, suspected that his parents and siblings were already aware of his homosexuality, and he perceived some tacit level of tolerance. When I asked Julio whether his family knew about his homosexuality, his response was, "Mmmm . . . I don't know. I think they do, but they never bother me at all. We have even touched on the topic. They tell me indirectly, mentioning people who have got [AIDS]. I imagine that they tell me so that I take care of myself, so that I seek information and all, but I have never experienced rejection from my family. Except for my older brother, who tells me—for instance, I make a certain gesture and he will say: 'You know what? It bothers me when you make that gesture. Be stronger, more masculine.' This bothers me but I don't dwell on it because it makes me feel bad, depressed."

Most interesting in Julio's case is that he was fully open as a homosexual man in other realms of his life. For instance, when Julio was offered the job that he had at the time of his interview, he disclosed his homosexuality right away. "When I started working, I told my boss that a friend of mine had been fired from his job for being *homosexual* and that I did not want that to happen to me. She said to me, 'There is no problem here; your life is your life, work is work.' She made me feel good." After crossing that barrier, he had revealed his homosexuality to everyone else in the office.

Julio had described his parents as people who were open about sexuality and with whom he could engage in dialogue. Yet, even when he strove for a more integrated lifestyle by telling friends and coworkers about his homosexuality, he could not be equally assertive with his family, perhaps because of the rules and expectations of "respect" that dominate family life. The strategy suited his family as well, except for his older brother, who was bothered by Julio for acting effeminate. But even this brother could not be direct, and instead of asking Julio if he was a *homosexual,* he had chosen to make Julio aware that some of his gestures were "not manly enough" and to ask him to change them. For Julio, relying on sexual silence at home, and being blunt and direct about his homosexuality elsewhere, seemed not to be incompatible strategies.

This last point marks a connection with cultural hybridity, as sexual silence has found a comfortable niche in the enactment of modern homosexual identities and yet is a strategy largely associated with more traditional ideas. In places where the development of gay identities is closely linked with the idea of "coming out," the use of sexual silence would be regarded as incompatible with modern homosexuality. In Guadalajara no such incompatibility existed.

Finally, some individuals thought of sexual silence, not as a permanent strategy, but rather as one that bought them time and allowed them to postpone the inevitable. This was the case for Gonzalo, a twenty-eight-year-old man who assumed that his family would eventually end up talking with him once they became fully aware of his homosexuality. Gonzalo said, "Look, I would really like [them to know] because it would take a weight off my shoulders. But I would not like it if there were rejection, given the majority of people's mentality. I know that my family—I really don't feel too good about [their possible reaction]. But sooner or later they will find out. I hope that day is really far away, given their mentality. I know they would not reject me, but there might be certain . . ."

"But you would not tell them directly?" I interrupted.

"No, I would not tell them directly, they will notice it sooner or later." Time, in Gonzalo's opinion, was an ally that might help postpone things long enough for the family's attitude to begin to change. Perhaps in time they would be at a point at which the rejection would be minimized. His fear was that if this dialogue took place prematurely, he could lose the support and love of his family.

Julio had no guarantee that an open dialogue about his homosexuality would ever take place. He was prepared to passively endure for as long as it took for his family to speak openly about his homosexuality, and he was willing to interpret the time elapsed as what was needed for them to be understanding. Although he wanted his family to speak openly, he took every precaution to keep his family from learning his sexual orientation. For instance, he chose to have only lovers who were masculine, in order to be able to bring them home and introduce them to his family as friends. Other participants made up stories that they thought allowed them to enact their transgressive behaviors without causing suspicion. In some of those cases, the suspicion was clearly there, but the stories ensured the continuation of sexual silence.

The Price of Silence

Although sexual silence was a convenient way of dealing (or, rather, not dealing) with sexual diversity and difference, it clearly had consequences for all parties involved. It was a major roadblock for the open acceptance of sexual diversity and for open family discussion about contrasting views on sexual matters, especially when they were not conceived to be part of the "normal" core. But, as the examples above demonstrate, silence also brought with it tacit tolerance and even support. Díaz noted this dual role in his discussion about silence in the enactment of Latino gay identities in the United States. Díaz concluded that "stories of family support were mostly stories of tolerance and non-abuse rather than of true acceptance" (1998: 90). Those who had achieved true family acceptance had had to engage in a "courageous and militant breaking of the homosexual silence. In these cases, men confronted their families, lovingly but firmly, about who their 'true' son was. Acceptance came when the family, courageously and against all kinds of cultural prejudice, met their children's challenge" (91). Yet, there were also considerable risks involved: "For many breaking the silence, even in families who already knew, was the beginning of a serious family conflict that led to disruption of family ties, including migration or expatriation" (92).

Individuals in Díaz's study had experienced the two opposite and extreme possible outcomes of breaking sexual silence: true acceptance or complete rejection. The problem is that individuals cannot necessarily predict what will happen once Pandora's box is opened. Unfortunately, when the family reaction was negative, men in Díaz's study risked losing access to their primary social networks. "Membership in such an extensive and resourceful social network provides individuals with a sense of security and social connectedness that protects them from both economic hardship and social isolation or loneliness" (1998: 94). When the price of openness can be so high, sexual silence appears to be a much more tolerable price to pay.

In my study in Mexico, sexual silence also contributed to the prevalence of a social environment that is not conducive to open, formal communication about sexuality among adults, and also one that strongly limits individuals' ability to engage in conversations about the topic with sexual partners. Individuals embedded in an environment dominated by sexual silence have few opportunities to develop a formal lexicon about sex, as well as strategies to bring up the topic and sustain a serious conversation outside specific settings such as therapy, or even the kind of interviews that I conducted.

One of the most extreme cases of the effect of silence on a couple was described to me during a conversation with a woman who cleaned the house of one of my study's participants. This working-class woman was in her sixties and she told me that she had never learned about the existence of sex until her wedding night, in the 1950s, when she was in her mid-twenties. As she and her husband departed on their honeymoon, her mother blessed her and mentioned, for the very first time, that her husband would "do things to her" and that she should not refuse. However, even then, she did not tell her what was going to happen. Her husband did not tell her either, and when the time came for sexual intercourse, he just asked her to undress. She had not the slightest idea about the nature of sex, and no one had ever shared with her any information about it.

She was so shocked at the idea of being naked in front of a man that she plainly refused and only slowly complied with her husband's desires over the following days. However, throughout what she described as a very traumatic experience, she and her husband never talked about the issue. Only much later, her husband told her that her refusal was exciting to him because it meant that she was truly virgin and innocent. In this case, her lack of knowledge about sex and her refusal were signs of her purity. He did not see postponing the consummation of their marriage as a problem because he was sure that she would eventually give in to his advances.

This example indicates another consequence of sexual silence: the shame and negative feelings about sex that many people develop and that have been labeled "sexual discomfort" in behavioral research with Latinos in the United States (Díaz 1998). Both sexual silence and discomfort have been blamed for creating what is seen as an inability among Latinos— including Mexican Americans and Mexican immigrants—to accept the role of sexuality and live their sexuality fully, without shame and internal conflict. Díaz (1998) has gone so far as to suggest that sexual silence creates a psychological split between sex and affection that among homosexual men results in a search for anonymous sex, loneliness, longing for a romantic relationship, problems practicing safer sex, and a deep-seated absence of affective intimacy in the context of sex.

Although I agree with the general notion that sexual silence comes with a price in terms of the inability to achieve full acceptance of sex, as well as potentially negative psychological effects, I would be wary of overly pathologizing the use of the strategy. Assuming that sexual silence is intrinsically pathological would presume that healthy sexuality and psychological well-being cannot be experienced in its presence. The only possible path left for psychological improvement, for integration of sex and affect, would be to break the silence. I would argue instead that sexual silence also has a productive side, not only in relation to the tacit tolerance that it creates but also in terms of sex itself. Individuals in Mexico often feel that sexual silence adds spice to the way in which sex and sexuality are experienced, because it contributes to a certain excitement associated with transgression.[11] Indeed, sexual silence also flavors cultural scripts about seduction, sexual passion, and the enactment of sex itself.

I now turn to discussing another strategy that seems tightly connected with the topic of communication and sexual silence and with the larger question of how Mexicans are socialized into sex. I am referring to the use of joking and humor as a socially acceptable way of establishing veiled communication about sexual topics—communication that does not break the rules of sexual silence.

SEXUAL JOKING: *LOS ALBURES*

Despite the common assumption in Mexico that maintaining silence about sexual matters is the proper thing to do, the topic of sex is frequently addressed in Mexican social interactions. The means whereby this can occur is humor, in the context of playful forms of interaction that convey camaraderie and trust and that foster a strong sense of bonding among friends, especially those of the same sex (prominently, although not exclusively, men).

The image of a group of men with working-class accents, gathered at an urban street corner to drink, smoke, joke around, and, particularly, joke about sex, has been invoked almost stereotypically in Mexican film for several decades. This iconography has appeared in low-budget films as well as in masterpieces by renowned international directors, such as Luis Buñuel's *Los olvidados*. This is one case where the stereotype seems to work: the representation of sexual joking is a faithful depiction of what traditional Mexican society considered to be the only acceptable medium for talking about sex. The image is inaccurate in that sexual joking is not exclusive to the urban working class. However, the popular perception is that the working class has developed the art of sexual joking most brilliantly.

Sexual joking, like sexual silence, plays a social role in Mexico that transcends what a naive observer might initially assume. Sexual joking is not just about telling jokes that concern sex. Instead, it involves an elaborate and sophisticated language in which phrases are carefully crafted to convey concealed, sexually charged messages about others participating in the verbal game. The listeners must in turn decipher the messages. Anyone who is directly affected must respond, not directly but with another sexual message hidden in an apparently irrelevant phrase—a phrase with a double meaning that wittily fits in the flow of the conversation. This is, in a nutshell, what Mexicans call *el albur*.

Albures, which were traditionally expressed by men and considered improper for women (except "bad" women), were invoked quite commonly in Guadalajara in mixed groups of male and female friends. The proper development of the form (i.e., the achievement of an actual conversation based exclusively on a string of *albures*) was quite an art and often acquired very erotic tones. Among men, *albures* could become extremely homoerotic, containing references to the male attributes, veiled requests for homosexual practices, sexual power struggles, and the like.

Octavio Paz made implicit reference to *albures* when he described "word games or battles—full of obscene allusions and double meanings. . . . Each of the speakers tries to humiliate his adversary with verbal traps and ingenious linguistic combinations, and the loser is the person who cannot think of a comeback, who has to swallow his opponent's jibes. These jibes are full of aggressive sexual allusions; the loser is possessed, is violated by the winner, and the spectators laugh and sneer at him" (1985: 40; see also Carrier 1972). His emphasis was on the homoerotic tone of *albures* and their use in power struggles in social interactions between men. In fact, this quotation is embedded in his discussion of male homosexuality, which he saw as related to male-male domination and described as being tolerated "on condition that it consists in violating a passive agent. As with heterosexual relationships, the important thing is not to open oneself up and at the same time to break open one's opponent" (Paz 1985: 40).

Furthermore, *albures* could also be used as a form of seduction—as a way to let potential sexual partners (male or female) know that one desires them. The use of *albures* for this purpose constituted a safe form of sexual communication because the listener could always pretend not to understand the concealed message, while the speaker could back out by saying that a phrase had no double meaning intended. *Albures,* then, are a safe antidote to sexual silence, but they also complement that strategy because they are an indirect, noncommittal, and rather tentative form of verbal communication about sex.

Although *albures* did not surface in the interviews for this study (which were considered to be formal conversations), they were constantly present in my everyday social interactions, particularly among groups of friends gathered at night for the purpose of play. I had the opportunity to see them being used as a joking game in group conversations but also saw them emerge in one-on-one dialogue. In the latter situation, their seductive role was central, and as Paz indicates, the choice of phrases and the ability to construct witty responses determined the relative power and perhaps even the sexual role preferences of the participants.

In the right context the question "¿Ya te levantaste?" (Have you got up already?) meant "Do you have an erection?" "¿Te meto eso en el carro?" (Should I put this in your car?) meant "Should I fuck you in your car?" Obviously, these could be innocent phrases that the listener chooses to interpret as having double meaning, thus resulting in a sexual joke. But they can also be said with intention, which would be indicated by a seductive tone of voice, hoping that the other person will interpret them as an invitation. If the interlocutor then responds with another *albur,* a string of sexual innuendos would follow, either as a joke or a seduction or both. The communication is both veiled and amusing and is anything but meaningless—it may foster camaraderie or be the ticket that will eventually lead two people to have sex with each other.

From the perspective of sex education, however, *albures* and sexual joking created a dilemma. Participants in my study were frustrated by the presence of joking and innuendo in conversations about sex that they hoped would be informative rather than playful. When people had a concern or were seeking to learn about sex, sexual joking constituted an unsatisfactory form of communication. Words such as *morbo, cuchicheo* (gossip), *frivolidad* (frivolity), *secreteo* (secrecy), and *albur* were repeatedly used in descriptions of the feeling of frustration that participants felt when they wanted to talk seriously to friends about sex. For several participants, this was particularly poignant during adolescence, when their friends seemed to be the only people they could approach to ask about things that adults were not telling them.

Ignacio, a thirty-year-old homosexual man, said that he had learned from his friends "[h]ow babies come, the first graphic depictions of what we had learned in school. But, in addition, it included the fantasies, the extra things." He then complained about the "gaps that exist in that kind of information" from friends and about the "environment of *cuchicheo* [gossip]" and "secrecy."

"Did you talk seriously or jokingly?" I asked.

"Over a background of basic, true information, it [the information] was handled as a joke or *albur,*" Ignacio responded.

Similarly, Gonzalo, a twenty-eight-year-old homosexual man, commented, "One begins to talk about girls, about the experience of each one of us, about wet dreams . . . but very superficially, very frivolously. We heard more from the older ones, but with no guidance." These examples point out a desire to talk and explore the topic seriously and an attempt to find guidance or support but also the inability to talk about sex with friends without joking, embarrassment, or guilt. For Elena, a fifty-three-year-old woman who was a high school teacher, these attitudes masked the fear that sex generated in the context of silence. She said, "[M]y students express laughter about sex [and also] fear of sex. Both things go together: laughter and fear."

In terms of HIV prevention and safe-sex negotiation, the cultural reliance on sexual joking and sexual silence was indicative of a major discrepancy between public health messages and social reality. While the HIV educational messages in Mexico, like everywhere else, have commonly advocated direct verbal communication and negotiation between sexual partners, the more common practice was either silence or indirect communication. The presence of this and other discrepancies is central to my discussion of HIV prevention later in the book. For now, I must note the need for health educators to consider whether *albures* could become a tool for future HIV education programs.

I am compelled to close this section by emphasizing the paradoxical role of sexual humor and *albures* in Mexican culture. On the one hand, they make the topic of sex a common one in everyday interactions. When used for the purpose of seduction, they indeed facilitate sexual communication. On the other hand, they also contribute to a perception that it is shameful to address sex openly or seriously. They support the notion that sex cannot be discussed in the same open manner as other human needs and activities.

(

This chapter has focused on two aspects of the sexual socialization of people in Guadalajara: sexual learning and the management of sexuality. The typical profile that emerges is that of children who grow up in an environment of sexual silence at home. They learn a little about the biology of sex in school but commonly have no formal access to information about the emotional aspects of sex and the range of expressions of sexual desire and sexual fantasy. They soon learn that sexual joking and *albures* are socially accepted forms of communication about sex, particularly with friends, and eventually develop the skills to participate in the game of joking.

As they grow, they also acquire a sense of "good" and "bad" from the collection of proscriptive messages about the body and about morality presented by adults. By the time they reach adolescence and adulthood, they have internalized these messages and begin to negotiate their sexual desires according to cultural expectations. They develop the skills, for instance, to participate in the enactment of sexual silence as a strategy to deal with sexual matters that might be socially criticized.

I must note that supporters of formal sex education and open communication about sex would likely dismiss the value of phenomena such as *albures* and sexual silence. They might judge them negatively as simply being repressive and inadequate, as remnants of a cultural past that require modernization. We have seen, instead, that these strategies also have

a productive side. Individuals who use them often obtain significant benefits in the form of belonging, enjoyment, seduction, and sexual pleasure.

Furthermore, without considering these strategies, it would be hard to
understand how Mexicans participate in the field of sexuality, as well as
how the replication of a core of "normality" has been ensured across generations. Indeed, in these strategies is a key that provides access to the logic
that guides many Mexicans' decisions in their adult sexual lives.

THE MEDIA, RELIGION, SOCIETY, AND THE STATE: INFLUENCING PERSONAL OPINIONS ABOUT SEXUAL MATTERS

In spite of the restrictions on formal dialogue about sex in their immediate social networks, Mexicans have extensive exposure to a variety of ideas and opinions about sexuality-related topics through the mass media. On television, for example, they follow the sexual lives of characters in dramas, sitcoms, and soap operas; they witness heated debates in talk shows; they learn about the positions of different social actors and institutions through newscasts; and they receive practical advice from televised interviews with sexologists and other experts. They have similar kinds of exposure listening to the radio or reading popular magazines and newspapers. Ideas about sexuality are also included in comments made by radio hosts, cultural programs that address sexual issues, and varied opinions advanced by writers and columnists.

This chapter is about the influence of these multiple sources of information about sex and sexuality on the opinions and ideological positions of Guadalajarans. I focus on their questioning of certain ideas, acceptance of others, contrasting of opposing positions, and adoption of norms and values that ultimately seemed to "make sense" within their own personal worldviews. Central to my discussion is the recognition that the media in Mexico, and particularly television, are having an unprecedented impact in shaping views about sexuality and gender. The ideas that they present often create enormous dissonance and prompt people to reflect on their own values and practices. This contrasting contributes to a more generalized questioning of traditional views. Via exposure to the media, "attitudes about couple's relations, family, work, sexuality, and other forms of everyday interaction are shaped by argumentative forms of culture and morality and less by the authority of tradition" (Cortés Guardado 1997: 109).

Furthermore, my analysis distinguishes between forms of influence within Mexico and those that come from the outside. I discuss examples of positions advanced in Mexico in locally produced media shows and by institutions that promote particular viewpoints and guidelines for behavior, such as the Catholic church and the state. I pay attention as well to the exposure to ideas arriving from other places, particularly the United States. As Gutmann put it: "Regardless of the extent to which U.S. television and film do or do not accurately reflect aspects of sexual experiences occurring in the United States, they are reference points orienting international viewers' attention to alternate sexual lifestyles and relations" (1996: 135). Television, in the words of another distinguished author, "imposes international culture and praises forms of life that imply, in a variety of ways, rupture with traditional schemes" (Monsiváis 1990: 173).

SEXUALITY IN RADIO AND TELEVISION PROGRAMS

Radio and television constitute the main sources of information and entertainment for the great majority of urban Mexicans. For Guadalajara, Cortés Guardado (1997: 90) reports that in a 1993 survey, 99% of Guadalajaran homes had at least one television and one radio, 65% had more than one television, and 70% more than one radio. The average for the same sample was 1.9 televisions and 2.5 radios per home.[1]

Similarly, a 1995 survey found that 80% of Guadalajara's residents listened to the radio and watched television on a regular basis. As sources of information, 44% preferred television, 37% preferred radio, and only 11% preferred reading newspapers. Respondents' average daily time spent listening to the radio was 3.5 hours, and slightly under 2 hours were devoted to watching television (3 hours on weekend days). Radio listening was more prevalent among the working class (79%, versus 68% among middle-class respondents and 56% among upper-middle- and upper-class respondents) (Cortés Guardado 1997: 92).[2]

Additionally, within these two media Guadalajarans had considerable choice. In 1994 there were forty-five radio stations in Guadalajara and there was regular airwave access to several national television channels and to three local channels, most of them controlled by the two largest Mexican television companies, Televisa and Televisión Azteca. During the 1990s there was a dramatic increase in access to cable and satellite television, particularly among the middle and upper classes, but not limited to them. In 1992 the state of Jalisco ranked third in Mexico in number of cable subscribers. By 1995 Guadalajara alone had 140,000 subscribers, which translated into an estimated cable television audience of 1 million people (or almost a third of the city's population) (Cortés Guardado 1997: 98).

Cable television had particular relevance in terms of the dissemination of imported ideas about a wide variety of social issues. Via channels such as Fox, Sony, HBO, CNN, Die Deutsche Welle, Discovery, Cinema Golden Choice, and MTV, viewers have ample access to ideas that are presented by television in Europe and the United States. As Cortés Guardado puts it: cable television "connects the subscriber to some of the most important channels of U.S. and Canadian television. This is particularly seductive to those who have their 'reference groups' in those countries and who are inclined to adopt their lifestyles or, at least, some aspects of their lifestyles" (1997: 98).

Through both regular and cable television, Mexican viewers have seen shows with a homosexual content: sitcoms such as *Ellen* and *Will and Grace*, or an episode of *The Simpsons* that depicts a cartoon version of John Waters as an openly gay store owner and that focuses on the question of whether Bart might be turning out gay. In American dramas and sitcoms—including *ER, The Practice, Beverly Hills 90210, Dawson Creek, Party of Five, Friends,* and *Melrose Place,* to name a few—they are exposed to the lives and tribulations of strong single mothers, people with HIV, emancipated working women, socially accepted unmarried couples, and sexually active single adults. In U.S. Spanish television talk shows, such as Univision's *Cristina* and Telemundo's *Tercel,* they witness discussions, often among members of the working class, about women's inequality, intergenerational sex, abortion, drugs, homosexuality, and extramarital affairs. And, increasingly, Mexican television and radio themselves are following suit by producing shows—local talk shows, soap operas, and investigative news reports—that present Mexican versions of many of the same debates. An example of the latter is a 1998 hour-long report on male homosexual life in Mexico City broadcast by a Mexican news cable channel.

In the next two sections, I discuss two Mexican programs that acquired a reputation for "pushing the envelope" about local issues related to sexuality and gender. One is a television soap opera called *Mirada de mujer* (A woman's gaze), which aired nationally in 1997 and 1998. The other is a Guadalajaran radio show called *La pitaya yeye* (The groovy pitaya-fruit), which aired for about a year on the University of Guadalajara's radio station in 1993–94.

Mirada de Mujer

Monopoly control over the production of Mexican soap operas was held for several decades by the Mexican communications corporation Televisa, which is the largest of its kind in Mexico and in Latin America. Within Mexico, Televisa was widely perceived to be unconditionally supportive of the Mexican government and, by extension, an active participant in the construction of the hegemony of the official political party, the Partido Revolucionario Institucional (PRI).

Televisa's soap operas, the *comedias* or *telenovelas,* are an adaptation in Mexico of the concept developed in the United States. They are also one of the corporation's greatest successes.[3] They are different from the U.S. soaps in that they are often shown during prime-time television. They also are short-lived, usually lasting several months, and not eternal like their U.S. counterparts. Commonly despised by men, at least publicly, the *telenovelas* have presented to several generations of women stories of love and deceit, of deep suffering, and of heroes and heroines striving to find happiness in the midst of all kinds of adversity. Some of the more popular *telenovelas* have played to the utmost fantasies of a working class craving the wealth of the rich. A common, and still successful, theme in the *telenovelas* is the story of the poor girl—the uneducated and submissive girl arriving in the big city from a small town *(del pueblo)*—who starts as the maid of a rich family and climbs up the social ladder to become the wife of the family's handsome heir. In this fantasy world, the girl is often played by a European-looking actress with light-colored eyes, fair skin, and blond hair, in complete disregard for the looks of the more "Mexican" or indigenous women that she is supposed to represent.

These basic features of the *telenovelas* are important in understanding why *Mirada de mujer* caused commotion among the Mexican urban middle class. This soap opera was produced by Televisión Azteca, which became a true competitor of Televisa in the 1990s, breaking the latter's monopoly over national commercial television. Television Azteca made an explicit effort to do something different, including producing some *telenovelas* that more faithfully represented Mexican reality, including its complexities and current challenges. *Mirada de mujer* was part of this strategy.

In direct contrast to fantasy-like representations of Mexican women's lives and discourses that reinforced the views of Mexican machismo, *Mirada de mujer* aimed at depicting realistically the lives of contemporary *mexicanas* and the gender inequalities that prevail in Mexico. More broadly, the writers sought to paint a view of Mexican society as seen through a woman's eyes, hence the name of the *telenovela*. When *Mirada de mujer* hit the airwaves, the soap opera was an immediate success, particularly among the middle class and the younger generations of Mexicans, who saw their lives captured for the first time on the television screen. Most uniquely, a considerable proportion of those who were hooked by the plot were men. Germán Dehesa, a well-known Mexican columnist, puzzled by the number of male viewers, commented: "*Mirada de mujer* has been followed, commented upon, discussed, vilified and exalted by a large number of men. Strange phenomenon" (1998: 5). Dehesa offered the following explanation: "men, no matter how preoccupied we are with macro-economics and the fluctuations in the oil market, have not failed to perceive that women have given up their passivity and blindness and now demand, with every justification, that their gaze be as valid as the masculine, in the extensive and never-ending task of deciphering the Universe, the world, reality and the human heart" (6). My only criticism of this comment is that in Mexico today it is not only men who would be concerned about the economy and the fluctuations in the oil market.

Mirada de mujer centers on the life of María Inés San Millán, the wife of a wealthy lawyer, who discovers that her husband, Ignacio, is having an affair with a younger woman. At the core of the story are the inequalities in the couple's relationship, which become blatantly evident as they emerge in the confrontation about the husband's extramarital affair and everything that follows, including the couple's divorce.

The couple's children are three young adults who live in the family home: Adriana, Andrés, and Mónica, all quite spoiled by the good life of their wealthy family. Over the course of the story, their lives provide the justification to address a range of social issues. Adriana is studying to become a lawyer and becomes pregnant by her boyfriend. She is faced with considering an abortion and decides against having one but ends up miscarrying after an accelerated wedding meant to provide legitimacy for her child. Having to choose between becoming a wife and pursuing her career, in the end she manages to do both. Andrés is suspected of being a homosexual, but it turns out that he is just inexperienced and shy with women. His relationship with his father is confrontational because Andrés wants to be a musician instead of a lawyer or a doctor, as his father would prefer.

He ends up creating a stir by falling in love, and secretly marrying, a black woman, which raises issues of racism within the story. Finally, Mónica, the youngest child, is an eighteen-year-old conservative and spoiled brat who has bulimia and desperately does all kinds of foolish things to try to keep her parents together, becoming in the process a puppet for her excessively and stereotypically conservative grandmother. Later in the story, a young man rapes her as she is leaving a party and she ends up having an abortion despite her religious, conservative values.

Other characters in the story helped diversify the range of issues with which the *telenovela* dealt, as well as the contrasting positions between different ideologies and generations. Along with Ignacio, María Inés's mother, Mamaelena, incarnates dogma and old *machista* positions. Her depiction is extreme but effective as the representation of what the writers would obviously like Mexicans to give up. In her role as mother, her goal is to bring her daughter and son-in-law together, at whatever price, even if she has to destroy María Inés and her children in the process.

María Inés also has two close friends, and a sister, who together form a solidarity network of middle-aged women, each facing different vicissitudes and preoccupations. Rosario is a housewife who is very much in love with her husband and who has a very active sexual life with him—a sexual life that becomes disrupted by her getting breast cancer and a mastectomy. This character is also used to depict postmastectomy depression and a woman's unwillingness to put her needs above the needs of her family. Consuelo, María Inés's sister, lives in Los Angeles and is beaten by her husband, whom she puts in the hospital when she attacks him in self-defense. Consuelo ends up having to confront his claim that it was an attempted homicide. Paulina is a sexually liberated, divorced woman, mother of two girls, who greatly enjoys sex and is obsessed by her efforts to stay young. In one of her affairs, she is battered by a lover and ends up acquiring HIV from him and later dying of an unrealistic heart attack, supposedly brought on by the stress produced by the news of her infection.

Finally, an important element of the story is that after her husband abandons the family house, María Inés falls in love with a young reporter, Alejandro Salas, who incarnates the idealized version of a non-macho Mexican man. He is a divorced father whose wife left him for another man and who is greatly supportive of equality in relationships. He is also everything that Ignacio is not and ends up providing a dramatic contrast with Ignacio's old-fashioned machismo. In the end, however, Ignacio is somewhat redeemed in that he recognizes the many mistakes that he makes throughout the story, often encouraged by Mamaelena (whom Alejandro Salas playfully dubs "Cruella Deville"). Together, María Inés and Alejandro are forced to confront the many social judgments imposed on a relationship between an older woman and a younger man, as well as the social perception that an abandoned wife does not have the same right as a husband to have extramarital sex.

This summary might explain why *Mirada de mujer* attracted so much attention. Many people thought that it was the ultimate television statement about sexuality and gender in Mexico. When I visited in 1997, I could not convince anyone I knew to get together with me on weekday nights between 9 and 10 P.M. They all had a daily date with *Mirada* (as people fondly began to call the show). But, as much as this *telenovela* promoted frank discussion of many social issues and inequalities in Mexico, the product was also imperfect. The writers regularly felt compelled to provide simple answers—answers that were often limited by the writers' perception of how far they could go without putting off their audience. In the end, they seemed wary of pushing too far and ended up choosing to walk a safer line by not touching deeply on issues that they probably found to be taboo, even in the context of their "liberal" script. In certain cases, they opened up a topic, only to close it rapidly once the frankness required to treat the issue became uncomfortable or too tense.

I offer here a few examples. Andrés was suspected of being homosexual, which caused María Inés to have a conversation with her friend Paulina about this issue. The *telenovela* carefully depicted the fears of a mother who is confronting the possibility of having a homosexual son, her interest in becoming informed by reading a book about homosexuality, as well as her ability to grow and understand. Yet Paulina soon after seduces Andrés and confirms his heterosexuality. The topic of homosexuality was immediately closed, and the *telenovela* offered no elaboration of what a homosexual life might be like or whether María Inés would have accepted a homosexual son. *Mirada* ended up indirectly supporting the notion that if you detect homosexuality early enough in a son, he can be redirected toward "normality." [4]

Andrés falls in love with a black woman from a rich Caribbean family, and their relationship puts racism on the table, as well as judgments against mixed-race couples. However, an upper-class, white-black relationship is not a very effective example in Mexico. First, there are very few blacks in the country. Second, the real victims of discrimination and racism in Mexico are the impoverished Indians. Getting to the true core of racism in Mexico would have required a relationship between Andrés, with his fair skin and European looks, and a dark-skinned, low-income girl of Indian background.

Finally, Paulina's acquiring HIV toward the end of the *telenovela* was easily interpreted as an indictment of freer women's sexuality. "That is what happens when a woman lives her sexuality freely" seemed to be the message. Although the writers were careful to indicate that she had usually used condoms and that she possibly became infected in the context of violent sex, judgment against her promiscuity was also made evident all along. Dehesa (1998) strongly complained about this twist in the story and sent a symbolic, playful message to the character when he wrote: "[Paulina], don't believe this, you getting AIDS. You will always live for me luxuriantly, generously, and bravely. The real final blow would have been for Mamaelena, and not you, to contract the virus. Her character was just like a virus." In this comment, he also faithfully represented how someone as intellectually oriented as himself became passionately involved in the story line of *Mirada*.

Regardless of its limitations, *Mirada de mujer* offered an alternative to the more common images presented in more mainstream Mexican *telenovelas*. The impact of these images was probably enhanced by the fact that that they were not coming from elsewhere—from distant and assumed-to-be-more-liberal places—but from within Mexican society as people see it today. These were not Norteamericanos showcasing their ideas but other Mexicans. Their issues could be those of anybody else in Mexico. As a working-class woman on a Mexican talk show put it, after commenting on her realization that she ought to change the rules and power relations in her marriage, "*Mirada de mujer* changed my life."

La Pitaya Yeye

La pitaya yeye was a one-hour daily radio show that began airing in Guadalajara on June 10, 1993. Broadcast by Radio Universidad, the public university's radio station, it was conducted by three witty men, one of whom was a member of a nationally recognized network of *moneros* (cartoonists). The show was an irreverent, humorous series of sketches and commentaries about all kinds of social issues considered taboo in Guadalajara, many of which were of a sexual nature. It aired during lunchtime, from 1 to 2 P.M. on weekdays and was very popular among young people due to its playful and transgressive tone.

In the show, the hosts freely improvised as they chatted with each other or responded to callers' comments and questions, created all kinds of different voices, and played prerecorded segments that had several regular fictional characters. Several of their segments were spoofs of existing television shows or situations in which they ridiculed the positions of politicians and other local and national public figures, including the Mexican president (who at the time was still seen as untouchable).

When I interviewed Luis Usabiaga, one of the three hosts, he indicated that sexuality was a central topic of the show from the outset "because sexual humor is a relatively easy thing to achieve." As the program developed, they realized that they were constantly crossing lines as they talked about issues that would normally be censored, and they decided to take the greater challenge of seeking a kind of sexual humor that was less superficial and that touched more deeply on sexual matters. Usabiaga also indicated that this was not hard for them, because as longtime friends they were used to being "pariahs" whose abrasive humor often caused scandal within their own social network.

To their surprise, many in their audience reacted positively to what they saw as a fun and humorous, and yet at the same time clearly serious, questioning of sexual repression. From presentations that they gave in high schools in Guadalajara, Usabiaga realized that young people were delighted to hear on the radio the kinds of ideas about which they joked with their friends and to know that *la censura* (censorship) had not taken the show off the air right away. In the eyes of many, the existence of the show was, in itself, a badly needed challenge to conventionality and a test of how far direct confrontation of social taboos could go.

Usabiaga added that, in part, the key to the show's success was that they made fun of everything and everyone at the same time as they validated alternative lifestyles. As an example, he said that the first reaction of local gay leaders to the show was very negative, because some of the sketches were overtly "campy," using stereotypes of effeminacy and making jokes about homosexuality. But he felt that the same leaders ended up understanding that this path contributed to changing social perceptions of homosexuality and promoting greater familiarity and acceptance. Interspersed in the humor, Usabiaga said, they were careful to place messages that questioned *homofobia* and aggression against *homosexuales*.

The hosts were certainly not shy about putting out messages about any number of sexual matters. On one occasion, I heard them provide a full description of the steps and techniques associated with fellatio. In their description of sexual acts, which were simultaneously humorous and "educational," the hosts also often commented on their own preferences and experiences with sex and made reference to their own bodies. Usabiaga recalled: "One day I found myself saying that the microphone stank . . . and then adding that it was perhaps because I had been doing sit-ups on it," which was a thinly veiled reference to anal penetration with a dildo or other object. "I later heard that many high school students had started listening after that, that they really enjoyed the reference, which was in part perhaps motivated by their *morbo* [their sick curiosity]." For Usabiaga, the use of *morbo* and *albures* allowed the show to make initial reference to topics that they made explicit immediately after. *Albures, morbo,* and sexual joking were the means to open up a more formal dialogue, which they often pursued in their explanations and discussions while, at the same time, maintaining a humorous tone.

A different strategy also used by the show, and closely associated with *albures,* was to make a remark that was meant to be interpreted as the opposite of what was being said. On one occasion they stated that "everybody knows that there are no homosexual relationships inside the Catholic seminaries," making reference to the widespread perception of sexual interactions in those schools. In their statements, they also drew links between sexuality and other social domains, such as religion and political corruption. The only problem with this strategy was that they often fell into the trap of using sexuality as a way to make fun of, or discredit, public figures (such as calling a politician *homosexual*).

Usabiaga stated that sometimes they went too far with the joking and the ridicule, with their own aggressions, to the point that "I would become scared by it." Their newly discovered freedom to express their ideas seemed to be somewhat unbridled, and they did not always measure the possible consequences. Most certainly, not all the social response to the show was positive, and the hosts received strong protests from some callers. Usabiaga's assessment, however, was that 95% of the calls were positive, "because we were not necessarily saying anything that you could not overhear while waiting for your bus in any corner in Guadalajara or at a soccer game." But some of the calls were aggressive enough to contain direct threats. "One person called saying that she was the daughter of an ex-governor, that she would find out where we lived, and that she could really harm us . . . this really scared us initially." Often, they decided to respond to negative calls openly on the show by using humor. Usabiaga mentioned, as an example, a time when a man called to say "Luis es puto" (Luis is queer). Instead of reading that message, they decided to read the caller's first name and say that he had called to see if Usabiaga had any time that afternoon to go out on a date. Other times they chose to directly confront the aggression. Some of their friends warned them: "At this rate you will get killed."

Finally, Usabiaga rejected the notion that the show's longevity stemmed from its protected status under the liberal umbrella of a university. He felt that although censorship in commercial radio is a very big barrier to free expression, shows like theirs are rare because of self-censorship among radio hosts. He also felt that *La pitaya yeye's* success was motivated by a widespread desire in the population for more openness and for social change. My interpretation is that, additionally, the show had enormous appeal among young people and those questioning Guadalajaran conventionality precisely because it opened a new venue to talk about sex, including some educational talk. In so doing, the show used a tone that was consistent with expectations about the use of humor in the discussion of sexual matters, but as preamble to delve into details about sexual practices and lifestyles. The show lasted one year and then was taken off the air, although not in the midst of any controversy. It did not have the opportunity to evolve enough for the hosts to see the realization of its full potential as an educational tool about sexual matters, and it is unclear whether Usabiaga and the other two hosts would have taken it further in that direction.

CHURCH AND STATE: INDIVIDUAL POSITIONS
ABOUT CONTRACEPTION AND ABORTION

Ideas about sexual matters in Mexico were also influenced by persons and institutions that made claims of expertise about sexual matters, delineated and promoted guidelines of moral behavior, or designed and implemented public policy. Urban Mexicans live in a social context in which alternative, often opposing positions about sexual issues are readily available, commonly through the mass media. In considering those positions, Mexicans are capable of explaining their own ideas and how they differ from the positions of different institutions or from ideas that they think Mexican society in general holds.

In my interviews and conversations, I often asked Guadalajarans to tell me what they thought about a number of issues, including abortion, monogamy, prostitution, casual sex, contraception, masturbation, homosexuality, and bisexuality. I begin here by discussing the contrasting attitudes about contraception and abortion, because they illustrate best the influence of institutional discourses—those of the Catholic church and the state—on personal sexual ideologies.

Opposition to contraception and abortion is at the heart of the Catholic church's position about sexuality. I expected that participants would readily talk about religion in discussing these two issues, but that was often not the case. Religion, Catholicism in particular, was mostly absent from my conversations about these issues, except when people wanted to point out values that they felt were Catholic contributions to Mexican traditions. I know this might surprise many readers, because Mexico is so commonly assumed to be heavily dominated by Catholicism and by the Catholic church and its ideas. I agree that it is, but there are some significant caveats.

Participants in my study, even those who thought of themselves as conservative, overwhelmingly supported the use of contraception. This support defied the long-standing opposition of the Catholic church against any attempts to prevent conception. The widespread support of contraception was fundamentally based on practical reasons. Virtually everyone in my sample believed that family planning was an economic necessity. Mexicans fully justified family planning and regarded the practice as being morally sound based on the argument that it is wrong to have children that one cannot support. In discussing his support of contraception, Julio asked rhetorically, "Why should I bring into the world a child for whom I cannot provide education and the material things that the child needs?" Dalia, who vehemently opposed abortion, said of contraception, "I agree with that. Imagine having fifteen *chilpayates* [children]. The situation is not such that you can have so many children. It is good to *planificar la familia* [plan your family], have them with love, or [not have them] by using prevention."

The phrase *planificar la familia* was introduced into Mexico in widely disseminated government-sponsored family-planning campaigns during the 1970s. It has become strongly embedded in Mexican discourse about contraception, along with the early campaigns' slogan, "la familia pequeña vive mejor" (a small family lives better), which made economic and practical sensibility a priority over moral or religious beliefs. The practical argument for contraception is powerful, especially when it is perceived as being supported by official government policy and by the majority of society, and this has created strong disregard of the Catholic church's position on this issue. As Gonzalo put it, "Even when the church says it [contraception] is wrong, that [you should do] what God wants, I don't think it [the church] is right. . . . One has to be realistic. One should have as many children . . . as one can support, not all that come." Even Ramiro, a working-class man who disliked the practice of contraception, had taken a pragmatic stance: "I feel it is wrong, but it is the only way and, well, *hay que entrarle* [one has to join in]," was his conclusion.

This is one case where the Catholic church's position was greatly over-powered by the combination of practical sense and official policy. It is also representative of the generally limited influence of the church on people's practical decisions, which Cortés Guardado, a local social scientist in Guadalajara, has explained in terms of the "laxity" of religious practice and his sense that "on average [Catholicism] fills a very limited space of people's everyday life, especially among the young adult population" (1997: 69). For this author, Catholicism continues to be a "social cement" and a "generalized point of reference" in Jalisco and Guadalajara, but also one that is mostly symbolic.

I agree with this assessment. However, this notion of Catholicism as a "generalized point of reference" requires further explanation. Catholicism in Mexico provides a social space for many, a spiritual space for some, and a decision-making tool for only a minority. In practical terms, the church's position has weakened as "religious truths fail to respond adequately to the multitude of dilemmas confronted in practical life" (Cortés Guardado 1997: 69). Furthermore, people see no incongruity between "religious truths" that are symbolic and practical decisions that contradict them. The explanation for this paradox lies in the flexibility and pragmatism that characterize the practice of Catholicism as a whole. I see this as related to Catholicism's "economy of sin"—wittily described by people in Guadalajara as a "sin now, pay later" philosophy, alluding to a credit card commercial—which leaves considerable room for individuals to act in their own self-interest and to postpone dealing with the religious consequences of their actions.

In supporting contraception, individuals were capable of proceeding according to what protected their self-interest most readily. In so doing, they also measured how others around them would perceive them—the social consequences—and evaluated whether they would be judged negatively or not. Having a sense that the practice of contraception was generally socially acceptable, and even sanctioned by public policy, greatly helped people make a practical decision that contradicted religious guidelines.

In relation to abortion, the story was very different. Even those who thought of reasons that justified some abortions held extremely negative views of the practice as a whole. They equated abortion with crime and murder and indicated that once a conception occurred it should generally not be stopped. Participants were emotional, and quite dramatic, as they discussed their personal positions about this issue. They used words and phrases such as *crimen* (crime), *crueldad* (cruelty), *tontera* (foolish act), *asesinato* (murder), *mal* (wrong), *malísimo* (terrible), *matar una vida* (killing a life), *¡no se vale!* (give me a break!), *fatal*, and *detestable*.

For some participants, the issue was cut and dry. Antonio said plainly, "It is a crime. If you don't want a child, use contraception." For Angel, "abortion is wrong. I believe life is one of the universal values, independently of what values define the structure. Life and freedom are universal values that no one has the right to take away." Ruth said that when you have sex without protection you have to be aware that a possible consequence is pregnancy. "Sexual relations require responsibility, and part of the responsibility is the possibility of pregnancy." And for Claudia, if a woman became pregnant she ought to accept it, period. "If you turn out to be pregnant, you just have to put up with it, because otherwise you are taking an individual's life away," Claudia said.

The distinction between acceptable and unacceptable abortions was strongly connected with notions of responsibility and a strong judgment against women's search for pleasure through sex. Andrea said: "It is terrible, . . . we are no one to take a being's life away. It is murder. Well, it also depends on the circumstances; I would think [it is not as bad] if there was a rape. But you should never have an abortion because of irresponsibility. . . . [The child] is coming due to your fault, for what you did, not for what [the child] did." In a similar vein, Ana commented: "If the mother has AIDS or was raped, well I would support it. But if a girl *anda nomás de acá para allá* [is just fooling around], it is wrong, because why would she be so *canija* [sly] and then not want the child? That's wrong." In the opinion of Martha, "[Abortion] is the most detestable thing I have seen in life. . . . I have always said that if you are good enough to be in bed [meaning 'to have sex'], then you are good enough to have a child." Others said that aborting meant "trying to erase your mistake through murder" (Lizbeth) or questioned why someone would have sex and not expect to have a child.

Still other participants focused on the rights of the fetus. They believed that life begins with contraception and assigned personality and feelings to the unborn child. Gerardo said that "it [the fetus] is a person who feels. That in itself would be a loss, because this being is going to be opposed to the fact that someone is going to take him out against his will." Esteban brought up a more spiritual perspective: "If you are conceived, you are conceived by a Supreme Being, a Grand Being, who gives you the opportunity to live. I believe that killing it [the fetus], that defenseless being who cannot even speak to defend himself, is a crime with all the aggravating circumstances. . . . Not even the cavemen did that!" In discussing solutions to the "abortion problem," participants referred most commonly to the use of contraception and sometimes to adoption. Some participants thought that in the absence of rape, disease, or danger to the mother, abortion should only be a last recourse when contraception had failed. This they justified by indicating that in such a case the sexual partners had at least tried to be responsible. Some were even more pragmatic and recognized that an abortion was preferable to subjecting an unwanted child to extreme poverty and suffering. Only a small minority justified the use of abortion on the grounds of individual rights or women's rights. Francisco, for instance, plainly said: "It should be exclusively a woman's decision." Some in this last group also felt that the legalization of abortion would be a way to prevent unnecessary deaths among women who currently resorted to clandestine abortions.

Finally, in one interesting view, Pedro sought consistency between ideas about contraception and ideas about abortion. Pedro said that "semen is life" and argued that if we accept this notion, there is no difference between contraception and abortion. People who accept contraception should then be prepared to also accept abortion. Using the same principle, however, Ivette argued that contraception and abortion were quite different: "[Contraception] is preventing a seed from joining the other, but in [abortion] the seed is already planted and you spoil it."

Despite the generalized opposition to abortion, as we saw above the signs of change in individual opinions and public discourse were already present. Abortion, however, continued to be a charged and difficult topic, and a majority of people felt compelled, at least initially, to abhor it. Among sexually active women, only Lola, who was twenty-four years old, acknowledged ever having an abortion (a total of three, in fact). This might not reflect the low frequency of the practice as much as the stigma attached to it.[5]

In my conversations about this topic in Guadalajara, I was struck by several absences. One was the lack of reference to the positions held by feminist groups in Mexico, for whom the fight to legalize abortion has been a major project. Similarly, even those who supported abortion to some degree rarely questioned the premise that "abortion equals murder." In this sense, transnational ideas about a "woman's right to choose," which were available in the media, were generally not palatable. Also, although the Catholic church's position on abortion prevailed, people rarely thought of religion as a reason to oppose the practice. Instead they invoked a personal moral stance. This seemed connected to the more general dismissal of religion as a basis for practical decision making. Finally, talk of governmental policies and laws rarely emerged in the discussion, except among those who pragmatically advocated legalization as a way to reduce women's mortality. The absence of consideration of state policies appeared related to the understanding that most abortions remain illegal, and thus to the perception that the state opposes abortion or has done nothing to change its status.

Indeed, the main difference in attitudes between contraception and abortion might be related to the position taken by the state in relation to these two issues. The state sanctioned contraception in 1974 and began to aggressively promote it, at the same time that the majority of the developing world jumped on the bandwagon of population control policies (LeVine 1993: 11). In relation to abortion, the federal government had blocked its legalization beyond those required by medical circumstances or justified by rape and had in fact overruled a local vote in Chiapas that would have made all abortions legal in that state.

In more theoretical terms, abortion seemed to remain in what Bourdieu (1994) calls "doxa," or the "universe of the undiscussed." Most of these participants felt no social pressure to question the notion that "abortion equals murder," which was then transformed into a "natural truth" even by those who took pragmatic positions about the issue. This taken-for-granted position was consistent with strong negative judgments about women's sexuality and with the notion that women should not seek sex for pleasure. Furthermore, feminists and legislators who promoted the legalization of all abortions not only were not convincing in an environment in which institutions as powerful as the state and the church opposed it, but were also judged negatively as being too radical. Ultimately, having a child was seen as acceptable punishment for a woman who acts in ways that society deemed "irresponsible." The idea that such a woman should have the right to manage her own body, and her own sexuality, and stop an unwanted pregnancy was truly unacceptable.

The situation of contraception was exactly opposite. State sanctioning of the practice, and its active participation in offering family-planning services and contraceptive devices, greatly opened up the issue for discussion. In this case, Mexico seems to have moved into what Bourdieu calls a "universe of discourse" or "argument," via the government's campaigns and programs and their contribution to the creation of a social language that disturbed previously existing premises. The expansion of a potential for acceptance forced the church and social conservatives to retrench and form an "orthodoxy" aiming to restore the "doxa" of opposition against contraception. They created loud groups such as ProVida (Prolife) that adamantly oppose family planning. Their position, however, had to compete with those of another powerful institution and of a variety of social actors within the "universe of argument" about the topic.

Thirty years after the issue was opened up for discussion, the orthodoxy opposing contraception appeared to have lost the battle. Contraception, practicality, and the protection of a couple's self-interest were now elements of what people called "responsible sexuality." Sexual pleasure, which was so strongly questioned in discussing abortion, was curiously absent. In characterizing contraception as a responsible act, participants somehow avoided acknowledging that nonreproductive sex is often performed just for pleasure. In the 1990s, notions of "responsibility" were popularly associated with contraception, but irresponsibility, illegitimate pursuit of self-interest, immorality, and murder continued to be associated with abortion.

THINKING LIKE THE REST: ADOLESCENT AND ADULT MASTURBATION

I now address another pair of issues that reflected broader influences on individual sexual ideology, in this case on the part of what individuals perceived were newly acquired attitudes that had become widespread in Mexican society. This desire to conform to norms and values regarded as being popular among a majority of Mexicans—or at least urban Mexicans—also applied to issues such as contraception and abortion. As we saw, in those cases people's attitudes seemed strongly influenced by the positions of institutions such as the church and the state. In the case of masturbation, however, institutions such as public schools and the state did not make any strong claims, and the Catholic church's opposition to adolescent masturbation was generally disregarded as being overly exaggerated and out of touch with contemporary reality.

In relation to adolescent masturbation, the main influence on people's opinions appeared to be the generalized perception that condoning this practice was a sign of modernity and an appropriate response to outdated moral traditions. Indeed, a majority of participants in my study expressed a positive opinion about adolescent masturbation, particularly among boys.

They had integrated into their discourse the perception that masturbation is a normal developmental stage marking the process of discovery of sex and of one's own body. This perception seemed influenced in part by a modernizing discourse about child development—a discourse that was advanced by professionals such as psychologists and sexologists through the mass media. The same professionals, however, rarely paid attention to adult masturbation and often operated under the premise that adults transfer into sexual intercourse the sexual energy that they previously invested in masturbation. Except for efforts within HIV prevention work, adult masturbation rarely formed part of the modernizing discourse of sexuality. When I raised questions about this practice, participants frequently expressed overt rejection.

Beatriz felt, for instance, that masturbation "is accepted until a certain age, but when you are twenty years old or older and you are still there, masturbating, well it shows some lack of control. It is like you can't find a partner and you reach a limit and so you masturbate. No way, when one is older one must think things over. There is no reason to masturbate past a certain age." In this view, adult masturbation was a sign of immaturity.

Gerardo, talking about what he would do should he realize that one of his children masturbated, said that he would not repudiate the practice and would try to ensure that the child understands that it should happen in private and be kept secret. The only possible problem he foresaw would be if the child masturbates "excessively." In that case he would approach a psychologist or a sexologist. In direct contrast with this acceptance of adolescent masturbation, Gerardo strongly rejected adult masturbation and said, "There is a time when it is normal. But later it is a vice. Like when adults do it." I asked him whether he masturbated and he said, "Sometimes. There are other times when I interrupt urinating and a drop [of semen] comes out. [When this happens] I try to distract myself." In search of consistency with his personal ideology, Gerardo actively discouraged himself from having fantasies that would lead him to want to masturbate. But sometimes he could not control his impulses.

This strong negative sentiment against adult masturbation was shared by Olga, who boldly stated, "Well . . . giving pleasure to yourself is a very egotistical practice. . . . Maybe men have the need to relax their genitals, and maybe they use masturbation as an excuse, but it is not necessary because men have such things as wet dreams, etc. So, I feel it is very egotistical." Although she focused on men, when asked about masturbation in women, she said the same principle applied but was unable to say whether she felt it was good or bad for women to masturbate. Finally, Javier thought that adult masturbation "is harmful, it is negative, because physically getting to ejaculation is not a problem, but [adult masturbation is] a way of evading reality, instead of having a woman. I have not masturbated since I was nineteen or twenty and now I am thirty-five."

I don't want to imply that this view prevailed in my whole sample. Sixteen participants spoke positively about adult masturbation and viewed it as a healthy practice, as a sexual alternative, as a way to fulfill one's fantasies, or as safe sex. Perhaps not surprisingly, this group included some of the participants who were most open about accepting sexual diversity, who practiced masturbation themselves, or who had received formal sex or HIV education.

What I find most interesting about the responses of those who opposed adult masturbation is that they rejected the practice on the basis of the symbolic meanings that they attached to the character of the person doing it. They constructed the "adult masturbator" as someone whose moral character is dubious, as someone who is incapable of intimacy with a love partner, is selfish, has a vice, is immature, or cannot control his or her (although mostly his) desires. Their views seemed entrenched in broader perceptions of the role of sex and intimacy in adulthood and in judgments against seeing sexual pleasure as a sole goal, exploring individual fantasies, or experimenting with any kind of self-provoked pleasure. Although they had assimilated the view that adolescent masturbation ought to be accepted and respected as a developmental stage, their views on adult masturbation were heavily influenced by more conventional perceptions of sexual vice and the evils of sexual desire—and, worst of all, unbridled sexual desire—outside the context of male-female couplings. For these participants, the construction of the adult masturbator as a bad person remained unquestionably valid.

THE IMPORTANCE OF BEING MODERATE

In general terms, expressed attitudes about contraception, abortion, masturbation, and other sexual matters reflected a desire among people to believe that their ways of thinking were socially acceptable. Similarly to the importance that many Guadalajarans gave to the notion of a core of "normality," they often also strongly valued being perceived as average in relation to their ideas, norms, and values about sexuality. In response to questions about how their personal sexual ideology compared to that of the rest of Guadalajaran society, more than half used terms indicating that they saw themselves as being moderate or average. This meant for them being placed, ideologically speaking, midway between liberal and conservative, and between traditional and modern.

The value placed on being moderate was evident in the justifications that participants gave for their position in the spectrum of possibilities. Beatriz, for instance, said that she was moderate, because "I am not *persignada* [fanatically religious, someone who is always making the sign of the cross], but I am also not acting on it [sex] and dating different people. [I am] normal." In the opinion of this young woman, being moderate meant not thinking conservatively—as a fanatically religious woman would—but also having control and not becoming a sexual libertine. Beatriz also explicitly associated moderation with normality.

Fernando made a similar evaluation. He concluded, "I would [probably] be [considered] a half-time liberal. This means that you can talk to me about anything. But my actions are very different. . . . I would restrict myself in some areas. If you tell me, 'orgies are great,' I would say, 'that's fine.' But if you told me, 'let's go to one,' then I would say, 'no way.'" Like Beatriz, this young man chose to emphasize the distinction between one's ideas and one's actions. His thinking was "liberal" but his actions were more conservatively in tune with his perception of what Guadalajaran society would expect.

Dalia said, "I am moderate. To me, a liberal person is one who agrees with things like abortion. Who aborts for whatever reason and does it whenever she wants. Or one who supports a congress of *homosexuales*.[6] You have to know what is acceptable and what is not. Not [do it] just because, or because you don't care what others do. That would be a very liberal person. A conservative person is one whose mind is plainly closed." For Dalia, being "moderate" meant an ideological middle ground between accepting everything, like a libertarian, and being "narrow-minded," like a conservative. Dalia also contrasted this stance with what she perceived to be the conservatism of previous generations: "I am very open to the new trends in sex. For me it is not bad talking about it. Our parents are like . . . sex makes them embarrassed, like they don't know what to say, or they think, 'why is she asking me?' . . . I hope our generation is more open."

Likewise, Andrea commented, "Well, I see sex as normal. Something that must take place." She meant that sex is a human activity that need not be repressed. "The puritans may think it [sex] is wrong. A normal person may think it is vital. And someone who is daring, sly, will see it as 'our daily bread.'[7] I don't think that I am so far out there that I would call myself liberal, but I am not conservative either; I am the middle point. I know what is good, what is bad, [and] how, when, and where [sex is appropriate]." Again, the emphasis here was placed on not falling into the trap of becoming "oversexed," which Andrea assumed a liberal would, at the same time that one recognizes that sex is a "normal human activity."

For some, being moderate implied the ability to navigate in both the world of tradition and the world of modernity, which would be consistent with the concept of hybridity that I discussed earlier in the book. For example, Antonio saw no contradiction between thinking and acting to some extent as a liberal but also doing so as a conservative. He first said: "I see myself as a quite moderate person and a bit liberal. I am not shocked by single mothers, divorced women, older women who date younger men, or older men who date young women. I am not shocked by prostitution or homosexuality." But he later added: "[I am] traditional. I am very conservative in my way of being, of thinking, of acting. I also like Mexican tradition." Francisco took a similar position. In response to my asking him to assess his ideological position about sex, he said: "Do you take combinations? . . . I am conservative but with liberal ideas in relation to prejudice and judgments about human conduct. But my essence is conservative."

Pedro went so far as to compare modernization to the "polishing" of traditional values. Change meant for him, not discarding the old ideas, but rather starting with them and transforming them into something new. "I am liberal but conservative. . . . I am liberal but take care of myself. I have freedom, but I limit myself. My values are traditional but not extreme, they are always absorbing something [new]—perhaps in my tradition 'yellow is yellow,' but it is becoming opaque, so I say, 'I want it to stay yellow, but I am going to modernize it, I am going to polish it.'"

Not everybody thought that such "cultural polishing" was possible, however. Ideological change, for Ivette, implied a conscious distancing from her upbringing. "I think I am at the middle point because I have my own ideas, liberal ideas, something like that. But I also carry what my family, what religion, inculcated in me. I think that is key. . . . I have been studying and separating myself a bit from my family; I have been learning new things. I have been comparing more what I have been told, what was inculcated in me, with what I am learning and thinking. . . . I don't like to be conservative anymore; in fact, I am of a conservative character with a tendency toward being liberal." Regardless of her desire for change, her comments did not imply discontent with the way her family thought; rather, they indicated her enthusiasm about the process of change that she had started for herself.

People who thought of themselves as ideologically moderate often were quite dissimilar. Being moderate included a wide range of positions, from conservative to liberal. But the use of the term "moderate" worked for them insofar as it allowed them to feel that their ideas were the ideas of the majority—that the average Guadalajaran would agree with them. Here the extremes were defined as "being liberal" (seen as synonymous with "libertine" or "emancipated," and thus of low moral worth) and "being conservative" (which in turn meant overly moralistic, narrow-minded, and antiquated).

The need for this sense of belonging to a core extended even to those who thought of themselves primarily as "liberal" or "modern," who were sometimes careful to state their agreement with some conservative values. Lola, for instance, remarked that she was "[l]iberal, but sometimes I have conservative outbursts. You could say that it is conservative or idealist that I want my partner to have [sexual] relations exclusively with me." In her opinion, monogamy belonged in the conservative realm of ideas. These self-defined liberal participants, like others in the sample, also tended to make sure that I did not perceive them as libertine. Gabriel, a twenty-one-year-old man, said that his ideas were "[l]iberal but with a limit. Liberal but not libertine. Modern."

MODERATION, FLEXIBILITY, AND IDEOLOGICAL CHANGE

This notion of moderation in relation to ideas about sex was also strongly valued because it is an ideological position that is flexible. By being moderate, participants did not need to adopt an immutable, fixed set of ideas about sex and sexuality: they could continue to believe in those traditional or conservative values that pleased them while simultaneously emphasizing and promoting the need for change where they saw fit. Being moderate provided room for individuals to reject specific practices that they did not personally like or to adopt new practices, without fearing that people would see contradictions in their ideology. In fact, except for a few cases, most participants in my study, including those who identified as "liberals," expressed some ideas and judgments that could easily be construed elsewhere as being conservative or repressive or as reflecting negative social attitudes toward sex. Some of those positions translated into a call for the outright repression of sexual desires that did not conform to a core of normative heterosexuality.

Regardless of participants' emphasis on "being moderate," I was struck by the extent to which the idea of "change" flavored their comments about sexual ideology. Participants were often at a stage in their lives in which they were struggling to make up their minds about their position on specific issues, and these struggles emerged in their way of reasoning about whether to judge and reject, or instead accept, specific sexual practices and ideas. They had to grapple with dissonance when they stated an idea that "had been inculcated in them" and then recognized that they did not necessarily agree with that idea and that they in fact thought differently. They would quite evidently establish an internal dialogue as they answered a question, and even seem puzzled when they realized that they did not agree with what they had learned or internalized—that they indeed had their own opinion.

For instance, in discussing prostitution, Olga, a twenty-year-old woman, began by emphatically saying, *"Es un mal"* (it's an evil). However, almost immediately, she added, *"Si me oyera mi mamá me mataba"* (if my mother heard me, she would kill me), and proceeded to provide reasons why prostitution must be accepted and regulated. In the end, she said, "We must be realistic; if it [prostitution] exists, we must make the best of it."

Ivette wavered in deciding whether she saw homosexuality as something good or bad from a moral standpoint. "In general we have been forced, we have been accustomed, to see it as something bad, as something that should not exist because it goes beyond the norms. But I believe that they [*homosexuales*] are people and are free to decide how and with whom they want to be in their lives. Sometimes one has an idea based on what they inculcated in you, but most of the time I think that, well, they are free to do as they like." She then continued, "[Homosexuality] is seen as something dirty, and people treat them as freaks . . . dirty. But the main point relates to God. God, according to people, gave us a gender and established the rules. So, if two people are not following the rules, *se están saliendo del jacal* [literally 'they are leaving the shack'] or are nonconformist, so they must change." In the end, her position about homosexuality was somewhat ambiguous. She supported the idea that *homosexuales* have rights and should be allowed to be as they want, but she also felt compelled to point out the disagreement between this view and what she had been told about homosexuality. She also seemed to become somewhat anxious as her perception of God's position made it into the picture and she realized that her opinion seemed to contradict what religion told her God commanded. In her last comment it is not clear whether it is society and God saying that homosexuals should change, or she herself.

My discussion of sexual ideology in this chapter is consistent with that of Bell, who considered that "[w]hat gives ideology its force is its passion."

Bell emphasized that "the most important, latent, function of ideology is to tap emotion" and believed that "not only does ideology transform ideas, it transforms people as well" (1990: 292). He applied these notions to the kind of "grand" ideologies that were advanced by scholars and intellectuals, by members of the educated classes, in an attempt to reshape the whole of society. My perspective, however, is more in tune with Gramscian thought—with a view that all individuals can and often do participate in the formation of their group's ideology. Gramsci (1987) believed that ideas and ideologies were not the exclusive property of the educated elites. Instead, he proposed that many individuals in a society engage in an intellectual process that leads them to what he called "spontaneous philosophy" and "critical awareness" and potentially causes them to become "organic intellectuals."

The examples that I have presented should demonstrate that individuals have the ability to analyze, and think about, a variety of sexual matters and to define where they themselves stand—whether they accept them or reject them and whether they agree with their society's position about any particular sexual matter. In this sense the examples point to processes of ideological change. The same examples simultaneously illustrate people's desire to conform and to not marginalize themselves because of their ideas and practices. This sometimes led people to adopt positions that were somewhat contradictory or that reflected multiple sources of influence.

Finally, cases in this and the previous chapter exemplify the interactive process through which individuals acquire knowledge and ideological positions regarding their sexuality and sexual behavior. For the analysis of these topics, not unlike my analysis of sexual identities in part 1, I have found it crucial to constantly pay attention to the interactions between the social environment and individuals—to the ways in which the social environment influences individuals and vice versa. The examples presented here have shown how institutions and organizations such as the media, the church, and the state influence personal sexual ideologies, and how those influences are exerted through debates and multiple discourses and positions presented on television and radio and in the printed media. In the chapter that follows, I begin to consider all of these issues together in analyzing how individuals conceptualize sex itself—the process through which they recognize that a sexual interaction is beginning, how they interpret their and their partners' actions, how they communicate with sexual partners, and how they leave sex to return to their everyday lives. This analysis offers a different filter to conceptualize how everything that has been covered so far in the book influences and flavors the content of individuals' sexual interactions. My discussion of what I call the "sexual moment" will also set the stage for the analysis of decisions made by individuals concerning the prevention of HIV and sexually transmitted diseases, which will be the goal and subject of the last part of the book.

THE SEXUAL MOMENT:
PATHS FOR THE ACHIEVEMENT
OF PLEASURE

"When does a sexual relationship start? How do you realize that sex has begun?" I asked Gonzalo, a twenty-eight-
year-old man who identified as homosexual during an
interview in late 1994. "I believe, mainly with the moment of that glance. . . . Seeing. *De la vista nace el amor*
[love is born from sight], one could say. So, the moment
you glance at the person . . . is when I believe sex begins. . . . Then you approach and start talking, and the
interaction of that type [sexual] is already beginning. You
start to know each other, and you slowly make your advances."

"What makes this different from a social interaction
not of a sexual nature?" I inquired.

"Your interest in knowing the person. In other situations you can approach and ask without having any [sex-
ual] interest. Maybe the other person has it, but you don't.
But that interaction was not sexual. It is simply a conversation and nothing else."

"So what tells you if an interaction is sexual?" I continued to press.

"The type of gaze and the type of questions. The eyes
say a lot and [also] the type of questions that are being
asked. When the conversation takes a certain level that
leads . . . it is like a question does not fit totally in the

regular conversation, and then you think, 'maybe there's a different kind of interest here.' But the glances are basic. Holding your gaze a bit longer than is normal is an indicator that there is some [sexual] intention, or at least an attraction toward the person. Whether the other wants to reciprocate or not is a different question."

Gonzalo, like many homosexual men in my study, believed that sex begins with a seductive gaze and mutual recognition of interest. Everything after that was already sex. Gonzalo also alluded to a certain kind of communication that facilitated seduction. Such communication was created with the body and by modulating the tone of voice, in order to make it evident that sex was happening, or the preparation for sex, and not a regular, nonsexual conversation. Having sex implied a personal transformation that allowed Gonzalo and a sexual partner to engage in an interaction that he saw as being different from that of other, everyday, nonsexual interactions. Although, as we will see, others had different views about how seduction happened and when sex began, the perception that a certain transformation took place in the transition between non-sex and sex was a common theme.

For Gonzalo, seduction was important to the experience of sexual pleasure. When I asked him, "What part of the sexual relation do you enjoy the most?" he responded: "Well, without leaving aside [the orgasm], to me what is most important is the moment of seduction: the caresses, the embraces, the kisses, the company. It is often more pleasurable than reaching the complete relationship [intercourse]."

During sex, Gonzalo emphasized the kind of fulfillment that he obtained from achieving a combination of sexual passion and love. These, he thought, were expressed mostly with the body and mostly without words. "It is definitely not a matter of asking, because it is not a questionnaire. Part of what makes [sex] attractive is that you discover little by little . . . at least for me, I reach a point of [just] feeling. When you touch a cheek, an arm, there is a response, you feel a vibration, a certain force that emanates, that tells you he liked it. If not, he did not like it. . . . [Also] saying a few words with sincerity, not just making them up, not pulling out a manual and reading them, but letting them emerge in the moment." Gonzalo, like others, felt that communication during sex is different from that dominating nonsexual interactions.

The rest of this chapter is devoted to an analysis of the themes contained in this example. As we will see, participants were not shy about sharing their opinions about this topic and had often thoroughly considered what made sex a pleasurable activity.

EXPLAINING THE SEXUAL MOMENT IN WORDS

Like Gonzalo, other participants talked about the nature of sex and the kinds of interaction and communication that they favored during sex. This proved to be a formidably challenging task for some of them, not because of a lack of understanding or due to shyness and reserve, but because they found it difficult to provide an explanation in everyday speech for what they perceived to be intense emotions and sensations. They knew exactly what they wanted to say but did not easily find plain words to express themselves. Indeed, they often resorted to poetic metaphors.

As my interviews and conversations about this topic progressed, I realized that the struggle had significance because it symbolized the demarcation between two different worlds in the experience of participants, non-sex and sex. I was asking them to describe, using the logic and language of rational, analytical thinking, what they perceived to belong in a considerably different realm of life experience. They felt that the space of sexual interaction was dominated by sensation, by a different kind of awareness in which the body had a primary role and where sensation created a special kind of communication. I realized as well that participants understood the existence of boundaries between these two worlds and ways to cross from one into the other. Furthermore, the separation between everyday life and what we call "sex" also represented a separation between the kind of "rationality" and language that dominate everyday life, and "unreasoned sensation," perceived to dominate during sex. Poetic language offered a bridge between the two.

The advantages offered by poetic language in describing "the erotic" were noted by Octavio Paz, the Mexican poet and philosopher, who argued that poetry, which he called "the other voice," is the only form of language capable of "naming the most fugitive and evanescent: sensation" (1993: 10). Paz portrayed poetic language as the best method that we humans have to verbalize erotic sensations: "a poem proposes a different kind of communication, ruled by laws different from those of the exchange of news and information. The language of a poem is the language of everyday life and, at the same time, that language says things different from what we all say" (12). Implicit in this perspective is the notion that sex is dominated by a logic that is different from that of everyday life. As Simon put it: "Sexual intercourse is often more poetry than prose as it represents a sequence of metaphoric gestures whose interdependencies or claims for coherence are rarely articulated" (1996: 144).

This distinction between the logics of sex and non-sex has also been noted in other theoretical accounts. For instance, Gold (1993), working on HIV prevention, focused on what he called "off-line" and "on-line" thinking about sex. He distinguished between the kind of reasoning and rational choices made "off-line," outside the sexual space, and what happened "on-line," while the person is sexually aroused and inside the sexual space. Watney referred to the awareness dominating the nonsexual space as "self conscious" (1990: 20). Simon described the sexual moment as "myth ('a story that is not history'—where the truth of telling is more important than the telling of truth)" and, as we saw above, as "metaphor ('a relationship between symbols that is not logical')" (1996: 148). Mitchell, using psychoanalytical language, talked about "an alternative realm [which] is created outside the usual objective reality, where the playful mutual surrender to the illusions of the other creates a kind of spell which makes passion possible—and which can easily be broken through noncompliance." He also depicted this "alternative realm" as an "altered state" (1988: 99).

I find this concept of "sex as altered state" to be most useful to capture the sense of a different logic and awareness during sex to which participants repeatedly alluded. Thinking of sex as an altered state helps depict not only the perception of a separation between sex and non-sex but also the kinds of transformations that individuals believed took place as they entered the sexual space and allowed themselves to seek sexual sensations and pleasure. It conveys as well a sense of the threshold that exists between the two kinds of space and of the agency required to enter the space of sex. This is the topic of the next section.

ENTERING SEX

In discussing the nature of sex, people in Guadalajara commonly perceived that they could recognize the moment in which an interaction became sexual—the moment when sex begins. They also felt that crossing the threshold into sex involved not only one's own sexual arousal and sensation but also taking someone else on the ride through seduction, or allowing oneself to be taken by a partner's seductive power.

Not everyone agreed, however, on the exact placement of the threshold between non-sex and sex. Participants had a variety of experiences with, and perceptions about, the point at which the transition into the sexual space begins. They emphasized different indicators of the moment of crossing. They also shared specific scripts that were defined to some degree by their sexual orientation. My study revealed a marked difference between the scripts favored to initiate sex between men and those that informed the initiation of sex between a man and a woman. Unfortunately,

I do not have enough information to identify any consistent patterns of initiation of sex between women.

The Man Wants, the Woman Resists

Participants' comments about how and when sex begins between a man and a woman seemed to be influenced by a cultural script that gave the initiative to the man and turned the woman into a reactive partner, one who is often expected to refuse—or at least to pretend to refuse—the man's advances. This script was used as a generalized reference point even by those men and women who opposed it—those who thought that women should have the right to initiate sex and that men should not judge this negatively.

The idea that men should always take the initiative was inserted in the larger set of norms about male-female relations that I described in chapter 2. During their socialization, many of the men had learned that men have the prerogative to have sex in order to experience sexual pleasure, to express love, or both. Women were told, by contrast, that the only justification for a decent woman to have sex is love in the context of marriage. Men were often in a position to decide what they wanted from any given woman: sex and pleasure or, instead, courtship and postponing sex until after marriage, with some shades in between. Women were advised to postpone sex until after marriage if they wanted to ensure that men would treat them seriously. Because men were seen to have the decision in their hands, they usually felt entitled to pursue casual sex with women whom they did not consider potential future wives. This privilege generally legitimated power imbalances in the relationships between men and women.

Even within marriage, men sometimes felt that the privilege of initiating sex was exclusively theirs and never the wife's. For instance, Remigio, who only had sex with his wife, said "a relationship starts when you [the man] begin to kiss and one starts to, how to say it, 'put the hand in the oven.' I think it is in that moment, when one starts and she does not do anything [to stop you]." Remigio referred here to the man's need to be forward and take risks, to make advances and make his desires known to his female partner. The wife then could respond either by accepting or by rejecting, and the man, in turn, interpreted the response. But the opposite, in Remigio's view, would be inappropriate. I asked Remigio, "Is it possible that it is the woman who starts?"

"I think it is possible," Remigio hesitantly responded. He then added, "But if it is the woman, I think that the woman never . . . she might not do it because she knows one is the man and . . . it would be really bad for a woman if she is the one who starts." Remigio concluded that it would be too strange, and ultimately bad for the woman, for a reversal of roles to occur, even if sex were happening in the context of marriage.

I previously described other cases that are not as extreme as that of Remigio but that are fundamentally based on similar premises. Those cases, which I briefly revisit here, indicate the extent to which this script of initiation of sex between men and women contributed to the management and control of Mexican women's sexuality.

In courting the girlfriend who later became his wife, Javier had been careful to manage their sexual desires so that he could believe that this woman was sexually modest while he also had some sexual involvement with her. He urged her to have sexual intercourse, and she refused. Javier took this refusal to mean that she was different from the other women who made advances to him at the bar where he worked and who readily agreed to have sexual intercourse. Instead of pushing further, Javier aimed at convincing his girlfriend to allow him to perform oral sex on her. But also, in an effort to help her protect her reputation, and thus her desirability, he did not allow her to ever touch, or even see, his genitals. Throughout this game, his girlfriend knew how to play her role well. She refused, but she also gave in to Javier's advances as much as she felt was possible without jeopardizing her status.

Esteban also reported carefully measuring when and with whom to initiate sex. He did not pursue sex with his girlfriend, because he wanted to marry her. Esteban saw her as a potential wife in part because of her sexual modesty. Previously, Esteban had seduced several other women. In those situations, he had initiated sex based on his perception that the woman in question would comply. Esteban's characterization of a woman as emancipated, seducible, or "potentially a wife" relied on her reaction to his advances. Women who initiated sex he automatically considered to be emancipated. With them he could engage in sex freely without regard for their reputations. With the rest, he had to measure whether to pursue sex or not. This he did based on incremental advances and assessments of the woman's responses. He would attempt to initiate sex if he assessed that the woman would be receptive. He would not if he decided early on, as with his girlfriend, that the woman was virginal and a potential future wife.

Esteban did not seem to realize that some of the women he managed to seduce were perhaps forced to pretend to be virginal with a different partner, whom they wanted to marry and whom they did not believe would want a woman who was not a virgin. Martha, for instance, had lost her virginity with a boyfriend who later abandoned her. In talking about how this happened, she felt compelled to emphasize that it was he who had taken the initiative and that she had given in to his advances as a result of alcohol consumption. "We had some drinks, became aroused—a little kiss here, a caress—and all of a sudden he saw me and said, 'You know what, I want to be with you.'" She never suggested that she herself had wanted to have sex or that sexual pleasure was a goal for her, although she recognized that she had become aroused. Martha now needed to pretend to be sexually inexperienced in order for men to take her seriously. Even women such as Lola, who lived her sexuality freely, were careful to pretend that it was always the man who was leading the process. This strategy helped ensure that men did not automatically disrespect them.

Men were not placed in this situation, as their prerogative to live a free sexuality was commonly accepted. However, not all women were sympathetic with men's freedom to have sex. Rosario, for instance, said, "Look, men are real bastards because they like to have sex just because they are horny, and they leave children dispersed everywhere. It makes me so mad!" Rosario's indictment of freer male sexuality equated the desire to have sex with irresponsible paternity. Andrea, criticizing casual sex more broadly, said, "I think it is quite wrong. I think God, or whoever created us, did not give us sex just for us to please ourselves, but for a reason, and the reason is to create a life. It makes no sense to do it 'just because' . . . sex today is just done because you have a boyfriend and it's the thing to do. And then you have another [boyfriend], and the same thing. People end up saying 'yes' always. It does not matter who it is, whether you love him or not, whether he satisfies you or not."

Reinforcing women's need to protect their reputations was also their being socialized to believe that love is a prerequisite for sex.[1] This did not necessarily mean marriage, but certainly it meant having a committed relationship with a man before sex could be considered. Ana, for instance, said, "I believe no one should do anything [sexual] without love, because they can then regret it. They may stop liking each other and start criticizing each other." Ana acknowledged that this was a learned idea. "I was taught that to have sex you have to give it all and that includes love and everything. So, if they are not in love with each other, why do it?" I asked her whether two people who had just met and had sex could experience love for each other. She responded, "No, because they don't know each other; they don't even know how the other is, their tastes or anything. They only saw the person there and they treated each other well, . . . but they don't know if the person is like that all the time." Clearly, her perception of love assumed the need to get to know the other person and the pursuit of a committed relationship.

Beatriz talked about this sequence. "When you see someone and you like him, and you get to know him and fall in love, and as time passes you develop an enormous passion for that person." Sex followed.

I do not mean to imply that no men shared these views. Despite their sexual freedom, they also learned that sex was better in the context of love. Adrián said, "I don't have sex without love . . . like I just met you and let's go to bed, that's not for me. If I know someone better, I [realize that the person] wants something more, [and develop] trust. . . . And there is an extra feeling. If you have sex with love you feel much more than if you have sex just for the sake of instinct; it is very different." In fact, the idea that sex is better in the context of love was nearly universal in this sample. Men in my study, however, tended to regard love as being important but not always necessary to justify sex. Instead, they considered the search for pleasure and sexual passion to be good enough reasons for someone to want to have sex and, like Esteban, were often on the lookout for opportunities to seduce women.

The Later, the Better
Given the script and values described above, it was often in the interest of participants in male-female sex to believe that the transition into sex occurred only when the interaction reached such physical intensity that it could no longer be regarded as being petting or a socially acceptable expression of love within courtship. However, people's opinions about what constituted an intense enough physical interaction to be called "sex" varied considerably.

For some participants, the transition into sex was marked by a certain quality of the touching between partners. Lola, for instance, said, "[Sex starts] with more involved caresses. For instance, kissing someone, touching his leg, coming close, when it is sex it happens more intensely, they are the same caresses but more intense." In a similar description, Ana used the words "affect" and *injundia*, a local term that denotes sexual intention, to describe the quality of caresses that can be interpreted as being sexual because they "feel different" to the players.

For others, like Beatriz, the threshold into sex was crossed only when there was some contact with the genitals. Beatriz said that sex begins when there are "caresses of your genital parts." Still others, like Ernesto, thought the threshold into sex was located at the point at which "there is penetration."

"What if a man places his mouth on a woman's genitals? Is that sex?" I asked Ernesto.

"As I said, to me sex is penetration. A mouth-genital contact—that is not sex," Ernesto concluded. For Ernesto, the premarital activity that Javier reported having with his wife would not have counted as sex. Javier certainly seemed to be in agreement.

Finally, one participant felt that orgasm was a requirement. Adrián argued that for sex to be called "sex" there needed to be "sexual climax." Sex could involve different types of activities, including penetration, but the crucial ingredient was that partners reach orgasm as a result of the interaction.

These varied interpretations suggest that it was often important for Mexicans to think of the threshold between sex and non-sex as occurring fairly late in the course of a sexual interaction between a man and a woman. Women and their male partners were frequently invested in believing that their sexual interactions were indeed not sexual. This notion was much needed in a context in which the protection of virginity and of women's reputations was essential.

Sex, in this view, was defined as the culmination of a lengthy process of courtship or seduction that led partners to want to have intercourse. Ana described this process leading to sex as one in which the partners "had some social contact, and then attraction, and something gave them the impulse to like something about each other. So they start touching, and then, they are ready to do what they have to do."

A sequence of events previous to sex was seen as necessary in interactions that were not transactional (such as a man's having sex with a prostitute) or performed just to seek pleasure (such as a man's having a one-night stand with an "emancipated" woman). The assumption was that individuals ought to have a connection before they consider the possibility of having sex together. For some people, the connection had to be extensive before sex could even be contemplated: partners should meet, get to know each other, feel attraction and make it evident, engage in some kind of courtship that indicates that the relationship is serious, express their affection through physical contact, and eventually (sometimes only after marriage) engage in what they think of as sex.

Most significant is that in this process the partners had multiple points at which to decide whether to continue on a path leading to sex (read "casual encounter" or "relationship between lovers") or whether to stop and postpone sex (read "courtship" and "potential marriage"). And yet, the separation between the two paths was not always clear-cut because people had developed ways for sex to be pursued at the same time that the pretense of sexual modesty was maintained.

Women could engage in a number of sexual acts without risking their reputations, provided that they resisted at least somewhat the man's advances and that they did not make any advances themselves. Men in these relationships could then pretend that their sexual partners were virginal and just giving in to their seductive prowess. Everything that happened before vaginal intercourse could be discounted as not being sex, even when such activity included, as in the case of Javier and his girlfriend, oral sex and other acts involving the genitals. In this regard Claudia said, "You can play, they say vulgarly, *te puedes dar una calentadita* [you can engage in arousing interaction]. And I say it is already part of the sexual relationship. But having sexual relationships is when you go to bed with him. When there is penetration." For some women, the notion that sex occurred only when there was penetration provided as well a means to simultaneously protect their reputations and their virginity.

Finally, some of these women perceived that sex truly began at the point at which they could no longer resist the man's advances and surrendered to his desire to have intercourse. Alicia said that sex begins "when you are *medio cachondones* [somewhat aroused] and you say, 'now.' They give you a little kiss, and murmur things in your ear, and kiss your neck, with more emotion. And then you say—one knows. . . . Like when they kiss you [in a certain way], a big beautiful kiss, then I think, 'no, this is it, I lose.'" "Losing" protected Alicia's reputation because it provided evidence that she had sex only because the man's seductive power was irresistible. In theory, no one could accuse her of wanting sex or initiating it herself.

This idea of "losing" or "giving in" had meaning regardless of whether the woman in question was truly resisting or pretending to resist for the sake of respecting the assumed script. Renata alluded to women's agency in this matter when she commented: "You start with caresses, a little kiss, a small embrace, and then it is up to the woman to decide if she wants to go further." Women such as Martha and Lola felt that they had a say regarding whether sex should happen, but they approached the task by taking the initiative in a veiled manner so as to be able to say that it was not they who were seeking sex and pleasure. Men happily lived with that strategy because they then did not have to question their partners' reputations or ask themselves whether their male prerogative to initiate sex was being undermined.

I end this section by noting that a majority of participants who said that penetration was a requirement for an interaction to be called sex also believe that the acts leading to penetration were part of the sexual encounter.

This means, for instance, that oral sex without penetration was not sex, but oral sex preceding penetration was a part of sex. This subtle distinction is important because it implies some kind of retrospective analysis in deciding whether a particular encounter was sex or not, as well as a constant measuring of how far partners can go before reaching the point at which the threshold into sex is crossed. In order to decide how to proceed, partners seemed to constantly ask themselves: Who is taking the initiative? Where is this interaction leading? Is he trying to go all the way? Is she resisting or complying? Is this now sex? This often silent dialogue became particularly important when partners were involved in a symbolic struggle in which one (typically the man) wanted to go further and the other (typically the woman) was expected to resist in order to protect her reputation (while also allowing for enough exploration for the encounter to be arousing and pleasurable for both partners). As we will see below, the initiation of a sexual encounter between two men was commonly perceived to be considerably different.

Man Seducing Man
A substantially different script was invoked when men spoke about initiating sex with another man, especially with a new partner. These men often referred to crossing the threshold into sex at the moment of mutual recognition, frequently in public spaces where other (nonhomosexual) people were oblivious to the sexual interaction that was developing.

Similarly to Gonzalo, in the introduction to this chapter, Rubén said: "For me, [sex] begins at the point that I see him [a potential sexual partner], even before there is any opportunity for physical interaction. That is, I am already living the experience. The smell of the person, the way he sits, his gaze, his hair, certain movements—all that can start the process for me. I live it. It is not like you have to take your clothes off and assume a certain position." In this case the subtle indicators of mutual interest— certain gazes and silent messages being sent back and forth—were highly eroticized. Engaging in this veiled dialogue marked the portal of entry into the space of sex.

The script in this case responded to the need to adapt to a social context that judged homosexuality negatively, where discretion and inconspicuousness were commonly required. Participants learned to make contact through a silent dialogue that was established via learned codes that denoted attraction and sexual intention. These messages traveled back and forth between potential sexual partners in social contexts where other people were unsuspecting. By engaging in such silent and somewhat subversive dialogue, and by conceiving it as charged with eroticism and sexual energy, these men perceived that a sexual interaction was already taking place—an interaction that might, or might not, evolve into physical contact and orgasm.

The script was so powerful that men played it out by the book even within the so-called liberated spaces, such as the gay bars and discos. There, glances being exchanged from one side of the bar to the other, seductive smiles, and other messages of interest were a constant feature of seduction and initiation of sexual moments.

Often, the enactment of a silent dialogue was complemented by an extra step that brought the bodies together and allowed for casual touching. For instance, when I asked Antonio when sex between two people began, he said, "From the moment that you are seeing each other, in the gaze, the brushing of a hand, at that point sex begins."

"Is it necessary to reach penetration?"

"No. I have had sex with someone without penetration."

Similarly, Angel said, "I believe it all starts with flirting, the glances, they sometimes really give it away, the way you dress, act, and a desire to try to call the person's attention to yourself. The person you choose. And if I like him a lot, it happens with glances, casually rubbing against each other, up to the moment."

"When do you know a sexual relationship is happening?" I asked.

"When we touch each other, kiss, because climax or an orgasm are not necessary to have sex. The fact that you are seeing each other, and embracing, and kissing, then I know that I am in the sexual relationship." For Angel, sexual touching was different from other forms of touching because of the awareness of attraction and the special quality of the touch. "[During sex] the caresses are completely different." He also emphasized that "suggestive movements toward the person" provided a sense of the intention and desire to seduce.

Although this script was more commonly described by homosexual men, I do not mean to imply that it was exclusive to them, as some of the heterosexual participants in my study made similar comments. Among the women, for example, Carmen indicated: "Sex begins with the body language, with seduction, the gaze, the brushing of bodies, the silences. It begins with physical closeness, slowly, a kiss on the lips, a kiss on the face, on the rest of the body."

"What is the minimum that must happen for you to say, 'I had sex with a person'?" I asked.

"Maybe it begins with a kiss, but it is a bit more than just a kiss. There doesn't need to be penetration for sex to happen. It can be the contact between bodies . . . a more intimate contact, closer."

Taking a different slant, Ruth said in response to my asking at what point sex begins: "It depends. At this point in my life I believe that I can start having a sexual relationship the moment that I meet someone."

"How does this manifest?"

"Well, I feel very attracted and I begin to fantasize. That is where it starts. He might not even realize it." Ruth allowed herself to transition into the sexual space when she realized her arousal and attraction for a man, even if the message had not yet been communicated to her potential sexual partner. I find this subtle difference between her and the homosexual men to be possibly related to gender-based differences in socialization. Her comments suggested the more reactive role that many women learn, and the premise that the man is the one supposed to be taking the initiative to seduce. In this case, however, Ruth's agency was made evident in her not needing the man even to notice her in order for her to cross the threshold and begin to experience the sexual interaction.

Although Carmen's and Ruth's comments are not significantly different in content from those of others quoted in the previous section, there is a subtle shift in tone that seems relevant. Carmen referred to her gaze as that of an active participant. The "brushing of bodies" seemed to be happening, not due to the whims of her male partner, but instead due to the desire of both. Ruth emphasized her ability to fantasize about a man and recognized the value of her own desires. Participants who spoke of the beginning of sex as connected with acts that took place much earlier than any kind of genital involvement or penetration, homosexual and heterosexual, appeared to acknowledge more readily their sexual desire and the idea of mutuality (in terms both of recognition of desire and of actions taken). They emphasized the opposite end of sexual interactions, compared with those who needed to believe that sex truly begins only when the genitals are visible and being touched or when penetration is allowed to happen.

In the following section I focus on the ways in which individuals characterized the transformation in awareness that took place during sex, as well as the forms of interaction and expression that they favored as a sexual encounter progressed.

INSIDE THE SEXUAL SPACE

Participants in my study held a common set of expectations about the course of events that should take place during sex. Such expectations were not only about the nature of the sexual acts but also about the emotions and the quality of the connection with sexual partners, as well as about the broader significance of actions taken by sexual partners in the context of a sexual interaction. In discussing this topic, participants presented an idealized version of sex—a version, in fact, that they might not have experienced themselves. However, although this version might not fully accurately represent the regular experience of sex, it is indeed descriptive of locally favored styles of sexual interaction and of shared meanings attached to sex. In presenting it here, I have organized my discussion around three themes: sexual passion, the flow of sex, and sexual communication between partners.

Reaching the Top of Mount Everest: Sexual Passion

The topic of sexual passion emerged constantly in my research in Mexico. People assigned sexual passion a central role in their assessments of sexual interactions. Its presence reflected strong mutual attraction, compatibility between partners, and high degrees of sexual satisfaction. Its absence was assumed to result in the opposite: sexual dissatisfaction, "bad sex."

Although this notion is most certainly not exclusive to Mexico, I soon realized that ideas about sexual passion there occupied a particularly core role in interpretations about sex. I realize that making this statement is somewhat tricky, because so many stereotypes about Latin and Mexican passion abound. Who has not been exposed to images of passionate, arm-waving *señoritas* or sombrero-clad Latin lovers that still appear in comedy in cinema and television? However, the role assigned to passion during sex, as the pages that follow attest, was more complex and powerful than what the stereotypes might suggest.

In their comments about sexual passion, participants had no shortage of words to describe its positive qualities: *fuerza increíble* (incredible force), *entrega* (abandonment and surrender), *ímpetu* (impetus, impulse), *instinto* (instinct), *explosión* (explosion), *ternura* (tenderness), *emoción* (emotion), *deseo* (desire). Encompassed by these words were the features that suggested the variety of roles that passion had in aiding the pursuit of pleasure during the enactment of sex.

Participants in my study alluded repeatedly to a strong need for *entrega*, or abandonment and surrender, to the flow of sex. A corollary to this idea was the need to suppress "rational thinking" if one was to experience *entrega*. Pedro, for instance, described sexual passion as "the reflection or the surrender of your internal whole, of you yourself as a whole." In order for passion and *entrega* to ensue, sex could not be dominated by the rules of rational logic and thinking. Instead, during sex the body was perceived to act with full force, while the brain was assumed to take the back seat and to support the kind of language that the body mandated. The language of the body was one of sensation and emotion—a language that required full body alertness in order to recognize one's own and the other's desires and pleasures, and the whims and needs that emerged as the sexual moment progressed. Although the language of the body was described as "nonverbal," it was not necessarily a silent language, but one in which words and sounds merely played a role different from the one that they have in everyday speech.

Sexual passion was also described as a "force, something that you cannot control," to use Ruth's words. In this role, several participants felt that passion is a motor that triggers a sexual response and enables the machinery of sex to be activated. Antonio said, "Without passion there is no response," and went on to comment that he defined it as "something strong, aggressive, and tender at the same time." Beatriz said, "If there is no passion, you don't develop the desire to do anything. Because passion kind of turns you on more, and you develop a greater desire to have sexual relations." Ivette indicated, "Passion is the feeling that pushes you to do it [sex]." Finally, Javier said, "Passion is your sexual spark. Your desire or sexual appetite, with some violence . . . not violence, but strength."

Passion was also assumed to be the origin of "intense sensations" during sex. Carmen, who used that phrase, said as well, "It is a moment when time stops, and stays like that, full of red colors and exciting sensations. It is marvelous." I interpreted Carmen's metaphors to indicate the experiencing of something equivalent to an altered state—the feeling that one "is not the same" during the sexual moment. Another similarly poetic metaphor invoked a different aspect of the intensity provided by sexual passion: "Passion is a fire that burns you but you don't want to move away from it." In this metaphor, Fernando introduced the idea that there may be a big price to pay for the sake of passion—a price that one willingly accepts in exchange for the intense pleasure that passion provides.

A slightly different aspect of the intensity of passion was related to the concept of "ecstasy." Ecstasy was seen as the prize waiting at the summit of sexual pleasure. Passion was the tool that allowed lovers to climb to the heights of emotion and sensation needed to achieve true sexual pleasure and communion between partners. "Ecstasy," as the summit, was perceived to be the moment when everything that can be involved in sex—emotion, desire, pleasure, fantasy, love, domination—coincided and took the shape of orgasm (ideally as a mutual and simultaneous experience). Elisa commented, "Ecstasy is the greatest, like being on top of Mount Everest." Fernando said, "Passion is very good because you reach something that is very high, very big. You feel an incredible force for the woman you are loving."

The intensity of sexual passion was also described as being ephemeral. In Eduardo's opinion, such intensity was related to "the fever, a momentary emotional explosion." He went on to say, "That's why a percentage of sexual couples confuse this momentary fever with love. That's how I see it." Elena used similar language in her description: "[P]assion may be exclusively the explosion of sexuality, or of emotions, without any respect for the other person."

These two comments alluded to a negative, darker side of the experience of sexual passion. "Passion might not last and might be just momentary, but it is worth it," seemed to be one message contained in these comments. "Passion may inhibit respect for the partner, as well as the realization that the feeling may be just temporary," seemed to be the other message. Other participants also recognized that sexual passion may have a considerable price as well as severe negative consequences. As an "uncontrollable force," passion was also perceived to be "obsessive," "self-destroying," "unbridled," "chaotic," "tumultuous," "aggressive," and "anxiety producing." In this sense, sexual passion was also dangerous.

Paz captured well this double role of sexual passion in Mexican sexual culture when he stated: "Like the god Pan, [sex] is creation and destruction. It is instinct: tremor, panic, vital explosion. It is a volcano and each one of its bursts can cover society with an eruption of blood and semen. Sex is subversive: it ignores classes and hierarchies, arts and sciences, day and night: it sleeps and only wakes up to fornicate and then sleep again" (1993: 16). Because of its dangers, participants regarded sexual passion as an experience that must be pursued but also controlled and correctly guided. The perception of two sides of sexual passion indicated people's need to strike a delicate balance during sex: to allow themselves to flow spontaneously in order to achieve true ecstasy but to control those aspects of passion that may be destructive or threatening.

In this management of passion there was a widespread acceptance that the price one sometimes (perhaps often) pays in exchange for sexual passion and sexual fulfillment is suffering. This theme has been constant in Mexican romantic songs for many decades: the lover who is trapped in the web of passion and whose desire is no longer reciprocated intensely feels the aftermath of true ecstasy. But the potentially negative outcome of pursuing sexual passion was seen as a necessary risk, and people gave themselves permission to engage in the game of passion with all its good and bad consequences. One might suffer, yes, but otherwise there would be little chance of experiencing the intense emotions and pleasures associated with sexual and romantic ecstasy.

I do not mean to suggest that participants always experienced sex with the intensity described in the previous paragraphs. They indeed were aware that ecstasy and sexual passion are not always present during sex. They also described sexual encounters in which sexual passion was absent or which they found to be unsatisfactory. Yet, participants saw no contradiction between the actual experience of sex and the goal of achieving passion and true satisfaction and ecstasy. Mexicans' discourse about sexual passion represented what they saw as ideal regarding the experience of sex, what one should strive for. This ideal seemed to open the door to a world of self-recognition, to an integration of the world of feelings and emotions with the rest of one's life. Much the same idea has been suggested by Lorde: "The erotic is a measure between the beginnings of our sense of self and the chaos of our strongest feelings. It is an internal sense of satisfaction to which, once we have experienced it, we know we can aspire" (1984: 54). In this sense, exploring the intricacies of sexual passion implied as well discovery (of self and other).

Ultimately, in thinking about sex, participants tended to share the view that passion offered many more benefits than risks, and that the abandonment and altered state that it could create were needed for sexual fulfillment. Marcela expressed this idea in the following terms: "[It] is like taking everything off, not only in the sense of taking your clothes off, but opening up and wanting to grab, and do, and touch, and eat, and undo, and submit, and think, and fantasize. It is the possibility of being and thinking anything—the moment when you can do anything you want, when someone awakens passion in you. It is a feeling of rapture, something you wish never ended."

"Can it be controlled?" I asked her.

"Well, it depends . . . oh no, I would not really want it to be controlled."

Similarly, Francisco put it in the following terms: "[Passion] is very important. . . . It is our ability to live a situation one hundred percent—so that it floods your conscience, and there is nothing that pulls you away from your passion." In these quotations, Marcela and Francisco refer to the connection between the discovery of passion and the ultimate achievement of sexual pleasure. They also begin to suggest sexual passion's function in helping individuals turn off the kind of "rational" thinking that characterizes everyday life, and passion's important contribution to the flow of sex, which are the topics of the following sections.

Rationality versus the Spontaneous Flow of Sex

"Passion is when you don't think about anything" was Claudia's succinct summary of the role of sexual passion as an inhibitor of rationality during sex. Providing more detail, Adrián thought, "No, definitely not, it is not good to [think during sex] . . . you don't know what's going to happen, you know nothing, and it is something irrational because you have it in you, let's say, as part of your nature." In this quotation, Adrián connects his sense that one should not think during sex with the need for spontaneity. Planning disrupted spontaneity and prevented the body from expressing what "you have in you," what is "part of your nature." This comment contained as well a reference to the "instinctual" aspects of sex, which for Adrián formed part of the "irrationality" of sex.

Adrián added later, "If you are a person who has too many complexes, then you are not comfortable. You can have sex just lying down and staying still, nothing else. That is, you don't use your imagination. I would say your mind increases things. Things emerge in the moment. . . . Your partner will respond, you communicate. Your imagination has no limit. To me it is something irrational." Adrián gave a role to the unleashing of the imagination during sex, which requires thinking, but this was not the same as thinking "rationally." It meant instead letting one's imagination construct the sequence of events on impulse. He saw the communication that takes place within sex as spontaneous, unplanned, and thus irrational.

In a similar vein, Olga stated, "I think it is hard [to think during sex] because you let yourself go with the passion. It envelops you, and it is perhaps hard to brake—there is a moment when it is inevitable, and it is irrational." Here again, the idea was that during sex passion takes over with full force. Individuals must allow themselves to flow, enveloped in the current. The use of the word "inevitable" points, as well, to a perception that passion, and the flow of sex, require some loss of control.

"Thinking," in the opinion of several participants, was something you have to do before and after sex, but not during sex itself. Elisa said, "You go where [sex] takes you . . . in the moment, but you think before or after, not during sex. [Then, you are seeking] ecstasy." Eugenio remarked, "You must think before, because you must think about who you are going to bed with. And afterward. But I am an enemy of cerebral relationships because you reduce the charm—it is not a matter of making sex cerebral." Rather than calling sex "irrational," Eugenio thought of it as "noncerebral."

Part of what was perceived to be rational, or cerebral, during sex had to do with thoughts and ideas that might emerge in forms that betray the spontaneous flow of a sexual encounter. This might, in turn, translate into saying words that do not contribute to sexual intimacy and arousal but instead "kill the moment." Interestingly, in providing examples about how rational thinking might show up during sex and "kill the moment," some participants made comments associated with health issues and hygiene.

Judith said, "It's necessary to allow yourself to be taken by the moment, by the caresses, not think that you are in a relationship, not pressure yourself [to think], because then it all dies. My partner used to do something that totally turned me off. We would start touching and she would say, 'Did you wash your hands?' She killed me with that. Now she doesn't do it." She went on to explain, "You are already aroused and they ask you whether you washed your hands and you feel the person is not thinking of you but thinking about hygiene. You think, 'You know what, let me turn around and leave.'"

Similarly, Enrique used the concept of "rational" thinking to make a specific distinction between passionate sex and safe sex. "[Sex] can be rational for some and irrational for others. Personally, I am [aware] of both and prefer rational sex."

"Tell me what happens in rational sex," I asked.

"In these modern times, one form of rational sex is safe sex," Enrique stated. He then explained that, in practicing "rational" sex, "You must first be aware of what you are doing. . . . It is best to use the methods that we have at hand such as condoms, lubricant, to prevent sex from destroying our lives." Enrique said this, however, not necessarily in defense of safe sex, because he then added: "Let me clarify that I am talking about sex without eroticism and without love. In it there is no surrender. It is only the flesh for the flesh and pleasure for pleasure." At this point, Enrique wavered and suggested that although his preference was to always use condoms during sex, condoms prevented not only diseases but also the potential for full surrender (entrega) and uninterrupted flow of sexual energy. He preferred the "rationality" of safe sex for health reasons but had a strong desire for the "irrationality" of passion and surrender. "When you are in love, you are generally faithful. So we could talk about the kind of security provided by faithfulness. And your entrega can be rational or irrational because it is the surrender of everything, anything goes, there are no secrets, no hidden corners. . . . Things present themselves. To me that is irrational because there are other things mixed in that to me are very valuable, even more valuable than sex." In Enrique's view, once passion took over in the context of love, "rational," safe sex had to be abandoned. I analyze the practical implications that these statements had for Enrique's life in chapter 11, in my discussion of relational aspects of safe sex.

In ideal terms, the image that participants associated with passion, pleasure, and ecstasy was one in which sexual partners surrendered to a spontaneous, partly instinctual flow of sex, which built sexual intimacy. Spontaneity and surrender implied a suppression of the kind of judgments offered by "rational" thinking. Participants used the word "rationality" to represent analytical, logical thinking—the kind of thinking that allows people to plan and make decisions in their everyday lives outside the sexual space. This is similar to what Gold (1993) would call off-line thinking. In this regard, rational thinking was perceived to "kill the moment" because it was a reminder of life outside sex and constituted a pressure to return to such everyday life. The sexual space was a special type of place, the site of a different kind of expression and awareness, one that had to be created and nourished.

A slightly different interpretation of the resistance to rational thinking during sex might be connected to the need to suppress judgment. I am referring here to the fact that sex requires individuals to engage with each other in intimate bodily interactions that do not commonly take place outside the sexual space. Imagine how it would seem, within contemporary Western societies, for a person to use her tongue to lick someone's chest, instead of simply shaking hands, when two individuals were being introduced to each other. Many of the types of interactions that happen during sex would appear extremely unusual and perhaps even ridiculous outside sex.

In the view of the sexual moment that was dominant in Mexico, rational thinking had a more positive role when it was seen to serve as a reality check or as a tool to avoid physical danger—but at the price of stopping the flow of sex. I discuss this point more extensively in the next section, in my examination of partners' dominant forms of communication during sex.

The Body Is Speaking

Participants talked about language and communication as they answered questions about how they let sexual partners know what they want to do during sex, and in turn how their sexual partners reciprocate. In these conversations, participants overwhelmingly emphasized nonverbal, bodily communication. Out of thirty-eight participants who contrasted the roles of verbal versus nonverbal communication during sex, only six felt that verbal communication should predominate. Four of these six were young women who had little or no sexual experience but who felt that partners should talk (perhaps reflecting a growing desire for greater gender equality).

Among those who emphasized verbal communication was Gabriela, who commented, "I believe in a combination of both [verbal and nonverbal communication]. You must talk of course. Talking is a complement to the relationship. I believe that you talk when you develop a real interest in the other person. Then you feel like talking." Gabriela emphasized in her comments the relational aspects of communication, as she herself was involved in a stable relationship with another woman. I asked Gabriela, "When two people are having sex, how do they tell the other what they want to do?" She responded, "With words."

"Verbal communication works?"

"Yes," she said plainly.

Similarly, Beatriz said, "I say it openly, say it at the moment. I believe that if two people have sex and they don't say what they want, they become frustrated, they don't feel good."

Holding an opposite perspective on gender relations, Ramiro emphasized his role as a man of delivering one-way verbal messages to his wife. "I tell her clearly what I want."

"And she? Does she tell you?" I asked.

"No, well, . . . if she accepts [what I want] she will say yes or no."

Ramiro did not believe in dialogue, but rather in a man's need to explicitly and verbally state his desires and commands. I must note that such control was perceived by other men to be possible through nonverbal, bodily language as well. Remigio said, "When one starts sex, one starts where you can. Then you just have to handle them [women]."

Those who favored nonverbal communication emphasized the ability of the body to express what words cannot. They recalled a kind of transformation that made the body more sensitive. In this regard, Angel said, "Basically your five senses begin to act, they become alert. You smell, taste, hear diverse sounds, . . . and these direct you as the [sexual] relationship develops." A conception of enhanced bodily alertness was also suggested in Ismael's opinion: "It is nice, because when you are concentrated, you do not want to miss anything by telling your partner, 'Do this or do that.'" Elena similarly stated, "[Sex] is something magical in that, how he sees me, how it feels to be next to this person, makes me vibrate from the toes up. In my last relationship, . . . I saw him and I trembled like a leaf."

The language of the body was expressed through an activation of all the senses, but the experience was guided through touch and movement. Isabel said, in relation to how she communicated during sex, "If it weren't verbal, . . . well, with the hands, caressing him, he would understand what I like." Fernando emphasized that he lets someone know what will happen during sex "through what my caresses communicate." Eduardo stated, "[Communication during sex] normally happens through gestures, ways of finding a position so that the other person gives you pleasure, and in theory you also try to provide pleasure. You measure your movements against those of the other person." These examples allude to the notion that a nonverbal dialogue takes place between sexual partners—a dialogue commanded by the body through its movements and caresses.

Within such dialogue, the body was assumed to be useful both to encourage and to refuse. Ivette said, "When you are in the act itself, if I want him to kiss me, embrace me, I give him a little help and move his arm like this, maybe he will realize it by intuition or will know that I want him to embrace me." Isabel said, "If I am embarrassed about saying, 'I don't like this,' I stop him with my hand and push him away. 'You know what, not that,' [I would say] but with my hands." These and other participants felt that the language of the body is powerful and quite sufficient to converse during sex and to make one's desires known.

¡Dime Más! Verbal Communication as Enhancer

Does this mean that for these Mexicans all is silent during sex? Is verbal communication assumed to be fully suppressed? Not necessarily. Supporters of nonverbal sexual communication believed that verbal expression can be a means to support the flow of sex through the use of erotic sounds and seductive words that contribute to arousal and that validate or question the actions taken by sexual partners. Adrián, for instance, said, "If you caress and you get a response or [your partner] tells you, 'You know, I don't like that,' or 'I love it.'"

"Can you talk during sex?" was my next question.

"Yes," he said simply.

"Verbally? Or in a different way?"

"Verbally. You can talk if you feel for the person. Concretely, you can say things that you feel."

For Elena, bodily language during sex need not exclude one's voice. "In a sexual relationship there is verbal communication, but in a lesser quantity than nonverbal communication. In nonverbal communication one uses the whole body to accept and reject, to induce and explore. There is much nonverbal communication, of a corporeal character. Sexual sounds help such communication, because they indicate satisfaction, and silence is the last thing that you want during sex: breathing, moaning, they are all very important."

Fernando mourned not having felt enough passion to express his feelings in words during sex, as a means to heighten the experience. He communicated through caresses but could not utter any words of love because he felt they would sound false. Fernando wanted dearly to feel enough sexual passion to speak up during sex: "[I]t is one of my main needs. To abandon myself and all. So that I can say things without them sounding false."

Javier, focusing on a different role of words during sex, brought into the picture the use of obscene verbal language in fostering sexual arousal. "[My wife] doesn't like us to talk in bed, we like to be guessing, enjoying, we don't like to talk because we lose concentration. [But w]hen we are close to orgasm, . . . I tell her things, dirty things, and she likes that. It makes her come faster and harder."

Taken together, these comments suggest that participants saw verbal communication as having a role during sex so far as it was supportive of the body's more dominant, nonverbal communication. This role was different from that of stopping sex when necessary, which is discussed in the next section.

¡Dije No! Verbal Communication as a Means for Refusal

Verbal communication was also seen as having the role of requesting certain actions, redirecting the flow of sex, or, if necessary, interrupting sex altogether when the body failed to convey refusal. Ismael said, "Sometimes you have to say it because you get tired of a position, but sometimes you want not to utter a single word. You might say it if you get tired or you are uncomfortable, but that almost never happens." Ruth felt that bodily communication was powerful, but verbal communication came in handy to applaud an action or to refuse when the body failed to convey the message: "[Y]ou can say everything or simply send messages [with the body]. For instance, in the responses that one has to a certain caress, a certain kiss, you are telling your partner what you like and what you don't. And if you liked something a lot and you want him to continue doing it, you can say it. Or if you dislike something and you don't want it to happen anymore, you can move away or say that it bothers you, that you don't want to do it."

Even in situations in which partners felt the freedom to speak, bodily language was perceived to have a more central and important role. Judith, who was Gabriela's partner, said, "[Gabriela] and I have always talked [about sex], since the beginning. We know each other well after all this time together and know what each likes and doesn't like. My communication with her is more based on kisses and caresses. She knows what I like and don't like, and if it is no, it's no."

"Said verbally?" I asked.

"Sometimes verbally and sometimes just with caresses," she replied.

In another example, I asked Esteban, "During sex, what happens if she starts doing something that you don't want to do, how would you refuse?"

"I try to let her know, holding her hand and saying, 'not this,' or moving my body to break loose," he answered.

Similarly, Marcela said, "You say, 'No, I don't want that.' Because it is not a matter of having to like everything . . . and those things must be clear to avoid entering a situation that is uncomfortable. [Also] with the movements themselves there are things that you feel, that you ask for without speaking. At times your body is screaming, 'Do this to me!' or 'I want to do this to you!' . . . I have also experienced times when I am with someone whose ideas I don't like but whom I like physically. Then I think, 'Look, let's not talk, let's just do.'" In this case, Marcela introduced the perspective that the balance between verbal and bodily communication might vary depending on the partner and the situation. She went on to say, "There are times when you don't need to talk. The movements themselves carry you. And there are times when you ask for what you want and also tell them what you don't want."

Talking about Sex outside the Sexual Space

Finally, similarly to Gabriela, whom I quoted above, some participants recognized that communication about sex outside the sexual space requires verbal language. This is the kind of communication that Gold (1993) would say happens while people are thinking about sex "off-line." Verbal communication was assumed to be particularly important in the context of relationships deemed to be long term or stable rather than casual. The goal was for partners to learn about the other's preferences, to reflect on what they enjoyed or did not enjoy, and to help them plan for the future of their sexual lives together. Elena said, "There can be full verbal communication about sex, but usually after the relationship happened. 'Look, I liked this, and this even more; do it this way, or that way; or you hurt me, or I hurt you, or tell me how.' But verbalizing this would happen after sex." Marcela stated, "In my current relationship we talk when we are not in the sexual relationship, right? We are eating or chatting in bed and we say, 'What do you like?' 'Well, I like doing such and such.'"

(

With some variation, the pattern that emerges from my data on sexual communication is the following: Most commonly participants gave a prominent role to nonverbal communication during sex and imagined a transformation that makes the whole body receptive to unspoken messages and capable of transmitting its own messages in return. They did not discount verbal communication altogether but assigned it specific roles as an enhancer of the sexual interaction; as a tool to ask for, or refuse, specific sexual acts; and as a form of communication about sex outside the sexual act itself. Those involved in public health and HIV prevention work should begin to see the implications of this pattern for their task.

REPRISE: SEX AS ALTERED STATE

Taken together, the views presented throughout the chapter characterized the space of sex as separate from that of everyday life. Included was the notion of a threshold that must be crossed, along with the idea that sex is a domain where individuals' awareness, reasoning, actions, motivations, and forms of communication are different. The transition from everyday life into sex implied a preparation for the body to dominate and for the mind to support the body in its endeavor. The space of sex was assumed, at least ideally, to be subject to abandonment to the whims of sexual passion and to the spontaneous dialogue established through bodily movement and supporting verbalization of feelings and sensations.

To describe this set of perceptions, I favor the metaphor of sex as an altered state—a state like those induced by drugs—because it provides a useful analytical tool to understand the shift in awareness that people perceived took place. The description of the sexual moment represented in my data implies that during sex, as in other altered states, individuals "are not the same" as when they are "sober." In this case, the altered state would be produced by an "intoxication" of desire, passion, feelings, and pleasure.

By extension, if individuals are not the same during sex as in their everyday life, they cannot be expected to make decisions with the same kind of rational thinking and planning that dominate nonsexual life. This is also a way of saying that the sexual moment has its own "internal logic" and "grammar" (Davies and Weatherburn 1991: 115) that allow the goal of pleasure giving and pleasure taking to become dominant.

I must clarify that I use the label "altered state" to refer to sex positively. I am well aware, however, that loss of control and abandonment to sexual passion during sex are precisely among the features of sex that threaten those who think of sex negatively. I have in mind here those who are generally opposed to the enactment of sex when it is not done for reproductive purposes or when it is done exclusively with pleasure and desire as motivations, at least outside heterosexual marriage. They might read in participants' accounts of sexual passion and pleasure a sign of recklessness or irrationality. I read instead an eloquent account of the wonderful and powerful human ability to experience joy and pleasure and to express feelings to others in intimate and fulfilling ways.

The notion of sex as altered state might also threaten public health practitioners, in Mexico and elsewhere, who believe that sex ought to be planned and rational so that individuals can avoid health risks. In fact, the "rationality" of decision making and behavior has been identified as a basic premise of much behavioral theory used in HIV prevention (Kippax and Crawford 1993: 266). Prieur et al. (1990) alluded to this premise when they stated: "If people don't behave 'rationally' that must be because they have lost their reason." These authors went on to problematize this assumption: "But the world is not that simple . . . a wider understanding of rationality is needed: including longing and love as motives for action" (quoted in Aggleton, Hart, and Davies 1991: 13).

Regarding sex, public health practitioners often assume that individuals should enter a sexual encounter having an explicit and negotiated plan with their sexual partners, that they should decide in advance what will and will not happen during a sexual encounter. But, as Davies and Weatherburn put it, this view is a "rather naive notion of negotiation . . . a notion which restricts negotiation to the explicit and verbal and ignores the implicit and paralinguistic. It sees the negotiation of a sexual encounter as a once and for all contract made verbally before or at the start of a sexual encounter and mediated only by the negotiating individuals' propensities, deficiencies and desires" (1991: 114). These authors go on to characterize sexual negotiation as one that "is continuous throughout the encounter, verbal and non-verbal and situated in a real physical and social context"

(114), and to highlight the various meanings that actions and gestures can take during a sexual encounter: "I love you; I hate you; I forgive you; do you love me; you are special; etc." (115).

I would expand this concept further to emphasize that sexual partners in Mexico tended to choose messages and communication that they perceived to contribute to the creation and recognition of pleasure. They hoped that their exchange would culminate in the achievement of sexual climax and ecstasy. The project of building ecstasy through a careful, yet spontaneous, sequence of actions was seen to dominate the interaction.

I would also argue that in recognizing a certain sequence of events that leads to pleasure and ecstasy, Mexicans understood local "rules of the game" that are commonly shared and that informed the staging of sexual moments (Simon 1996). This metaphor of sex as "staging of dramas," as Simon calls it, requires not just the "performance of a role" but also the constant interplay between actors. It also requires a dialogue in which competing meanings are contested, completed, and redefined (Simon 1996), which, in the Mexican case, appeared to be done mostly nonverbally.

This is to say as well that in establishing a sequence of events that help them achieve and maintain the "altered state" of sex, sexual partners appeared to engage in the complicated task that Gagnon and Simon (1973) call "sexual scripting." They used "cultural scenarios"[2] to inform their actions, but they also became active participants in contributing to the transformation of cultural scenarios or scripts through their own desires and personal interpretations ("intrapsychic scripting") and the dialogue and mirroring taking place with sexual partners ("interpersonal scripting"): "Even within the context of overtly sexual acts, pleasure or satisfaction is determined in critical ways by sociocultural meanings that occasion the sexual event and by the personal meanings occasioned by that event. The pleasuring capacities of the sexual event are the result of effective performance of the actor's interpersonal script and its embodiment of elements of the actor's intrapsychic script. In the necessary interplay between these two levels of scripting, the derived pleasure most often proves to be complex rather than pure" (Simon 1996: 29).

This last concept is connected to what Kippax and Crawford (1993: 255) call "shared meanings," which are understood by sexual partners and by the groups in which they socialize. Sexual partners operate within the limits of available cultural scripts, but they help change the limits as well. "The very possibility or necessity for creating interpersonal scripts transforms the social actor from being exclusively an actor trained in his or her role(s) by adding to his or her burdens or interaction the task of being a partial scriptwriter or adapter. Actors become involved in shaping the materials of relevant cultural scenarios into scripts for behaviors in specific contexts" (Simon 1996: 41).

Constructing pleasure and engaging in the flow of passion seemed to offer participants enormous benefits, personal and interpersonal. Participants often referred to a communion with others that they achieved by allowing the "collision of bodies"—as Dowsett (1996: 173) calls it—to take place as they spoke the language of sensations and pleasure. In this sense, the altered state of sex was perceived to be, not just about individuals, but about the shared space and dialogue created by the relational (Dowsett 1996), by the interaction within the "sexual dyad" (Davies and Weatherburn 1991: 113; Kippax and Crawford 1993: 267; Levine 1992: 195).

Pablo was particularly eloquent about the benefits of achieving communion with a partner in the context of a spontaneous flow of passion. "I really like it when you don't talk, when you just feel what you are doing. Then I feel affection for someone . . . there is no need to explain anything. Everything flows nicely and, sexually speaking, I feel really well in those moments. . . . It's like you two are one person in bed." Pablo strongly recognized that for him this was powerful energy. "You can say everything just by seeing him, by touching him. What awakens in people? I really don't know. When you see him naked and touch him, it is like there is a strange language. . . . Your energy is compatible with that person's, they mix." This spontaneous communion seems to be related to the ideas expressed by Simon: "For both self and other, the eroticized sexual act often represents an act of offering and possession of what can only be wholly offered or ever truly possessed: the intrapsychic experience of another person. 'Did you really want it?' 'Did you really enjoy it?' These questions are asked repeatedly, if silently" (1996: 48).

Additionally, Pablo felt that when the signs of such communion with a partner developed spontaneously, he could enter the sexual space comfortably. "I am a difficult person in terms of approaching someone or being approached. When you meet someone, there is always something in the air. What's going to happen? . . . With people [with whom I really enjoyed sex] it was great because there was no need for definition, we never had to talk, we engaged with each other in a lovely way and it [sex] was very fluid."

In these and in other comments Pablo seemed both puzzled by and marveling at his ability to achieve the altered state of sex and to reach the ultimate heights of communion with a sexual partner. His puzzlement had to do in part with the counterintuitive notion that when ecstasy is achieved during sex, it is not so much from what the partners do but rather a certain "excellence" in terms of how they communicate and help each other feel pleasure.[3] Achieving ecstasy seemed to imply the confluence of conditions that ensured that sexual partners "fully meet" in the sexual space. It also seemed to involve, at a more personal level, a sense of illuminated self-knowledge.[4]

Finishing this chapter with these quotations from Pablo is rather poignant for me because Pablo was HIV-positive and died after I finished my study. I present them here as an invitation to reflect on the power of sex and sensation as we delve into the subject matter of the last part of the book, which focuses on the creation of HIV prevention programs and the practice of safe sex in Mexico. In the chapters that follow, I analyze, among other topics, the apparent disconnection that existed between the views of sex and sexual negotiation presented here and assumptions commonly made in designing HIV prevention programs in Mexico.

PART 3   AIDS AND HIV PREVENTION

Like people in practically every other country in the world, Mexicans were confronted in the early 1980s with the need to respond to an emerging HIV epidemic and to initiate an often unwelcome, yet crucial, public dialogue about the topics of sex and sexuality. In Mexico AIDS and HIV prevention have been, since the mid-1980s, the motor powering most social discourse about sex and sexuality. The epidemic put squarely on the table contrasting, and often strongly opposing, ideas and values about all kinds of issues related to sexuality and forced the public at large to participate in the discussion.

The topics of AIDS and HIV prevention in Mexico are particularly relevant for the arguments in this book in two different, yet complementary, ways. One is that they allow us to see the convergence of many of the issues that I have covered so far—sexual identities, roles, socialization, ideology, and perceptions of the sexual moment—because they all seem to play a part in determining the outcome of specific sexual encounters in terms of HIV risk. This convergence, as demonstrated by the cases contained in this last part of the book, has immediate practical implications for the search for solutions to the spread of HIV in Mexican cities such as Guadalajara.

Discussing HIV prevention and the onset of the AIDS

epidemic in Mexico is also significant in a more general way. AIDS came to complete the history of Mexican sexuality in the twentieth century because it opened up a dialogue—full of debate and ideological arguments—that transformed the field of social relations regarding sexuality in Mexico. After the debates created by the government-sponsored policies on birth control in the mid-1970s, AIDS became the first new nationwide arena of social contestation of ideas and values about sex and sexuality.

Since around 1985—which marked the time when AIDS became a topic of public interest in Mexico—discussion about what to do regarding AIDS and HIV prevention has constituted a central force driving Mexicans' reflections on issues of sexual diversity and homosexuality, gender inequalities, marital relations, sex education, sexual identity, and even larger questions about the meanings of cultural modernity and the loss of traditional values. AIDS made the schisms between groups with opposing ideological positions more evident than ever and prompted people who held various political and ideological positions to enter the discussion and advance their particular views about Mexican sexuality. These players proposed alternative pictures of the future of Mexican sex and sexuality, pictures that seemed extremely different from each other and that included all sorts of imaginable strategies—from the promotion of condom use and sex education to calls for a retreat into silence about sexual matters and a return to old-fashioned "moral traditions"—as antidotes against the epidemic.

The chapters contained in this part of the book focus on the insertion of HIV prevention into the larger landscape of sexuality that I have presented throughout. In them, I analyze the availability of tools for HIV prevention and how participants in my study were using, or not using, protection against HIV. I analyze how they made decisions about HIV prevention, especially during the moment of sex. I also address more fully the contradictions and incompatibilities that seemed to exist between the dominant HIV prevention messages and educational strategies in Mexico and the realities of Mexicans' sexual lives. The analysis of such contradictions implies as well reflections about the incompatibilities between the goals of health promotion and HIV prevention, on the one hand, and the expectations that individuals had regarding the sexual moment and the kinds of expressions of desire and experiences of pleasure that take place within it, on the other.

For this analysis I rely both on the narratives provided by participants in my study about specific sexual encounters and on my account of specific HIV prevention activities that were taking place at the time of my study in Guadalajara and the state of Jalisco and, at the national level, in Mexico City. Narratives provided by participants typically contained not only an account of the sexual encounter but also individuals' own analysis of the situations surrounding the encounter and the reasons behind the outcome in terms of safety, or lack of safety, against HIV transmission. The same participants were also capable of assessing how they learned about AIDS and HIV prevention and the effects that their knowledge and skills had in determining their awareness about the disease and their sexual behaviors.

Before turning to that analysis, I characterize the range of responses to AIDS and the variety of actors who have participated in the ideological debates about HIV prevention strategies since the mid-1980s. This will help me to place decisions made by individuals about HIV prevention in the larger political context regarding sexual matters that existed in Mexico in the mid-1980s and 1990s. In addition, this information will complement what we know already about the cultural landscape of the country during the last two decades of the twentieth century.

RESPONDING TO AIDS:
HIV PREVENTION WORK IN MEXICO

INITIAL REACTIONS

Although the first news about AIDS in the United States arrived in Mexico early in the 1980s, few people had heard of the disease until 1985. The announcement of Rock Hudson's diagnosis, and the subsequent series of newspaper articles about the existence of AIDS cases in Mexico, placed the disease on the chart of local social and health problems. They also yielded an initial wave of reaction in the pages of the print media and over the airwaves of radio and television broadcasting. This initial discourse in Mexico about AIDS was extremely negative. As Mejía (1988) pointed out, the first attempts by Mexican reporters to cover AIDS were tainted by moralism and by a condemnation of sex and of homosexual practices. These early articles also openly blamed people with HIV for acquiring the disease.

From 1983—when the first case of AIDS was reported in Mexico (Rico, Bronfman, and del Río-Chiriboga 1995)—through 1985, Mexican government officials made no statements about AIDS. However, as a result of the publicity that AIDS received in 1985, and the rumors about an epidemic that was out of control, public health officials were forced to break their silence in 1986. A report by the secretary of health read: "Mexicans have *no reason to be alarmed* by the acquired immunodeficiency syndrome that has reached high incidence in other countries, because, of 63 detected cases, only 17 have been confirmed" (Mejía 1988: 31, my emphasis). The official view was that the disease did not represent a problem for Mexicans, and the commentary aimed to justify the lack of state response to confront it. This view was confirmed by the opinions of physicians and public health officials who stated that most Mexicans were not at risk because "the population of Mexico does not belong to the risk groups" (Mejía 1988: 31). Because of the small number of cases, "it makes no sense to redirect large amounts of economic and human resources . . . to combat the malady when there are other diseases [to attend to]," in the opinion of Ruiz Palacios, another doctor speaking to the media (Mejía 1988: 31).

Also in response to the news about AIDS, a wave of antihomosexual rhetoric and actions took shape. Stereotypical views of *homosexuales,* combined with ignorance about the disease, promoted a discourse of condemnation of people with AIDS (Mejía 1988). Fear of the disease resulted in discrimination against people with AIDS and the systematic violation of the human rights of people with HIV in hospitals, clinics, and their workplaces. There are multiple reports and testimonials from this time about doctors and nurses who would refuse to come close to a person with AIDS, would deny treatment and care, and, in extreme cases, would leave patients without any sanitary care or food for days for fear of catching the disease (Alvarez 1988; Cárdenas 1988; Robledo Valencia 1988). After 1985, when the HIV antibody test became available, there were also publicized cases of people who were fired from their jobs after testing positive, often without their having given consent for the test.[1]

In this atmosphere of condemnation, soon after the initial responses to the AIDS epidemic in Mexico took place, community-based groups initiated actions to counteract the negative social perceptions of AIDS and to begin addressing HIV prevention. The Secretariat of Health followed and joined in those efforts in 1986.

WHO HAS AIDS?

At the time of these responses, it is likely that the number of AIDS cases in Mexico was still quite small. However, this changed in subsequent years, as cases began to be diagnosed around the country and the numbers rapidly grew. In a nutshell, this is how the picture of the AIDS epidemic in Mexico looked in early 1995, at the time that I was completing my fieldwork: As of November 1994, Mexico had reported to the World Health Organization 20,453 cases of AIDS (INDRE 1994).[2] Most of these cases had been reported in large urban areas and tourist resorts. The areas most affected were Mexico City, which accounted for over a third of all cases, and Jalisco, with 13% of the cases, which were concentrated mainly in Puerto Vallarta and Guadalajara.

A majority of cases had affected men (84%), and particularly men with homosexual or bisexual behaviors (41% of all cases,[3] and 68% of all the cases among men for whom the category of transmission was known). Among women (who accounted for 14% of all cases), 51% were thought to have acquired HIV through blood transfusions and 47% through heterosexual sex.[4] According to Magis Rodríguez et al. (1998) the proportion of cases among women is larger in rural areas of Mexico than in urban areas, where a majority of people with AIDS are men.[5] I must note that the category of HIV transmission was not known for approximately 25% of the total number of AIDS cases nationally, which raises some questions about the validity of the estimates.[6]

In Jalisco, among the 2,558 AIDS cases reported by 1994, 77% were among men and 23% among women.[7] Also, among the 1,395 cases for which the cause of transmission was known, 55% included homosexual or bisexual behaviors.[8] Similarly to the national figures, these data must be read with some caution, because the cause of transmission was not known for 46% of the reported AIDS cases.[9]

It is also noteworthy that in a majority of cases of AIDS in Mexico, the transmission of HIV had happened through sex (85% of all cases for which the mode of transmission was known). Blood transfusions and blood donation (via the reuse of the same needle with several donors) constituted a significant form of transmission until 1987, when the blood market became regulated.[10] Injection drug use was responsible for a tiny proportion of AIDS cases in Mexico (1%), mostly in the northern, border states (Uribe Zúñiga, Magis Rodríguez, and Bravo García 1998). Finally the age group that had been most affected by AIDS in Mexico included those between twenty-five and thirty-four years old (41% nationally, and 61% in Jalisco).[11]

As for the number of people infected with HIV living in Mexico, the estimate provided for the end of 1997 was 180,000 (UNAIDS/WHO 1998). Around the same time, Magis Rodríguez et al. (1998) offered an estimated range of between 116,000 and 174,000 persons infected with HIV in Mexico. Assessing the pace of the AIDS epidemic in Mexico, these same authors argued that although the increase in the number of AIDS cases in Mexico was exponential between 1988 and 1991, it had stabilized by 1996, with an average yearly increase of 4,000 cases.

Taken together, these data suggest that the AIDS epidemic in Mexico has mostly affected young people, mostly homosexual and bisexual men in urban areas, and that the transmission has been mainly sexual. The data also indicate a trend toward an increase in the number of infections among women, particularly in rural areas, and in the number of cases of heterosexual transmission. Fortunately, the seroprevalence of HIV is still low in many places around the country, even among homosexual and bisexual men. In Guadalajara, for instance, a study conducted around 1990 reported a seroprevalence rate of 13.5% in a sample of men recruited in gay bars and discos (Izazola-Licea et al. 1991),[12] and no recent reports suggest dramatic increases in this rate. Needless to say, epidemiological data alone do not capture the full impact that AIDS has had in Mexican society and culture. I now turn to an account of the ways in which different social actors and groups organized to respond to the emergence of the epidemic, and the measures that they envisioned could stop the spread of HIV in Mexico.

THE PLAYERS IN HIV PREVENTION WORK

Getting Organized: CONASIDA and the Nongovernmental AIDS Groups

After the initial denial about AIDS in the Mexican government waned, international pressure from the World Health Organization resulted in the first official effort to combat the spread of the disease. In 1986, the Mexican government created the Consejo Nacional de Prevención y Control del SIDA (CONASIDA), the National AIDS Council, which was made official by presidential decree the following year (Mejía 1988). The Panamerican Health Organization (PAHO) had asked governments to establish national AIDS councils that would administer international prevention funds channeled through its AIDS program (Pérez Franco 1988; Sepúlveda 1993). CONASIDA was to become the recipient and administrator of the bulk of the international money for AIDS prevention that flowed into Mexico.

In Guadalajara, the state government created its own AIDS office: the Consejo Estatal del SIDA (COESIDA), State AIDS Council. Although independent from CONASIDA, this office was to implement in Jalisco the policies that CONASIDA defined at the national level. CONASIDA, however, had no power to ensure a minimum standard of quality of government services in places other than Mexico City, where most of its efforts were focused. In fact, COESIDA's director reported to Jalisco's secretary of health and not to CONASIDA's executive director in Mexico City. As a result, governmental AIDS policies in Jalisco were directly dependent upon local politics regardless of the nature of the mandates being dictated in the nation's capital.[13]

By the time CONASIDA was created, a number of existing homosexual and lesbian groups around the country (labeled *grupos civiles,* "civil groups," or *organizaciones no gubernamentales,* "nongovernmental organizations," or NGOs) and some newly created AIDS-specific groups had already begun independent efforts to fight AIDS in specific communities. The first civil groups to respond were those that had organized to fight for homosexual rights in the late 1970s and early 1980s. All of them involved small numbers of people who had been politicized by a very incipient gay and lesbian movement, mainly in Mexico City but also to a lesser degree in other cities, including Guadalajara. Two Guadalajaran groups became involved in AIDS prevention efforts: the Homosexual Pride Liberation Group (GHOL), a homosexual men's group; and Patlatonalli, a lesbian group.

Between 1985 and 1990, activists formed a first generation of NGOs that had an exclusive focus on AIDS and HIV. Homosexuals and lesbians, prostitutes, blood donors, and people with HIV and their relatives made up the bulk of volunteers involved in these groups around the nation (Díaz Betancourt 1991). As in other countries, the people responding to AIDS were those already affected or those who could see the threat of the disease close at hand. In Mexico City, several of these groups grew as a result of the renewed emphasis on nongovernmental action after the 1985 Mexico City earthquake, and some, like Brigadistas contra el SIDA (Rescue Workers against AIDS), had originated from the homosexual participation in the postearthquake rescue efforts.

In Guadalajara, several AIDS NGOs initiated activities beginning in 1987. The leaders of these Guadalajaran groups were mostly homosexual men, medical workers, and heterosexual women. Between 1993 and 1995, during the time of my research, there were five community-based NGOs in the city that had an exclusive focus on fighting AIDS and providing services to people with HIV: Azomalli, CHECCOS (Humanitarian Committee of Shared Efforts against AIDS), DIATIB (Diagnosis, Treatment, and Biomedical Research Group), Familiares y Amigos de Personas con SIDA (Relatives and Friends of People with AIDS), and Ser Humano-Guadalajara. Each one of these groups had a specific emphasis on services, research, or emotional support, and all had some small component addressing HIV prevention. The two groups that had more full-fledged prevention programs were CHECCOS and Ser Humano.[14] During my research, I had contact with all of the active AIDS NGOs but worked more closely with CHECCOS, whose efforts I describe later in more detail.

These AIDS NGOs operated with tiny budgets and their efforts were fundamentally based on volunteer work. The money that supported their limited infrastructures often came out of the pockets of their leaders or from small private donations. In 1993, noticing the success of groups in Mexico City, they were just beginning to seek funds more formally through grant proposals. By 1995, they had received small grants that amounted to a few thousand dollars.

In addition to the state programs and the AIDS NGOs described above, there was a third force shaping HIV prevention efforts in Guadalajara and the rest of Mexico. Conservative groups dedicated to the promotion and maintenance of what they called "sound moral values" began questioning the messages and discussion about sexuality that were beginning to emerge in Mexico. They opposed open dialogue about sex and sexuality, condemned homosexuality, and abhorred the use of contraception and, by extension, of condoms as an HIV preventive measure.

No Sex, No Condoms: The Conservative Groups' Counterattack

From the time of their establishment, the efforts of governmental and civil programs were aimed at confronting the negative discourse that initially emerged around AIDS and the people who had it. CONASIDA relied on the messages that other countries were creating. Targeting the Mexican population as a whole, the agency rapidly jumped on the bandwagon of promoting condom use and the avoidance of unprotected sexual intercourse. The NGOs did the same, often explicitly targeting specific population subgroups and tying their messages to the larger goal of reducing the inequalities suffered by sexual minorities, women, and sex workers.

As these responses took shape, the political right in Mexico reacted vehemently against AIDS education. The Catholic church and conservative groups felt that CONASIDA's media campaigns promoted sex, promiscuity, and depraved sexual practices. In response to the safe-sex campaigns developed by CONASIDA, they undertook a variety of political actions. They began by expressing their outrage to the media, but their outspoken declarations proved to be mostly ineffective and self-marginalizing. They soon began to implement more sophisticated oppositional strategies. They filed lawsuits targeting the officials responsible for the safe-sex campaigns, which generated considerable attention nationwide. They also initiated their own AIDS media campaigns. In the late 1980s, a group of conservative, wealthy women in Mexico City formed a group called Enlace, which promoted a conservative version of HIV prevention that included only abstinence and heterosexual marriage as the sole morally acceptable strategies to avoid HIV infection.

Also in Mexico City, a conservative group named ProVida —"Prolife," mocked as "ProSIDA" ("ProAIDS") by the more progressive AIDS activists—which predated AIDS and had been founded in 1978 by a coalition of groups opposing abortion and reproductive rights, became a boisterous opponent of CONASIDA's efforts. In 1989, the group filed a lawsuit against CONASIDA and the Secretariat of Health, charging that the governmental AIDS program promoted promiscuity (Sepúlveda 1993). It also organized a political march on the Secretariat of Health during which participants burned condoms.

The attorney general declared that ProVida's charges were unjustified, and the ruling on the lawsuit favored the educators. In other cases, however, the conservative groups had greater success. A year before, CONASIDA had gained the support of famous Mexican actors and singers to participate in a television campaign with the slogan "Disfruta el Amor. Hazlo con Responsabilidad" (Enjoy love. Do it responsibly). After a press conference, and before the campaign's release, the conservative groups initiated a controversial debate that resulted in the publication of more than 1,500 newspaper articles (Sepúlveda 1993). As a result, the largest Mexican television network refused to air the ads and took punitive measures against the actors and singers involved. CONASIDA compromised and created a new ad that said only, "Inform yourself." According to Jaime Sepúlveda, who was the undersecretary of health supervising CONASIDA at the time, "the ad was so mediocre and inexplicit that the audience was left with uncertainty about what the message was about" (1993: 138).

In the opinion of Edgar González Ruiz (1994: 107), a Mexican journalist, the measures taken by the television company were representative of a "kind of censorship that is intentionally exercised by powerful companies and that is presented as part of their business policies." The same author argues that there were close ties between members of what he called "the ultraconservative groups," large businesses, and the more radical factions of the Partido Acción Nacional (PAN), the conservative political party. González Ruiz also documented the direct effect of the pressures of powerful conservative forces on politicians and elected officials. Given their financial clout, conservative groups managed to affect policies through pressure and direct influence upon officials who were part of the same social and economic elite to which the members of the conservative groups belonged.

Placing Roadblocks in Guadalajara

In Guadalajara, soon after CONASIDA placed billboards promoting condoms, local conservative groups strongly expressed their opposition to the governor of Jalisco, who immediately ordered the billboards to be removed. A similar outcome resulted from pressure from members of AFOP (the Power of Public Opinion Alliance)—a local conservative group of women that was nicknamed Las Damas de Blanco (The Ladies in White)—when they realized that COESIDA was distributing condoms and brochures describing their use at the annual, month-long Fiestas de Octubre (October Fiestas) in 1993. The only large condom campaigns that had not been successfully blocked by conservative groups in Guadalajara were the television ads and condom advertising that were broadcast on national television, because the local groups had no power to interfere with electromagnetic waves coming directly from the nation's capital.

The conservative groups presented themselves as the voice of all of Guadalajara's population. Invoking religious values, morality, and what they claimed to be true Mexican values, these groups dismissed alternative viewpoints. In their discourse they aimed to create feelings of guilt and shame among those who did not agree with their ideas. Because their positions were extreme and inflexible, their vociferous statements easily triggered debate and caught the attention of the media.

Additionally, members of the conservative groups relied on their social connections and wealth to develop political clout. Backed by their social position, they negotiated directly with top officials and politicians and affected public policy, even when the officials disagreed with their ideas. In one instance, the governor of Jalisco prohibited the development of underground private parties similar to the "raves" in the United States and acknowledged that he had made his decision under pressure from "moralist ladies" (González Ruiz 1994: 93).

Finally, as in Mexico City, the conservative groups advanced their own claims as experts about AIDS. They backed Enlace's campaigns promoting abstinence and fidelity and supported the group's posting of billboards throughout Guadalajara. A Catholic nun initiated Piapid, a church-based group that opened an AIDS hospice. The group promoted compassion for people with AIDS and simultaneously condemned condoms and safe sex. The conservative groups' claim of expertise on HIV prevention, combined with an emphasis on "sound moral values," made their message attractive to the media, which could safely report information about AIDS that they judged to be noncontroversial.

During the time of my study, COESIDA and the local AIDS NGOs censored themselves, ever mindful of the certainty of opposition should they make their more progressive views widely public. These progressive AIDS educators shied away from any activities that might trigger a conservative reaction. In this social climate, even basic informational and outreach efforts, such as passing out brochures and condoms in public places, were perceived to be potentially controversial.[15] Yet, despite the dominance of a conservative social environment in Guadalajara, CONASIDA's media campaigns had been successful in putting out the basic message about the danger of AIDS and the utility of condoms. Working with small numbers of people, the nongovernmental AIDS groups had also been able to engage their clientele in a more thorough exploration of sexual negotiation skills and of a variety of sexual behaviors and desires that were consistent with HIV safety.

THE NATURE OF THE WORK

From its inception, most progressive HIV prevention work in Mexico focused heavily on the dissemination of basic information about transmission and condom use. This seemed to be a logical first step to facilitate the initiation of behavioral changes in the Mexican population. Only a small fraction of Mexicans had access to more in-depth individual or group strategies. An exception is TelSIDA, CONASIDA's national AIDS hotline, a program with a broad reach that also aimed to help individuals deepen their knowledge, personalize it to assess their individual risk, develop strategies, and acquire new skills. Between 1989 and 1995, TelSIDA's operators were prepared to tailor the delivery of information about AIDS and safe sex to the specific situations and needs of individual callers (Carrillo Rosado 1997).

A 1988–94 report by CONASIDA listed the following educational services: mass media campaigns using radio, television, billboards, and bus and subway advertisements; printed materials, including brochures, posters, and stickers; TelSIDA; and pre- and post-test counseling for HIV antibody testing (CONASIDA 1995). Around the same time, Mexico City AIDS NGOs mainly carried out a combination of street outreach, distribution of educational brochures and condoms, informational talks, and safe-sex workshops. They also participated in radio and television talk shows and interviews, provided some telephone information, had developed a monthly newspaper supplement about AIDS and produced a *radionovela*.

In Guadalajara, HIV prevention programs were similar, although smaller and more informal than those developed in Mexico City. COESIDA-Jalisco had failed to implement mass media informational campaigns or to help disseminate locally the posters and billboards developed by CONASIDA because of the opposition of the local conservatives. Before 1995, the state government justified the lack of local campaign work by arguing that budget limitations prevented mass media advertising.[16] In the case of Guadalajara's AIDS NGOs, the groups did what they could with a committed workforce of volunteers but also with very little money and with very loose organizational structures. Their programs were largely intuitive and unplanned, and their provision of informational talks, their interactions with the media, and their distribution of brochures were, overall, reactive rather than proactive.

During 1994, there were only three large social events in which COESIDA and the AIDS NGOs had considerable presence, and which were becoming standard venues for HIV prevention activities in the city. One was a candlelight march in May to memorialize people who had died of AIDS, which had become a yearly tradition. By focusing on compassion for the sick and using a format that was not incompatible with Catholic church philosophy, the groups had managed to attach to the march a mass in Guadalajara's cathedral. The second event was the distribution of AIDS information and condoms at the Fiestas de Octubre, where both COESIDA and the NGOs had informational booths. The third was a weeklong series of educational and fund-raising activities organized around the commemoration of World AIDS Day on December 1. In those events, the NGOs and COESIDA managed to mobilize enough attention to make AIDS a relevant formal topic in the mass media. The rest of the year, however, AIDS was treated only in isolated articles in newspapers and reports on the radio; when a scandal ensued due to the conservative groups' outrage at HIV prevention messages; or in national television ads and talk shows broadcast from Mexico City. The availability of nonsensationalist news about AIDS and AIDS education for the population at large in Guadalajara was scarce.

Reliance on Advertising and Social Marketing

Up to the mid-1990s, a majority of HIV informational work throughout Mexico centered on the dissemination of basic messages about the perils of HIV and about condom use. Using social marketing techniques, the campaigns aimed at creating awareness, suggesting options, and triggering action through simple, direct messages that most commonly used the imperative verb form. Statements such as "pónte un condón" (put on a condom), "infórmate" (inform yourself), "participa" (get involved), and "habla con tus hijos sobre el SIDA" (talk to your children about AIDS) were typical. The goals of these messages and campaigns were to inform, warn, and sensitize the Mexican population and to promote "social participation" in the fight against AIDS (CONASIDA 1995: 670).

Rico, Bronfman, and del Río-Chiriboga (1995) described the evolution of messages in CONASIDA's campaigns. The first campaign presented a drawing of a corpse with a tag attached to its toe bearing the phrase "Died of AIDS." Other pieces during 1987–88 included a matchbox with the slogan "I don't play with fire," which alluded to risk taking, and a poster with the slogan "Enjoy love. Do it responsibly." The authors are careful to point out that, for the first time in Mexico, in this explicit campaign "the word condom was mentioned in the mass media in our country" (645). Another 1988 message stated, "AIDS is not a moral problem, it is a public health problem," and was accompanied by the phrase *"Preservativo o condón* [the two Spanish words for 'condom']: The name does not matter. What matters is that it saves lives." Needless to say, these messages created furor among the conservatives.

The same authors suggest that, due to the violent conservative reaction, in the years that followed, CONASIDA aimed to establish a more conciliatory tone in its messages. Between 1989 and 1992, the agency began using neutral messages such as "Don't you think you should become informed?" and "This [different volunteer activities] is what I am doing. What are you doing?" which were stated in television spots by a variety of people involved in the fight against AIDS. The goal now was to promote social participation and the desire to seek AIDS information in one-on-one interactions with AIDS professionals (Rico, Bronfman, and Río-Chiriboga 1995: 646).

Other efforts at the time included a campaign targeting parents. This campaign showed a child asking questions about AIDS while a father read a newspaper (his face hidden behind the newspaper). When the father put the newspaper down, the spot revealed his eyes to be covered by a blindfold. The slogan that followed read "Quítate la venda" ("take off the blindfold," meaning "open your eyes") and suggested that parents should call TelSIDA for information. During this second phase of its mass media campaigns, CONASIDA decided not to promote condoms directly and openly any longer.

In the opinion of the more progressive activists and educators, the shift in strategy reflected a deliberate taming of the previously bolder messages in order to avoid more negative reactions by the conservative groups. González Ruiz (1994: 51) claimed that CONASIDA was now consulting with Enlace, the group that exclusively advocated abstinence and fidelity, members of which the author claimed were now reviewing the campaigns for approval. The net result was that, with Enlace putting out their own mass media campaigns and CONASIDA becoming less bold, direct messages about condoms and safe sex vanished, as the more progressive NGOs did not have the money to create their own sex-positive mass media campaigns.

In Rico, Bronfman, and del Río-Chiriboga's opinion (1995), CONASIDA was in a bind and would never find a way to please everybody, or anybody at all. Referring to a 1989 forum aimed at measuring societal opinions about what HIV prevention messages to broadcast, they said, "CONASIDA was severely criticized by liberals and conservatives. The former emphasized that the information on AIDS was insufficient, while the latter remarked that condom promotion induced promiscuity. The few who applauded the campaigns were branded as being pro-government" (1995: 646). Governmental HIV prevention work had become the center of debates about sexuality, morality, modernization, sex education, and the relations between civil society and governmental policy.

Theories of Behavior

In their informational work, HIV educators in Mexico made several assumptions regarding the sequence that followed after individuals' exposure to basic information and to social marketing messages. The messages were designed to tell people what to do, in succinct and simple terms. They also aimed to convince their audience that everybody was adopting the desired behaviors, which is an extension of product-marketing techniques used in advertising.[17]

The premise was that basic information and social marketing messages create awareness of susceptibility to the disease and provide a course of action for individuals to follow. Such awareness, in combination with the newly acquired knowledge, was assumed to change attitudes, translate into motivation for the use of protection and the intention to enact behavioral changes, and ultimately result in changes in sexual behavior (Rico, Bronfman, and del Río-Chiriboga 1995: 647). As in other parts of the world, HIV educators in Mexico adopted a linear model that began with the dissemination of information and social marketing messages and was believed to culminate, somewhat automatically, in the enactment of safe sex and condom use.

Mexican HIV prevention educators were often trained in disciplines such as public health, psychology, and communications and had been exposed to social psychological models and behavioral theories developed in the United States, as well as to an emerging "global" discourse on HIV prevention. Their strategies seemed consistent with the premises made in theories such as the health belief model (Rosenstock 1974a, b; Janz and Becker 1984; Rosenstock, Strecher, and Becker 1988), the theory of reasoned action (Fishbein 1967, 1993; Fishbein and Middlestadt 1987), the stages of change model (Fisher and Fisher 1992), and social cognitive theory (Bandura 1977, 1986, 1987; O'Leary 1985; Strecher et al. 1986). Considered as a block, these theories claim that human behavior can be explained and predicted by individuals' knowledge, awareness about a problem, beliefs, attitudes, intentions, and abilities (commonly represented by the concept of "self-efficacy")[18] in the context of environmental supports and constraints. These theories focus on the behavior of isolated individuals who are also assumed to be "rational actors" who are fully in charge of their actions. Within a kind of "economy" of personal and environmental forces affecting an individual's behavior, the theories propose that behavior can be changed by deliberate actions (or "interventions" in public health lingo). Such interventions aim to increase individuals' level of knowledge and awareness and to convince them to change their beliefs, attitudes, and intentions (i.e., acquire those that are conducive to a "healthy behavior").

The behavioral theories also suggest the need for programs that provide individuals with new skills and that simultaneously increase their belief in their ability to enact behavioral changes. This is also often done using two modes of intervention. One involves more diffusion of information—for instance, telling people how to use a condom or messages such as "you can do it, it is easy if you know how," or "everybody is doing it," which is assumed to "normalize" a specific action. The other involves one-on-one dialogue or group discussion, in sessions or workshops where individuals have an opportunity to practice a new behavior through role playing.[19]

Working within the assumptions of these theories, models, and techniques, governmental HIV prevention educators in Mexico initially created the kind of simple directive messages to which I referred in previous sections. Later the agency shifted to using its messages to trigger actions that would lead individuals to seek more information, testing, or counseling or to become involved as volunteers in the fight against AIDS. In the shift the agency seemed to recognize that mass media campaigns could only do so much and that for individuals to continue the linear path toward behavior change it was necessary for them to obtain more in-depth information and skills. These are the topics of the next two sections.

More Information, Please

Soon after the first HIV prevention programs began, Mexican HIV educators realized that the dissemination of basic information about HIV and of directive slogans was insufficient to ensure behavioral changes. Gloria Ornelas, executive director of CONASIDA, declared in 1988, "It is not enough to provide information. That does not guarantee a change in conduct" (Pérez Franco 1988: 309). Undersecretary of Health Jaime Sepúlveda argued that "information is a necessary condition, but is not sufficient to modify behavior" (1993: 134). Similarly, Rico, Bronfman, and del Río-Chiriboga stated, "By then [1988], it was considered that to modify behaviors, the first step was the delivery of information; now we know that information is a necessary condition, but is not sufficient to modify behaviors" (1995: 645).[20]

These writers, who directed the design of HIV prevention programs at CONASIDA, were mostly unable to propose new options. In Ornelas's case, as an alternative she proposed further provision of information in face-to-face interactions. Rico, Bronfman, and del Río-Chiriboga (1995: 650) recommended raising awareness about susceptibility, convincing people that "the solution was in their hands," and creating social commitment. In a 1988–94 report of activities, CONASIDA officials stated: "It is known today that information is insufficient to modify behaviors and that it is necessary to complement mass media dissemination programs with strategies that manage to sensitize and create awareness through affection. This is achieved through communication interventions conducted face-to-face and in groups, and with actions and mobilization in which society is fully involved" (1995: 676). Generally speaking, for HIV educators in Mexico, the alternative to disseminating simple information and messages was simply the provision of more detailed information, via printed brochures, radio and television shows, presentations and other face-to-face interactions, including one-on-one counseling.[21]

The new goal was to facilitate the process of behavioral change by helping individuals deepen their knowledge and obtain cognitive tools that were perceived to be necessary for the implementation of HIV prevention.[22] The nature of these more elaborate messages is well represented in the text of brochures published in Mexico in the late 1980s and early 1990s. These brochures were often based directly on materials published outside Mexico. In their translation for use in Mexico, the educators typically did little to question the theoretical and cultural assumptions that informed the original messages or to ask whether the recommendations that they made would be effective in the Mexican cultural context.[23]

Furthermore, the information provided in brochures typically was written using a strictly medical tone, focusing on the more scientific aspects of the disease. The brochures containing general information usually discussed the nature of HIV, its modes of transmission, its interaction with the human immune system, HIV testing, and the stages of the disease (as classified by the World Health Organization).

Information about how to use a condom or about safe sex and alternative nonpenetrative sexual practices was commonly provided in separate brochures altogether, and again, these often maintained a strictly medical tone. They rarely discussed how condoms and safe sex could become integrated in an individual's sexual and affective life, or how the use of these strategies could compete, or be made consistent, with other aspects of sexuality and sexual desire. Information about condoms and safe sex was kept separate so that educators could select whether any given person should, or should not, have access to text that was deemed "sexually explicit" and thus perhaps of a strictly adult nature. Educators could then avoid being negatively judged as sex promoters—or, even worse, as promoters of homosexuality—because they could say that the information about sex was made available only to those who requested it. Furthermore, medical language justified the impartiality of the health educators' efforts and helped them defend their positions as "experts." The irony is that medical information about the virology and immunology of HIV, and about the classification of stages of AIDS, was often of little use to people making decisions about what to do sexually and how to do it.

When educators ventured into proposing alternative paths of behavior in brochures targeting the general Mexican population, they felt compelled to emphasize that sexual abstinence was the best option, followed by monogamous relationships (assumed to be not risky by nature), and only then followed by condom use and safe sex. In making these recommendations, they often stated them succinctly, in bullet point format, without much elaboration. The assumption was that condom use and safe sex were the solutions of last resort for people who could not be abstinent or involved in monogamous relationships. This in itself marked a contradiction between the brochures and the simple messages that CONASIDA broadcast on billboards and in spots on radio and television, which initially focused mostly on condoms.

The messages contained in the brochures also seemed to legitimize a separation between "good" and "bad" people regarding their sexual behavior. Good people should be able to abstain or be monogamous and not have to worry about AIDS. Monogamy was assumed to be inherently not risky, and educators paid little attention to the sexual partners' previous risk or to the need for HIV testing in order to obtain evidence of seronegativity. Bad people would have to resort to the messiness of condom use and negotiation. Bad people, however, were offered access to "safe sex" (meaning mostly nonpenetrative sex) as an option. This meant, by extension, that the eroticization of nonpenetrative sexual practices was assumed not to be relevant for monogamous couples—the premise being that they were heterosexual and ruled by fidelity and unprotected penetrative sex.

This informational strategy, however, was changing in the mid-1990s, when educators began searching for a more balanced way of addressing the menu of strategies for protection. In a brochure targeting university students, for instance, CONASIDA said, "Given that the sexual path [of infection] is the most common, you must adopt sexual practices that reduce for you the possibility of contagion. These can range from abstinence to the practice of so-called 'safe sex,' which means that you avoid exchanging fluids such as vaginal secretion, pre-ejaculatory fluid, semen and blood during sexual contacts; avoid penetration; or use a latex condom in all sexual encounters involving penetration." Note that the definition of safe sex here is broad, stated in terms of the avoidance of fluid exchange, and is offered to everyone as an option. The brochure continued with a suggested course of action: "Choose with your partner the preventive option that is best for you. Don't take risks. Remember that one single sexual contact with someone infected with HIV, even if you can't tell, may be sufficient to infect yourself. Talk with your partner. Demand that your [male] partner wear a condom. Ask him. Overcome your shame and the fears and put it on." [24] Note that all these recommendations are stated using the imperative form.

Embedded in this short text, as in many of the messages advocated by HIV prevention educators in Mexico, were expectations about how sex should happen outside the context of "fidelity." The emphasis was on planning and open communication. The educators assumed that negotiation and verbal sexual communication, and overcoming feelings of sexual shame and fear of sex in general, are prerequisites for HIV prevention. The educators also assumed that individuals had the intrinsic power to ask for, even to demand, the use of condoms. This view contradicted the emphasis that many people placed on nonverbal sexual communication, as I described in chapter 8.

In another example, a brochure on safe sex published by the NGO Abrazo and entitled "No coja riesgos. El SIDA mata" (Don't take risks. AIDS kills)[25] made similar assumptions and moved to promote greater acceptance of sexuality:

> All human beings have the right to adopt and enjoy our sexuality in accordance with our preferences and principles, so long as we live it fully and responsibly. It is very important to have open communication with our partner or with the people with whom we relate [sexually].

> It is not safe to have sexual relations with people whose true health status we ignore. In any case, [there is a need] to protect each other with a condom.

> Monogamy is ideal to guarantee [having] a sexual relationship without risk for contagion. If you have decided to have intimate contact with a person you do not know well, you must take the following into account.

The brochure then provided information about sexual practices that involved low and high HIV risk, promoted condoms as "the only barrier that can protect the couple from sexually transmitted diseases," and suggested the use of water-based lubricants. The brochure ended with what sounds like a more political exhortation: "Live your love fully, with the respect demanded by your integrity, your partner's and life's! Sex is love, not death. Don't take risks, AIDS kills." Here, the AIDS educators were ready to call for a shift in sexual mores—for the recognition that Mexicans should feel entitled to have sexual desires and enjoy sex. To do so, however, individuals needed to learn to communicate openly about sex and negotiate verbally with their sexual partners.

Note that much of the discussion in these brochures assumed condom use to be a fairly simple and straightforward task. They mostly ignored any interpersonal barriers or difficulties that could emerge in the implementation of safety measures. Considering those issues would emphasize a contradiction between messages that indicated that condom use was simple and messages about how to overcome barriers that might make condom use complicated.

If Not Information, Skills

During the time of my study in Guadalajara, the more elaborate messages about safe sex and sexual negotiation had not yet appeared in the brochures distributed by local AIDS groups but had already filtered into the

presentations, interviews, workshops, and training sessions offered by local HIV prevention educators. The educators had begun to recognize that
medical information alone would not achieve the kinds of changes desired
unless other broader changes also took place regarding the ways in which
people thought about and practiced sex.

HIV educators had also begun to emphasize skills needed to accomplish
what HIV prevention messages proposed: assessing the risk of specific situations, planning sexual activities, establishing open communication with
sexual partners, and negotiating condom use. Mexican AIDS educators
were increasingly adopting the view that decisions about sex and safe sex
needed to become more rational and, by extension, that sex itself required
some rationalization as well. This change was further perceived to be a move
toward a greater acceptance of sexuality and sexual diversity in Mexico and
toward demystifying the topic of sexuality via more open and broader communication about sex, including communication between parents and their
children. Educators launched a critique of what they saw as the more antiquated aspects of Mexican sexuality: traditional gender roles associated
with machismo and the silence that surrounded sex education and the practice of sex itself. In their view, the combination of knowledge about HIV and
new ideas about sexual planning, communication, and eroticization should
simultaneously result in increased self-determination, behavioral change,
and a change in social norms about sexuality.

These ideas were consistent with the notion of "self-empowerment,"
defined as "the ability to act more rationally and purposefully in the pursuit of self-determined interests" (Aggleton 1989: 222), which is consistent with the concept of "self-efficacy," the cornerstone of social cognitive theory (Bandura 1977, 1986, 1987). The premise behind self-efficacy
is that behavioral changes greatly depend on individuals' belief in their
ability to take action and the increasing successes that they achieve as they
implement new behaviors in a stepwise fashion. Broadly speaking, in promoting new skills, HIV prevention work also promoted rationality, sensibility, self-interest, and individuality (Aggleton 1989; Altman 1993), and
these characteristics were regarded as being means to modernize sexuality
in Mexico—a country that greatly values collectivity and the interpersonal
aspects of social (and sexual) relations, as the discussion in previous chapters attests.

Learning How in Guadalajara

In Guadalajara in 1993, CHECCOS had the most developed HIV educational program among the local AIDS organizations. Attending to a popu-

lation with diverse sexual persuasions, the program was beginning to emphasize the need for individuals to choose among a variety of strategies. In her 1998 bachelor of arts thesis in psychology, Martínez López, who coordinated the group's education activities, wrote: "Taking into account the existence of sexual diversity, options must be provided so that the audience itself determines the best alternative for self-protection: abstinence, mutual fidelity, safe sex (nonpenetrative sexual relations), or the use of implements to reduce the risk of sexual HIV transmission (such as the masculine and feminine condoms)" (1998: 81). Between 1992 and 1993, the group offered on average five educational talks per month, conducted four HIV multiple-session classes, staffed six informational tables at public events, provided information over the phone to a few callers every week, and published six educational brochures (216). A 1994 report of activities estimated that the agency had distributed 600,000 copies of their brochures that year to the public and to other groups in the city and elsewhere (218).[26]

The classes at CHECCOS were offered to groups of between twelve and twenty-five participants. Each class included seven to nine sessions, each one four to five hours in length, over a two-month period. The training covered basic information on HIV, HIV transmission, and testing, plus discussions of sexuality that were directly taken from workshops developed by sexologists in Mexico City. Included were exercises questioning what is "normal" and what is "natural" in sex, offering basic sex education, analyzing individuals' own "behavioral sexual expressions," and discussing the topic of sexual preference based on the Kinsey scale. The training also dealt with attitudes toward people with HIV and services for people with AIDS, and it smartly tied the HIV prevention and AIDS service sections together by forcing group participants to reflect on loss and on their own mortality. Such reflection simultaneously promoted awareness about the need to stay safe and the need to be sensitive to the emotions experienced by those living with HIV.

During the class's last session, the group engaged in a "safe-sex eroticization workshop." Participants were exposed to information on the risk of a variety of sexual practices, were taught how to do sexual negotiation, and received information on the use of condoms and other sexual implements. In an attempt to validate the possibility that training participants might have sexual desires not met by safe sex and condom use, they were asked to mourn the loss that safe sex involves and affirm that they have new options. They were told that it was easy to enjoy safe sex and condom use for penetration. They also role-played different dyadic situations in which they had to convince an unwilling partner to practice safe sex or use a condom.

I participated as an observer in one of these classes and was invited to lead a section on HIV transmission for the group of trainees. Most of the participants were young people who were students and either wanted to know more about the disease or wanted to do volunteer work or social work as part of their school programs. There were also a few gay men and staff members from organizations other than CHECCOS who did not find in-depth AIDS training at their workplaces. As Martínez López put it, "CHECCOS was the first AIDS NGO in Guadalajara that opened an ongoing training space, both to its volunteers and to the public at large" (1998: 227). CHECCOS aimed at creating peer educators—that is, community members who could "replicate" the information as volunteers or as informal educators in their own social networks. A premise of their formation was that they themselves needed to acquire the necessary skills, in terms of sexual acceptance, sexual communication, and sexual negotiation, in order to teach others how to do the same.

The training gave some participants the first opportunity they had ever had to discuss the topic of sexuality formally. It also offered the first chance for them to ask themselves the question, "What do I really like when it comes to sex?" or "What am I likely to like when I start having sex?" (some of the younger participants had never had sex). Some of the trainees were quite shy at first but became more playful as the training progressed. Some were also meeting open *homosexuales* for the first time or telling a mixed group of people about their homosexuality. The training rapidly acquired a tone of transgression. In the end, breaking the rules about sexuality seemed to be a liberating experience for the participants.[27]

Martínez López stated: "the training allowed the opening of a space of actualization, knowledge, self-questioning, reflection and psycho-educational enrichment." She also indicated that participants "gained awareness about the problem, learned the information, revised their attitudes about the disease and the patient, death, sexuality, and the risks of acquiring the virus." This process, she argued, "generated an internal change that allowed participants to stop feeling distant from the problem and become agents of change in their communities, family and society" (1998: 225). The author also concluded that the training provided participants with options for self-protection within sexual diversity.

In this case, the AIDS educators sought to help participants learn more about their own sexuality and, in the process, to change their attitudes about sex in general. In accomplishing this task, they were often confronting long-standing, sex-negative values, and battling against deeply internalized ideas about sex that they regarded as conservative, traditional, old-fashioned, and incompatible with HIV prevention. The educators' goal was that participants become more inclined to making decisions that fit the model of planned, negotiated sex that they were promoting.

The educators were also attempting to foster changes in Mexican sexuality, as part of the larger project of "cultural modernization" within which most progressive HIV prevention efforts were embedded. Greater awareness about sex, planning, and verbal communication between partners were expected to counteract "old" patterns of silence, machismo, inequality, and negative or moralistic attitudes about sex. By adopting the dominant, global discourse that prevailed in international HIV prevention work, the Mexican educators trusted that sex in Mexico would become more consistent with the "modern" version of sex that they perceived existed elsewhere.

In the two chapters that follow, I examine the use of the measures proposed by HIV prevention educators in the context of actual sexual encounters in Mexico. Chapter 10 focuses on the use of information about HIV transmission, attitudes about condoms, availability of condoms, and risk assessment—that is, on the use of the tools needed for effective HIV prevention before the enactment of sexual encounters. Chapter 11 addresses interpersonal dynamics that compete with HIV prevention during sex, as well as the incompatibilities between the public health discourse on HIV prevention and the relational and emotional needs associated with sex.

RESPONDING TO THE MESSAGES:
GUADALAJARANS' USE
OF HIV PREVENTION TOOLS

HOW MUCH DO YOU KNOW? BASIC INFORMATION ABOUT HIV TRANSMISSION

Participants in my study had varying levels of knowledge about HIV and its transmission and about condom use and safe sex. In general terms, all were aware of the basics: they could name the disease, they knew it was serious and transmissible through sex, and they were aware that condom use helped prevent it.[1] In fact, in participants' narratives about unprotected intercourse, only rarely did lack of information and awareness factors determine the outcome.

René, who knew very little about sexuality and HIV, offered one such example. He was a young heterosexual man who had his first sexual experience at age fifteen (four years before the interview) with a woman whom he met at a party. "We started talking there, and went out. And then it happened." Six months before the interview, he had another similar experience. He went to a party to have fun and meet women and ended up having sex with one later that same evening. In neither case did he consider using condoms or any other form of protection against disease or pregnancy. When I asked him if he had heard about AIDS, he said: "I've only heard about it. I still don't know what that is."

"Do you know how it is transmitted?"

"The truth is, no, I don't."

"Do you know how to protect yourself against the disease? How to avoid it?"

At this point, René said succinctly and directly, "You must have the sexual relationship with a *preservativo* [condom]." He also added that he had seen a condom before but never used one. In response to a question about whether using a condom worried him or not, and whether he found it important, he stated: "I think it is necessary, because one doesn't know with whom *uno se pueda meter* [one might become involved]. *Ya pues,* they say that with time, like that [AIDS] starts showing up in you. Sometimes it might be necessary to use it [the condom]."

"You said you have never used one; why is that?"

"I don't know, I am not attracted to that."

"And you are not scared about AIDS either . . . ," I began to say, but he interrupted and shot back, "Ah, I tell you. You know people more or less. With them perhaps [there is no danger]. But the others, one doesn't know *ni como andan* [what their situation is]." René separated women about whom he could "more or less tell what their situation is" from women about whom he felt he knew nothing.

"If you are with a woman whom you know, you are not afraid of having the sexual relationship?" I further asked René.

"No, not really," he responded.

René's interpretation included some perception of the separation between emancipated and sexually modest women, among whom some could be seduced to have sex. I asked him, "Is it easy or hard [to find women for sex]?" René responded, "Well, some are *dificilonas* [somewhat difficult], you see. But I have met others who [are willing] to do it when you first meet them, and then it becomes easier. . . . Some inspire more respect than others, you can tell right away. With the ones that are more *aventadas* [daring], [you can pursue sex] more openly."

Yet, even with these women, René felt no worry once he felt he knew them. The sexual encounters to which he referred had been with women he had just met at parties. René found a way to trust his intuition and develop some sense of the person as he seduced her. The result of this brief, friendly interaction gave him enough trust to avoid feeling the need to think about condoms.

René had never had any formal conversation about sex with anyone in his life. Informally, he had talked with friends right around the time that he had his first sexual encounter. René had discovered masturbation by himself, but he said that he did not practice it any longer. Now he put his energy into finding women with whom he could have sex. This shift seems consistent with the view that masturbation should be a transitional practice and not one that adults should continue to pursue.

René's lack of assessment of potential risk was similar to that of others who were more knowledgeable. He shared with them, however, a sometimes unwarranted reliance on intuition and trust. But in his case this seemed to be compounded by inadequate knowledge about HIV and AIDS, as René was poorly equipped to make informed decisions regarding HIV prevention.

René was one of three participants in my study who knew little or close to nothing about AIDS and HIV transmission. And yet, René was still able to pinpoint the role of condoms in preventing this disease about which he felt he knew nothing except that it was deadly. This should not be surprising given that, as we saw in the previous chapter, messages about the deadly character of AIDS and about condoms had been emphasized in most mass media campaigns. This finding is consistent with survey studies that showed that most urban Mexicans had at least a basic awareness and information about AIDS, and that they obtained their information from mass media campaigns disseminated through billboards, television and radio, and, to a lesser degree, from printed materials.[2]

Many participants in my study knew more than just the basics. Regarding their levels of knowledge about AIDS and HIV and their access to sources of information, they can be divided into three broad groups.

1. Those with a basic level of knowledge. This group includes people who knew about the existence of AIDS, could name the disease, and knew that it is life threatening and potentially deadly. They recognized a connection between sex and AIDS, and sometimes between blood products and AIDS. They did not necessarily understand what caused the disease and how it was transmitted, but they knew that they could avoid it by using condoms. In some cases they had questions about casual contact and transmission, although, in general, they did not fear catching the disease in ways other than sexual contact.

For instance, Martha, in response to my asking about how much she knew about AIDS, said, "Actually, very little. I would say, really very little. Well, [you get it] if you don't take care, if you don't protect yourself, in blood transfusions, but I am not very involved in all of this."

"Do you know how it is transmitted sexually and what to do to protect yourself?" I asked.

"What do I know?" she asked rhetorically. "To protect yourself . . . should I say it?" she continued shyly. "You must use condoms. I think that is what is being promoted and is the little I know. Because for transmission to happen it [is required] that you have sex with an infected partner and not use protection."

I also asked Ramiro, "Have you heard about AIDS?"

"Yes. It is incurable. It is very dangerous," he responded.

"Do you know how you get it?" was my next question.

"Well, no . . . I have not had much information about that," responded Ramiro.

"Do you know how to avoid it?" I continued.

Ramiro said, "I have heard that only by using condoms." Ramiro was married and for that reason did not feel the need to use condoms.

2. Those with an intermediate level of knowledge. This second category includes participants who knew the basics and had also gathered some additional information, usually from the printed media. They could name HIV as the virus that causes the disease. They knew that HIV is transmitted in specific ways and that casual contact is not risky. They could talk about HIV-antibody testing and about the role that nonpenetrative sex has in HIV prevention. Some of them used terms such as *grupos de riesgo* (risk groups), *promiscuidad* (promiscuity), and *abstinencia* (abstinence). Their sources of information were mostly television, radio, newspapers and magazines, and, among students, presentations at school and assigned readings.

One example in this category is the following. Talking about HIV transmission, Javier stated: "[Transmission happens] through sexual contact, blood, and transfusions. I know it is anaerobic, it dies with oxygen. So there has to be some really intimate contact. It is transmitted from mother to fetus." Javier went on to talk about the bodily fluids that transmit HIV. "Semen, vaginal, blood. I believe saliva doesn't [transmit HIV], it has very little [virus] or almost none."

Similarly, Esteban said, "It is a very complex topic. [AIDS] is a disease that concerns us all. It is a disease caused by a virus that enters through a direct route, either blood or sexual contact. . . . I know that it is a virus that unfortunately has very different codes in each person. And [the variation] makes it hard to have a vaccine. I know it is a very complex problem and one that should concern [all]: *bisexuales, homosexuales,* and *heterosexuales.*"

"Do you know how to protect yourself against the virus?" I asked Esteban.

"There are methods. For instance, a man can use a condom. I think it is the only way to avoid transmission. The safest is abstinence. But that is so hard for human beings. And you can get infected through blood."

3. Those with an advanced level of knowledge. This final group included those who had a fairly sophisticated understanding of HIV transmission and safe sex. They could clearly identify the relationship between HIV transmission and blood products, perinatal issues, and sexuality. Some of them had sought training as volunteers in AIDS organizations or had contact with people who worked in the field of HIV prevention. Others were professionals who were interested in the topic. Yet, some were well educated and sexually active and had felt the need to learn more in order to make better decisions during their sexual encounters. In general, these participants could address the erotic aspects of safe sex, which they saw as involving much more than condom use alone.

An example of the level of knowledge held by participants in this category is the following quotation from a woman participating in a discussion group with elderly people at a local clinic. This woman, who clearly had professional training, said about AIDS, "It is a disease that is caused by a virus and that is contagious. It is transmitted mainly through sex because the microorganism is in the blood. Then, besides sexual contact—it is also in fluids such as vaginal secretions and semen. It is also in saliva. But contagion only happens when there is a wound. For instance, in a kiss, if it is a, let's say, light kiss, superficial, there is no transmission. But if it is a deep kiss, there can be transmission. Fundamentally [transmission happens] through sex and from syringes, when someone who has it [HIV] uses them and then someone else uses them. . . . But this happens if the syringes are not sterilized. If they are sterilized, I think there is no problem, because this is a fragile virus that is rapidly destroyed. All of us should demand disposable syringes when we get a shot or go for a blood test."

Carmen provided another example. She had volunteered in a lesbian group and had participated in several AIDS workshops. Carmen said, "It can be prevented in many ways. To begin with, not thinking that sex is only penetration, but playing with your body without any exchange of bodily fluids. There are so many games and ways in which one can enjoy and be erotic! Just the rubbing of bodies together, using latex gloves to touch, and, to penetrate, the condom. Using latex cutouts for oral sex."

A majority of the participants had levels of knowledge about AIDS that fit in the first two groups in this classification. Having information was not always sufficient to ensure safety, however: several of the participants who had considerable knowledge about HIV were engaging in potentially risky sexual practices. The disregard of knowledge about HIV will be apparent in the description of cases of unprotected sex that I present in the remaining part of this chapter and in the next.

HOW DID YOU LEARN? SOURCES OF INFORMATION ABOUT AIDS AND HIV

Most participants in my study had learned the basic information about AIDS and HIV from television. Very few had read articles about AIDS in newspapers and magazines. Among them, some were confused by conflicting information in such articles.[3] Because the media were often sensationalist or ill-informed about AIDS, people who relied solely on television and newspaper articles for information were sometimes exposed to scientifically inaccurate information or news that blew matters out of proportion. Gonzalo, for instance, said that he had learned what was safe by himself, "reading magazines, browsing through newspapers, looking for information even in foreign medical journals, trying to find out if there was something new, listening to the news. But often [the information] was contradictory: 'this is not true anymore, this is safe, this is not safe.' It wasn't specifically known what you could really do. There was a rumor that you could get it when you had a tooth pulled out. Given that I have had lots of problems with my teeth, I said, 'Oh my God! Maybe it already happened to me.' So I tried to seek out more information, by myself."

"Did you have any access to brochures or campaigns?" I asked Gonzalo.

"Not then. There was always the issue that those things were [socially] banned . . . that AIDS only affected *homosexuales*. . . . So, trying to get information, picking up brochures, was like acknowledging that you had reasons to believe that you could have it [and thus that you were homosexual]. That kind of reaction could have happened at home. I read, sought out information, but left everything at work. I would not take it home."

Gonzalo was referring to his seeking information in the late 1980s. Although the situation was changing by 1995, his comments illustrated what might still be a common phenomenon. The stigma associated with AIDS and homosexuality still prevented some people from finding answers to important questions about risk and protection. The overall lack of conversation about sex did not help either.

It is striking that, of all the participants, excluding those who volunteered with an AIDS organization, only one reported learning about AIDS and HIV via an educational program. Participants had had little or no contact with any of the brochures, events, information lines, talks, workshops, and training sessions offered by Guadalajaran AIDS organizations. These were mostly absent also in participants' narratives about initial sources of information about AIDS. This finding made me wonder about what "distributing 600,000 brochures"—as a 1994 report by CHECCOS described—meant in reality (Martínez López 1998: 218).

A 1993 opinion survey conducted by the University of Guadalajara's Center for Opinion Studies asked the question, "What governmental or private organizations that specialize in AIDS treatment and prevention do you know?" The secretary of health was mentioned by 24%, COESIDA by 23%, and CHECCOS by 0.8%. A full 22% said that they had never heard of any AIDS organization (Cortés Guardado 1997). The only NGO that had made it into the awareness of a tiny percentage of the sample was CHECCOS.

Despite their claims as a social force in the city, CHECCOS and the other NGOs seemed to constitute a source of information and a space for socialization into a culture of prevention and safe sex for a small minority that included students, volunteers, *homosexuales* and *lesbianas,* and people with AIDS and their friends and families. Furthermore, some of the people who participated in workshops or as volunteers in AIDS organizations had become interested in them only after realizing that they had been exposed to HIV or had been in high-risk situations. The timing was problematic because information about AIDS and awareness about the need for protection should reach individuals before they engaged in high-risk sexual behaviors.

Considering how most participants in my sample learned about sex and sexuality, it should not be surprising that many had never formally sought to learn about AIDS and HIV. If individuals did not have formal channels to learn about sexuality and to discuss it openly in a serious manner, then they likely lacked channels to formally address the topic of HIV transmission and protection. Overall, people's acquisition of information about AIDS seemed to be incidental rather than an active and planned activity. This assessment applies as well to their acquisition of skills regarding safe sex and condom use, as the next section demonstrates.

CONDOM MECHANICS

Similarly to what has been reported elsewhere,[4] participants in my study expressed a variety of views about the virtues and limitations of condoms as a protective measure. Although many found that condom use could easily be integrated into their sexual lives, others had quite negative feelings toward condoms. One common complaint was that condoms are not infallible, with the implication being that therefore they are not worth bothering with. For instance, a woman in a focus group with elderly people said, "They say that there are people who were born regardless of their parents' using a condom. Condoms can break, so there is not one hundred percent security." Opponents of condoms in Mexico, such as the conservative groups and the Catholic church, used this same argument. It helped them justify their disagreement with condom promotion in terms that were palatable even to those who did not otherwise share their conservative views about sex. For instance, after the World Population Conference in Cairo in September 1994, one of the local television channels gave fifteen minutes of free time to the Catholic archbishop of Guadalajara, Juan Sandoval Iñiguez, to broadcast a message to the local population during the daily newscast. In his speech, the archbishop strongly warned his audience that condoms are not always effective, and thus that condom use did not constitute prevention against HIV. This was the only "scientifically oriented" fact the he used in his speech, the rest of which was focused on the virtues of morality and respect for traditional Catholic values.

The same message appeared in a brochure by Piapid, a Guadalajaran group associated with the Catholic church that ran an AIDS hospice. The brochure asked the question, "Do condoms prevent AIDS contagion?" The answer provided was, "No [in bold, italicized capital letters in the original]. Despite the false information that we often hear, even the condom manufacturers recognize that the use of condoms only reduces the probability of contagion, and *does not prevent it completely*. If you have sexual relations with or without a condom with a person who could be sick with AIDS, *you are playing with your life and with your family's*."

Therefore, as a way to support the promotion of monogamy and abstinence, people in Guadalajara were able to invoke the view that condoms are not always effective—a view that was also expressed by some participants. The position of the older woman quoted above, however, was more pragmatic. She added, "But of course [condoms] are a form of prevention for people who cannot lead a virtuous life."

Some participants expressed dissatisfaction with condoms because they experienced difficulties using them correctly, commonly because they had not learned the steps involved in putting one on and possible measures for troubleshooting. For instance, Ismael tried to put on a condom during a sexual encounter, but without really knowing how to do it. Ismael stated, "She asked me to put on a condom. I used it but it stayed inside her. I was looking for it [laughter]. I was pretty angry and I never wanted to use it again."

Participants such as Ismael, who had no formal instruction on condom use or on the nuances and details of safe sex, navigated haphazardly through the complications of condom use in sexual encounters. Gerardo, a heterosexual man who had premarital sex with his current wife, had to figure out condom use without anybody's help. When I asked him if he knew how to use a condom, he said, "You discover it more or less by yourself."

"Have you ever had a brochure that describes what to do to avoid breakage?"

"No. You just put it on with the lubricant that it already has."

In his case, the incorrect use of condoms and spermicide resulted in an unwanted pregnancy that forced Gerardo and his girlfriend to marry. In fact, condoms were not their favorite contraceptive because his wife felt pain from the friction (they did not use any extra lubrication) and because his satisfaction was diminished. He explained the problem by saying that his foreskin was pulled back by the condom, which increased the friction on the head of the penis and reduced pleasure.

This case illustrated two additional problems. One is that the condom use messages in Mexico were rarely complemented with information about the need for additional water-based lubrication (and about the potential damage that condoms can suffer from the use of oil-based lubricants). This might be changing, however, as newer educational brochures include information on local brands of water-based lubricants. The other problem is that the existing brochures on condom use were often copies of educational materials written in the United States, which rarely considered condom use for the uncircumcised penis. Although my research in this regard was not exhaustive, I have seen only one brochure in Mexico that addressed this issue. This brochure's recommendation was, "Before putting it on [the condom], lower the foreskin as much as possible." The attempt here was to make the uncircumcised penis look like a circumcised one before putting on the condom. The issue for Gerardo, instead, seemed to be the need to use enough lubricant inside the condom to allow the foreskin to move more freely over the head of the penis despite the condom, thus protecting it from friction that uncircumcised men often find to be excessive when the foreskin is kept lowered.

Another common complaint about condoms had to do with the interruption of the flow of sex created by the need to put on a condom right before penetration. AIDS organizations in Guadalajara taught in their workshops that condoms should be available and visible throughout the sexual interaction. This measure had been fully adopted by several participants. Esteban said that, in casual sexual encounters, "I would have it [a condom] next to me, in a drawer in the bedside table. Ready to be opened."

"Do you usually have condoms with you?"

"At home, in my bedroom, and also here at my business . . . even in my truck." However, not everybody reported the same strategy or having ready access to condoms.

Esteban, like other men, believed that a condom could be silently introduced into the encounter at the appropriate moment without interrupting the flow of sex and without verbal negotiation. Yet, the messages about condom negotiation did not validate this strategy, which seemed to be common among the men who effectively used condoms. There was a contradiction between a message of "verbal sexual negotiation" and many people's expectations about the flow of sex. In fact, the silent introduction of condoms was more consistent with the kinds of spontaneity and unpredictability favored by participants and which I described in chapter 8.

In more general terms, by far the most common objection to condom use among participants in my study was loss of satisfaction. Several men and women in my sample complained about this issue, using popular phrases such as "using a condom is like taking a shower with a raincoat" (Javier) or "eating a candy with the wrapper on" (a middle-aged woman in a focus group). In one case, dissatisfaction with condoms was presented as an incentive for monogamy. Ramiro said, "It is easy to use them, but in any case it is not the same. You don't feel the same. I have not liked to use them. That is why I don't get involved with other people, only with my wife."

Even some of the participants who used condoms regularly recognized that condoms are a barrier—if a necessary one—and that they would prefer overall not to have to use them. Yet, in presentations, workshops, and training sessions such as the ones provided by CHECCOS in Guadalajara, the mantra was that "condoms are erotic and fun and can contribute to sexual pleasure by enhancing sensitivity." The problem is that this message alienated people who disliked condoms. It left little room for them to validate their negative feelings about the protective device and then move on to figure out how to make the best of having to use them, or take specific steps with a partner to allow them to discontinue their use.

During the time of my study in Guadalajara, individuals could access condoms in the following ways. They could buy them for the equivalent of approximately one dollar apiece in a number of drugstores—but not all—and supermarkets around Guadalajara. Some stores placed the condoms where customers could select among several brands without needing to ask for them. In others, condoms were kept behind the counter, and people were forced to ask someone to bring them out. A second alternative was to obtain free condoms from COESIDA or from the AIDS NGOs around the city, at their locales or when the organizations had events or informational tables. The third was to go to clinics and family-planning organizations.

In all of the above cases, condoms were available mostly during the day. The situation was different at night, past the regular closing time of 9 P.M. To my knowledge, except for one homosexual disco that made it a point to have a bowl with condoms displayed, no other places where people socialized at night made condoms available to their patrons. Also, Farmacias Guadalajara, the largest chain of drugstores in Guadalajara, which also had the largest number of twenty-four-hour drugstores, refused to sell any form of contraception, including condoms, because of the religious values of the family that owned it (González Ruiz 1994).

Yet, as is often the case in Mexico, there was a creative alternative. Pablo narrated his encounter with a black market in condoms that operated at small stands right outside some Farmacias Guadalajara. After meeting a potential sexual partner, Pablo realized that he had no condoms at home. On their way there at three in the morning, he asked his partner to stop at a Farmacia Guadalajara. He went inside to buy condoms and his partner waited in the car. The clerk told him the official line that condoms were not sold in that establishment but added, in a lower voice, that he should ask the flower lady outside. Pablo approached the woman and asked for a condom, which she gladly sold him for the outrageous price of twenty pesos for one condom, the equivalent of about U.S. $6.50 at that time.

Some of the flower stands, which were commonly located outside these drugstores and other businesses, were often open this late because flowers are a traditional element of Mexican *serenatas* (serenades). These serenades usually involve a man who shows up outside his lover's, or intended lover's, house with a *mariachi* band or a guitar trio and flowers to declare his love. Just as there were spots in town, including the famous Plaza de los Mariachis, where music bands could be hired for *serenatas* at all times of night, there were also flower stands where the required flowers could be purchased. In an example of the integration of the needs of modern life with Mexican traditions, the flower stand operators had realized that those in need of flowers were often also in need of condoms. If they could get away with greatly overpricing the flowers, they could also do the same with the condoms.

TAKING CHANCES: HIV RISK ASSESSMENT

After information and knowledge about HIV and condoms, another requirement emphasized by AIDS educators in Mexico and elsewhere was individuals' realization of personal risk and awareness of their susceptibility to the disease. The assumption was that such awareness would prompt individuals to use their knowledge to examine their past sexual behaviors and decide whether they needed to be tested, as well as to plan their future sexual encounters and make sound decisions that would help them stay safe against HIV transmission.

This task has been commonly labeled "risk assessment" in HIV prevention programs, and it involves the ability to use knowledge about AIDS and HIV in an organized manner to analyze the risk of any given behavior and sexual situation. In my work with HIV prevention at the San Francisco AIDS Foundation in the late 1980s, we used a simple exercise that described the nature of this task. The exercise involved asking three questions. The first one was, "Is HIV present in the encounter?" The second involved asking whether there was any exchange of bodily fluids that could have an infectious concentration of HIV. The third question was, "Is there a path for the virus to enter the body?"

In Guadalajara, the information required to answer these three questions was commonly covered in educational brochures and in presentations, workshops, and training classes. The assumption was that individuals could make informed decisions by assessing risk and could develop personalized strategies to reduce the risk of any given situation. For the first question in this risk assessment exercise, the implication was that individuals learn the HIV serostatus of their partners through disclosure. In the absence of this knowledge, they ought to stick to safe sex (or, as advocated by some of the messages in Mexico, to monogamy). Questions two and three became relevant in the absence of information about the partner's serostatus, or when there was a reason to not trust a partner's answer—the fact that people lie about other things was invoked as a reason for avoiding blind, uninformed trust. The goal of questions two and three was the selection of sexual practices that did not involve the exchange of fluids in which HIV could be concentrated at infectious levels (namely blood, semen, and vaginal secretions). This meant avoiding contact between the potentially infectious fluids and possible points of viral entry (namely, open cuts or sores and mucous membranes, particularly in the genitals) (Carrillo et al. 1992).

Put in those terms, the task sounds rather simple, and in the late 1980s I myself was a true believer that anyone could use this kind of risk assessment straightforwardly to stay protected. However, the problem with this assumption appears to be that a medical, fact-oriented analysis of risk is often at odds with the more intuitive forms of risk assessment that many people favor as they conduct their sexual lives. Through means other than the information contained in the medical form of risk assessment, participants in my study often decided that their partners could not possibly have HIV.[5] They sometimes later found out, particularly in this city where seroprevalence was low overall, that the sexual partners they assumed to be HIV-negative were in fact HIV-negative. They took such confirmation of their intuition to mean that they could rely on assumptions, rather than facts, in order to decide when not to use protection against HIV.

In contrast with this popular strategy, at the time of my study in Guadalajara the local messages often repeated an early dictum of HIV prevention in the United States: "You have to assume that all your sexual partners are HIV-positive." The alternative to making such an assumption is captured by what HIV educators in English-speaking countries have labeled "negotiated risk" (Kendall 1995). In this second scenario the task is for the sexual partners to have a conversation prior to the sexual encounter, to disclose their serostatus or knowledge of previous risk, to create encounter-specific guidelines, and, in longer-term relations, even to get tested prior to discarding the use of protection. In the more liberal use of the negotiated-risk scheme, educators and activists have recognized that some individuals might be prepared to assume "some risk," and that from a public health perspective "some risk" is a better alternative than "much risk."[6] The assumption here is that always having "no risk" might be unrealistic for some, and that what U.S. AIDS educators call "harm reduction" may pay off as an overall goal, in lieu of a zero-percent-risk approach.

In Guadalajara, in the mid-1990s, the discourse of "negotiated risk" and "harm reduction" was not present. However, the strategy being promoted there coincided with the premise in negotiated risk that open, verbal communication prior to a sexual encounter is needed for the risk assessment process to work. This emphasis contrasted sharply with the more intuitive, silent assessments that often informed decisions about what to do with any given sexual partner.

A good example of the use of intuition was offered by Gonzalo in his narration of the process leading to a casual sexual encounter with a man whom he met one night at a *disco gay*. Like others in the study, Gonzalo believed that a sexual interaction began with eye contact that triggers seduction. He was one of the participants who seemed to fully transition into the sexual space after "that special gaze," and he greatly enjoyed the sensations that engaging in seduction produced. Once seduction started, his awareness was transformed and he began to flow with the interaction. During sex, he fully relied on bodily communication and he emphasized liking the process of discovery, the back-and-forth communication that took place as bodies began to touch.

In discussing his motivation to stay protected during sex, he squarely stated that he would not have sex without a condom unless he had full assurance of the other person's HIV status. Gonzalo said, "[T]he thing is that if you are really expecting to carry on a [sexual] relationship, you have to put it [the condom] on. If I am not sure of my situation, and the other person's, despite how much I want him, [I don't do it]. To avoid causing [him] damage, I protect myself, expecting that the other person, if he really wants to be with you, he will not cause you damage." He followed with a comment about how this last statement mostly applied to situations in which sex is tied to love, "because when it is just passion perhaps you don't even care. *Se te sube tanto la pasión* [the passion climbs so much] that you are not interested [in condoms] and do not protect yourself."

Two years before the interview, Gonzalo experienced a great passion upon meeting a stranger at a gay disco. "This person did not live here. They[7] had come just for a weekend. They were staying in a hotel. We started talking, we danced a little, and I got the idea. After embracing, kissing, touching, passion erupted, and they suggested, 'Let's go to my hotel.' I thought about it for just a moment, not long, and I said to myself, 'This guy is from out of town and he won't come back. There will be no other opportunity.' We went to their hotel, to his room . . . where we *estuvimos* [literally 'were,' meaning 'we had intercourse']. When it happened, when we got to the moment of the relationship [penetration], I did not have protection." Note that, according to Gonzalo's account, they never uttered the words, "Let's have sex." Sex was always indirectly implied, which allowed for the silent flow and game of sex to happen and provided a potential exit should one of the two decide not to continue with the encounter. Gonzalo used these indirect references to sex even in his account of the experience, as he used the word *estuvimos* as an indirect way of saying "we had intercourse."

I asked Gonzalo whether his partner had condoms available. "No, there was nothing there to use for protection. But being there in the moment, the relationship took place anyway." Again, note that "the relationship took place"; it is not something that he and his partner did (or were responsible for); it took place, it happened to them.[8]

"Did you think at any time in making this decision whether there was any danger? Did you do any kind of assessment?" I asked him further.

"Yes, but I perhaps did not really consider it. But I tried anyway to not finish inside this person . . . to avoid any situation. And in fact, it happened quickly, and we finished later by masturbating."

"Were you ever worried about this after the encounter?"

"Yes, it worried me but not much because, I don't know if I am wrongly informed, but I understand that, although there is risk as well for the one who penetrates, the risk is higher for the one who is penetrated. So, given that I did not finish, maybe there was no opportunity [for me to get infected]. *Esperamos en Dios que no pase nada* [God forbid anything bad will happen]." Gonzalo rightly assessed that risk is lower for the insertive partner but incorrectly assumed that the key to reducing the risk for him was not to ejaculate inside his partner—that his becoming infected was more likely if he ejaculated.

Gonzalo's decision was also influenced by his intuitive assessment of the person he had just met. "He was an upper-middle-class person who worked for television. He had a certain level, he had to protect a certain image. He was young, not too old. He seemed to be a healthy and clean person. That is the evaluation that I made. If he had been a different type of person, I would not have done it."

"What type of person would've made you feel mistrustful?"

"Look, people of a certain group. Although some people in television are like that. But with people who are hairstylists, I would never do it. First of all, people who seem to be malicious, who show a lot what they are [homosexual] or who go from one person to the next [who are promiscuous]—you can tell, even in the features of their faces. You can tell whether someone has been very *corrido* [literally 'run,' meaning very sexually active]. His looks. He must look like a clean and nice person. If he is not clean or healthy, I would not do it either. It would need to be someone who, I can tell from talking, needs to protect an image and that he will respect you, that he is respectable. If he isn't that way, I wouldn't do it."

It is relevant that in a different part of his interview, in talking about his choice of partners for long-term relationships, Gonzalo had said, "For me to have a relation with a man, he needs to not be *obvio* [literally 'obvious,' meaning effeminate], because sooner or later someone will realize that you are going out a lot with this person, they will have to know him. If they get to know them, they should meet a person who is not effeminate, who is good-looking, with *buenas costumbres* [good habits and morals], not in terms of socioeconomic level, that is not important." Gonzalo was concerned that an effeminate partner would interfere with a basic strategy of his homosexual life, which was to live a double life among nonhomosexual people and introduce a partner as a good friend. Should this "good friend" be effeminate, people would begin to wonder. Effeminacy in a man threatened Gonzalo in other spheres of his personal life and translated into suspicion of HIV risk.

"What about his education and social class?" I asked.

"Definitely too. He must have a certain cultural and educational level. Logically, people like that [more educated] have more knowledge and use more protection."

"And what about social class?" I pressed.

"I believe that in Mexico social class is really tied together to a certain level of knowledge, not education, but knowledge. Having a certain social class allows you to move further in school, to have a certain level in your studies, more than other people. It is true that a person can have knowledge and culture in other ways, but it is harder to trust someone who did not study anything beyond secondary school. So, social class does have a great influence," was Gonzalo's conclusion on this topic. He was more tentative about this issue, as he seemed to feel that social class should not be a reason for discrimination.

Gonzalo's decision was informed by a number of criteria, but clearly his intuitive assessment that this man was respectful and desirable, and thus trustworthy and HIV-negative, had considerable weight. In fact, Gonzalo ignored the most important indicator of risk—the fact that his partner was willing to have unprotected sex with a stranger about whom he basically knew nothing. He would apply this criterion freely to someone who caused suspicion, someone who was dirty, effeminate, poor, badly educated, someone he assumed to be promiscuous, but not to this respectable-looking partner. Underlying his criteria were not only attitudes about hygiene but also attitudes about education and social class. Furthermore, these images seemed to be intertwined with internalized homophobia. A person who was working class, who had a stereotypically homosexual profession, and who was effeminate would also fall automatically, for middle-class participants like Gonzalo, in the category of the sexually undesirable and potentially risky.[9]

Although my emphasis here is on Gonzalo's intuitive and inaccurate risk assessment, the example touches on a number of other factors influencing his decision that seem related to sexual silence, perceptions of the sexual moment, bodily communication, passion and seduction, love, sexual identities, ideology, HIV information, condom availability, and trust. That a collection of factors was related to decisions made at the moment of sex seemed to be true of almost every account of unprotected sex in my study. However, I would argue that it is often possible to detect one specific factor that tilts the balance of the outcome in terms of HIV risk. In this account such tilting possibly happened when Gonzalo concluded, from his intuitive assessment, that this sexual partner was respectable and trustworthy, despite his willingness to engage in unprotected sex with a stranger, and that the potential risk could be disregarded.

Gonzalo had spoken before about his standards regarding condom use and sexual negotiation in a way that greatly contradicted the sexual experience analyzed here. Gonzalo had said, "Everyone that I have been with has always wanted to use protection."

"Who speaks normally about protection, you or your partner?" I asked.

"Normally both . . . usually, when you get to a point in which you are moving to other kinds of situations [meaning sex]. But eventually, before reaching the point [of sex] we start talking, to tell our experiences, like 'aren't you fearful about AIDS?' 'Are you afraid of AIDS?' And I say, 'Yes, I am very afraid about such issues, so I usually try to do something else, with protection or such things, and just certain practices.'"

"Where do you get condoms when you need them?"

"Mmmmm . . . I buy them in the drugstore."

"Do you carry them with you when you go out?"

"Yes, in fact I didn't before. But *a la hora de la hora* [when the time came], the moment arrived, just before having intercourse proper, and [the brief dialogue], 'Do you have protection?' 'Yes?' 'No?' If not, 'You know what, *mano* [buddy], let's finish up just with masturbation. And nothing else.' I have started carrying protection recently."

"So, before you didn't carry condoms, but you refused to have anal sex?"

"Right, except for that one time." Gonzalo was fully aware that his reasoning and standards had not informed any of his decisions the night of the sexual encounter that he related. He had even considered taking an

HIV test after this encounter but had not done so because he was fearful of the possibility of a positive result.

The potential consequences of this kind of intuitive risk assessment were most palpable in an account that was provided by Pablo, the only participant who disclosed being HIV-positive in my study. Pablo had gone out to a gay bar and was talking to a man. Closing time was approaching and he asked this man whether he wanted to leave with him. The man agreed and said he wanted to go for a walk, but Pablo was wary about the area where they were. The man then suggested taking a taxi and once in it he gave the driver his own address. Upon arrival, they went straight to this man's room. "He grabbed my hand and, blah, blah, blah, I began asking him questions. I wanted to know more about him and I asked, and he showed me some of his [creative] writing," Pablo reminisced.

This scene made Pablo feel comfortable. "I then started feeling quite good with him. Right? When you move from just meeting someone to actually become intimate. Right? I really like being comfortable and we did that for a while; we were chatting for a while and he would grab my hand, touch my face. And we would tell each other about our lives and after about half an hour to an hour he got up to use the bathroom, and I did the same, and then we began to have more contact." The seduction that had started a few hours before at the bar was now concretizing in a sexual encounter. But, as in the encounter related by Gonzalo, neither partner had ever mentioned the idea of having sex. "I think we both knew what was about to happen, since we had come to his house."

At this point, Pablo began experiencing some anxiety and tried to avoid the act of penetration. He was allowing sex to flow spontaneously and without controlling it but was also aware that they did not have condoms. Pablo did not want his partner to penetrate him without one. "I tried to postpone it as much as possible, we took off our shirts first, and we were *cachondeándonos* [making out] for a long time, and then we started touching more, and we got to the point where he said, 'Let's go to the bed,' and we did."

"Were you naked?" I asked.

"Not yet, when we went to bed, he took all his clothes off and we were naked in bed, embracing, for a long time. And the funny thing is that no one was saying, 'Do you have a condom?' And I was thinking, 'I am letting myself be carried away. What will happen? What will happen? And I am drunk, I have four beers in my system.' I became very anxious and felt cold, and when it was all about to happen [anal sex], I told him, 'I don't want this to happen this way.'"

"You said it verbally?" I inquired.

"I said, 'Do you have condoms?' [He said,] 'No, I don't.' 'Me neither.'"

"And what happened then?"

"He said that he chose people quite well and that I should not be anxious, that nothing would happen. So, he was going to penetrate me and I told him, 'No.' He responded well. [He said,] 'I respect what you decide.'" Pablo's sexual partner seemed to be thinking that Pablo was afraid of him, instead of thinking that Pablo could pose a risk to him.

Using verbal communication as a refusal strategy, Pablo managed to stop before unprotected anal sex happened. Yet, he experienced considerable discomfort because, aided to some degree by the effects of alcohol, he was feeling good about abandoning himself to the flow of sex. His having to think about condoms and to stop his partner from penetrating him without a condom was a severe disruption of such flow. After stopping and taking a break, his partner began stimulating Pablo with his tongue, by licking his whole body, including his anus.

"Did you have an ejaculation?" I asked.

"[Yes]. When we masturbated."

In the end, the encounter involved no HIV risk. But this only happened because of Pablo's ability to refuse unprotected anal penetration. Besides the other factors that could have tilted the balance in this sexual encounter—alcohol consumption, respect for the flow of sex, and Pablo's lack of disclosure of his HIV-positive status—most salient is Pablo's partner's willingness to have unprotected sex because of the inaccurate assessment that he made. Because Pablo was a nice, middle-class guy who seemed to be respectable, his partner assumed that he could not have HIV. He decided to trust his intuition that Pablo was "fine." Pablo was horrified by his partner's assumption because he knew that this man would be engaging in this behavior without the slightest awareness that he was about to expose himself to HIV during anal sex.

It should be evident that the assessments in the two examples discussed here, which were fairly typical in my sample, did not involve the use of concrete or objective medical indicators. The only one who assessed risk correctly was Pablo, as he knew the risk that he posed to his sexual partner. Pablo's assessment was not only correct but also concordant with the HIV prevention messages available to him, and he was capable of verbally refusing unprotected penetration. We will see later that Pablo was less successful under different circumstances involving strongly defined sexual roles.

Contrary to what some of the messages in Guadalajara at the time promoted—planning, HIV testing, disclosure of serostatus, verbal negotiation, choosing sexual practices in advance, and setting limits—some of the individuals involved relied on their intuition and were ready to relax the guidelines of safety in the absence of any intuitive red flags. Those red flags would have risen if a potential partner had somehow evoked the person's stereotypes about who has HIV (in Gonzalo's case, working-class, effeminate hairdressers).

(

The bottom line about HIV risk assessment and the rest of the prevention tools promoted by HIV prevention educators in Guadalajara is that their availability did not always guarantee that a person who was knowledgeable, had learned the necessary skills, and was motivated to stay safe would do so. A main limitation was that the tools offered were frequently incompatible with the ways in which people thought about sex, about sexual decision making, and about the sexual moment. They also seemed to compete with people's expectations regarding their sexual partners and the ways in which they assessed other aspects of their relationships.

The HIV educators in Guadalajara were mostly focused on convincing people that public health recommendations regarding safe sex and condom use worked. Although they were somewhat aware that people used intuitive forms of reasoning to make decisions about sex, they did not seem to realize how powerful and dominant these forms of reasoning were. They felt that once individuals learned about the perils of HIV and the advantages of open communication, they would easily adopt the methods being proposed: to engage in verbal communication with partners, find out the necessary facts, and conduct a medically sound risk assessment. By trusting that this task could be straightforwardly accomplished, they failed to realize that intuitive reasoning, along with an emphasis on spontaneity and discovery, was associated with expectations about sex that ran deeply in the local sexual culture. They also failed to realize that intuition was an accepted tool to assess the overall value of a potential or new partner. They assumed instead that intuitive assessments were relied upon simply because of a deficiency in knowledge, skills, and education.

Furthermore, the HIV educators did not realize that intuitive assessments were generally connected to the development of trust, which, as we will see in the next chapter, was an important relational aspect of sex. In this case, in preparation to enter the sexual space, not having to talk about anything, not needing to suggest that sex was beginning, contributed to a sense of fulfillment and a spontaneous flow that people valued. Gonzalo's example also suggests that the forms of reasoning that I discussed throughout this chapter had a function in the pursuit of sexual pleasure, and that there was a competition between relational needs and HIV prevention. This competition is still rarely considered in HIV prevention in Mexico and elsewhere.

Programs such as the CHECCOS training classes were trying to find deeper ways of conducting the task of HIV prevention education and to insert HIV prevention within what educators' perceived to be a larger need for sex education. But they had also accepted without much questioning or adaptation the core premises of prevention theories, methods, and messages developed elsewhere or with a particular professional slant (that of social psychology, public health, sexology, or communications). They saw their task as changing (and implicitly modernizing) people's ideas about sex by influencing their attitudes, beliefs, skills, and ultimately sexual behaviors as part of an explicit process of "rationalization" of such behaviors. They failed to consider that such a modernizing project might not be needed in order to help people reduce their risk and that the "irrationality" of sex is not intrinsically problematic. I continue this exploration of discrepancies between the practice of sex and the methods of prevention in the next chapter, where the focus is on the relational and situational aspects of individuals' and couples' decisions about HIV prevention and sexual behavior.

TRUST, LOVE, PASSION:
THE RELATIONAL CONTEXT
OF HIV RISK

I have presented two contrasting views of the sexual moment. One emerges in Mexicans' discourse about sexual desire, seduction, sexual passion, and love. This is a discourse that emphasizes emotions and relational dynamics during sex and shows the high value assigned to seeking validation, satisfaction, and communion with sexual partners. The second view is contained in the highly medicalized discourse of HIV prevention. In this case, rationality, informed decision making, individuality, and self-determination are typically emphasized, along with the view that sexual health and the avoidance of disease should be a top priority during sex. In Mexico, while the former view of sex highlights spontaneity, mutual surrender, and abandonment, the latter has stressed self-control and the need to contain sexual passion.

In this chapter, I examine the discrepancies between these two views of sex. I point out the pressing need for their integration within HIV prevention work—for the realization that they are not intrinsically in opposition to each other. Indeed, people in Mexico who were successful at implementing HIV prevention measures commonly did not follow the guidelines of rationality suggested by the more common preventive messages and instead adapted them to fit within their own preferred ways of having sex and of communicating with partners during sex.[1] In doing such adaptation, they learned how to simultaneously fulfill their sexual desires and protect their health in the process, most commonly by introducing HIV prevention measures in ways that did not disrupt an otherwise spontaneous flow of sex. They used protection without needing much previous, explicit verbal negotiation.[2]

For this analysis, I have found it necessary to consider relational aspects of sexual interactions that have typically been ignored in the design of HIV prevention programs because of the programs' strong focus on individual behavior.[3] I pay attention to styles of relational negotiation that do not involve verbal communication but that sexual partners effectively use in obtaining what they want from their social and sexual relationships (Mane and Aggleton 2000). I found that before and throughout a sexual encounter, people interpret the desires, intentions, roles, and expectations present, and even the trustworthiness and overall character of their sexual partners. Every action and response on the part of sexual partners becomes meaningful for constructing an understanding of the encounter and its significance (Ferrand and Snijders 1997).

I also consider in my analysis cultural scripts and their role in informing sexual partners' interpretations during a sexual encounter, as well as the forms of reasoning (which Guizzardi, Stella, and Remy [1997] label "pragmatic rationality") and the logics governing individual and relational decisions during sex. Because cultural scripts typically have been learned and internalized over a long period, and because they are broad and related to the sexual encounter as a whole, people tended to invoke them more readily than the health-related scripts outlined in HIV prevention messages. Several authors have suggested that people rely on cultural scripts, and on the logics that accompany them, in interpreting all kinds of situations that emerge in the context of sex (Bastard and Cardia-Voneche 1997; Ingham and van Zessen 1997; Ahlmeyer and Ludwig 1997; Campenhoudt and Cohen 1997; Díaz 2000). Cultural scripts become particularly useful when individuals are responding to a situation with which they are not familiar. In discussing actors' spontaneous analysis of situations and their courses of action, I pay attention to the interactions between the sexual partners (both as separate individuals and as a dyad) and the social contexts in which they have sex. I also focus on people's simultaneous roles as subjects of social norms and social expectations and as agents who help transform those roles and expectations (Campenhoudt et al. 1997).

Similarly to the cases that I presented in the previous chapter, my analysis here relies on accounts of sexual encounters and behavioral strategies described by participants in my study. As they recalled sexual interactions, participants provided a great deal of personal analysis of the situations surrounding these sexual encounters and were often aware of the discrepancies between their actions and what they had learned they should do in order to ensure protection against HIV. Generally speaking, when such discrepancies arose, participants showed some retrospective discomfort or preoccupation about their inability to implement what they knew about HIV prevention. Some tried to understand what had led them to take HIV-related risks. Nonetheless, they also justified their actions during sex by arguing that there is a difference between one's motivation to stay safe and the realities of a sexual encounter. This was a way of saying that other important needs competed with sexual health. The unfulfilled desire to enact protective measures against HIV transmission in light of other relational needs was frequently not perceived to be illogical. Instead, inconsistencies in the use of safety measures were framed within a longer list of everyday experiences involving competing needs, priorities, situations, and desires. I begin my discussion of these issues by contrasting the call for self-control in HIV prevention messages with people's expectations about sexual passion and spontaneity.

SEXUAL PASSION AND SPONTANEITY

Carmen was one of the women in my study who possessed a sophisticated understanding of HIV and safe sex. I quoted her view on the eroticization of nonpenetrative sex in the previous chapter. Although she strongly supported the practice of safe sex, she was aware of the difficulties involved in enacting it. She said, "People can go to ten safe-sex workshops and say, 'Surely this will help a lot; I won't have sex anymore without protection,' but then it is difficult to propose to the sexual partner to have sex with protection. It is difficult to do it in real life."

I asked Carmen more about this issue. "What barriers exist against staying protected during a sexual relation?"

She responded, "Well, I think there can be many barriers. Surely everyone misses the taste of semen, of vaginal fluids, of the whole body, and it is hard to think of a barrier, of latex.[4] I still find it quite difficult. Although I have not had sex without protection, it has been hard to learn to maintain it because—it is true that one can read books and go to workshops, but living it is not easy."

"When did you start using protection?"

"Since I attended a workshop. About six years ago."

"Are you consistent in your practice? Do you use it all the time?"

"Look, the truth is that I didn't when I had contact with this girl, even when we both attended the safe-sex workshop for women. *Ay!* I don't know what happened, truly."

"What do you think happened?" I pressed.

"It happens that you disconnect from things and you are so *apasionado* [passionate], wanting the person so much that you forget."

"Was that the only time? Has it ever happened with a man?"

"It almost happened with a guy. But fortunately I said [no]. But it was hard, very hard, to tell you the truth."

Carmen's comments spelled out the tension between the kind of rationality required for the implementation of safe sex and the abandonment and spontaneity that sexual passion facilitates.

Similarly, Pablo talked about the health risks that he took under the spell of passion and that he felt led him to becoming infected with HIV. "I love to experience passion—in the past I let myself be carried away by passion, I did many stupid things." He felt that this happened during a time of "self-destruction." He had just told his family that he was a *homosexual* and this created tremendous conflict. He felt guilty and angry at the same time that his sexual energy was boiling inside looking for an outlet. "I repressed sexuality so much that I could not direct it, like someone would come and put things in motion and there was all that effervescence. When I went back home in December [for Christmas, a time that is often emotionally loaded], I had an *acostón* [a casual sex encounter] with some guy. I was really drunk that night. Many things started happening and I— has it ever happened to you that you feel like you are doing things outside of yourself? I am trying to explain to you the sensation of not having control of yourself, and you are seeing things happening [from the outside]."

Pablo's experience is reminiscent of the kind of loss of self-regulation reported by Díaz (1998, 2000). Pablo lost control and became a spectator of his own actions, of his own unbridled passion. He had met this man in a bar and had ended up going back with him to his apartment, along with another two men. Once there, both pairs began making out in the living room. Then the other couple went into the bedroom. Pablo and his partner followed them a few minutes later. The man ended up penetrating Pablo without a condom and ejaculated inside his body.

Throughout the interaction, Pablo said, "one of the others was trying to tell me something with his eyes." Pablo added that when he and his partner came into the bedroom, "this guy continued looking me in the eyes; he was trying to tell me not to be there, that I should leave. I was looking at him too but had no will; we were just letting ourselves get carried away."

"Because of passion?" I asked.

"I believe so, because alcohol does things to you; it *alborota las hormonas* [stirs up your hormones]." The other couple left as soon as Pablo and his partner started having anal sex. When they finished, Pablo noticed something strange on his partner's back. "His back had many big *granos* ['pimples' or 'spots']. I felt fear." Later, Pablo grimly stated, "When I saw his back, it is like I read my future. I don't know if he had it [AIDS], but seeing his back told me many things and I felt lots of fear." Motivated by his fear, Pablo took an HIV test a few weeks later, which yielded a positive result. He speculated that the man who kept looking at him during the sexual interaction, and who was a friend of the man with whom Pablo was having sex, probably knew something about this man's HIV status and was trying to warn him. Whether this particular partner infected Pablo cannot be known. What is clear is that Pablo had interpreted, retrospectively, what he thought were signs that should have told him that he was putting himself at high risk. Pablo relied on intuitive reasoning and could not get himself to ask any questions. Nor did he dare to stop the sex, which was happening in a context of alcohol consumption, silence, spontaneity, and high and uncontrollable passion.

These two cases make reference to the two sides of sexual passion that I discussed in chapter 8. Spontaneity, sexual passion, and loss of control were greatly favored. Their presence was taken to mean that sex was good and that sexual partners were compatible. The same features, however, were regarded as being problematic in situations in which control was perceived to be needed, such as in making decisions about HIV risk and safety. Carmen had been capable of refusing unprotected sex in a sexual encounter with a man, but the same had not applied in an encounter with a woman, where she perhaps also perceived a lower risk. Pablo, who also reported instances in which he remained in full control while also experiencing passion, had been unable in this case to articulate his fear and to stop the sexual interaction. He attributed this failure to his emotional state and to the dynamics of spontaneity and sexual passion.

Additionally, in these two accounts, there might have been other factors affecting the outcome—factors that depended on the roles taken by each sexual partner, their unfamiliarity with the type of situation, and even power differences during the sexual encounter. Expectations of sexual passion and spontaneity, however, were perceived to fundamentally support the decision not to stop the encounter—"to kill the moment"—or to attempt to change its course in response to fear (in Pablo's account) or to a more general perceived need for health safety (in Carmen's example). Allowing sexual passion to dominate as a way of maintaining the flow of sex might be connected with the fragility of sex's separate reality that my analysis in chapter 8 suggested. As Alhmeyer and Ludwig put it: "Intimate communication . . . is highly vulnerable to the impact of everyday reality. Minor signs may suffice to make a sexual intercourse collapse or prevent it from getting started" (1997: 34). In relation to sexual passion, deciding whether to introduce or not the use of protective measures against HIV was equated with a larger decision that might lead the whole sexual encounter to "fail" from the viewpoints of connection, intimacy, and the fulfillment of sexual pleasure.

ROLES, IDENTITIES, POWER

In the context of a spontaneous, often silent initiation and enactment of sex, people often relied on intuitive assessments and assumptions about what their sexual partners desired. Some of those assumptions were determined by perceptions of the sexual identities and roles of the actors involved. For instance, Osvaldo, a young homosexual man, had a history of sexual interactions with male cousins with whom he had initiated his sexual life as an adolescent. These interactions began with playful mutual exploration of their bodies and had segued into a long-term relationship with one of Osvaldo's cousins that involved anal penetration, with Osvaldo as the receptive partner. For several years after initiating these sexual encounters, neither one of the two identified as *homosexual*. They both continued to assume that they were "regular" young men continuing what had started as adolescent sexual playfulness. Osvaldo, however, was moving in the direction of being sexually interested only in men. The cousin was going in the opposite direction. He had moved in with a girlfriend and was now living in a different city. He came to see Osvaldo periodically, and then they would have sex. In these encounters, the cousin tended to take a dominant role that determined the flow of the sexual interaction, usually culminating with Osvaldo being anally penetrated.

Osvaldo had adopted the identities *homosexual* and *gay* three years before his interview, at age eighteen. During the first two years after choosing these new identities, he knew little about AIDS. "A year ago I learned what exactly it [AIDS] was. How it is transmitted, why it is transmitted, and everything. . . . The first year was a year of *desmadre* [excess]. I would have sex with people without caring."

"Did men ever ask you to use a condom?"

"Some wore one, some didn't. For instance, my cousin never wore one until now that there is more awareness that *homosexuales* are a source of infection." Before Osvaldo adopted a homosexual identity, neither he nor his cousin saw a need for a condom. Only now that Osvaldo was *gay* and his cousin was aware of the risk posed by *homosexuales* had they begun using condoms. However, the cousin's desire for condoms was not consistent. "Sometimes he does not want to wear one, but I ask him to. . . . First, he was the one who put one on, because of fear, because he knew that I was entering the world of homosexuality and going out to bars. He was scared. . . . Interestingly, now when he comes for the weekend, he does not want to use one. And I tell him, 'Put one on because I am scared.'" Osvaldo had become very fearful of HIV and often believed that he had symptoms of the disease. After learning that HIV could be transmitted through oral sex, he had decided to stop practicing it with most sexual partners except for his cousin, whom he considered to be safe in that regard (perhaps because the cousin did not identify as *homosexual*). His fear, however, was large enough to now make him feel that his cousin could pose some risk during anal sex. "Now that he lives far away, I don't know with whom he is involved," remarked Osvaldo. This made Osvaldo become assertive.

His fear of AIDS and his assertiveness, however, had not prevented Osvaldo from having unprotected sex with an openly bisexual man the weekend before our conversation. He had been trying to meet up with him for a while, but an encounter had not taken place because the man was always with his girlfriend. This time, the man called Osvaldo and asked to meet him at a gay bar that was also frequented by gay-accepting *heterosexuales*. Osvaldo assumed that the man would come with his girlfriend, but he came alone. "I thought, 'What's up! He wants me for something.' His girlfriend's best friends were there. They were making sure that we did not do something foolish. I tried to stay calm. I was calm. We were sitting with our arms crossed, looking at each other [across the table]. He grabbed my hand. We came back to my house. He said, 'I want the opportunity to be alone with you.' We ended up parked by the side of a road. We did it there, without a condom."

"And why did you do it without a condom?"

"I felt too much trust. I said, 'I am not worried because this boy'—you know I have never seen him cruising. So, I don't know why, but I did not want [a condom] either."

"Did you have them?"

"No, well we did. No, we didn't, now that I think about it."

"And what did you do?"

"Everything. Intercourse. He penetrated me. In fact, I am sexually *internacional.* I have no parking problems [i.e., no problems assuming either role]. I don't have one single preference. But I almost don't like to be passive anymore." Osvaldo commented that he now tended to have only nonpenetrative sex, but in this case he seemed to measure the risk of this encounter by his perception of his partner's lack of promiscuity. He assumed that this man, being a bisexual man who had a girlfriend, did not pose the same risk as an openly homosexual man. This assumption, compounded by his strong desire for an encounter with this man and the anticipation that ensued, had made him not consider condoms.

Osvaldo was annoyed by the implications of this recent encounter, particularly given where he stood in terms of fear of HIV and HIV testing. "I will let six months go by [and get tested]. I am a hypochondriac. I begin to notice something wrong with my body and I start hallucinating that I have AIDS. Like one time I felt that I was losing my hair. And the first thing I thought is 'AIDS.' My last test was in July [the interview took place the following February]. And since July, this was the first time that I had sex without a condom. To some degree, I am actually taking care of myself. . . . But this time, because it was him, I put my hands in the fire."

"And he didn't ask for the condom either?"

"No, he didn't ask."

I continued to challenge Osvaldo to think about the specific situation during this encounter. "Let's talk about this moment when you were deciding to do this. What prevented you from asking for a condom? What was your reasoning? How did you make this decision?"

"Well, in part it is that I really wanted him."

"And what does that mean?"

"That I was stubborn about getting him."

"And what does that mean in terms of the condom?"

"In terms of the condom? That I trusted that he could not have anything [AIDS]. I was sure that I still had a negative result six or seven months after." Osvaldo felt he did not pose a risk to the other. "And so it happened. I took a step further without saying, 'Put on something.'"

"And what do you think would have happened if you asked?"

"He would have put one on. But it is strange that he did not ask me for one. He didn't care. I have to avoid thinking about that. I have a feeling that he had fought with his girlfriend and he wanted to escape to go with someone and—it is so wrong—he knew that I was willing to give it all to be with him. I had that feeling. At some point I told him all that I feel for him, but he never said what he feels for me." Osvaldo was realizing, as he spoke, that his partner's attitudes contradicted the image that he had of him.

"And you never talked about AIDS?"

"No." .

Osvaldo's intuition was that this had been a window of opportunity that might not be repeated. Not only did he trust that his partner posed little risk due to his bisexuality, but the same bisexuality gave the partner a more dominant role and put Osvaldo in a more submissive position. This seemed to be further compounded by a certain vulnerability that resulted from feeling that he was the one who wanted the other more, the one who was willing to "give it all to be with him." Furthermore, because this was a man who had a girlfriend, Osvaldo seemed to have readily assumed the role that many women in Mexico are forced to adopt when they feel the need to obtain or retain a male partner.

In an even more striking example regarding sexual roles, Pablo had an encounter involving unprotected anal sex that made him feel immensely guilty. Pablo had not managed to disclose that he was HIV-positive or stop his partner's advances to penetrate him during the encounter. The day after the encounter took place, Pablo called me to tell me about it, seeking an objective way to analyze what had happened.

When he would pass by on his way to a nearby bus stop, Pablo would notice a young *albañil*, a construction worker, at a site near his house.[5] He was attracted to him and puzzled because the man seemed so masculine and yet also seemed to be sending out what Pablo interpreted to be signals of interest. One afternoon, as Pablo was walking back home past the construction site, he saw the man standing by the sidewalk. He said hello to him and they started talking. The man seemed to be so hot after working under the bright Guadalajaran sun that Pablo instinctively offered to give him a glass of cold soda. But, by the way he said it, he made it clear to him as well that he was offering much more. The man accepted the offer and walked with Pablo toward his apartment.

As soon as they entered the apartment, they embraced and began to make out. Pablo felt greatly overpowered by this man's masculinity (a perception that seemed to be exacerbated by differences in social status between the two men). The man's masculine presence immediately defined the tone of the interaction, as well as the roles of both actors. Pablo willingly accepted a submissive role. The man forcefully adopted a dominant role. Pablo greatly enjoyed the situation, except when he realized that the encounter was leading to anal penetration. Within the roles that they had adopted, Pablo found no way of suggesting the use of a condom or stopping his partner's attempt to penetrate him without one. He considered the need to tell him that he was HIV-positive as a solution of last resort, but he feared that the partner would react negatively and violently. Pablo became concerned about having to disclose his serostatus while this strong stranger was on top of him, completely in physical control of the interaction. So he remained silent, continued enacting the expectations of his adopted role, and let the man penetrate him until ejaculation.

When Pablo called me, he was trying to make sense of what happened. He justified his action to some degree by saying that his partner also had to assume responsibility for his own protection. Yet, he had concluded that his own mistake was to allow things—his "fantasy"—to advance to a point at which he could not step out of his willingly adopted, submissive role. Pablo had clearly experienced a lack of power that he felt was associated with the strong masculine stance demonstrated by the other man.

Pablo referred to the man as a *chacalón*, a term used by Mexican *homosexuales* to describe masculine, working-class men who are often dark skinned and have Indian features. He found his partner's looks very attractive and liked the man's willingness to enact the dominant role that Pablo expected of him. Pablo puzzled over how he could experience something like this again, something so very special, but without having to worry about his inability to introduce condoms or refuse unprotected anal sex when he adopted this chosen, submissive role.

Pablo's role in this interaction resembled the roles that some women had in sexual encounters with men. Remember Martha, who had been seduced by an old boyfriend and was now resisting having sex with a new boyfriend out of fear of developing a reputation as the type of woman that men would perceive to be readily available for sex. That was the type of woman with which Osvaldo's and Pablo's roles were most closely associated. In a sexual encounter between a man and a woman, however, the male prerogative to initiate sex, as well as the perceived need for women to be sexually modest, greatly shaped expectations about when and how a condom was used, as well as who suggested using it. Martha, for instance, said that it would be hard for her to request the use of a condom because it would signify that she was sexually experienced. She saw this as an action that would be difficult to accomplish while she was also actively trying to resist having sex and to appear to be virginal. The logic of her reasoning was informed by social expectations about male and female roles, which defined who was supposed to do what during sex. In this sense, the inability of a nondominant sexual partner to request, or demand, the use of a condom was often already defined by the time a sexual encounter commenced.

This power differential between sexual partners has been noted in HIV prevention work as a major cause of HIV risk, particularly for women. It is commonly believed that such a power differential is always involuntary.[6] The assumption is that power differentials lead directly to HIV risk when the more powerful partner does not want protection and when the other partner is "powerless" to change that, which could be one conclusion in analyzing Pablo's sexual encounter with the construction worker. Yet, Pablo also felt that the power differential was productive from the point of view of sexual pleasure and actively played a part in constructing it. He strongly valued an encounter in which his partner could fully take control and dominate, where he could "be taken." In this sense, he was an active participant in creating the roles that intrinsically contained the power differential, and he indeed enjoyed what the power differential provided for the sex. Similarly, Osvaldo interpreted that his not asking for a condom symbolized his willingness to "give it all" to this desirable bisexual man. For Martha, as for other women, not asking for a condom was part of a broader strategy to maintain her status as decent, to be able to be sexual without risking her reputation. Her initial resistance to sex and her gradual acquiescence contributed to her desirability and to the couple's passion and arousal during sex.

The sexual partners who were taking a so-called submissive role were also exercising some degree of agency. As a result, separating how much in these encounters results from oppression—oppressive forms of gender inequality and the exercise of one partner's power and the other's inability to confront it—and how much from the partners' mutual search for sexual pleasure or justification is complicated. All these issues seemed to be so entwined that it would be unfair to judge all power differentials as being intrinsically malign and thus always oppressive by definition.

Furthermore, we ought to consider the degree to which these roles and interactions are emblematic of the diversity of sexual partners' identities, which suggests the need to avoid assuming, as Terto notes in relation to homosexuality, that groups sharing one form of attraction are "a monolithic and homogenous group, a single population group" (2000: 66).

Taken together, these findings suggest that a variety of roles, identities, and levels of power are always to be expected and that HIV prevention measures need to be made to work in their presence.

SENTÍ CONFIANZA: THE ROLE OF TRUST

The theme of trust has emerged repeatedly in the accounts of sexual encounters discussed throughout this chapter. Participants commonly viewed trust as a basic ingredient needed for sex. They often also recognized that "trust in a sexual partner" was a central force informing their decision not to use condoms or practice safe sex. I have concluded that the relationships among trust, sex, and HIV prevention in Guadalajara were far from simple. The connections among these issues seemed to be embedded in complicated cultural scripts that involved people's perceptions of the roles of love, intimacy, fate, self-sacrifice, passion, sexual modesty, and the flow of sex, and which were often in direct opposition to the public health discourse about HIV prevention.

In order to characterize such cultural scripts about trust in the context of decisions about HIV prevention, I have separated my analysis into two parts. First, I consider views about how trust was related to sex and HIV in nonmarital relationships that participants perceived to be stable, long-term, and not casual. Second, I focus on views about the same topic but in casual sexual encounters.

The Trust-Love Connection

The cultural script that tended to inform the enactment of sex in non-marital, stable relationships was the following. Despite the sexual liberties granted to men, participants had commonly been socialized to accept as true that sex was best and only fully justified when it constituted an expression of love for a partner. The internalized need for this justification was particularly strong among women, who were often also concerned about maintaining their status as "decent" and sexually modest. Participants who utilized this script emphasized needing to experience feelings for a partner and anticipating that the relationship would be long lasting before engaging in sex. In this context, one of the indicators that demonstrated that love was developing was trust in the sexual partner.

The need to experience love, and thus trust as well, resulted in two kinds of scenarios. One involved "real love," a label that I would apply to situations in which participants were truly experiencing feelings of love for, or at least infatuation with, a partner, and such feelings motivated their decision to have sex. The second implied what I call "socially determined love," or situations in which participants were under pressure to convince themselves that they were in love as a way to justify acting on their sexual desire (which might, or might not, be love related). Clearly, it is sometimes hard to separate the relative weight of each of these types of emotional involvement in a specific situation, as participants could simultaneously experience some degree of both.

Trust and love were both explicitly connected with a third concept that is relevant here: self-sacrifice. Some participants viewed their willingness to do things that might be against their own personal interest, sometimes at the request of their partners, as an indicator of their trust, and in turn of their love, for that partner. Those actions were occasionally described as "doing stupid things in the name of love."[7] To make things more complicated, one form of self-sacrifice that participants associated with the development of trust and love was agreeing to have unprotected sexual intercourse. This idea appeared to be strengthened by the perception that condoms and safe sex contradicted the goals of intimacy and interpersonal connection, which were also seen as basic ingredients of the development of love. Completing the script was the common perception that asking for a condom or for safe sex revealed oneself as being sexually experienced, which defeated the efforts of those participants who were trying to be sexual without jeopardizing their reputation as sexually modest.

In all senses, public health messages informing the promotion of condom use and safe sex directly opposed idealized perceptions of "what sex should be like," particularly in the context of love. Overall, the ability to practice safe sex in the context of ongoing or steady relationships was easily hindered by the many layers of meaning and interpretation associated with trust, love, desire, self-sacrifice, and commitment, as well as by social expectations about how individuals with specific sexual roles and practices should manage them. Additionally, a series of issues regarding risk assessment, negotiation, and sexual communication could be found embedded in the opposition trust/love/intimacy versus HIV prevention/safety. The expression *sentí confianza* (I developed trust) was used as shorthand to represent all these complicated issues combined. Developing trust thus constituted a central organizer determining priorities and decisions during sex in a long-term relationship and marked the incompatibilities between individuals' motivation and intention to stay safe and other emotional, relational, and physical needs that they looked to sex to fulfill. When those other needs were higher on the list of priorities than concerns about HIV, it was easy to dispense with condom use and other safety measures, especially since they seemed to diminish the sense that love and trust were present in the relationship.

Within the circular logic of the cultural script (trust leads to love, love to sex, sex to more trust and love), it was difficult to insert the recommendations of existing HIV prevention messages because they all seemed to invert the cycle (safe sex and condoms indicate casualness about sex and a lack of love, and they can also create mistrust, which in turn reduces the ability to justify sex). Getting rid of condoms meant that trust was developing, that the sexual partners were falling in love, and that the relationship was becoming strong and intimate. Wanting protection against HIV meant the opposite: that love and trust were not developing and, by extension, that the relationship was threatened and the desire for sexual interaction was not fully justified.

One example of how this played out is the following. Around the time of my interview with Martha, she was tempted to have sex with a new boyfriend but actively resisted in order to protect her reputation. He was good-looking and seductive. She recognized that her desire to have sex with him was motivated by how much he aroused her but emphasized that her main motivation for sex was her love for him. Besides the threat to her reputation that her suggesting condom usage might provoke, it would also threaten the perception of love within the relationship. This, in turn, would further invalidate her desire to have sex. The cycle was completed with Martha's integrating her sense of sacrifice into her justification for why she would have sex—unprotected sex. When I asked Martha, "Have you ever talked about AIDS with your boyfriend?" she responded, "No."

"If he didn't want to use protection, would you still have intercourse with him?"

"I believe I would," she stated straightforwardly.

"Why?"

"Because I love him very much. I think I would do it."

"So, love would be stronger than fear?"

"I think it would win me over," she concluded.

Within this line of reasoning, which seemed self-reinforcing, there was practically no room for her to demand condom use, or perhaps even to consider it. The price Martha seemed most ready to pay was potential HIV risk, which also fit well with local ideas about the acceptance of fate.[8] Martha's trust in her partner implied her believing that he would not do something maliciously. But it also implied her accepting that trust can always be betrayed and that one cannot always control the occurrence of betrayal. Her previous boyfriend, to whom she "sacrificed" her virginity, had indeed

abandoned her. The awareness of potential betrayal symbolized a romantic view that personal sacrifice is a potential price that you may have to pay
for love. Martha seemed to fully accept this romantic view, particularly
since it also supported her conviction that it was love that motivated her
desire for sex.

The use of this strategy was certainly not exclusive to women. Some of
the men also saw trust and love as required signs indicating the strength of
a relationship. In their cases, however, the need to be perceived as sexually modest was absent. The emphasis instead was on the power that love,
trust, and self-sacrifice had as indicators of commitment. For heterosexual
men, this commonly meant that a woman was worthy of being courted for
marriage, which in turn meant postponing seduction and sex (which, for
them, was also a form of self-sacrifice). For homosexual men this meant
being capable of establishing intimate connections. In a social context in
which homosexuality was highly sexualized, and where there were many
social barriers to establishing long-term homosexual relationships, these
men sought reassurance that their relationships were not purely sexual—
that they could last and prove that loneliness need not be a consequence
of homosexuality.

Antonio, for example, thought of himself as dominant in his relationships with men, but he also saw love as a powerful force to which he had
to surrender his will. He associated this need for surrender with passion
and with the strengthening of his relationship to his current boyfriend.
Antonio and his boyfriend had been going out for a month but had known
each other for two years. Antonio was aware that his boyfriend had had
considerable risk for HIV during those two years. Antonio received a negative result when he took an HIV test, motivated by his wanting to protect
this new boyfriend. The boyfriend had never taken an HIV test and refused to take one out of fear he would receive a positive result. He did not
want them to use condoms either. Antonio had agreed to engage in unprotected anal sex with him (both in the insertive and in the receptive
roles).

Antonio explained that love was the main reason for him to continue
assuming a risk that he knew to be possibly high. He stated, "I believe [I
had unsafe sex] because I am in love. If I were not in love, I would not
have sex with him."

I asked him, "What does love do in relation to protection [against
HIV]?"

"What does love do? It blinds you, it closes doors, it cancels opportunities, because the only thing you see is that your world is that person, and

you look for a way to be with that person. I already told you, normally I do not let anyone penetrate me, and . . . he has asked [to penetrate me] and I have allowed him to. [I say this] so you realize what love causes."

"Has he ejaculated inside you?"

"Yes. I have [also] ejaculated inside him," Antonio affirmed.

In this case, his sacrifice was not only about unprotected sex but also about being penetrated, which was not his usual preference. Antonio made two additional statements that indicated the degree to which he believed that love justified sacrifice and took his power away. First he said, "I might get really hurt because I love him." Then he added, "He is now my world, my new toy, my crystal ball, my everything. It is stupid, but he is. I am the kind of person who doesn't like to lose. I have never lost. And I consider myself to be very fortunate, to have a very strong character. Yet, he has made me fall badly. For him I have been drunk and have been caught crying. Just so you have an idea of how things are." Antonio believed that the power of love was large enough to justify his willingness to pay the large price that he was aware he might pay should his partner be HIV-positive. Love had a blinding power, had a life of its own, and took a central role in determining his actions.

For Juan, another homosexual man, the focus was not on his own power but on his efforts to give it up while, at the same time, demonstrating that he could make a man fall in love. Juan needed to prove to himself that he could conquer "a real man." He sought to enact to perfection his adopted and idealized roles as woman and *pasivo*, to demonstrate to a partner that he could provide him as much satisfaction as a woman, or more. He believed condom use in this type of relationship would interfere with the development of trust and love and with the roles that he wanted himself and his partner to take. During a conversation with him and one of his friends, I posed the following scenario for Juan to consider. "Imagine that you initiate a relationship with a partner and he tells you that he has been at risk in the past and wants to use condoms. What do you do?"

"I use them, but only one month or two. Not any longer than that. Making love with a condom is not like being with a person but more like being with a bag. I don't like it." Here he made reference to his dislike of condoms in general, his willingness to be temporarily docile (as he imagined a woman ought to be), but also to his desire to ultimately impose his will and abandon condom use (as he also imagined a woman should do).

I then asked him, "And how do you decide when to stop using them?"

"Well, time passes by and one says, 'Okay let's start doing it without a condom.' My last partner got mad at me when I said that, but in the end we did it." Here again, he alluded to the imposition of his will. Juan perceived that his partner would give in to unprotected sex as a result of his desire and as a logical outcome of increased familiarity.[9]

I protested, "Listen, but if he had been at risk [previously], the fact that he is with you for a month does not take the risk away!"

He immediately shot back: "Yes, but one develops trust. It is trust that one has in him and then one falls in love. And then you think, 'Well, I will die from something anyway.'" Juan did not deny the risk involved but was certain about his decision, because he regarded his need for trust and love as priorities and as justifying the price he was willing to pay. Like Martha and Antonio, Juan emphasized his acceptance of fate, which he inscribed within a romantic ideology that might justify the thought, "My love is so great I would die for it."

Finally, Enrique, who thought of himself as a fairly modern and liberal person in relation to sex, reported having unprotected anal sex with a boyfriend once they decided that they were pursuing a long-term relationship. Enrique was strongly focused on ensuring that love was developing and thus that his relationship was growing. He said he really wanted to make this relationship work and feared becoming lonely as he aged.

When I first met Enrique, he was involved in a three-year relationship with a previous partner, with whom he did not use condoms for anal sex (they both had received negative HIV test results at some point in their relationship). Enrique had been cautious and used protection and practiced safe sex in a few extramarital affairs and, later, with all sexual partners after he broke up with his lover. However, when he met his new partner, who refused to take an HIV test, he ended up giving in to his partner's desire to stop using condoms once he became infatuated and his need for commitment became stronger.

At the time, Enrique was a volunteer at an AIDS organization, and he experienced great discomfort that stemmed from the contradiction between what he preached and what he was now doing. He approached me feeling extremely guilty about the lack of protection and seeking to find a way to bring condom use back into his relationship. Enrique felt that he was being forced to throw out the window the assessment of risk that he had made, in order to prove to himself and to his partner that he trusted him and thus that he loved him. Enrique concluded that he could not continue living with the contradiction and decided to turn things around by asking his partner to be tested or to reinitiate the use of protection as acts of love for Enrique. Rather than de-emphasizing love, Enrique aimed to find a way to redirect how love was expressed in ways consistent with HIV prevention measures.[10]

Affronts to Fidelity

The threat that condom use posed to trust in long-term relationships also took a different form. Requesting a condom could be easily construed as meaning "I don't trust that you've been faithful" or "I have been unfaithful." This was especially the case if this happened after the partners had already not used condoms on previous occasions, or when the sexual partners had known each other for some time and presumed that they trusted each other. For instance, Eduardo felt confident about condom use but expressed his awareness about the possible misconceptions that women may develop when their partners propose using protection. I asked him, "Is it easy for women to accept condom use?"

"Mmmmm . . . it generates a lot of mistrust. I feel the reaction is, 'This bastard, he probably fucks around a lot' or 'You don't trust me; if you are a saint, why don't you trust me?' The psychological barrier is very strong. People misinterpret [asking for a condom] as a lack of trust in them."

Antonio commented as well on this topic. In discussing his boyfriend, I asked him, "What would happen . . . if you introduced the use of protection? If you said, 'You know what, I am worried about risk and want to use a condom.'"

He responded, "Trust would be lost. Why? I live alone. He lives with his family. I see him for a moment at night, just for a while, or maybe I don't see him at all [on any given night]. The moment I say, 'Let's use a condom,' he will think, 'You are cheating on me with someone else.' And that would not be true. That's what I mean about [losing] trust."

This issue would be particularly poignant in an already existing relationship in which one of the partners indeed becomes worried about his sexual activity with other partners or fearful as a result of suspecting that the other might be incurring risk outside the relationship. What might appear to be a straightforward task regarding the protection of one's own self-interests and health may indeed threaten the continuity of the relationship. The worried partner might feel compelled to continue having unprotected sex with the other, instead of asking for condoms and, in turn, having to deal with the topics of suspicion, mistrust, infidelity, and dishonesty. In the case that the suspicion is about a more dominant partner, the worried partner might also be unable to request condom use out of fear of a negative, even violent, reaction.

Instant Intimacy

In general terms, participants recognized more readily the need for condoms and safe sex in casual sexual encounters and were often able to implement those measures. However, when they were not successful, trust was often a justification, even in situations involving sex with a stranger about whom they knew very little. Such decisions were heavily influenced by intuitive risk assessments; assumptions about a person's hygiene, respectability, or class; and individuals' desire to believe that they choose their sexual partners well. Additionally, there seemed to be a connection between trust and the desire to achieve intimacy, even in the context of a one-time sexual encounter. Similarly to the function that trust had as an indicator of love and commitment, in this case trust could function as an indicator of intimacy and of the potential for achieving sexual passion, abandonment, and enjoyment. Trust was seen as an ingredient ensuring sexual pleasure. It also helped avoid experiencing sex as an "empty" or "impersonal" event.

Adrián, Osvaldo, Pablo, and other men who participated in casual sexual encounters (not with prostitutes) indicated, at one point or another, that trust and intimacy were important elements of all sex, not only sex in the context of long-term relationships. Those who enjoyed casual sexual encounters often seemed to share an understanding that actors aim to establish a connection during the moment of sex, a level of intimacy, that is significant—even if it is also ephemeral—and that is confirmed by the intensity of sexual passion. The bottom line is that these participants tended not to talk about their casual sexual encounters just in terms of the sensations or the acts, nor did they speak of their casual sexual partners in ways that denoted objectification (an exception being Javier, who spoke of "using" or "manipulating" women for his own pleasure). Instead, they emphasized the intensity of the moment, the communication between bodies, and the ability to feel and make the other feel. Similarly to their discourse about sex in the context of love, when they talked about casual sex they often emphasized the relational aspects of their encounters.

Regardless of whether people did manage to experience a sense of intimacy and connection in their casual sexual encounters, it was important to them to seek it, even only as a justification for sex. This would seem to be a requirement in a cultural context where, traditionally, there have been strong judgments about the pursuit of sexual pleasure, and where sex was considered fully justified only in association with love and marriage. Individuals, however, did seem to genuinely experience strong connections with their sexual partners even in situations in which they intuitively knew that their sexual activity might not lead to anything beyond that encounter. They also often entered these casual encounters with openness toward the possibility that they might be the beginning of longer-term connections.

In this context, an important ingredient that facilitated the creation of instant intimacy and connection was the feeling of trust in the person—trust that allowed the casual sexual partners to abandon themselves to the flow of sex, let their bodies discover each other, and experience pleasure. If something else happened afterward, if a more involved relationship ensued, it was important for them to construct this partner as trustworthy from the beginning. If nothing else developed, they could at least retain the memory of an intense, passionate, and fulfilling encounter within an environment of trust.

Placing blind trust in a stranger might seem, by all practical standards, inherently risky. Yet, participants narrated cases in which they were able to manage their trust—and all that came with it—and their wariness of risk in ways that suggested that they were willing to walk a line of "informed uncertainty." When they were proficient in this task, they often knew when to stop and change course as the risks began to exceed what seemed comfortable to them. Arturo offered one example of this type of risk management, as he reported having become capable of trusting casual partners and pursuing intimacy with them while also keeping an eye out for red flags that told him when to stop.

Arturo had begun having sex with men at age sixteen. Since then he had engaged in many casual interactions, mostly with men whom he met on the street. Several of these partners were married and had wives, and at least a couple of them had attempted to have unprotected anal sex with him without disclosing that they were HIV-positive. In these casual relationships, his trust would hold up to the point that he became fearful of his safety, both physical and health related. This simultaneous emphasis on trust and caution had helped him avoid having anal sex without condoms in situations that he later realized would have been quite risky.

His ability to stay safe failed only in situations in which he had not managed to measure the risk because his trust was combined with other feelings and emotions that he perceived were also predominant at that moment. Explaining why he had unprotected sex with a man he had just met, Arturo said he felt safe with him. "The other thing was mostly my trust in him and—I place myself in a situation of *valemadrismo* [not caring], and on the other hand *ni modo, si pasa ni modo* [acceptance of fate]. . . . And after this guy, I entered a period of *ligue y autocastigo* [cruising and self-punishment]." During that period in his life, Arturo lost perspective on how to use his ability to react to any red flags of potential risk in casual sexual encounters in which he trusted his partner.

Similarly to what happened in long-term relationships, asking for a condom during a casual sexual encounter had the potential for creating mistrust and prompting rejection. Absent in this case, however, were concerns about cheating and fidelity. For instance, in a conversation with a group of homosexual men in a café, one of them said that when he asked for a condom, men tended to think that he was suspicious and not that he wanted to protect them. In response to this comment, another man added that, indeed, when someone had asked him to use a condom in a casual sexual encounter, he had felt offended. When I asked him why, he said that he did not know fully, but that it was as if his sexual partner did not trust him or was suspicious that he was HIV-positive. He was offended about his partner's assumption that he could be HIV-positive. Yet, was that not the message that was commonly put forward in HIV prevention programs in Mexico—that individuals should assume that every sexual partner is HIV-positive and proceed to have safe sex? This man also said that in the encounter to which he was referring, he never considered that his sexual partner might be asking him to put on a condom in order to protect him. In other words, he fully trusted that his partner, about whom he knew nothing, could not be HIV-positive.

In this context, a partner who directly requested condom use and safe sex tended to generate distrust and concern, which is the opposite of what is needed for effective HIV prevention. Mistrust emerged most readily when participants interpreted a request for protection as an indicator of promiscuity or HIV-positive status, or suspicion of the same. Actions that from the point of view of HIV prevention should denote responsibility, caring, and trust meant instead that a person was sexually experienced, promiscuous, risky, and thus not to be trusted. They could also indicate that the person asking for protection was suspicious, cold, and lacking the ability to trust the other and establish intimacy. The irony is that, unlike Arturo, participants were often not able to see the red flags of potential risk after deciding that they trusted a partner. This happened even though the trust was frequently sustained by inaccurate assessments—by the perception that the person was nice, clean, serious, or sexually modest or inexperienced—and when the very same "trustworthy" partner was willingly engaging in unprotected intercourse without reservation. It is ironic that, regarding HIV risk and prevention, individuals often ended up trusting someone when they should not, and not trusting someone else whom they should.

Another irony is that when individuals put on a condom or requested one, or when they stuck to only having safe sex or nonpenetrative sex, their sexual partners commonly complied. Although some Guadalajarans reported encountering sexual partners who refused to use protection, in most cases they had witnessed docility once protection and safety from HIV were introduced. All that it took was for one of the sexual partners to take the initiative. Even the man in the previous section who was offended when a partner requested a condom ended up complying and using one during the sexual encounter. I must note that "asking for safe sex or protection" ought to be interpreted broadly to encompass requests made with verbal language, bodily language, or a combination of both.

Nevertheless, lack of refusal by sexual partners did not guarantee that at least one of them would take the initiative to bring safe sex or condoms into the context of a sexual encounter. This was particularly true for women who had learned never to initiate sex or to take the initiative during a sexual encounter. Individuals would likely not take the initiative to ask for protection if they feared that their partner would refuse or react negatively, or if the action could be read as a sign of their own sexual experience, promiscuity, or even HIV status.

A common frustration among participants who emphasized the practice of safe sex was their feeling that they often found themselves having to be the ones taking the initiative to request safety. One participant, for instance, reported being worried about the fact that out of ten sexual partners only one had asked for the use of condoms during sex. Eugenio, similarly, complained that sexual partners did not ask about condoms, even at the moment in which a condom was imminently needed. Eugenio said, "I have not met anyone who rejects condoms, but I have always been the one who has suggested it and who has had the condom. Curiously, I have never found anyone who says, 'I have condoms' or 'Here is my condom.'"

"But they have accepted it," I commented.

"Yes, which indicates that they do know [about the need for them] already. But believe me that it has been disappointing to be in bed with someone who wants to have sex and who never asks whether you have condoms. When I see that things are quite advanced and there is no question asked about condoms, I feel terribly disillusioned, to the point of losing my arousal. I say, 'How is it possible!'" Eugenio was the sole participant reporting that the absence of a request for condoms made him "lose his arousal," as the opposite scenario was more common—that condoms were seen to represent a loss of satisfaction. The implication of this docility in terms of HIV prevention is that ensuring that at least one partner takes the initiative to introduce safety and protection in a sexual encounter might be enough to also ensure that the encounter progresses without HIV transmission risk.

ARE YOU REALLY GOING TO STAY WITH ME?
OTHER COMPETING NEEDS

In order for the initiative to ask for condoms and safe sex to be present, at least one of the sexual partners ought to have HIV prevention in mind as the initiation of a sexual encounter approached, or during sex itself, regardless of whether this was communicated or not to the partner or partners. However, this clearly was not always the case. Some participants lacked a deep-seated awareness about HIV, in particular those who had little knowledge about the disease or no sense that the health problem pertained to them. For others, however, the problem was that HIV prevention occupied a lower rank in comparison to other priorities connected with the relationship between the partners or with the situation in which the specific sexual encounter was occurring.

This competition among priorities was evident in several of the cases that I already discussed, particularly when a desire to be with a partner overrode any other needs, or when participants felt a strong need to adopt a role or protect an identity or reputation. Yet, participants reported several other reasons why HIV prevention would fall off the map once it competed with other, more powerful needs. Even well-informed and motivated participants occasionally did not consider the need for HIV prevention when they were strongly preoccupied with a different relational issue. Sometimes they realized this lack of awareness only when they found themselves analyzing the encounter as they conversed with me.

Lola, who was having a relationship with a married man, provided one example of this phenomenon. Lola had extensive sexual experience and felt confident about her ability to negotiate sex and to use protection against HIV and practice safe sex. She talked openly about the topic of safe sex with male coworkers and friends and felt that her strong personality aided her in this regard. She also reported having no problems taking the initiative during sex with men. Discussing the use of protection, she said, "I am not very passive and I usually take the initiative, and I can say whether I do or do not want what is about to happen." In previous relationships, she was able to have conversations about contraception prior to sex and had provided condoms for her partners.

She never considered using condoms with her current partner, who was married to another woman, because when their relationship started they were very concerned about his marital problems and wondering what it meant for them to become a couple under those circumstances. Lola said that "this dominated our emotional space at that moment, more than any physical issue. We didn't think about it until later. In fact, I am expecting a baby. And [when we found out] we became fearful and [said] '*chin*' [fuck]! We have thought about taking an AIDS test, both of us. Although we have an idea [that we are both negative], you can never be sure whether you are healthy or not." Lola's partner claimed to not be having any sexual relations with his wife and to be in the process of divorcing her.

"You never thought about the need [for condoms]?" I asked.

"No, I tell you that based on these other *rollos* [issues] that we had, the difficulties of what we were doing, [our preoccupation was] 'OK, what's going to happen next?' And you start bonding emotionally with this person and you are far more worried about other things. 'Are you really going to stay with me? Or what are you going to do?'"

Lola had mentioned earlier that protection against AIDS was very important, so I asked her how she dealt with the discrepancy. Lola answered, "Yes, but I did not consider this to be a casual relationship. There was already more of a relationship with this person." Like other participants, Lola associated condom use more readily with casual relations and less with longer-term relations in which partners already knew each other and trusted each other. Lola then added, "I don't know, it was irresponsibility on my part," recognizing that there was some inconsistency between her ideas and her decision. "You don't think about it."

Lola then told me about the role that she took with her male coworkers, who were somewhat fascinated by having her work alongside them as a truck dealer. When they talked about their unprotected sexual adventures, she was quick to educate them about AIDS. She also talked to them about their double standards regarding male and female sexuality and questioned their inability to stick to monogamy (which she believed women more readily did). She concluded, "I can reflect more when I see someone else's case rather than my own."

Julio, in a different example, talked about the first time he had sex. He was twenty years old and went to one of Guadalajara's largest shopping malls with his sister. He was already aware of his attraction to men but had never had any sexual interaction. At the mall, he split up from his sister and went into a store to buy a stuffed animal. "In the store I saw a young guy who turned to look at me. We were exchanging glances, and he proposed that we go and have sex. I said yes. I did not use any protection, because it was my first time, I was very badly informed, and everything else, it was my first experience. We went to his house and had sex."

In part, his not considering protection against HIV was related to a lack of information. Julio learned much more about HIV soon after, and a group of newly acquired friends gave him some brochures published by COESIDA, the local government AIDS agency. However, the other key words in this account are "everything else." Julio used these words to indicate that there was much else going on for him at that moment when he was about to have his first sexual encounter. HIV concerns did not figure highly in the list of issues that he was negotiating, both with himself and with his partner. He was there to discover sex, and HIV had no room in his thoughts at that moment.

SEX VERSUS THE HIV EDUCATORS' VIEW OF SEX

It is troublesome that in their creation of health promotion messages, Mexican AIDS educators—like their counterparts elsewhere in the world—constructed a version of sex that ignored some of the practice's most central relational aspects. The AIDS education version of sex appears particularly inadequate if we consider the many personal meanings that people attach to sex, as well as what Mitchell (1988: 102) describes as the "relational issues and struggles" that are played out within its realm. Such issues, the same author explains, are shaped by a "sense of being 'driven' . . . [which provides] a natural vocabulary for dramatic expressions of dynamics involving conflict, anxiety, compulsion, escape, passion and rapture" (103). Through dramatic expressions, "[s]exuality takes on all the intensity of passionate struggles to make contact, to engage, to overcome isolation and exclusion" (103). Crossing, along with someone else, from everyday life into the realm where sexual energy and expression dominate opens the door to experiences and sensations that contribute enormously to individuals' knowledge about themselves, others around them, and the world in general.

The stories told in this chapter suggest it is unrealistic to assume that, in order to accomplish the laudable goal of sexual health, individuals should fully rationalize sex and emphasize "self-interest" over everything else, and in turn sacrifice much of what sex gives them. Instead, the question is how healthy measures can be incorporated functionally into sex without disturbing the practice's romantic and pleasurable roles in people's relationships.

Additionally, HIV prevention work has tended to ignore that risk and risk taking—understood broadly and not just in terms of HIV or health—

constitute important ingredients that help people achieve their goals in the pursuit of connection and sexual pleasure.[11] This takes several shapes in Mexico. First, in a social environment in which transgression is often highly eroticized, perceptions of risk and danger are easily associated with sexual pleasure (Kendall 1995; Watney 1993). Second, my data suggest that people in Mexico strongly valued transcending isolation through the kind of contact with others that sex entails, and this required taking certain "good risks." Such "good risks" placed individuals on a course to achieving intimacy and pleasure, encountering others in the most personal way, validating aspects of their broader lives, and experiencing sensations of sexual passion and ecstasy that would not be available to them otherwise. To achieve these goals, individuals had to open up to the possibility of establishing a special and different connection with someone else, either casually or in the context of a long-term relationship. The inability of much HIV prevention work in Mexico, and elsewhere, to distinguish between "good risks" and "bad risks"[12] within sex—the latter referring to health and safety risks—and the tendency among public health professionals to consider all risk to be intrinsically damaging are also at the core of the incongruity between people's ideas about sex and those of public health practitioners.[13]

People's acceptance of the risks inherent in sex also implied awareness that throughout an encounter there might be interferences of many kinds—misinterpretations and disagreements between sexual partners and negative feelings and even ill intentions, which could kill the pleasure and connection and turn the event into a frustrating or traumatic experience. They knew that the sexual interaction might mean something very different to their sexual partners—for instance, whether sex was performed just for pleasure or for love—and that in the end they could suffer. In order to participate in voluntary sexual encounters, they learned to manage these potentially damaging consequences. These adults understood that the only alternative was to avoid sex and relationships altogether, which they considered the worst of all options. They were aware that some forms of risk taking constitute an intrinsic element of sex that cannot just be wiped away by health messages that aim to cleanse the practice from all risks indiscriminately.[14] As Mitchell puts it: "Because sexual excitement entails such a powerful physiological response, and because the full emotional responsiveness of each other, in contrast to the physical presence of that other, can never be taken for granted, sexual encounters always contain elements of risk and implicit drama. Will the other be there, and in what way? When sexuality approaches true intimacy, an unritualized search for open emotional exchange, one places oneself in the other's hands (the double meaning intended)" (1988: 107).

In this view of sex, individuals place themselves in the position of surrender, both to their own and to the other's sexual desire. They experience the other as "very powerful, and thus very dangerous," and they seek, through sexual release, "reassurance against abandonment and betrayal" (Mitchell 1988: 108). They engage in "the dramatic play between the visible and the hidden, the available and the withheld, the longing and revelation" (108), in building sexual passion, and they enter the world of the erotic through the "creation of [an alternative] realm, in which one's pleasure is not hostage to the wishes and values of the other" (113). Accomplishing all of this—which is consistent with the views of sex, passion, and intimacy of participants in my study—carries considerable personal risks that are accepted as necessary ingredients of sex.[15] These forms of interaction also represent relational (and, to some degree, developmental) functions of sex, which have little to do with the sanitized public health version of the practice commonly contained in HIV prevention messages.

A REFORM OF HIV PREVENTION EDUCATION

Rather than continue attempts to make sex more planned and rational, HIV educators in Mexico might need to pause, reconsider the premises of their current efforts, consider the strategies used by Mexicans who are successful at implementing HIV prevention measures, and begin to define new educational strategies.[16] Much of this work would likely prove to be somewhat counterintuitive. Instead of absolute self-control, people might need to learn how to continue highlighting sexual passion and abandonment without giving up the ability to recognize warning signs for unwanted health risks. Instead of simply being taught how to plan ahead and verbally communicate with their partners, individuals would need to identify how they carry out negotiations about other aspects of sex and relationships and apply those same skills to staying safe throughout sexual encounters.

This is not a call to abandon the dissemination of basic information about HIV transmission, to stop teaching people how to use condoms, or to ignore the importance of communication about sex in long-term relationships. Those ingredients are needed, but they ought to be integrated within the totality of meanings—social, relational, personal—that Mexicans attach to sex (Parker and Carballo 1990; Parker, Herdt, and Carballo 1991). In other words, the knowledge and skills needed to carry out

HIV prevention properly need to be contextualized within the reality of people's sexual lives, with all their wonderful moments and also their complications. This means, for instance, that rather than attempting to convince everyone that condoms are the norm and are quite erotic, it might be more productive to recognize that they indeed frequently constitute a barrier to intimacy and pleasure and to emphasize that nonetheless they are a necessary measure to prevent potentially deadly diseases such as AIDS. Such bluntness might open the door for a more honest discussion about how condoms can realistically be included in penetrative sex, about the negative meanings that they have acquired in terms of trust and love, and about the medically sound steps needed before dispensing with them in relationships.

This integration might mean, as well, abandoning the linear and static model of sexual behavior that informs much HIV prevention work in Mexico—the sense that information leads to awareness and motivation, which in turn lead automatically to safe behavior. In this model, once a person decides to practice safe sex or use protection, the process is implicitly perceived to be stable and irreversible. The reality of sexual behavior and risk for many people is not so simple. Even those who are reasonably effective at protecting themselves and others find themselves in situations and relationships in which these abilities become threatened or impaired.[17]

Furthermore, because some of the causes of risk do not directly depend on individuals' motivation or desires but are subject to relationship dynamics, and because relational dynamics are embedded in a social and cultural context that strongly influences them, a focus on longer-term changes and structural changes is also badly needed. These kinds of goals could be tied to efforts to reduce inequality, discrimination, poverty, and other social ills found to create HIV risk (Parker 1996b; Parker, Easton, and Klein 2000; Díaz 1998, 2000). Such efforts could ultimately aim to foster a social context with greater sexual equality, where people can live their sexuality more freely, where women can become stronger actors in their relationships with men, where men can become more humble about their roles within those relationships, and where those who are excluded from a dominant core of "normality" can achieve acceptance. These are large, utopian goals that are not likely to be achieved as a result of HIV prevention work alone. HIV prevention work in Mexico may play a role in working toward their realization, however, without losing sight of the more urgent, immediate need of fighting the epidemic.

Promoting Self-reflection

Most immediately, the kind of contextualization that seems needed would require efforts that help people personalize what they know about AIDS, consider ways in which such knowledge can be integrated into their sex lives, analyze how prevention measures might play out in the context of their sexual and emotional relationships, understand situations that could make them vulnerable, recognize social and cultural constraints that limit their ability to stay safe, and envision strategies to seek sexual fulfillment while also protecting their and their sexual partners' health. The range of possible answers to the question, "what might work for you?" might be quite broad. For instance, some individuals might conclude that they can indeed introduce safe sex and protection silently, by adopting certain bodily positions during sex. They might also realize that, given a partner's refusal to use a condom or avoid doing a certain sexual act, they would need to "kill the moment." Others, however, might conclude that any request for safety or protection would be greeted with anger and even with violence. Their strategizing might require asking themselves whether change can occur within the relationship and whether the relationship is worth maintaining.

Additionally, as individuals and groups reflect about these questions, they might also realize ways in which the social and cultural system does not support prevention. Such realization could be used to help them acquire a role as social actors who can help construct new sexual mores, educate future generations of Mexicans differently, and demand more supportive social services as citizens (see Paiva 2000).

Promoting self-reflection as a tool in HIV prevention work requires considerable flexibility from the educators. Despite reasonable efforts on the part of the HIV educators, a possible answer to questions about whether people indeed want to avoid the potential of HIV infection could in the end be "no." If the response is negative, at least room would be created for individuals and couples to examine why the potential risk of receiving HIV, or passing it on to others, is not important to them. If they want to stay safe but are failing, they can analyze how risk is created in specific situations, in encounters with particular partners or types of partners. Through reflection, they could begin to understand how HIV prevention needs compete with other personal and relational needs, as well as what factors influence—personally or socially speaking—their participation in sexual contexts that involve high risks.

By emphasizing self-reflection, I do not mean to suggest a need for therapy or for what HIV educators sometimes call "case management." For a majority of those in my study, the more immediate personal need seemed to simply be more opportunities for guided discussion. Some might also require some practical support, perhaps in the form of social services, in order to initiate broader personal changes. Overall they needed to access the same kinds of solidarity that seemed to exist in other spheres of everyday life, such as in women's support for each other in confronting the realities of their relationships with men, or the support that *homosexuales* provided each other in enacting their stigmatized identities.[18]

Balancing Cultural Change

Perhaps the most difficult challenge is for HIV prevention educators to reconcile their preconceived ideas about possible future directions for Mexican sexuality—their ideas about cultural patterns that they think ought to change—with people's desire not to lose culturally accepted forms of interaction that contribute to sexual pleasure. These can include power differentials and voluntary forms of domination and submission, or the reliance on spontaneity and nonverbal language to enact unplanned sexual encounters. Mexicans were also wary about the possible undermining of their orientation to the collectivity and their personal styles of interaction as a result of the promotion of individuality, rationality, control, and self-regulation.

In envisioning cultural and social changes, and even structural changes, my findings strongly suggest that caution is needed before swiftly embarking on a kind of "modernization" that would make Mexican sexuality become fully like the version commonly proposed by the dominant medicalized, global AIDS discourse. I am suggesting here that the assumptions of globalization might need to be turned upside down to consider that Mexican sexual culture, and that of other parts of the so-called developing world, contain features that might benefit the populations of rich Western countries. Such change in premises would in effect transform the globalization of ideas and practices about sexuality and HIV prevention into a two-way street.

My assessment is that Mexican cultural expressions such as *albures,* sexual silence, and the local emphasis on seduction and nonverbal communication, as well as local scripts about abandonment, loss of control, surrender, sexual passion, and spontaneity, could be used as tools in HIV prevention work. Currently, most of these aspects of Mexican sexual culture are deemed to be barriers rather than resources, even when they do not inherently contradict the goal of sexual health. Their inclusion in HIV prevention work is related to what Freudenberg described as "[identifying] elements of the culture that can support prevention and risk reduction, and [helping] populations to question other elements that increase risk" (1990: 596).

Finally, in promoting cultural change, I would warn against regressive structural change strategies that could increase sexual repression. The public health profession has a history of reliance on the regulation of human activities and on prohibition as a means to achieve its goals, sometimes even when those strategies inadequately limit individual freedoms. The temptation to use policy and legislation to repress is always particularly strong in relation to sexual issues, because they are so often controversial and already negatively judged.

Adapting Existing Models

Self-reflection is a feature included in a number of existing educational models, from Bandura's (1977, 1986) "self-efficacy," to "self-empowerment," to Freire's (1988) "consciousness raising" (or *conscientização*, the original word in Portuguese), to "community organizing" (Minkler 1997; Altman 1994; Wohlfeiler 1997) and "community mobilization" (Parker 1996b). However, although these concepts share some commonalities, they also suggest considerable differences with regard to the goals of reflection as defined by the varied ideological persuasions of their proponents. My analysis suggests that using them in Mexico would require some adaptation.

For instance, in considering "self-efficacy" or "self-empowerment," one would need to be wary of the individualistic assumptions that accompany these concepts and that could be incompatible with Mexicans' collectivist orientation. In considering "consciousness raising," avoiding predefined answers to open-ended questions would be crucial, as the principles of the method are otherwise defeated. A model of "community organizing" should ask who decides what changes are important, whether the directions considered are locally relevant, and how long it would take before positive effects are realized or before attending to HIV risks becomes central to the organizing agenda.

The overall advantages offered by programs that are based on collective self-reflection, however, are nicely illustrated by a program targeting low-income students attending night school in São Paulo, Brazil (Paiva 2000). This program, based on Freire's educational method (1988), used various creative techniques to generate discussion. The goal was to transform participants into "sexual subjects" (Parker, Barbosa, and Aggleton

2000), meaning here individuals with the ability to question gender scripts that regulate heterosexual relationships in Brazil, and who can envision how to counteract oppressive forces that limit their ability to stay safe. Students analyzed how the "sociocultural context regulates their sexual lives," and "how social forces can frustrate individuals' intentions to practice safe sex and control their own sexual lives" (Parker, Barbosa, and Aggleton 2000: 219). They also discussed sex education, sexual roles and identities, sexual scripts, eroticism and the meanings of sex, and the conditions that prevailed within their own sexual contexts. The most immediate goal was to provide tools for HIV safety. The larger goal was to turn participants into "citizens"—that is, social agents who could act on behalf of their groups and communities and, for example, demand free condoms, improved sexual education in local clinics, and better treatment by medical personnel who had disregarded their needs.

This program seems close to the kind that would help contextualize HIV prevention measures for Mexicans such as those in my study, particularly if it contained an additional ingredient: considering how power differentials and current gender roles may contribute to the mutual search for pleasure when neither partner is attempting to damage, or take advantage of, the other. Like Parker, I believe that such a program could be a part of a larger effort, because "no single intervention, nor even integrated set of interventions, can in fact be adequate in responding to the risks posed by HIV/AIDS" (Parker 1996a: 63).

An advantage offered by this kind of program is that it simultaneously works at the level of individuals and couples in need of safety (the more immediate goal) and promotes larger cultural and social changes (a longer-term goal). The work could be framed overall by the search for social equality and health. In the case that concerns me, the task implies working with the full complexity of many of the issues that I have discussed, including sexual identities and roles, sexual socialization and education, sexual ideologies, sexual communication, and the interplay between power, domination, oppression, and desire, and then tying these issues to HIV prevention.

(

There is no doubt that the social responses to AIDS and HIV prevention have constituted important forces shaping recent discourses of sexuality in Mexico. But, despite their transformative role, HIV prevention programs so far have not led to an in-depth discussion, grounded in lived sexual experience, about the many points of connection between sex, sexuality, gender relations, social inequality, health, modernization, and social and cultural change. This absence leads me to pursue one final question: Given the historical evolution of ideas and practices related to sexuality in Mexico in the twentieth century, how can we expect sex and sexuality in Mexico to change as the twenty-first century begins to unfold?

Conclusion   **New Opportunities in a New Century**

THE QUESTION OF CHANGE

Practically everyone in Guadalajara with whom I spoke about sexual matters had something to say about the need for cultural change. The nature, quality, and depth of the changes desired varied considerably among individuals, but those who were willing to discuss sexuality seemed to agree on one idea: that Mexican sexual culture contains some values and customs that they considered to be old-fashioned and obsolete.

Questions about cultural change have flavored much of the discussion and debate about sexual matters in Mexico throughout the twentieth century, especially as growing numbers of Mexicans became exposed to alternative ideas arriving from the north. Members of every generation of twentieth-century Mexicans have questioned some of their parents' ideas and practices about sexuality, family, and gender relations. In the process they have been confronted with deciding what they want for themselves, whether to accept values that they believed to prevail in what they often regarded as the "more advanced" parts of the world, or whether to create something new that is more uniquely Mexican. Their reflections have been flavored also by the diversity of positions taken by those in Mexico who have chosen to submit their ideas for consideration within the realm of public opinion. These people include those who have openly promoted change and questioned what they see as obsolete ways of thinking, as well as their counterparts—those who have felt threatened by change and have feared that emerging values would contribute to the dissolution of an imagined cultural core of *mexicanidad* and "sound Mexican morality."

In Guadalajara, in the last decade of the twentieth century, the desire for change was most clearly present among those who thought that prevalent cultural values regarding sex and sexuality were oppressive to them, and thus detrimental to their lives. Among them were women who suffered from their unequal status in their relationships with men. Recognizing the greater freedom that society granted men to enact their sexual desires, these women often debated whether to pursue a similar degree of freedom for themselves or instead to make men understand a need for restraint, or both. Some men also questioned the inequality between men and women. These were men who were beginning to realize that their own privileged status reduced women's potential for growth and fulfillment, and who struggled with how to be fairer while also protecting their own sense of manhood.

A similar desire for change was evident in the comments by *gays, homosexuales,* and *lesbianas,* men and women who were becoming increasingly tired of the social pressures that forced them to hide, and of the fear of being discovered and rejected. For them the question of change included debate about how to make the best of their situation and how to promote social acceptance of their lifestyles and identities, but without disrupting their sense of belonging in Mexican society or creating a separate gay society.

Hope for change in the management of sexuality in Mexico also came into view when Mexicans, young and old, complained about having discovered their sexual desires in isolation and without much guidance, in ways that made them feel immensely lonely. They wished that adults had given them honest and open advice, especially when they first began experiencing sexual desires. As adults, they were making inroads by holding increasingly open conversations about sexuality-related topics, but they were simultaneously careful not to disrupt prevailing expectations of silence and complicity in dealing with sexual difference and of discretion and respect within their own social and family networks.

The need for change was, as well, a main thrust of the efforts of HIV educators. These practitioners aimed to prepare individuals to enact their sexual relations differently, with more openness and acceptance of their sexual desires but also with a strong emphasis on the protection of their health, greater individual control, and a certain personal power to look after their own interests. Their work was an example of the modernizing projects of professionals and health activists in Mexico—psychologists, sexologists, doctors and nurses, public health workers, feminists, gay and lesbian activists, and family-planning counselors—who have focused on drawing connections between sex and individual well-being and have been confronted by the opposition of conservatives invested in preventing change.

For most people, however, how to effect change regarding these and other issues related to sexuality was not always immediately clear. In each of these examples a person's desire for change did not automatically translate into clear-cut strategies for easy or direct implementation. Change often implied the potential for severely negative personal consequences for those who decided to pursue it in their own lives. Fear of those consequences, plus the pervasiveness of cultural scripts that supported the status quo, frequently limited individuals' ability to envision how to remedy the inequalities from which they suffered.

Furthermore, it was not uncommon for affected individuals to become active participants in the replication of the social conditions that oppressed them in the first place. When they did, it was often precisely because they had internalized norms and values that curtailed their ability to confront the status quo directly. Instead, they developed indirect strategies that gave them something close to what they wanted, perhaps imperfectly but without confrontation.

For instance, women who desired a status more equal to that of their male partners sometimes used negotiation strategies with those partners that perpetuated their subservience. Instead of confronting their male partners directly, they obtained some limited power by playing out roles that seemed consistent, at least superficially, with social expectations of submission and dependence. They were forced to engage in careful manipulations that guaranteed that their partners' sense of manhood, and their self-image, stayed as intact as possible. That way, they reduced the potential for conflict and helped their male partners save face.

They sought the solidarity of other women who understood their situations and appeals for change but were also careful to ensure that their own efforts, and the support provided by others, did not disrupt their relationships with men to the point that those relationships became threatened. And they were often suspicious of the more organized strategies advanced by the local *movimiento feminista,* which was commonly thought to be too radical and to seek a kind of confrontation and separatism that many perceived to be counterproductive.

A similar argument could be made about the middle-class Guadala-jaran *gays, homosexuales,* and *lesbianas,* many of whom led double lives in order to avoid potential social rejection. These men and women commonly believed that Mexican society would change and begin to accept homosexuality when the visibility of heterosexually acting homosexuals increased. But they rarely took steps to disclose their same-sex attraction to those who were close to them, out of fear of negative responses and the potential disruption of their most precious and tight connections. Overall, they were also opposed to organized efforts to confront *homofobia,* the formation of a Mexican gay and lesbian social movement, and the creation of gay-specific institutions and neighborhoods. They feared that any such strategies would result in isolation and in unwarranted conflict with their families and nonhomosexual friends and colleagues. Instead, these men and women were often willing to play by the rules of self-imposed silence as a way to ensure veiled social tolerance.

Despite those limitations, there were signs in Guadalajara and Mexico that cultural change was occurring, sometimes at a very rapid pace, and that some of the inequalities that prevailed regarding the status of women and sexual minorities were being addressed and debated. There were also signs, however, that change in social attitudes about some sexual matters was incredibly slow, as in the case of abortion and women's reproductive rights. In the pages that follow, I will examine the factors that seemed to determine differences in the pace of change, as well as the selective nature of the changes that were taking place.

CULTURAL HYBRIDITY AND CHANGE

I have argued that the evolution of ideas about sex and sexuality in Mexico has been characterized by the hybridization of Mexican sexual culture: new values and ideas are in constant interplay with those that preceded them, because the former are not always regarded as a replacement for the latter. In this context, cultural change is strongly flavored by the adaptations that are needed for new and old to coexist. New values and practices need to be made consistent with those traditions that Mexican society values as part of a perceived cultural core. Nevertheless, the cultural core also requires some constant revision in order to stay current and to fit within the logics of cultural innovation. In this sense, the idea of an untouched cultural core is an illusion.

Giddens has argued that the need for these reinterpretations of tradition indicates that the coexistence of old and new that is implied in the concept of cultural hybridity is a fallacy. "Justified tradition is tradition in sham clothing," says Giddens, and he contends that the revision of tradition is a sign of the kind of reflexivity that characterizes modernity (1990: 38). Instead of the coexistence of tradition and modernity, he suggests that the constant examination of social practices in a modern society ultimately changes the role of tradition as the "inertia of habit" is overcome. The path toward modernity, and the abandonment of tradition, are then considered to be inevitable.

In regard to sexuality in Mexico, Giddens's view supports that of Mexican authors such as Monsiváis (1990, 1993), Bellinghausen (1990), and Bautista (1990), whose writings suggest that modern ideas about sex and sexuality are winning out over traditional values. These authors see the signs of modernity in the existence of cultural expressions such as Mexican feminism, a local gay and lesbian movement, and the emergence of a local sexual revolution in the 1970s. However, not everybody has emphasized or accepted this view. Other authors writing about sexuality in Mexico have noted the contrary by focusing on what they believe are living expressions of traditional Mexican sexuality—such as gender roles and machismo—which has led them to conclude that Mexican sexuality remains mostly dominated by old, traditional values. Carrier (1995), for instance, equated the absence of U.S.-style gay communities and institutions, and the fact that homosexual men in Mexico still recognize and emphasize gender roles in their sexual relations, with an absence of widespread modern homosexuality.

My work suggests that Mexicans such as those in my study were neither fully abandoning what they consider to be traditional values nor accepting them as an immutable given. Instead, they seemed to be engaged in contrasting the ideas that were inculcated in them when they were growing up with newer ideas to which they are now exposed as adults. In these personal reflections, however, Mexicans seemed to strongly favor the search for ways to adopt contemporary values while at the same time respecting core traditions (or at least appearing to respect them). This respect translates, in my opinion, into the presence of mixed attitudes that might appear to contain contradictions but that individuals managed to hold with some coherence within their own worldview. This last feature is a characteristic of cultural modernity with respect to sexuality in Mexico that does not fit well with Giddens's more general views on modernity.

In this sense, my work and conclusions are consistent with those of scholars such as Gutmann (1996) and LeVine (1993), whose empirical data repeatedly suggest that Mexicans desire new forms of social interaction but also greatly respect the rules and proscriptions imposed by traditional values, roles, and identities.[1] My work is also consistent with that of authors such as Prieur (1998), who shows that even for the people adopting traditional customs, new ideas are beginning to affect their interpretations about their identities and their practices.[2]

Many Mexicans appeared to have mastered the accommodations required in the interplay between new and old—a mastery that would be hard to account for if we pay attention to only one side of the coin, the survival of old values or the adoption of new ones. I would argue against observing the nature of cultural change in Mexican sexuality through a lens that allows exclusively for the analysis of surviving expressions of Mexican tradition, because the only logical conclusion from the sole use of such a lens would be that sexual culture in Mexico remains premodern. Similarly, I would also argue against paying excessive or exclusive attention to the strong desire for and adoption of ideas and practices arriving from the outside. Mexican sexual culture would then appear to be fully on a path toward "Americanization" and toward the abandonment of ingrained traditions. And finally, although I clearly advocate analyses that attempt to account for the interplay between the two, I would also argue that such analyses must be done carefully in order to avoid, as García Canclini warns us, automatically developing the view that contemporary culture in Mexico is skipping modernity to become conveniently postmodern. In García Canclini's opinion we need to resist the temptation to read postmodernism in the "pastiche and bricolage" (1995: 6) that might at first glance appear to characterize contemporary Latin American cultures.

Current views about "globalization" provide a different lens to examine the tension between new and old. A number of examples throughout this book attest to signs of the effects of globalization on Mexican urban sexual culture, particularly in terms of the instantaneous access, most predominantly among the middle and upper classes, to ideas and expressions of culture from many different places (most readily from the United States).[3] With the advent of the Internet, which was becoming popularized around the time that my study ended, and with the constant bombardment of images and ideas in the mass media, Guadalajarans are as much a part of the global phenomena of sexuality as their counterparts in many other cities around the world.[4]

However, as we also saw, ideas and practices that are accessed through globalization are usually reinterpreted before they are integrated into Guadalajarans' ideology and lifestyles. In this regard, notions of locality continue to be of clear importance, even in the context of rapid change and globalization.[5]

Two interesting examples of this tension between globalization and locality are offered by the global proliferation of a particular style of gay dance clubs and the recent fad of male strip shows for women (further popularized by the film *The Full Monty*). Both of these expressions of sexual culture have emerged in Guadalajara. Any foreign visitor patronizing these places could easily characterize the decor, the rules of interaction, and the cultural expressions as being basically the same in Guadalajara as they are in any other metropolis. Yet, if they paid closer attention, they would also begin to recognize the reinterpretations, sometimes subtle, sometimes rather obvious, that give a local flavor to the very same practices. My analysis in Mexico suggests that, rather than aiming to strictly separate the global from the local in relation to sex and sexuality, contemporary research in places like Mexico benefits from the simultaneous consideration of both and from a certain flexibility of interpretation that accounts for the interplay between the two. What results from foreign influence and what is developed locally are then accounted as parts of processes of cultural change within which the two are considerably entwined.

CULTURAL TRANSFORMATION AND PUBLIC OPINION

Among participants in my study, much of their explicit contrasting of ideas about sexual matters appeared to be prompted by their exposure to social debate and to ideas about alternative sexual identities and lifestyles shown by the mass media, particularly television and radio. For men and women in Guadalajara, exposure to images and ideas that were new to them triggered a fair amount of thinking. They provided them with tools to question their own values, including those that they had internalized during their socialization, which their parents probably hoped would fully inform their views about sex and sexuality as adults. As a result, most ended up developing personal positions on a variety of issues that allowed them to participate in social debate (and, by extension, to contribute their two cents to the formation of public opinion). For example, a debate about AIDS on a popular nighttime talk show had the power to trigger enormous response and further discussion among its audience; the tribulations of an abandoned wife who refused to accept the expectations of her role, as was the case of the character of María Inés in *Mirada de mujer*, would become daily office or school talk among those who watched this popular *telenovela*. The availability of discussion about sex, sexuality, and gender in the mass media made these acceptable topics for conversation.

In this sense, the mass media have become a core space for the shaping of public opinion about sexual matters in Mexico. Social actors of all kinds have learned that participating in this core is extremely important to disseminate their positions and to place them on the table for public discussion. The list includes progressive Mexican social movements, such as the feminist groups and gay and lesbian groups, which have exerted some of their most effective influence by presenting their positions through the media. Even in a context of opposition to, and sometimes social condemnation of, the work of these groups, they manage to find spaces within the media where they can present alternative viewpoints directly to a broad audience.

These groups used the media in addition to other, more traditional organizing tactics and political advocacy. Generally speaking, participants in my study felt opposed to these groups and saw them and their tactics as "too radical." In their indiscriminate disregard of progressive social movements, these middle-class Guadalajarans failed to recognize that, through the media, the groups provided viewpoints that would otherwise be totally absent in public debate about sexuality-related topics. In the case with which I am most familiar, the small movement promoting gay and lesbian rights, the leaders of local groups, because of their power to speak in the media, were instrumental in opposing regressive or oppressive policies and had gained access to local politicians, thus also contributing to the promotion of change within the realm of politics, which is the topic of the next section.

THE REALM OF POLITICS

In 2000, Mexico experienced a dramatic change in its political system. The election of Vicente Fox Quesada to the presidency marked the end of the PRI's seventy-year regime and the first time that PAN, the conservative party, obtained presidential power. The process leading to this change, however, was well under way at the time of my study. By that point, the PAN had already won several state governorships and mayoral races. Jalisco elected a PAN governor and Guadalajara a PAN mayor in 1994. At the time, because of the generally conservative orientation of the Panistas, the increasing political power of this party was raising concerns among those promoting progressive changes in the arena of sex and sexuality.

In Jalisco, however, despite some policy flops concerning gender and sexuality issues that seriously backfired—such as an initial attempt to prohibit female governmental employees from wearing *minifaldas* (miniskirts) in public offices—the PAN also took some pragmatic measures. For instance, the leaders of local AIDS NGOs feared that the PAN would greatly reduce, or eliminate altogether, the local COESIDA, the state governmental office on AIDS. They were opposed to that outcome even though they had constantly protested the ineffective work of that office under the PRI state governments. Instead of limiting it, the new government appointed a progressive doctor to head it—a doctor who had previously participated in community-based AIDS work locally. In her negotiations with the new governor, the new head of COESIDA managed to form a progressive team that was now composed mostly of educators and activists who had previously worked or volunteered with the local AIDS NGOs, including several openly gay men. This change would have been impossible under the PRI.

Another interesting example has to do with the status of the gay discos. Past PRI city governments that were new in office had felt compelled to close them as a way to demonstrate their commitment to morality and order, only to provide them with new permits a few months later. However, as soon as the new city government took office in 1994, Pedro Preciado, the most outspoken gay leader in Guadalajara, obtained an audience with the new mayor and a commitment from him not to close the gay venues at all. As a result, the gay venues remained open and undisturbed. Someone like Preciado did not have the power to mobilize a large group of activists but could claim to speak on behalf of "the movement" and, by extension, on behalf of all Guadalajaran *homosexuales, gays,* and *lesbianas.*

The effects of these kinds of social movements within the political arena were even more evident in Mexico City, where at least one openly lesbian candidate was elected to the local legislature during the 1990s, a woman became mayor in 1999, women have been appointed to head two of the largest national political parties, and sexual orientation was included in local antidiscrimination ordinances (Medina 1999). During the 1990s, the doors were opening for the promotion of a kind of cultural change that results indirectly from the acquisition of political power by members of oppressed groups and from the creation of policy and legislation that favor equality and promote equal rights.

As the PAN's power grew, however, and the party implemented repressive policies in a number of places, the potential for regressive change seemed greater (González Ruiz 1994). But the responses to repression seemed to be increasing as well, often supported by the perception of widespread and rapid changes in public opinion about some issue, such as homosexuality. For other issues, such as abortion, changes in public opinion seemed to be rather slow. I now turn to outlining what might explain this difference.

CULTURAL LEAPS

One of the features of cultural change in Mexico that I find paradoxical is the accelerated pace at which changes occur in some aspects of culture compared with other aspects. At the level of individuals' lives, as several of the cases that I have analyzed throughout the book exemplify, some people managed to achieve fairly dramatic changes in their personal situations within short periods of time. They questioned the condition that oppressed them and moved forward toward creating new situations that allowed them to live their sexuality more freely. They often did this without becoming isolated and without abandoning aspects of Mexican social, collective life that they valued. In this sense, their paths and experiences question stereotypes about the inability of Mexicans to enact change regarding sexual issues.

Take, for example, the case of Miriam, who was able to confront her husband's homosexuality and explore more fully her sexuality with male lovers after her divorce, without suffering social stigma or negative judgment on the part of her family. Or consider Enrique, who, in scarcely three years, was able to obtain the support of his parents regarding his homosexuality, bring his male lover into the family network, live with him openly in a house owned by his father, and even request his parents' help when he and his lover were having difficulties that could potentially have resulted in violence.

The rapid nature of cultural change in some issues was even more dramatic when the change happened at a broader social level, and especially when the normalization of new ideas took place within the media to which most Mexicans had broad access. I discussed in chapter 7 the relevance of the *telenovela Mirada de mujer.* A more recent example, the *telenovela La vida en el espejo,* which aired in Mexico in 1999, offers a striking example regarding the normalization of homosexuality. One of the show's central characters, Mauricio, was the eldest son in an upper-class family in Mexico City. The audience got to see this young, masculine man negotiate the process of realizing his homosexuality, accepting it, telling his family about it, falling in love with another masculine man, and eventually bringing this man as his partner into the family. Mexicans were presented with depictions of romantic affection between these men (although not of explicit sex) and of their eventual incorporation as a couple into the family network, which would still create a stir in many places. The Mexican television network Televisión Azteca, which produced and aired this *telenovela*, seemed not to experience negative reactions from its audience or advertisers that could have led them to consider canceling the show. They broadcast it in full during prime time, five nights a week over a period of around four months, to a large national audience.

Explaining how these changes take place in Mexico is complicated, because they seem to involve the spontaneous emergence of a certain momentum that sends the country at an unpredictable moment into what I call "cultural leaps." These leaps seem to happen when different courses of thoughts and ideas coincide and turn into a strong need for local questioning and a search for alternative views. When such a need emerges, those who are invested in cultural modernization seem to rely on whatever is internationally regarded as being on the cutting edge and to then reinterpret it and adapt it to fit into a contemporary Mexican reality. In the process of reinterpretation and adaptation, those promoting change may in effect "skip over" the political struggles and social processes that validated those ideas elsewhere. They can present new views and lifestyles as epitomizing what "anyone in a more modern world would think"—as a logical and already proven outcome of social debate about the issue. In so doing, they offer what might appear to be radical images within the Mexican cultural context without having to take a gradual or more measured approach.

The introduction of new ideas in this fashion often relies on the element of surprise. In the case of the story line regarding the character of Mauricio in *La vida en el espejo*, the writers were careful to portray him during the first few weeks as a regular man who was experiencing some internal conflicts regarding his lack of interest in having sex with his girlfriend. There was some talk about impotence. There were some allusions to his being "less of a man"—perhaps even some veiled insinuations that he could be *maricón*. This was all consistent with expectations about how the issue would be handled in a context of sexual silence. But suddenly, everyone in the *telenovela*—Mauricio's girlfriend, his future male partner, the rest of his family, and, through them, the *telenovela*'s audience—was confronted with Mauricio's realization of his homosexuality and his decision to acknowledge the truth and explore what it means to acquire an identity as a Mexican *gay*.[6] Without any warning, people watching this *telenovela* were receiving images that presented an alternative view about how homosexuality could be handled in contemporary Mexico. They were forced to think about the issue as a result of gaining access to serious and open treatment of the topic—discussions that included different characters' reactions, both negative and positive, as well as Mauricio's strategies in dealing with his new life—and ultimately received a powerful message about the need to openly accept and integrate a son's homosexuality into the fabric of Mexican family life.

The enactment of this kind of cultural leap seems to build upon an already widespread attitude about the desirability for cultural modernization. The overall social acceptance of portrayals of homosexuality and of other sexual matters in *La vida en el espejo* might be connected with a widespread need to believe that the country has achieved a level of cultural sophistication that grants it membership in the modern, global world. This would be related to the pride felt by many Mexicans, particularly in the middle and upper classes, in the fact that the country is able to hold public discussion about difficult and controversial topics. In the case of homosexuality, extramarital sex, and other sexual matters, although many people might be opposed to the ideas being presented, or would choose to handle the same issues differently in their own lives, they simultaneously might cherish the presence of those ideas as an indication of Mexico's modern character.

Finally, and perhaps most significantly, the fact that these ideas and images are being presented in shows that are produced in Mexico makes a large symbolic difference. The audience realizes that these are not U.S. television characters acting in a foreign social and cultural milieu, from whom they can establish distance. Instead, in these shows viewers see Mexican characters facing contemporary issues and using strategies that the viewers can then identify as being relevant for the management of their own lives. As a result, many Mexicans are exposed to a certain cultural modeling that shows them how modern Mexicans could (and perhaps should) deal differently with sexual matters—the mistakes that they might make and the tribulations that they might face in the process, but also how they can change as they confront more honestly and directly a diversity of issues that they cannot continue to ignore.

IDEAS THAT EVOLVE SLOWLY

In direct contrast with the example presented in the last section is the lack of cultural change in matters such as abortion and a woman's right to choose. This issue has been raised in the Mexican television shows that I have analyzed. Women who decide to have an abortion also appear routinely in U.S. shows as exercising an accepted and normalized right. And yet, as in the case of those who participated in my study, many Mexicans remain unequivocally opposed to the practice.

In my discussion in chapter 7, I argued that the difference between attitudes about abortion and attitudes about contraception in Mexico is related to the role that the Mexican government played in the normalization of contraception. I also argued that the acceptance of contraception has been supported by pragmatism and the widespread belief that financial considerations justify the prevention of conception. In fact, among the few in my sample who talked more pragmatically about abortion, practical decisions were an ingredient of the justification that they offered. Yet, mostly absent in their considerations were any ties between the practice of abortion and women's rights.

These ties were also absent in the *telenovelas* that I have analyzed, where abortion was presented overall as a moral dilemma, where a woman had to balance her practical self-interests with those of her unborn child, and where abortion ultimately was justified only in the case of a character who had been raped. And, even then, she underwent a painful and difficult process before finally concluding that she should not have the child. In two other cases of women characters who became pregnant—young women who wanted to study and have their own careers—both decided that the morally sound decision was to have the baby and pay the price of their misfortune or carelessness. And, in both cases, the situation was resolved when they miscarried. They emerged from their tribulation without children but also with their moral characters intact.

In my opinion, this is one case in which cultural change is very slow because the topic of abortion continues to be extremely charged for many Mexicans, particularly for two reasons: the association of abortion with murder, and social ambivalence about women's sexuality and their right to seek sex for pleasure the same as men do. As opposed to male homosexuality, about which more Mexicans seemed to be ready to make some concessions and to consider such acceptance to be a sign of cultural modernization, legalizing abortion remained an option that people like those in my study felt they could never support. They feared that supporting abortion might make them appear to be in favor of murder and to be sexual libertines. This is one topic about which many Mexicans seem to have little desire to be like people in countries where abortion is legal and where a woman's right to abort is more openly accepted (even if also heavily contested). Furthermore, in contrast to issues for which Mexican traditional ideas are perceived to be signs of "cultural stagnation," abortion seems to fit in the realm of issues about which many Mexicans think people in places like the United States have gone too far. They read signs of "moral decay" in the acceptance of abortion in other places and not signs of "cultural advancement."

This is to say, as well, that within the complicated dynamics of cultural change in Mexico, people have learned to be selective. Different actors within Mexican society manage to calculate when the risk of change can be afforded and when to seek refuge and comfort by upholding traditional ideas that are perceived to denote the nation's "high moral standards." I believe attitudes about abortion are representative of the latter, and thus the desire for cultural change regarding attitudes about this practice is minimized.

ISSUES THAT REMAIN UNTOUCHED

In the course of my research, there were two other issues that Guadalajarans like those in my study rarely brought into their discussion of cultural change. One was any questioning of family relations and of the role that the immediate and the extended family played in their lives. They commonly assumed that a strong connection with their families, at whatever price, was not only justified but also necessary. The other was related to the nature of sex itself and the cultural scripts that I discussed in chapter 8. I will address here the question of family, and I will return to a discussion of the nature of sex in the next section.

I was constantly surprised by the fact that participants in my study had rarely questioned their relationships with their families, even in situations in which the family was a strong source of discomfort and conflict. Taylor (1978, 1986) and Carrier (1972, 1976, 1989a, 1995) noted this phenomenon in their analysis of homosexual life in Guadalajara and Mexico City in the 1970s, and surprisingly little has changed since then. Other authors have written of a similar phenomenon among nonhomosexual people. The sense is, overall, that the Mexican family continues to play a central role as a source of practical and emotional support. Unmarried individuals still face the expectation that they live with their families unless they are in a different city (which is precisely what prompts some to pursue work or school elsewhere as a justification for moving out of the family home). For married individuals, the families of the couple continue to be central to their social activities on an ongoing basis. This often requires frequent and regular visits and time spent together as a family clan (Cortés Guardado 1997).

My surprise regarding the lack of questioning of the role of the family is related to Mexicans' exposure to images and ideas about how people in the United States negotiate and manage their family relations, which stand in great contrast with the more commonly accepted Mexican style. This issue is relevant here because the Mexican family, as I noted in chapter 6, is often the source of informal, but powerful, socialization and regulation of the sexuality of their children, even during their adulthood. An emphasis on guidance and protection means preventing daughters from engaging in sexual behavior before marriage and helping them maintain their social status as decent. It also means providing some freedom to the sons but making sure that they do not acquire "vices," fall victim to "bad women" who prey on them, or become involved with undesirable people (often meaning *homosexuales*). "Guidance," in this context, is commonly not dissimilar to direct control and even repression.

Emotional and practical dependence on the family was pervasive. A majority of unmarried participants in my study continued to live with their parents or other relatives. This severely limited their ability to live their sexuality freely and put tremendous pressure on them to hide from their families any signs of having sexual desires or any evidence that they were in fact being sexual. The expectation that family life is a top priority was also present in the media. In the two *telenovelas* that I discussed above, one of the main problems that emerged when one of the parents decided to have an extramarital affair (in one case the father, and in the other the mother) was the threat that their actions posed to the integrity of their families. In both cases, central concerns were how to avoid the dissolution of the family and how the parents could protect the interests of their children. In both cases there was a premise that divorce irreversibly affects the family and, by implication, some negative judgment against parents who place their self-interest over the interests of their children. Note, however, that all "the children" in these two shows were eighteen years old or older, all still living in the family home. Yet the writers chose to emphasize that their parents' utmost responsibility was to protect them from family dysfunction. The parents' desire to divorce was deemed to be secondary, even when the children were old enough to become independent.

In *La vida en el espejo*, the writers lightly suggested at several points that the children were adults already and that they could take care of themselves. However, despite the fact that the three siblings end up taking partial control of their own lives (without financial independence), and defining their own paths apart from their parents, the emphasis on the importance of the family continued until the show's very end. And, in an interesting twist, the same emphasis was offered as a justification for why parents ought to accept the decisions made by their children regarding their choice of partners and lifestyles, regardless of the parents' opposition to those choices. The younger son in the *telenovela* ends up marrying the woman whom he made pregnant, the daughter decides to live out of wedlock with her boyfriend, and the older son establishes a homosexual relationship. But in the show's final scenes, all six of the younger generation are shown sitting at the table with the now divorced parents and their new partners.

Given this emphasis on the maintenance of, and respect for, the family, people in my study were invested in finding ways to make their desires for change consistent with family life and were responsive to the social expectation that they keep their ties with their families strong. At stake were not only their sense of belonging within their families but also considerable material and practical support (Murray 1987). This is perhaps, in part, why they so feared engaging in any open communication or confrontation that could jeopardize their family relations, or even taking actions that would put them in the position of having to lie to their families. This explained to a large degree Martha's reluctance to have sex with her new boyfriend, because she feared that her sexual activity not only damaged her reputation but also created more opportunities for her family to realize that she was no longer a virgin. It also explained much of the resistance that *homosexuales, gays,* and *lesbianas* felt toward constructing a more integrated identity in which they could be more open about their same-sex attraction. Those in my study like Pablo, Antonio, Lola, Esteban, and Marcela, who had managed to disclose their premarital sexual activity or their homosexuality to their families, were truly testing the waters of what seemed to be one of the strongest taboos in Guadalajara: open communication within the family about sexual activity, sexual diversity, or alternative lifestyles.

THE PERMANENCE OF SEXUAL INTIMACY

Another issue about which people rarely indicated a desire for change was the nature of sex itself. My discussion in chapters 8 and 11 suggested the existence of a shared view among participants about the ingredients that make sex pleasurable. This view reflected expectations about sexual passion, spontaneity in the flow of sex, and bodily communication as tools for experiencing ecstasy.

Mexicans who desired change regarding sexual inequality spoke of an older view of sex in which experiencing orgasm and ecstasy was seen as a male prerogative in sex between a man and a woman or as the prerogative of the dominant partner in male homosexual relations (lesbian relations were ignored altogether). Cultural change in this regard was perceived to imply a recognition that both sexual partners should have the right to achieve sexual fulfillment and that it was the duty of both to not only seek their own pleasure in sex but also to provide it and help ensure that their partners experienced sexual ecstasy as well.

On the other hand, participants recognized that the goal of mutual pleasure did not necessarily require change in the forms of interaction during sex that included power differentials—a partner's dominance and a partner's receptiveness to such dominance during sex between two people—or change in well-favored forms of bodily communication. A certain inequality between partners was perceived to be an intrinsic element of sex and an ingredient for the buildup of sexual pleasure. I must clarify that this view of role differentials involved more than a definition of who dominates and who is dominated, or who penetrates and who is penetrated. First, dominating was not necessarily the same as exerting power or controlling. Second, the different roles were often seen as being self-selected. Third, the idea of a role differential seemed somewhat connected with a desire for one partner to "hold" the interaction and provide structure and direction (summarized in the notion of "taking the other") and for the other partner to be responsive and be "taken." These ideas seemed to refer to the interactions taking place during sex as a whole and not just to the acts of vaginal or anal penetration. Finally, these roles were not always seen as permanent or immutable, and some participants felt that the roles (the dominance and submission) could shift in their sex with a particular partner even within one single sexual encounter, or with different partners.

Participants overall were unwilling to consider altering these ingredients of pleasure even when they were presented with a different view of sex that was contained in messages about the health implications of their sexual behavior. As we saw, expectations about the transformation of sexual behavior into a planned behavior dominated by individual rationality and self-interest were commonly perceived to be unrealistic and in direct competition with the view of sex that people favored.

One possible explanation for this resistance seems related to the argument advanced by Giddens (1990, 1991, 1992), who regards sexual and romantic relations in the context of high modernity to be a refuge from the highly impersonal social relations in other aspects of modern life. According to this view, individuals experience within sex and romance a kind of intimacy and trust in other people that are now unavailable in other domains of everyday life, where relations are dominated by calculations of risk and a socially created need to trust abstract institutions. I would argue that the idea of "sex as refuge" is somewhat present in Mexicans' views about sex, but with an emphasis that differs from that contained in Giddens's analysis. The difference, in my opinion, stems from the emphasis that Mexicans place on collectivity, which seems to reduce the perceived separation between sexual intimacy and other forms of intimacy encountered in everyday life outside the sexual space.

Although the realm of sex was recognized as a separate domain of human experience—one dominated by the body and its forms of expression—for Mexicans the separation between non-sex and sex was not necessarily as abrupt or dramatic as Giddens's analysis suggests. This is to say, as well, that the spontaneity and relational flow that Mexicans valued during sex were also strongly present in everyday interactions, the difference being that the former implied a higher level of intensity—the creation of an altered state and full bodily involvement. The latter was perceived to involve spontaneous, and somewhat unconditional, camaraderie, fondness, and affection, seen in ideal terms as devoid of the calculations and boundaries that Giddens attributes to friendship in the context of high modernity. In Giddens's view, such calculations result in a need to make conscious decisions to pursue and create interpersonal trust, commitment, and intimacy.

In Mexico the emergence of these features in relationships was thought to be more spontaneous. Mutual exploration, friendship, and even sex and romantic relations were perceived to result from a certain willingness to devote time to socializing and meeting new people, among whom new friendships and romantic relationships spontaneously emerged. My interpretation is that, among Mexicans in my study, the resistance to changing sex was embedded in a larger resistance to any alteration of the overall spontaneous nature of their interpersonal relations, sexual or otherwise, and their collective orientation, in light of the growing pressures of modernization.

HIV PREVENTION AND CHANGE

As I discussed with participants the nature of their sexual encounters, I came to understand that those who successfully implemented preventive measures against HIV often learned the required information and the proposed strategies for protection and then made them consistent with the version of sex and interpersonal relations that they favored. This meant that they were not following the educators' recommendations regarding planning and negotiation. They were instead managing to engage in culturally accepted forms of seduction leading to sex, and in spontaneous sexual interaction, while also maintaining awareness about possibly risky situations. They knew how and when to introduce the use of protection and to avoid potentially risky behaviors, but without disrupting the body-dominated flow of their sexual interactions. I suggest that paying attention to this ability is crucial in revising the strategies of protection that are being promoted. In my opinion, such revision implies helping people achieve two goals: (1) learning how to keep awareness about HIV risk in the back of one's mind in order to be able to recognize red flags of potential risk and (2) being able to act when a red flag is raised by taking the initiative to introduce protection or refuse to engage in behaviors implying HIV risk (but without assuming that this requires explicit negotiation).

I do not mean to minimize the constraints to this agency that might emerge when differences in power between sexual partners are involuntary and too large to be manageable, and when refusal to comply with a partner's desire could result in violence or the potential for forced interactions. As my discussion of these issues in chapter 11 indicates, addressing these constraints ought to be inscribed in larger questioning of gender and power relations, via the analysis of lived experience and of specific relationships. This, I argued, might constitute the bridge between individuals, sexual dyads, and their social environment, as well as the trigger to generate participation in larger efforts to effect social, political, and cultural change.

As an example of the ways in which professions—such as public health, medicine, and psychology—attempt to promote cultural modernization, I have pointed critically to HIV prevention efforts that tend to oversimplify sexual behavior; adopt foreign models, ideas, and practices without questioning the premises behind them and adapting them to Mexico; and disregard local cultural expressions. In making this critique, however, I do not mean to invalidate the progressive intentions and partial success of efforts such as those of CHECCOS, which I discussed in chapter 9 as an example of community-based AIDS work in Guadalajara. Improving those efforts would require (1) greater flexibility on the part of the educators to consider locally preferred forms of sexual interaction; (2) greater sophistication to attend simultaneously to sexual partners' immediate relational and health-related needs and to larger and longer-term cultural changes; (3) increased ability to generate a response among program participants that translates into personal and group agency, activism, and "citizenship" (Paiva 2000); and (4) an aptitude to convey the complexity of the issues at hand and work with such complexities in defining realistic strategies. In my opinion, for the educators to be successful, they ought to approach this revision of messages and strategies through dialogue with the people and groups for whom the programs are meant. Educators must create a two-way street of communication and reflection, and facilitate processes of change, rather than offer predefined strategies and attempt to convince people to accept them.

Based on the conversations and interviews that I conducted for this study in Guadalajara, my prediction is that people would surely demonstrate untapped abilities to link HIV prevention with personal needs, relational issues, cultural norms and values, and situational constraints. They might also problematize assumptions previously made in HIV prevention work; become interested in exploring more deeply the topics of sex, sexuality and gender; and begin envisioning alternative strategies for protection and personal forms that are based on their own realities. They might also elucidate possible forms of participation in the promotion of social change. In effect, this contextualization would shift the emphasis from individual behaviors imagined to happen in a social vacuum to behaviors that are immersed in the "social and cultural representations" shaping them (Parker 1996a).

Finally, and more generally, the specific case of HIV prevention work should raise questions about how to improve the role of the health professions in fostering cultural changes in sex, sexuality, and gender in Mexico. My call here is for greater discussion about how to innovate while simultaneously appreciating what local sexual cultures offer and while carefully scrutinizing the premises of models and theories that arrive in Mexico from other places. The health professions can then indeed become a conduit for dialogue, engage in a balanced comparison of local culture with global discourses, and contribute a Mexican perspective to the increasing worldwide exchange of ideas and practices.

IMAGINING THE FUTURE

I have finished writing this book precisely at the turn of the century, at a moment that many around the world have thought of as an opportunity for change and renewal, an opportunity to imagine a better future. In the case of Mexican sexuality, I believe that imagining its future will require further analysis of the many issues discussed in this book.

I highlight here the wonderfully complex interplay between tradition and modernity, which, in Mexico, as in other places in Latin America, has given rise to unique flexibilities of interpretation. Mexicans' classification of sexual identity, and changes in awareness about different groups of people and sexual lifestyles, are strongly influencing people's senses of themselves and others. Available sexual scripts and rules of interaction are constantly being contested and transformed. Individuals are ever more consciously contributing to modifying available scripts through their own reflections and via the enactment of their own sexual and romantic relations.

Increasingly diverse actors are shaping new ideas, norms, and values about sex and sexuality in Mexico. The list includes the mass media, politicians and policy makers, leaders of social movements, religious leaders, intellectuals, professionals, and educators, as well as common people. Some of them are fostering change; others are trying to prevent it. Most believe that their ideas ought to be present in the field of public opinion and policy making, and that they can either contribute to promoting "leaps in modernization" or prevent them from happening.

As the twentieth century closed, the need to understand how ideas and norms about sexuality in Mexico form was becoming increasingly pressing, particularly in light of the growing, widespread access to global sexual culture. In this regard, I have found it of utmost importance to examine how a local emphasis on modernization mixes with a strong local need to protect *mexicanidad* and how this mix plays out in social selectivity about what changes and what does not.

Although, at first sight, such selectivity might appear to be almost random, upon examination it seems instead to be determined by intricate factors that at times generate momentum for rapid change. In some instances, a single historical event, such as the increased social discussion of homosexuality that resulted from the unfortunate emergence of AIDS, was enough to trigger considerable cultural change.

Envisioning the future of Mexican sexuality requires the ability to recognize the many subtleties of local interpretations—to imagine which global values, ideas, and practices will be appealing and how they will reemerge, now adapted to fit in the local cultural context. As I have previously argued, such subtleties seem to contain the key to understanding what makes sexuality and its processes of change particularly Mexican. I do not mean to suggest that similar analyses would not be relevant in other countries, as in fact they have proven to be useful in other places in Latin America and might be useful even in countries like the United States where modernity is assumed to be not only widespread but normative.

During the past seven years, I have been humbled by the many instances of change that I have witnessed regarding sex and sexuality in Mexico. This sense was strongly present when I participated in gatherings and parties where homosexual and heterosexual people socialized without the presence of boundaries or negative judgments created by their differences. I felt the same when I saw women like Ema recognize the source of their oppression in their relationships and take appropriate action to proudly initiate new lives, including new sex lives. I experienced a similar feeling when I observed men like Enrique negotiate lives as self-accepted *gays* who managed to retain the love and support of their families and to achieve something close to a fully integrated gay lifestyle. And the same sense emerged when I watched depictions of new and more contemporary Mexican ideas about sexuality on national television or when I learned about the passage of laws against sexual and gender discrimination in Mexico City, which is probably a precursor to similar developments in the rest of the country. Together, these and many other examples that I discussed in the book offer a hopeful view of the willingness of Mexicans to seek change. They also should cause us to question stereotypical views about Mexican sexuality that still abound.

At the same time, during these seven years I was also challenged by the many constraints that Mexican people continued to encounter in their efforts to effect personal change. Examples were the negative comments that *homosexuales* and *lesbianas* had to endure about their lifestyles and the profound misconceptions that many people had about same-sex attraction; the negative judgments against women's sexuality and against the pursuit of sexual pleasure in general; the open reactions of men against changes in the status quo that could limit their power; and the overt and often aggressive negative reactions to change from the most reactionary groups within Guadalajaran society. The road leading to sexual equality in Mexico still seems to be rather long. It is my hope that the ideas presented here provide an additional viewpoint within the highly contested field of Mexican public opinion about sexual matters—that this book adds my "two cents" to the discussion and encourages reflection and a desire to better understand the many forces shaping sexuality in today's Mexico.

Appendix 1   Descriptions of Interview Participants

This is an alphabetical list of the men and women whom I interviewed for this study. The list does not include individuals with whom I had short, casual conversations in the context of participant observation, nor people attending discussion groups. All the names are pseudonyms.

Adrián: A lower-middle-class man, age twenty-five, who identifies as *bisexual*. He moved from a small town to Guadalajara, where he is currently a college student.

Alberto: A forty-year-old, upper-middle-class man who identifies as *homosexual* and *gay*. He owns his own business and lives with a long-term male partner.

Alfonso: An upper-middle-class salesman, age twenty-eight, who identifies as *homosexual*.

Alicia: A twenty-five-year-old woman who identifies as *normal*. She supports herself working in a clothing store and lives with her mother.

Ana: A twenty-year-old college student who identifies as *heterosexual*. She lives with her mother and four siblings in a lower-middle-class neighborhood. She has never had sexual intercourse.

Andrea: A college student, age eighteen, who hesitantly identified opposite-sex attraction as *heterosexual*. She has never had sexual intercourse. She lives with her middle-class parents and two siblings.

Angel: A twenty-four-year-old man who is a graduate student in the basic sciences. He lives with his brother in a rented apartment in a middle-class neighborhood. He identifies as *bisexual*.

Antonio: A twenty-five-year-old man who identifies as *gay*. He has worked since age nine and is now general administrator at a corporation. He lives alone in a rented apartment in a middle-class neighborhood.

Arturo: A twenty-two-year-old man who identifies as *gay*. He is a college student and lives with his family in a working-class neighborhood. He is active as a volunteer in an AIDS organization.

Beatriz: A young woman, age eighteen, who is a college student from a middle-class family. She lives with her parents and one brother. She has never had sexual intercourse.

Carmen: A family counselor who, at age thirty-three, identifies as *heterosexual*. Her identity includes a sexual interest in women and she has participated in lesbian organizing. She has an apartment in a middle-class neighborhood.

Claudia: A young woman, age twenty-three, who works as an employee in a construction company. She is single and identifies as *normal*.

Dalia: A nineteen-year-old woman who is a student in a private college and who lives with her middle-class family. She is exclusively attracted to men but does not self-identify as *heterosexual*.

Eduardo: A twenty-seven-year-old man who identifies as *heterosexual* but who also has a sexual interest in men. He works and lives with his middle-class family.

Elena: A fifty-three-year-old woman who owns a house in a lower-middle-class neighborhood, where she lives with some of her high school students. She identifies as *heterosexual*.

Elisa: A middle-class college student, age twenty, who volunteers at an AIDS organization. She identifies as *heterosexual*.

Ema: A forty-year-old woman who lives with **Gregorio** and their son in a lower-middle-class neighborhood. She does clerical work in a clinic.

Enrique: A twenty-year-old man who identifies as *gay*. He is a volunteer at a local AIDS organization. During the time of the study, he moved out of his middle-class family home to live with a male lover in a house owned by his parents.

Ernesto: A college student, age eighteen, who identifies as *heterosexual* and *normal*. He lives with his middle-class parents, both of whom work, and his three siblings.

Esteban: A twenty-three-year-old man who identifies as *hombre* (a man) and as *heterosexual*. He is a college student and also helps out in a family business. He lives with his family in a middle-class neighborhood.

Eugenio: A forty-eight-year-old man who identifies as *homosexual*. He is a university professor and lives in his own apartment in a lower-middle-class neighborhood.

Fernando: A nineteen-year-old, middle-class college student. He lives with his mother and his brother.

Francisco: A twenty-two-year-old man who identifies as *heterosexual*. He is a psychology student in a public college and he lives alone in a room that he borrows.

Gabriel: A twenty-one-year-old man who sells clothes to support himself, his mother, and two siblings. He lives with his family in an upper-middle-class neighborhood. He identifies as *gay*.

Gabriela: A thirty-four-year-old medical doctor who owns a house, where she lives with her partner, Judith, and their two children. She married a man at age twenty-three. She identifies as *gay* and rejects the label *lesbiana*.

Gerardo: A thirty-one-year-old, married man who works as an engineer. He supports his wife and four children and lives with them in the house they own in a lower-middle-class neighborhood.

Gonzalo: A professional man who identifies as *homosexual* but who is careful to explain that this label does not pigeonhole him into a fixed category. He is twenty-eight years old and lives with his middle-class family.

Gregorio: A thirty-six-year-old man who identifies as *heterosexual* and who lives with Ema and their son in a lower-middle-class neighborhood. He works as a manager in a small company.

Ignacio: A thirty-year-old, middle-class professional who works as an accountant. He identifies as *homosexual* and lives with his family, which he described as being "very traditional."

Irma: A thirty-one-year-old married woman who lives with her husband and children in a lower-middle-class neighborhood. She is a housewife.

Isabel: A lower-middle-class woman, age thirty-two, who identifies as *heterosexual*. She works as a secretary. She is single, has never had sexual intercourse, and lives with her parents and three sisters.

Ismael: A thirty-four-year-old, married, middle-class man. He identifies as *hombre* (a man). He knows the term *heterosexual* but does not apply it to himself.

Iván: An eighteen-year-old, middle-class student who identifies as *homosexual* and *gay*. He lives with his parents and a sister in an upper-middle-class neighborhood.

Ivette: A college student, age nineteen, who has never had sexual intercourse. She lives with her parents and three siblings in a lower-middle-class neighborhood.

Javier: A thirty-five-year-old man who lives with his wife and their two daughters and who identifies as *heterosexual*. A veterinarian by training, he now produces motivational videos. He worked previously as a singer in a bar, where he met his wife.

José: A twenty-four-year-old man who identifies as *bisexual*. He is single and lives in a working-class neighborhood.

Juan: A man who identifies as *gay* and is twenty-eight-years old. He works as a cook and lives in a working-class neighborhood.

Judith: A thirty-five-year-old, upper-middle-class professional who identifies as *gay* and who lives with her partner, **Gabriela,** and their two children.

Julio: A young man, age twenty-five, who works and lives with his lower-middle-class family. He identifies as *homosexual*.

Lizbeth: A college student, age eighteen, who comes from a middle-class family. She thinks of herself as *heterosexual* and has never had sexual intercourse.

Lola: A twenty-four-year-old single mother who lives with her daughter in her mother's house in a middle-class neighborhood. She supports herself working as a truck dealer.

Lourdes: A middle-class woman in her mid-thirties who identifies as *lesbiana*. She has participated in women's and lesbian organizing.

Luis: A working-class, eighteen-year-old man who has sex with men but does not identify as *homosexual* or *gay*. He is a salesperson in a furniture store and lives with his family.

Marcela: A twenty-six-year-old woman who has a primary sexual interest in men but also has sex with women. She is a researcher at a private university and lives with her boyfriend in a middle-class neighborhood.

Margarita: A nineteen-year-old, middle-class college student who lives with her parents and two younger siblings. She identifies as *heterosexual*.

María: A twenty-three-year-old, middle-class woman who is unemployed and who lives with her family. She identifies as *normal*.

Mario: A twenty-nine-year-old man who identifies as *homosexual*. He works for the government and lives by himself in a rented apartment in a lower-middle-class neighborhood. He has been involved in a relationship with a married man for eight years.

Martha: A young woman, age twenty-four, who works in her upper-middle-class family's business. She identifies as *femenina* (feminine) and does not know the term *heterosexual*.

Miguel: A twenty-one-year-old man who identifies as *normal* and who has sex with other men. He is a college student and has a girlfriend.

Miriam: An upper-middle-class woman in her forties who was previously married to a man who was sexually interested in men. She now works as a psychotherapist.

Olga: A twenty-year-old, middle-class woman who is a student in a private college. She identifies as *heterosexual* and lives with her parents and eight siblings.

Omar: A thirty-five-year-old man who identifies as *homosexual* and *gay*. He works as a female impersonator at a gay dance club and lives alone in a lower-middle-class neighborhood.

Osvaldo: A twenty-one-year-old man who works as a store employee. He identifies as *homosexual* and *gay*. He lives with some of his siblings in a middle-class neighborhood.

Pablo: A thirty-two-year-old man who identifies as *homosexual* and *gay*. He is the only interview participant who revealed being HIV-positive. He lives alone in an apartment in a middle-class neighborhood.

Pedro: A thirty-one-year-old man who identifies as *homosexual*. He is an employee at a hospital and rents a shared apartment in a lower-middle-class neighborhood.

Ramiro: A twenty-seven-year-old, married man who works in a factory. He has two children and lives with his family in a small, one-bedroom house in a working-class neighborhood.

Raúl: A nineteen-year-old man who identifies as *gay*. He works in a factory and lives in a working-class neighborhood with his family.

Remigio: A peasant who lives in the outskirts of Guadalajara with his wife and two children. He has an extremely low income.

Renata: A twenty-nine-year-old, single woman who identifies as *heterosexual*. She lives with her lower-middle-class parents and two siblings.

René: A working-class young man, age nineteen, who lives with his family. He discovered sex at age fifteen and seduces women whom he meets at parties.

Rodrigo: A twenty-nine-year-old, upper-middle-class man who identifies as *homosexual* and *gay* but who is attempting through therapy to become *heterosexual*. He lives by himself in a rented apartment.

Rosario: A young college student, age eighteen, from a lower-middle-class family. She lives with her mother and her grandmother.

Rubén: A middle-class man, age thirty-five, who identifies as *homosexual*. He lives alone, but he also supports his parents and three nephews.

Ruth: A schoolteacher, age forty-two, who lives with her children in a middle-class neighborhood. She identifies as *heterosexual*.

Appendix 2   Methodology

GENERATING THE DATA FOR THIS BOOK

I arrived in Guadalajara in September 1993 and left in late August 1995. Upon arrival I contacted professionals working in the field of HIV prevention and a few people whom I knew from previous visits to the city. Within a period of four weeks, I had begun making social contacts either through my volunteer work in AIDS organizations or by participating in social activities with individuals who had no connection with AIDS work. Once I was situated in a variety of initial social circles, I began collecting field notes, recruiting participants for individual interviews, and exploring the possibility of organizing some discussion groups about sexual topics.

During the two years that I spent in Guadalajara, I engaged in participant observation and conducted sixty-four in-depth interviews and three discussion groups. Most of the interviews and the three discussion groups took place during the first year. I continued performing participant observation during the second year while also analyzing the interview and discussion-group transcripts.

People in Guadalajara were generally accepting of my role as a doctoral student conducting research on sexuality and showed interest in discussing the topic. Such interest opened up opportunities to recruit potential participants for my interviews. Except for a few heterosexual men who refused to be interviewed about sexuality, or who felt that they had nothing to contribute, most of the men and women whom I approached expressed interest in participating.

Contrary to stereotypes that prevail in the United States about Latin American countries—the notion that sex is a taboo subject in that part of the world—initiating one-on-one or informal group conversations about sexuality was fairly uncomplicated. As the quotations throughout the book suggest, people who participated in interviews answered the questions openly and, with few exceptions, did not find talking about sex inordinately embarrassing. This facility, however, did not apply to structured group discussions. Although people overall were willing to have informal group conversations about sex with their friends or acquaintances—particularly if those conversations involved humor—they were wary about having to reveal intimate details of their own sexual lives in structured group discussions with strangers. They reacted with suspicion to invitations to attend a discussion group and often proposed that a one-on-one conversation was a better option for them. This limitation forced me to reconsider my original research plan, which involved holding several focus groups in addition to the individual interviews.

Individual Interviews

I recruited individuals for interviews using two separate strategies: (1) approaching participants from the various social networks to which I gained access and (2) publicizing my study by distributing leaflets in homosexual bars and discos and participating in interviews for local radio stations and local newspapers. In those interviews I asked people who were interested to call my personal telephone number. If I was not around to answer the phone, an answering machine instructed them to leave a message or to call again later. Overall, the public's response to my request was positive, and I only received one negative, possibly threatening message.

I gave potential interviewees the option to talk to a man or to a woman. I hired a young woman who had recently graduated from a social psychology program and who had been referred to me by CONASIDA in Mexico City. A majority of participants did not express objections to being interviewed by a person of the opposite sex, regardless of their being told that some of the questions were of a sensitive nature. For this reason, I conducted most of the interviews for the study. Also, throughout the interviews, participants were given the option to refuse to answer any questions. However, with some minor exceptions, participants were generally willing to answer all questions.

Although the interviews were open ended, I used a short questionnaire to initiate and guide the conversation. This guide included questions about the following general topics: sexual socialization, sexual identity, personal definition of sex, sexual communication, knowledge about AIDS and safe sex, and sexual ideology. The interviews had a conversational format and there was flexibility to depart from the scripted questions as needed. This format contributed to building rapport and, in my opinion, greatly contributed to the openness and trust that characterized the interviews.

There was no specific order in which to ask the questions. However, I and my assistant were careful to ask questions about a person's individual sense of their sexual orientation or identity prior to engaging in any discussion about sexual identity categories. The goal was to avoid shaping self-perceptions of identity or suggesting labels that the interviewees could then adopt even if they were hearing them for the first time. As much as possible, we elicited labels of identity that the participants themselves used, and then we used those labels throughout the rest of the interview. For instance, if a person said that she identified as "*normal*," we continued referring to her identity using that label later in the conversation.

On average, the interviews lasted between sixty and ninety minutes, although some were longer than two hours. Most of the interviews were recorded on audiotapes and then transcribed verbatim. There was only one person who refused the use of a tape recorder, and there were two interviews that took place spontaneously, when I did not have a tape recorder available. In those three cases, I took extensive notes right after the interview finished.

Overall, participants were lower middle to upper middle class, young, and single and had at least some high school education. Participation was less likely among older, married men and women and among women who identified as lesbians. This limitation had two important consequences. One is that my data about the identities and lifestyles of lesbian women are scarce. The second is that I did not have any opportunities to talk with married individuals who were having an extramarital affair at the time of my study.

Participant Observation

I conducted participant observation in several settings and with people belonging to different social groups. Of particular importance was my work as a volunteer in CHECCOS, a local nongovernmental AIDS organization, as well as my participation in the social networks that CHECCOS members maintained.

Participant observation at CHECCOS, as well as at other AIDS organizations with which CHECCOS collaborated, provided me both with background information about HIV prevention activities in Guadalajara and with insight into the development of educational programs in the city—both their potential and their limitations. Furthermore, the development of friendships and ongoing social relations with CHECCOS members and with other people within a variety of social groups provided me with important data, throughout an extended period, about how individuals interpreted their sexuality and integrated protection against HIV in their sexual lives. Participant observation in this context allowed me to observe changes in perceptions about sex and HIV prevention as the social conditions surrounding individuals changed. It also allowed me to gain insight into and analyze, jointly with the people involved, the conditions influencing sexual encounters. Included were encounters involving risk for HIV transmission where at least one of the sexual partners intended to stay safe and felt efficacious about his or her ability to practice safe sex.

Some of my conversations in this regard resulted from social interaction with people whom I initially interviewed and who afterward talked to me about topics related to the interview as their personal situations changed. Sometimes, these individuals would contact me specifically to tell me new information about their successes or failures with HIV prevention measures or to report more information about their sexual lives in general. Other times, these updates emerged in conversations taking place during social gatherings. In these cases, the initial interview plus the opportunity to observe changes in perceptions and practices over time proved to generate rich and useful data.

The contexts in which participant observation was conducted incorporated a wide variety of people: those who were familiar with HIV prevention and those who were not; men and women of different ages and social classes; people who practiced a diversity of homosexual, bisexual, and heterosexual behaviors and who had a variety of ways of specifying their sexual identities. Overall, however, the majority of people whom I met in the context of participant observation were lower middle to upper middle class and young (eighteen to thirty-five years old, although the age range spanned from sixteen to sixty-two years old) and had at least some high school education.

Participant observation for this study took place literally at all times of the day and night: during working hours in offices and public places, during meals with different groups of people, after hours in parties and outings to local hangouts, bars, and discos. In all of these contexts, the topics of sex and AIDS were commonly present, although it was generally regarded to be a more appropriate topic of conversation for nighttime social gatherings. As part of my ongoing observations, I also had the opportunity to witness interactions between individuals that included active sexual cruising and veiled seduction (particularly in homosexual circles), to participate in conversations about sexual situations and about conflicts with sexual partners, and to carry out more theoretical discussions about HIV transmission and sexuality. Thus, participant observation yielded rich data on the everyday role of sexuality and AIDS in local social interactions and provided me with a unique opportunity to follow the history of several of my informants over a period of several months.

In a more general sense, participant observation also allowed me to account for sexuality as immersed in the social and political environment in Guadalajara. This perspective was advantageous because I could study local debates about sexual norms and values, talk to people about their own personal perspective, and observe the rapid pace of social and cultural changes taking place in Mexico. Participant observation provided me with a more general view that helped me understand the place that sexuality occupied in everyday life.

Discussion Groups

I conducted three discussion groups in a local clinic with people attending a diabetes self-help group and two social groups for the elderly. A total of fifty-five people participated in the three groups. The diabetes group included people of low- to middle-class background, and most participants were between twenty and fifty years old. The two social groups for the elderly included mostly lower-middle- to middle-class people, aged sixty or older.

Because of the nature of the setting, the large size of the groups, and the fact that group members knew each other, these discussion sessions can hardly be called "focus groups" in strict methodological terms. Although the discussions took place behind closed doors in a meeting room, they were subject to interruptions by the clinic's staff and by newcomers who arrived late to their regular group meeting and who could not be turned away. Despite these limitations, the groups with elderly people provided some interesting insight into the values of the older generation, to which I would have had no access otherwise.

People in the diabetes group were quite diverse and their responses were similar to those of others in their same age range, and thus did not reflect differences caused by their chronic medical condition. However, I have used the data from this group with caution, principally because many of the participants seemed to know each other quite well, which might have limited their willingness to express opinions that could have put them on the spot in front of the rest of the group. Nevertheless, their interaction provided an opportunity to observe discussion about sexual norms and values, which was similar to that in other settings where I performed participant observation.

In my original research plan I anticipated holding ten structured focus groups with different kinds of people. However, the concept of a "focus group" appeared to be quite foreign to people in Guadalajara, and most participants expressed interest only in the individual interviews and not in any kind of formal, structured group discussion. People offered several reasons for their refusal to participate in focus groups: lack of time, not wanting to go to a specific location, and, ultimately, being prepared to disclose personal information about sexuality in private but not in a group. Interestingly, in private, one-on-one conversations, participants showed great willingness to volunteer intimate information about themselves and about their sexual lives, often beyond my original expectations.

DATA RECORDING AND ANALYSIS

Both the interviews and the discussion groups were audiotaped and later transcribed verbatim. To ensure confidentiality, participants were asked not to use any names or personal references, and any such information that slipped through in the audiotapes was omitted in the transcripts. Access to the audiotapes was strictly limited to the interviewers and to the transcriber. All participants quoted in my writing were given pseudonyms.

Data resulting from participant observation were recorded in field notes, which I wrote within a few hours after the events to ensure greater reliability. Field notes were organized by date and by event.

The transcribed text of all interviews and discussion groups, along with the field notes, were pooled together into a single database to be coded. Before beginning this activity, I read the interviews in full and created a coding guide. Using the original text, I created individual files containing selected passages (usually questions with their answers and sections of interviews addressing a single topic). I coded these individual files by assigning keywords from a single comprehensive guide that covered all the themes that emerged as I read the transcripts for the first time.

This process resulted in a new database with more than 1,000 entries. I used this database in the analysis by conducting automated searches of individual keywords or combinations of keywords that allowed me to identify patterns of response and commonalities of experience, as well as differences. For instance, a search on homosexual identity and power provided all the entries that contained commentaries or narratives in which both topics emerged and there was some connection between them.

Additionally, I considered each interview as an individual case study, to analyze more generally the ways in which participants integrated their sexuality into their lives, the logics that they followed to accomplish such integration, their personal history, how they had acquired a sexual ideology, their definitions of their sexual identity and classifications of the identities of others, and the role that HIV prevention measures played in their sexual lives, among other topics of analysis. This allowed me as well to examine both consistencies and contradictions within individuals' own ways of thinking and acting, and how they made sense of the sexual world surrounding them and of their role in that world.

Reliance on Narratives about the Past

As illustrated by many of the examples in the book, my analysis often relied on accounts of sexual encounters and individuals' recollection of the situations in which they took place. It also relied on individuals' recollection of their sexual upbringing and on the way in which they were socialized about sexual matters. I am aware of the limitations that retrospective accounts offer, given individuals' inevitably flawed memories of the past and the revisions that may be made to allow individuals to make the past consistent with their present reality, identity, and ways of thinking. For the purposes of my analysis, however, the facts reported were often less important than the reasoning and logic used in the reporting.

This is to say as well that despite the possible distortions introduced by retrospective accounts, the data also provided an interesting view of people's understanding of their current sexual lives at the time of the study. In this sense, details about a particular event that were omitted, forgotten, or embellished to fit better into a person's recollection of the event were sometimes less important to my analysis than the individual's way of speaking about the event and his or her explanation of the logic informing actions taken at the time of the event. The latter provided me with insight about interviewees' reasoning, of their view of the world, and of their understanding of the sexual culture into which they were socialized and in which they participated, which have all been crucial ingredients in my analysis.

In studying individuals' logics or reasoning, however, I am aware of the inevitable effect of formal participation in an interview, which likely makes participants feel compelled to provide answers, explanations, and justifications that help them come across as thinking, rational people. This feature of qualitative interviewing might contribute to the emergence of what Stephen O. Murray, in a review comment, called "some artificial consistencies and non-salient categorization schemata." Despite this limitation, my assessment is that the examples that I selected for quotation generally reflected people's usual ways of speaking about these topics, particularly since their comments or reasoning did not differ much from those occurring in informal conversations about the same topics (where people were not necessarily "on the spot," feeling that they ought to produce articulate comments).

Finally, I am also aware that, in reporting their sexual behaviors and levels of HIV risk, individuals might be tempted to omit reporting practices about which they were embarrassed or that threatened their identities. This problem is inevitable in any kind of research in which individuals are asked to report retrospectively on their sexual behaviors. In relation to my data, however, in addition to data collected in interviews, I gained access to detailed information about sexual encounters provided by people with whom I developed considerable rapport over a period of time. Because of my training and of my conscious attempts to demonstrate a lack of judgment about sexual matters, I developed a reputation as someone to whom anything could be told. I realize this characteristic of my interactions does not eliminate the problem of self-reporting, but I believe it generally helped in reducing it as much as is possible in this kind of research.

LIMITATIONS

As with any other study, quantitative or qualitative, readers should exercise caution about generalizing my findings to Mexicans not living in Guadalajara or whose demographic characteristics are radically different from those of the participants in this study. This would be of particular importance when considering rural Mexican settings as well as people who are at either extreme of the income scale: people who are very poor or economically marginalized and people who are very rich. As I have already mentioned, an additional limitation of this study is the low participation of married, middle-aged people and of lesbian women. Finally, although the study suggests the existence of strong generational gaps in terms of sexual norms and values, it does not fully explain their nature nor their effects on sexual behavior. This limitation resulted from the greater participation of younger people—people who belong to the generation of Mexicans who were about to initiate, or had recently initiated, their sex lives in the mid-1990s.

Thus, the results of this study should be regarded as referring to a fairly young, urban Mexican population marked by a variety of sexual identities and sexual behaviors, including homosexual (mostly male), heterosexual, and bisexual. It is my hope that this work sparks the interest of researchers in undertaking more empirical studies on the topic of sexuality and AIDS in Mexico with a variety of populations.

Notes

INTRODUCTION

1. Throughout the book, isolated Spanish words and phrases appear in italics.

2. I use the terms "sex" and "sexuality" as separate but complementary. By "sex" I mean sexual practices and behaviors. By "sexuality" I mean the larger effects that the quality of being sexual has on individuals' lives, including their interpretations of sexual identity, the meanings they attach to sexual desires, their selection of sexual partners, their ideas and values about sexual matters, and so on.

3. In Mexico, the nicknames *tapatío* and *tapatía* are used to refer, respectively, to men and women from Guadalajara. Since there might be confusion as to whether these words include those who have moved to Guadalajara, I have chosen instead to use the term "Guadalajaran," which should be understood to include all city residents. This distinction is important because a considerable number of people in my study lived in the city but were not born there. They belonged to the large sector of immigrants from other parts of Mexico who make up approximately half of the city's population (Cortés Guardado 1997).

CHAPTER ONE: MEXICAN SEXUALITIES

1. I use *homosexual* as a generic term to refer to Guadalajarans who had adopted a separate identity based on their same-sex at-

traction and sexual behavior. At the time of my research, this was the word that people most commonly used to refer to themselves or to others who shared the identity formed around same-sex attraction. *Homosexual* was followed closely by the terms *lesbiana* and *gay*. Note that these are the Spanish versions of these words, which I use to avoid implying that they mean exactly the same as the equivalent words in English.

2. Throughout the book, quotations given in English from sources published in Spanish are my translations unless otherwise noted. I have kept some of the original text in Spanish (and supplied the translation in brackets) or provided the original Spanish word in brackets when I deemed it important for readers who speak Spanish to have access to words representing cultural concepts that do not translate well and to nuances that are lost in translation.

3. As Renato Rosaldo notes in his foreword to García Canclini 1995, evolutionism assumes that "social formations at any single point in time can be ordered chronologically from ancient to modern in a way that corresponds to a parallel moral ordering from inferior to superior. From this perspective, the modern becomes all that is secular, innovative, economically productive, and democratic" (p. xiii).

4. Since this incident, the number 41 has been recognized as a way of invoking homosexuality. Among boys, for instance, it was common in the 1970s for one to punch another in the arm while saying, "Forty-one!" The other boy was supposed to respond by punching back and stating, *"Safo!"* (meaning "not me!" or "no way!"), thereby reassuring others of his masculinity.

5. *Lagartijo* is the masculine version of the word *lagartija*, which means "lizard."

6. *Jotitos* here is the diminutive plural of the word *joto*, which is an old derogatory term used to refer to effeminate men in Mexico.

7. Cortés Guardado (1997) comments on the phenomenon of secularization but sees it, not as exclusively Mexican, but rather as part of worldwide changes.

8. *Criollo* is a term applied in Mexico to the people of Spanish decent who were born in Mexico. Before the war of independence, the *criollos* did not have the same rights as the *peninsulares* (Spaniards born in the Iberian Peninsula). This was a major motivation for the *criollos'* desire to become independent from Spain.

9. *Mestizo* is a term applied to people of mixed Spanish and Indian heritage.

10. For more on the high value placed in Guadalajara on the European side of its traditions, see Riding 1986: 405.

11. The word should be *respetuoso,* "respectful."

12. See essays in Bellinghausen 1990.

13. Riding makes a distinction here by social class. "The past remains alive in the Mexican soul. Not all Mexicans of all regions and all classes are alike: in the provinces, they resent the imposition of what they consider the Aztec-rooted *mestizo* culture, and the middle-class minority struggles to shake off the past, sacrificing the present for a future of Americanized value and rewards" (1986: 19). Similarly to other authors, Riding assigns the upper classes a special role in bringing U.S. values into Mexico. "The children of the middle-class and affluent families began traveling and studying abroad, learning foreign languages and adopting American fashions. Industrialization and urbanization also shattered a once dominant provincial way of life, spawning new attitudes and behavior" (345).

PART ONE: SEXUAL IDENTITIES

1. This contrasts, Giddens argues, with the kind of limited reflexivity required in premodern societies: "in pre-modern civilisations reflexivity is still largely limited to the reinterpretation and clarification of tradition, such that in the scales of time the side of the 'past' is much more heavily weighed down than that of the 'future'" (1990: 37).

2. I borrow here the term developed by Rubin (1984) to refer to the assumed correspondence between biological sex and expectations regarding demeanor and sexual roles.

CHAPTER TWO: GENDER-BASED CATEGORIES OF SEXUAL IDENTITY

1. The list includes Döring (1990), González Rodríguez (1990), Gutmann (1996), Lamas (1990), Ponce, Solórzano, and Alonso (1990), Carrier (1972, 1989a, b, 1995), Moreno (1990), Riding (1986), Taylor (1978, 1986), Prieur (1998), LeVine (1993), and Murray (1995).

2. For similar analyses in other Latin American countries, see Parker 1991, 1999; Lancaster 1992; and Fry 1985.

3. The terms *pasivo* and *activo* used as descriptors of the sexual role in a sexual relationship between men are almost exclusively used in the homosexual world. Traditionally, heterosexuals have regarded *maricones* as being the receptive partners in anal sex but do not necessarily use the *pasivo/activo* distinction. The association between homosexuality and a receptive role is discussed by Carrier: "Because of the lack of stigmatization in Mexico of the anal inserter participant in homosexual encounters, most Mexican males are not fearful of bisexuality. They do not believe that 'one drop of homosexuality' makes one totally homosexual as long as the appropriate sex role is played; that they must show erotic distance toward other

males as long as they are masculine, and play the inserter role in homosexual encounters. . . . Thus, although heterosexuality is considered superior to homosexuality in Mexico, a Mexican male's gender identity is not necessarily threatened by his homosexual behavior" (1989a: 227).

4. Similarly, Parker and Carballo argue that in the context of Latin America, "sexual activity, in same-sex as well as opposite-sex interactions, may actually be relatively unproblematic, and may translate into a high degree of bisexual behavior without ever being transformed into a distinct bisexual identity" (1990: 501).

5. In his discussion of the term *buga*, Balderston compares it to the Caribbean term *bugarrón* and wrongly assumes that it is used for men only and to mean "straight-acting, but willing to fuck gay men" (1997: 192). *Buga* is used by homosexual people in Mexico to refer to heterosexual men and women, and its meaning is, as the *Oxford Spanish Dictionary* correctly defines, roughly equivalent to "straight." In Guadalajara and the rest of Mexico, *bugas* are assumed to lack sexual interest in people of their own sex.

6. It is quite astonishing that, in a situation in which a married woman has an affair, she may maintain the role of "virtuous" with her husband and family (as long as they do not find out) while playing the role of "common" woman with her lover, with whom she would then be allowed more sexual exploration. A common and derogatory way of stating this is the phrase "my prostitute, your wife," which refers to the fact that a second man may turn a virtuous woman into a common one and thus attack the husband. This is a form of revenge between two men, the woman being only the instrument.

7. A man interviewed in Döring 1990 discusses this issue: "There are many who have their spouses just to keep them 'in their place' [to control them], to have relations with them as our fathers and grandfathers had them. And so they need an extra lover, to do with them what they cannot do with their wife" (168).

8. See Mitchell 1988 for a psychoanalytical discussion about why men tend to do this to certain female sexual partners. Mitchell states: "Prostitutes or women declared inferior and devalued are appealing precisely because one need not worry about pleasing them, meeting their standards, gaining their approval for one's own impulses and desires" (113).

9. A psychoanalyst interviewed in Döring 1990 provides a similar view when he comments: "Men experience the fact that a woman takes the initiative, for instance, or her desire for physical experiences beyond what is classically expected from a woman, as something that is tremendously threatening. . . . The man is active, the woman *must* be passive" (50, emphasis in the original).

10. A national study reports an increase of 10.5% between 1976 and 1987 in the proportion of women who work (26.9% in 1976 and 37.4% in 1987) (García and

Oliveira 1992). One study in Guadalajara found a 25% increase between 1982 and 1985 in the number of working women in a small sample (González de la Rocha 1989). The author points out, however, that female work in the city is undervalued: "even when female work is basic for survival, it is undervalued and women have little autonomy and authority. Many women who were receiving a salary had to work furtively because their husbands prohibited their leaving the house to become involved in duties that are not domestic. By contrast, men have greater 'freedom' to act and control their salaries" (161).

11. This is a widespread problem in Mexico, as in many other places, as women strive for greater participation in the work market. Döring states, "In our milieu, the incorporation of women in the work market has not included her liberation from tasks that have been traditionally regarded to be feminine: caring and education of the children, caring of the sick and the elderly, maintenance of the home (work such as cooking, cleaning, washing clothes, going to the market, etc.)" (1990: 25).

12. Up to this point, Ema seemed to be using strategies aimed at expressing discomfort or getting things done without confronting her more powerful partner. These strategies were similar to those reported by Cornwall and Lindisfarne: "Women accidentally-on-purpose burn toast to express their displeasure with their spouses; or they have headaches to resist sexual demands" (1994: 25).

13. Although there is a sense in urban Mexico today that the overtly effeminate men tend to be working class, this was not always the case. There is historical evidence of the multiple meanings that being *maricón* or *joto* could have earlier in the twentieth century. The identity could be that of a working-class man who dressed as a woman and lived in a bordello; a cultivated artist whose mannerisms were heavily affected but who was also regarded as elegant and eccentric; or a man who passed as "normal" in his work but who was overtly effeminate when participating in social networks where *camp* was acceptable. This variety of lifestyles associated with being a *maricón* or *joto* in Mexico is discussed amply by Monsiváis (1998).

14. The lack of a negative response might indeed be related to loss of power. Like women who are the subject of *piropos* by strangers, a man had to absorb such sexual objectification in silence. He was, in some way, being "feminized." I thank Steve Murray for this observation.

15. Even the less colloquial language used historically to refer to these men is by no means neutral: *anormal* (abnormal), *desviado* (deviate), *afeminado* (effeminate), *mujercita* (little woman), and *degenerado* (degenerate). For discussion of the meanings of the different terms used to refer to homosexuals colloquially and formally, see Taylor 1978; Carrier 1989a, b, 1995; Murray and Dynes 1995; Buffington 1997.

16. Gutmann (1996) points out that besides the association with homosexuality, these terms have the additional connotation of cowardice and are used to refer to a

man who, although not suspected of being homosexual, is thought of as being "less of a man."

17. See the work of Prieur (1998), who interviewed several men who led lives as *normales* but who had sex with effeminate men who went through excruciating efforts to pass as women. Some of the masculine partners in these relationships were in almost complete denial about their involvement in sex with men. Such denial seemed to be a convenient way to pursue sex with men without confronting the meanings of their attraction for their own sex.

18. Buffington (1997) makes reference to the proactive adoption of effeminacy among men in Mexico since the turn of the century. His analysis of this issue is based on criminological records of the first half of the twentieth century. Buffington states that "adult male sexual inverts (as turn-of-the-century observers described effeminate men) flamboyantly asserted their difference, often taking suggestive, feminized nicknames like 'la Golondrina' (the swallow) and 'la Bicicleta' (the bicycle)" (1997: 121). Similar examples appear in Novo 1979, a memoir about the life of men with homosexual behaviors in Mexico City in the 1930s.

19. *Torterías* are small eating places that serve Mexican sandwiches made with *bolillo* or *telera* (types of French bread) stuffed with a diversity of fillings. These establishments are associated with traditional Mexican urban culture, the old parts of Mexican cities, the life of the poor, and alternative lifestyles.

20. Carrier characterizes men in his research who identified with the *internacional* role in the following terms: "The author's data suggest that most of them are masculine rather than feminine and during the early years of their sex lives play only the 'activo' sexual role—the 'pasivo' sexual role being incorporated later as they become more involved in homosexual encounters. Many 'internacionales' state that although they may play both sex roles, they nevertheless retain a strong general preference for one over the other" (1989a: 231).

CHAPTER THREE: NEW FREEDOMS, NEW BOUNDARIES

1. Chauncey (1994: 13) points out that the shift toward accepting the division between homosexuality and heterosexuality took place in the United States between the 1930s and the 1950s, by which time this division had replaced the division of men into "fairies" and "normal men." In Mexico this new classification did not replace the previously existing one, but instead it was superimposed upon the previous gender-based division.

2. Nevertheless, the term *joto* is commonly used in informal conversations and can be mildly to strongly derogatory, depending on the tone in which it is used. *Joto* can

also be a friendly, casual way for homosexual men to refer to each other (similar to the use of the word "faggot" among gay men in the United States).

3. *Manflora* is the feminine of the word *manflor,* which, applied to men, is the equivalent of "pansy."

4. Mayate is the term used within the homosexual milieu to refer to masculine men who have sex with men, sometimes for money, without identifying as *homosexual* or *gay.* See Prieur 1998.

CHAPTER FOUR: SUBTLETIES OF INTERPRETATION

1. It may be argued that the transition from one system of categorization to the other in the United States is not complete—that there are many people, especially among ethnic minorities, who think of sexual identities in terms that are based on gender roles or that resemble hybridity. However, it is also undeniable that the hetero/homo/bisexual division dominates in mainstream classifications of sexual identities, as well as in the discourses about sexuality in the popular media.

CHAPTER FIVE: NEGOTIATING EVERYDAY LIFE

1. This notion has been used in work in other Latin American cities. See Parker's description (1999) of the superimposition of a gay grid in Rio de Janeiro and Fortaleza in Brazil.

2. Disclosure would risk the loss of the considerable practical support that families provided: housing, food, clothing, as well as services such as cooking, washing, ironing, housecleaning, and so forth. A feminist woman interviewed in Döring 1990 said, "Mexican families function as job agencies, social security cushions, etc. When people lose their job, someone in the family helps; if they lose their home, they go home to their parents; if they have a child outside marriage, the child is taken to the grandmother; etc. The family continues to provide for many aspects which in other societies, the more developed ones, the more industrialized, it does not" (101). For more on this topic see Murray 1987, 1995.

3. See the description of the movement's characteristics and achievements that Pedro Preciado, a Guadalajaran gay activist, provided in a 1993 interview with Carrier (1995). When I talked with Preciado in 1994, he felt that the efforts of the gay and lesbian groups had waned considerably and that the leaders, including him, were severely burnt out. This in part had to do with the draining experience and enormous defeat that the activists suffered when they attempted to organize the International Lesbian and Gay Association (ILGA) conference in Guadalajara in 1991 (Carrier 1995: 186).

1. Bandura provides a sobering reminder about an equivalent situation in the United States: "In the sexual domain, our society has always had difficulty talking frankly about sex and imparting sexual information to the public at large. Because parents generally do a poor job of it as well, youngsters pick up their sex information from other, often less trustworthy and reputable, sources outside the home or from consequences of uninformed sexual experimentation" (1987: 4).

2. Other authors in Mexico have noted this phenomenon. Döring stated: "Usually, the family does not talk about sexuality, even when it constitutes the context where the socialization process starts. [Talking about sexuality] is only done when there are traumatic events that break the implicit agreement not to talk about 'that' unless it is absolutely necessary, which happens when there is an accident or disease among one of the family members, or when something else happens that breaks the balance assumed to be good by the family" (1990: 237).

3. In LeVine's study (1993) in Cuernavaca, none of the younger women ever discussed the topic of menstruation openly with their mothers, and instead they obtained information about it from older siblings and friends. Yet, once they began menstruating, their parents took explicit measures to limit their freedom of movement as a way to prevent them from falling into the temptation of having sex with a boyfriend. The adolescent girls had to find ways to circumvent their parents' control in order to interact socially with boys.

4. Moreno mentions the absence of information about the emotions connected with sexual awakening in girls, and of any explanation on the part of parents that sexual feelings were connected to the genitals, with "the part of our bodies that many did not name because they were not even given the freedom to assign it a name" (1990: 41).

5. The words *morbo* and *morbosidad* in Mexican Spanish convey a combination of sexual intent, obsession, joking, and sexual double entendres. They imply referring to sexual matters in a tone that is lurid, ribald, and off-color.

6. Dowsett (1996), in his study of male homosexuality in Australia, provides an interesting account about how the experience of the body and its desire, of actual sexual exploration, constitutes an important source of information about sexuality for boys. In a more negative sense, a study with young people in Peru found that for young men and women their "own sexual activity is their main source of information about sexual health, that is, they learn from their own experience of unplanned pregnancy and STDs [sexually transmitted diseases]" (Cáceres et al. 1997: S76).

7. Sexual coercion was identified as a significant problem in the study conducted with young people in Peru (Cáceres et al. 1997; Cáceres, Marín, and Hudes 2000).

8. Forrest et al. report a similar phenomenon in a study with Hispanic men in the United States. Most participants "had never discussed sex or STDs with their fathers." Fathers typically just provided the message to "be careful." One participant said, "We have more knowledge than our parents. Now we learn more from our friends than from our parents." However, the conversations that these men had with their friends appeared to be less than perfect. "Several participants said that it is difficult, under ordinary circumstances, for Hispanic men to have a serious conversation about AIDS or sex. They noted that when these topics come up in casual conversation, friends always start joking and making wisecracks" (1993: 114).

9. See also LeVine 1993 and Gutmann 1996 for additional analyses of the transmission of values about sexuality from one generation to the next in the Mexican context.

10. The HarperCollins *Spanish Dictionary* translates this word as "womanizer," which is the most modern use of the term. However, in this context the term would also refer to a man who is a bit of a gigolo or a swinger, who has no problem conquering women, and who has no desire for a stable monogamous relationship with any of the women whom he dates.

11. The value placed on transgression as an erotic practice has been noted by Parker (1991) in his extensive research on the sexual culture of Brazil.

CHAPTER SEVEN: THE MEDIA, RELIGION, SOCIETY, AND THE STATE
1. Riding reports, "Mexico has become a nation of television watchers, with even the poorest semi-literate viewers receptive to the sophisticated stimuli of programs and advertising. Television is now the principal influence on the cultural, political and economic attitudes of the population at large" (1986: 456).

2. Riding refers to the role that radio had in the 1920s in fostering the internal globalization of Mexican culture across regions of Mexico. He also points out that, through the radio, "[t]he invasion of Mexico City by Guadalajara's mariachi music began soon afterward" (1986: 450). This suggests that the arrival of the radio in Mexico played a role in the construction of the type of Guadalajaran-based *mexicanidad* that I discussed in chapter 1.

3. Indeed, Mexican soap operas are widely popular in many other countries around the world.

4. In a more recent *telenovela, La vida en el espejo* (Life in the mirror), the same production team included a central male character who is homosexual. See the conclusion for more on this *telenovela*.

5. Cortés Guardado indicates that 7,576 abortions were reported in Jalisco in 1992 and that the Secretariat of Health in Jalisco has estimated that 75 clandestine abor-

tions are performed daily in the state, or around 30,000 per year total. In Cortés Guardado's opinion, the latter figure is most likely an exaggeration. He concludes, however, that what "cannot be denied [is] that abortion is quite common in Jalisco" (1997: 138).

6. Dalia was referring to attempts to organize the ILGA conference in Guadalajara in 1991, which I described in chapter 1.

7. Andrea is alluding to the phrase *el pan nuestro de cada día,* "our daily bread," a line in the Catholic prayer Our Father. This phrase is commonly used in Mexico when a person wishes to remark that someone wrongly sees as a basic need something that is not.

CHAPTER EIGHT: PATHS FOR THE ACHIEVEMENT OF PLEASURE

1. Cedillo Nolasco and Morales Delgadillo refer to this socialization of contemporary women in Mexico. They note that women are taught not to disassociate emotion from sensation and that contemporary Mexican women learn to be critical of men's sexuality because "they [men] can have sex without love or with anyone they want" (1990: 51).

2. Simon defined "cultural scenarios" as "the instructional guides that exist at the level of collective life. . . . Cultural scenarios essentially instruct in the narrative requirements of specific roles. They provide the understandings that make role entry, performance, and/or exit plausible for both self and others; they provide the who and what of past and future without which the present remains anxiously uncertain and fragile. The enactment of virtually all roles reflects either directly or indirectly the contents of appropriate cultural scenarios" (1996: 40).

3. I have borrowed this term, "excellence," from a quotation by Lorde that seems extremely relevant here: "This internal requirement toward excellence which we learn from the erotic must not be misconstrued as demanding the impossible from ourselves nor from others. Such a demand incapacitates everyone in the process. For the erotic is not a question only of what we do; it is a question of how acutely and fully we can feel in the doing" (1984: 54).

4. Simon argues, "We often experience our sexual selves as coming from within largely because the moment is illuminated with a sense of knowing yourself as you have always been for the first time, knowing yourself in an especially confirming way" (1996: 138). Simon goes so far as to suggest that the "intensity of feeling [perhaps also of sexual passion?] derives not from revealing ourselves to the other, but in revealing ourselves to ourselves. The other is merely the occasion" (153).

1. These cases occurred in banks, private corporations, and state companies such as PEMEX, the state's petroleum company. In one legal case involving PEMEX, after months of legal battles, a federal court ordered that the worker be reinstated in his job, establishing an important legal precedent against discrimination (Galván Díaz and Luna Millán 1992; Pereyra 1992).

2. This figure was perhaps but a fraction of the total number. At the time, the Secretariat of Health estimated a rate of underreporting of AIDS cases of more than 50%. By the end of 1999, the number of reported AIDS cases was 42,762 (figure obtained from the Amigos contra el SIDA website, www.aids-sida.org/esta distica.html, accessed on 3/29/00).

3. By the end of 1999, there had been a small decrease in this proportion to 37% (figure obtained from the Amigos contra el SIDA website, www.aids-sida.org/es-tadistica.html, accessed on 3/29/00). However, according to Magis Rodríguez et al. (1998) there is some evidence that this proportion is probably an underestimation.

4. This ratio began to reverse in subsequent years, given that the number of cases of HIV transmission through blood transfusions dramatically decreased when testing of blood products became the norm in 1987.

5. Magis Rodríguez et al. (1998) indicate that although the epidemic is still primarily urban, there has been a trend toward *"ruralización,"* as the number of AIDS cases in towns that have a population of 2,500 or less increased from 3.7% in 1994 to 6% by 1997.

6. This figure had dropped to 18% by the end of 1999, which suggests some improvement in AIDS epidemiological surveillance in Mexico (figure obtained from the Amigos contra el SIDA website, www.aids-sida.org/estadistica.html, accessed on 3/29/00).

7. By May 1997, the number of AIDS cases in Jalisco had increased to 3,678, and the proportions by gender were 79% for men and 21% for women (figures obtained from COESIDA's Boletín Mensual Epidemiológico, at the website sida.udg.mx/org/coesida/boletin/mayo-97.html, accessed on 3/29/00).

8. This figure had increased to 58% by May 1997 (figure obtained from COESIDA's Boletín Mensual Epidemiológico, at the website sida.udg.mx/org/coesida/boletin/mayo-97.html, accessed on 3/29/00).

9. The problem with collecting data about causes of transmission among AIDS cases in Jalisco appears to be getting worse, as the proportion of cases for which the cause of transmission was unknown had increased to 56% by 1997.

10. In 1998, according to Magis Rodríguez et al. (1998), 13% of AIDS cases could be traced to blood transfusions or donations.

11. Magis Rodríguez et al. (1998) report that 78% of the men with AIDS and 73% of the women were between twenty-five and forty-four years old at the time of diagnosis.

12. This same study found seroprevalence rates of 25% in a similar sample in Mexico City, 12% in Merida, 9% in Acapulco, 7% in Tijuana, and 2% in Monterrey.

13. This structure is typical of the relationship between the federal government and the states' governments in Mexico. The states often create offices that are parallel to those at the federal level, and the federal offices establish a coordination function that does not involve direct supervision.

14. Since the time of my study, a number of new groups have emerged. I do not account here for efforts initiated in Guadalajara after 1995.

15. Altman alludes to this "subversive" aspect of simple AIDS educational actions when he states: "Because AIDS affects disproportionately those who are marginalised by virtue of sexuality, gender, behaviour, ethnicity or wealth, organising around AIDS tends to disrupt existing structures and discourses of power. In the developing world . . . the provision of even basic information or support to those who are infected can require actions which are politically radical" (1993: 1).

16. A common complaint among members of NGOs concerned what they saw as the political careers of the officials who had led COESIDA. In their view, these officials perceived their work directing COESIDA as a springboard for their political careers, and not as public service. This began to change in 1995 when the newly elected PAN government took office. See the conclusion for details about this transition.

17. This type of approach is criticized by health educators who believe that social change happens as a result of individuals' ability to question the social conditions surrounding them by developing a "rational insight into their lives," as Brown and Margo state. For these authors, "health education programs often rely on techniques that manipulate behavior rather than facilitating individuals' and groups' abilities to influence and control their physical, social and economic environments" (1978: 9).

18. For Bandura, "self-efficacy is concerned with people's beliefs that they can exert control over their motivation and behavior and over their social environment. People's beliefs about their capabilities affect what they choose to do, how much effort they mobilize, how long they will persevere in the face of difficulties, whether they engage in self-debilitating or self-encouraging thought patterns, and the amount of stress and depression they experience in taxing situations." This

author relates the concept of self-efficacy to a combination of self-protection, self-regulation, self-motivation, self-guidance, and self-assurance. In this theory, the acquisition of self-efficacy is regarded as dependent on a person's belief that he or she can take appropriate action as needed. "When people lack a sense of self-efficacy, they do not manage situations effectively even though they know what to do and possess the requisite skills. Self-inefficacious thinking creates discrepancies between knowledge and self-protective action" (1987: 1).

19. See Bandura 1987. This influential author is one of the strong supporters of strategies that provide both an "awareness and knowledge of the profound threat of AIDS" (1987: 4) and "guidance on how to translate [individuals'] concerns into efficacious actions" (5). His model strongly relies on what he calls "social modeling," which he feels "ought to be designed to build self-assurance as well as to convey rules for how to deal effectively with troublesome situations" (6). In Bandura's opinion, role playing constitutes an initial "simulated situation" in which individuals "need not fear making mistakes or appearing inadequate.... The simulated practice is continued until the skills are performed efficiently and spontaneously" (7).

20. See also Castro 1989.

21. The emphasis of HIV prevention programs on the dissemination of information became the standard in many places besides Mexico. See Aggleton 1989; Bandura 1987; Freudenberg 1990; Patton 1990; and Kippax and Crawford 1993. Some of these authors criticize the emphasis on information dissemination and favor instead interventions that provide personal awareness of risk and skills to enact new behaviors (including practice of those skills through role playing). Others are critical of the latter approach as well. They question overall the emphasis on individual behavior and favor instead an emphasis on the relational and environmental factors affecting behavior and on the meanings that sex and drugs acquire in the context of interpersonal and group relations.

22. This goal was consistent with what Bandura felt was a prerequisite for self-efficacy regarding HIV prevention. Bandura claimed that "what people need is sound information about how AIDS is transmitted, guidance about how to regulate their behavior, and firm belief in their personal efficacy to turn concepts into effective preventive actions." "To be more effective," Bandura suggested that "health communication should instill in people the belief that they have the capability to alter their health habits and should instruct them how to do it" (1987: 3). This last notion is intrinsically connected with the idea that if educators convince people that they are capable of taking an action, they will.

23. Parker notes a similar problem in Brazil, where directly translated materials that focused "on restricting the sexual repertoire" were counter to a local "emphasis on *fazendo tudo*," or "doing it all" (1993b: 79).

24. This undated, but recent, brochure is produced by CONASIDA and simply called "Para universitarios" (For university students). The brochure also contains information about social participation and asks students to join the fight against AIDS by volunteering or doing their "social service"—a requirement in most Mexican universities—with CONASIDA or by becoming peer educators in their own social networks. The brochure indicates that its creation was supported by the Panamerican Health Organization and the World Health Organization.

25. This title implies a double entendre. Adding the word *con* so that the title reads "No coja con riesgos" changes the meaning in colloquial Mexican Spanish to "Don't fuck riskily."

26. The number seems to be an exaggeration for several reasons. First, the total population of Guadalajara is around 3.5 million. Second, the cost of printing and distributing that number of brochures bears no correspondence with the organization's extremely limited budget. Third, in 1998, and with a much larger budget and staff, CONASIDA printed approximately 800,000 brochures to be used in Mexico City and in the rest of the nation.

27. Indeed, the tone of the training was so transgressive in the Guadalajaran context that when similar training was offered by Ser Humano in mid-1995, the police were contacted anonymously and told that the organization was going to be holding "a homosexual orgy" in its locale. A squad team showed up ready to close down the place. Fortunately, the educators were quick to contact the state AIDS council, and the police were convinced that what was being offered was HIV prevention training.

CHAPTER TEN: USE OF HIV PREVENTION TOOLS

1. This is consistent with research findings about AIDS knowledge in Mexico. A national survey conducted by CONASIDA in the late 1980s (Izazola et al. 1989) showed that 98% of respondents had heard about AIDS, 83% knew AIDS was an infectious disease, 73% knew the disease was caused by a virus, 93% knew that a test was available to find out if a person is infected, and 97% knew that the disease could be transmitted through sex with an infected person. Regarding transmission, 97% indicated that the disease can be prevented by avoiding sex with an infected person, 70% said that reducing the number of sexual partners was a preventive measure, and 65% said that AIDS could be prevented by using a condom during sex. The survey also revealed that 70% could identify a condom when they saw one. The figures were even higher among students, homosexual men, and health care workers.

2. A national survey by Izazola et al. (1989) indicated that 73% of respondents had heard messages about AIDS on the radio, 72% on television, 50% had read mes-

sages in newspapers, 23% in magazines, 9% in brochures, and 4% in books. See also Ramírez et al. 1994; Sepúlveda 1993.

3. In a national survey conducted in the late 1980s, over 70% of respondents had heard or seen messages about AIDS on radio and television, but only 9% had read AIDS-related brochures, and 36% had never seen a written message. Of the sample, 93% had never seen any small media promotional materials containing AIDS messages such as posters, matchboxes, stickers, ashtrays, or key chains (Izazola et al. 1989).

4. In a study of men with homosexual behaviors in Ciudad Juárez: "Sixty percent of the respondents had negative opinions (n = 113) and 40% (n = 75) had positive opinions about condom use. Individuals who had a negative opinion of condoms reported less use of condoms than those who had a positive opinion" (Ramírez et al. 1994: 171).

5. In U.S. settings like San Francisco, some HIV-positive people have reported using a similar strategy to decide that a potential partner is also HIV-positive, which they have taken to mean that there is no need for protection (Díaz 1999).

6. See Watney 1993.

7. Throughout this account, Gonzalo tried to speak about this person using the feminine article—which would apply to the word *persona*, which is feminine—or neutral articles and pronouns. His choice of words indicated that he did not want to specify that this person was a man and he had mastered, like others in my sample, the art of speaking neutrally. Here I have used the plural to achieve the same effect (mimicking current colloquial practice in the United States). Gonzalo was not consistent as the narration continued, and eventually he started referring to his partner using masculine forms.

8. This is consistent with Díaz's (1998) findings. Latino gay men in his San Francisco study often disassociated themselves from responsibility for their decisions during sex by thinking of sex as something that happened to them, not as something they did.

9. Gold (1993) argues that relying on stereotypes—positive or negative—in assessing how much risk a partner poses is probably more common during moments of intense sexual arousal, which he calls "being on-line."

CHAPTER ELEVEN: THE RELATIONAL CONTEXT OF HIV RISK

1. This idea is consistent with the notion that individuals are actors who interpret perceived norms and adapt them to fit their own life situations. See Campenhoudt et al. 1997 for more on this issue.

2. In this sense, my findings are at odds with those of researchers who believe that verbal communication is crucial to ensure condom use, such as Alhmeyer and Ludwig, who, focusing on European societies, suggest, "Without having talked about it at all, it is very difficult to bring the condom in" (1997: 36).

3. See the articles in Campenhoudt et al. 1997 for a more comprehensive theorizing of the relational aspects affecting HIV prevention measures.

4. This alludes to a connection between the exchange of fluids and perceptions of sexual intimacy, seen here as a barrier to condom use (Cohen and Hubert 1997).

5. For an account of sex between men among construction workers in Mexico, see Liguori, González Block, and Aggleton 1996. These authors provide interesting evidence of sexual games among the workers at a Mexico City construction site— sexual games established through *albures* and casual touching.

6. For discussion of this issue see Sobo 1995; Parker 1996a, b; Cáceres et al. 1997; Cohen and Hubert 1997; Gogna and Ramos 2000; Mane and Aggleton 2000; Paiva 2000; and Parker, Easton, and Klein 2000.

7. This same connection is present in Sobo's (1995) study with impoverished African American women in Cleveland. Sobo found that women were able to identify situations in which they or their friends acted against their self-interest when they felt they were in love with a man who was doing things that negatively affected them, such as cheating on them.

8. Note that I use the phrase "acceptance of fate" and not "fatalism." I consider it important to distinguish what constitutes a culturally based sense of resignation to events regarded as being uncontrollable from the kind of pessimism that the word "fatalism" implies.

9. This is consistent with the view that "[n]ot using condoms also has a strategic sense. . . . [It may] be the expression of the wish for increased intimacy and total mutual trust. The use of condoms then is a type of information for the partner regarding the state of the relationship" (Bastard et al. 1997: 55). A similar phenomenon has been noted by Parker (1993a).

10. Davies and Weatherburn refer to this difficulty of turning the request for safe sex into an expression of love. "It is assumed that the individual will want to have safer, non-penetrative sex as an expression of love for the other. But this tendency is contradicted by the deeply rooted symbolic meaning of penetration as an expression of the same love. It is this contradiction that lies at the heart of the problem of safer sex" (1991: 114).

11. See Davies and Weatherburn 1991 and Levine 1992 for more on this issue.

12. I have borrowed this term from Watney 1993.

13. Bolton extends this idea to the field of AIDS-related sex research in general and adds an interesting point. "Sex consists of both, pleasure and danger, but, by focusing on risks, too many of the positive dimensions of sexuality have been ignored along with the richness and complexity of behavior in this domain. Sex research has been the servant of repressive, antisexual forces because of this narrow vision" (1992: 153).

14. Kendall (1995) discusses this issue further using Giddens's conceptualization of the historical creation of the modern concept of risk—the notion that risk as we know it today in Western societies is a product of a modern sense of control over the outcomes of events taking place in our lives and a sense that we can control the outcomes through our behavior. Based on this notion, Kendall offers a characterization of risk that involves its involuntary nature, the acceptance that risky behavior is a part of everyday life, the cumulative nature of isolated risks, and individuals' ability to make rational choices and consciously adopt certain risks. However, during sex, some risks might not be rationally evaluated. As Kippax and Crawford state, "many sexual episodes take place without forethought and decision-making, at least at the conscious level . . . , action may precede thought and intention. There may be no deliberation, no intention to act in a certain way" (1993: 266).

15. Bastard et al. suggest that "the aim of handling the risk [for HIV infection] is not necessarily health preservation but part of the relationship's language" or "the expression of relational strategies" (1997: 55).

16. My critique of HIV prevention work in Guadalajara presented in the remainder of this chapter necessarily draws not just on my fieldwork but also on my training as a public health educator and my eleven years of hands-on experience designing HIV prevention programs. (Most of my work has been in San Francisco—at the San Francisco AIDS Foundation and the STOP AIDS Project—though I have also assisted in the creation of HIV prevention programs in Mexico and Latin America.) Of course, as I have argued, the social and cultural context in Guadalajara has its own characteristics and requires distinctive approaches. However, at least in a general sense my practical experience has given me perspective on the challenges confronting AIDS educators. That there are indeed some similarities to these challenges as experienced in different parts of the world is also suggested by the close fit between some of my own critiques and suggestions and those that have been put forward by authors from a range of countries in practically every region in the world.

17. For more on the topic of linearity of behavior see Kippax and Crawford 1993 and Ingham and van Zessen 1997.

18. The role of solidarity in HIV prevention work has been highlighted by Daniel and Parker (1993).

1. For instance, women in LeVine's study (1993) hoped that their daughters would have more equality in their relations with men (more than what their own generation had achieved) but also carefully conveyed to them the urgency of a woman's need to protect her social status as decent and indirectly suggested to them that their relations with men would be unequal by definition. Men in Gutmann's study (1996) desired not to be identified with the image of the Mexican macho but were careful not to appear to be *mandilones,* men who are subservient to women. They were trying to craft new identities as men and wanted those identities not only to reflect their fairness but also to express that they still were the ones with power over women.

2. *Mayates* in Prieur's study (1998)—masculine heterosexually identified men who had relations with the *jotas,* the effeminate men who tried to pass as women—were becoming aware that their behavior could be seen by others as resembling that of middle-class *homosexuales.* The *jotas* themselves embodied the traditional and stereotypical role of *maricones* (unmanly men) but were aware of their membership within the larger world of Mexican homosexuality and understood that their identity was one among other options within that world.

3. In a field such as the study of sexuality, rarely do we consider how the process works in the opposite direction, from the so-called developing world to the rich industrialized countries. I would argue, in that regard, that some of the analysis included in this and other work conducted in developing countries might prove to offer important analytical tools for research conducted in places like the United States, not only with ethnic minority populations but also in the social mainstream.

4. See Altman 1996; and Parker 1999. While this book was in press, a new book by Altman (2001) focusing specifically on sexuality and globalization was published. See also Boellstorff 1999; Larvie 1999; Povinelli and Chauncey 1999; and Rofel 1999.

5. Some analyses are strongly focused on locality and criticize analyses of globalization for oversimplifying the forms in which Western culture influences local cultures in the developing world. For instance, in Thailand, Jackson (1989, 1997) has noted the culturally bound integration of homosexual behaviors into Thai identities, which, he argues, cannot be simply explained by what he calls the "borrowing" of Western sexual identities. Similarly, Balachandran (1997) has mapped complicated arrangements of homosexual identities in India and has emphasized that the emergence of gay spaces is related to a uniquely local geography where the notion of "gay" intersects with an Indian "cultural ethos."

6. Mauricio's realization of his homosexuality is triggered by his attraction to a Mexican man who teaches at Stanford University and is visiting Mexico City to teach a seminar at Mauricio's university. Mauricio's first reaction is to deny his

desire and accelerate the plan to marry his girlfriend, but he soon realizes that he ought to confront his homosexuality, tell his parents about it, and live a *vida gay* (a gay life). In this *telenovela,* the character of Jim, the Stanford professor, allows the writers to depict ideas about modern gay identities and lifestyles as they imagine them to be in the United States. Jim first becomes the person guiding Mauricio through the process of self-acceptance and later also becomes his lover.

Bibliography

Abramson, Paul. 1992. "Sex, Lies, and Ethnography." In *The Time of AIDS: Social Analysis, Theory, and Method,* edited by Gilbert Herdt and Shirley Lindenbaum, 101–23. Newbury Park, Calif.: Sage Publications.

Aggleton, Peter. 1989. "Evaluating Health Education about AIDS." In *AIDS: Social Representations and Social Practices,* edited by Peter Aggleton, Graham Hart, and Peter Davies, 220–36. New York: Falmer Press.

Aggleton, Peter, Peter Davies, and Graham Hart, eds. 1990. *AIDS: Individual, Cultural and Policy Dimensions.* London: Falmer Press.

———. 1994. *AIDS: Foundations for the Future.* London: Taylor and Francis.

Aggleton, Peter, Graham Hart, and Peter Davies, eds. 1991. *AIDS: Responses, Interventions and Care.* London: Falmer Press.

Ahlmeyer, Heinrich W., and Dominique Ludwig. 1997. "Norms of Communication and Communication as a Norm in the Intimate Social System." In *Sexual Interactions and HIV Risk,* edited by Luc Van Campenhoudt et al., 22–43. London: Taylor and Francis.

Almaguer, Tomás. 1991. "Chicano Men: A Cartography of Homosexual Identity and Behavior." *Differences* 3, no. 2:75–100.

Altman, Dennis. 1986. *AIDS in the Mind of America.* Garden City, N.Y.: Anchor Press, Doubleday.

———. 1993. "Expertise, Legitimacy and the Centrality of Community." In *AIDS: Facing the Second Decade,* edited by Peter Aggleton, Peter Davies, and Graham Hart, 1–12. London: Falmer Press.

———. 1994. *Power and Community: Organizational and Cultural Responses to AIDS.* London: Taylor and Francis.

———. 1996. "Rupture or Continuity? The Internalization of Gay Identities." *Social Text* 14, no. 3:78–94.

———. 2001. *Global Sex.* Chicago: University of Chicago Press.

Alvarez, Rubén. 1988. "Pacientes y médicos. Entrevistas." In *El SIDA en México: Los Efectos Sociales,* edited by Francisco Galván Díaz, 161–69. México, D.F.: Universidad Autónoma Metropolitana.

Balachandran, Chandra S. 1997. "Cultural Geographic Issues in the Study of 'Gay' Spaces in India." Paper presented at the First International Conference, Beyond Boundaries, Sexuality across Cultures, July 29–August 1, Amsterdam.

Balderston, Daniel. 1997. "Excluded Middle? Bisexuality in *Doña Herlinda y su hijo.*" In *Sex and Sexuality in Latin America,* edited by Daniel Balderston and Donna J. Guy, 190–99. New York: New York University Press.

Bandura, Albert. 1977. *Social Learning Theory.* Englewood Cliffs, N.J.: Prentice Hall.

———. 1986. *Social Foundations of Thought and Action.* Englewood Cliffs, N.J.: Prentice Hall.

———. 1987. "Perceived Self-Efficacy in the Exercise of Control over AIDS Infection." Paper presented at the NIMH Drug Abuse Conference, Women and AIDS: Promoting Health Behaviors, Bethesda, Md.

Bastard, Benoît, and Laura Cardia-Voneche. 1997. "From Rational Individual to Actor Ensnared in a Web of Affective and Sexual Relations." In *Sexual Interactions and HIV Risk,* edited by Luc Van Campenhoudt et al., 127–34. London: Taylor and Francis.

Bastard, Benoît, et al. 1997. "Relationships between Sexual Partners and Ways of Adapting to the Risk of AIDS: Landmarks for a Relationship-Oriented Conceptual Framework." In *Sexual Interactions and HIV Risk,* edited by Luc Van Campenhoudt et al., 44–58. London: Taylor and Francis.

Bautista, Juan Carlos. 1990. "¿El fin de la democracia gay?" In *El nuevo arte de amar,* edited by Sergio Bellinghausen, 125–27. México, D.F.: Cal y Arena.

Bayer, Ronald. 1989. *Private Acts, Social Consequences: AIDS and the Politics of Public Health.* New York: Free Press.

———. 1994. "AIDS Prevention and Cultural Sensitivity: Are They Compatible?" *American Journal of Public Health* 84, no. 6 (June): 895–98.

Bell, Daniel. 1990. "The End of Ideology in the West." In *Culture and Society: Contemporary Debates,* edited by Jeffrey C. Alexander and Steven Seidman, 290–97. Cambridge: Cambridge University Press. Originally published in Daniel Bell, *The End of Ideology* (Cambridge: Harvard University Press, 1988).

Bellinghausen, Sergio. 1990. *El nuevo arte de amar.* México, D.F.: Cal y Arena.

Blackwood, Evelyn. 1986. "Breaking the Mirror: The Construction of Lesbianism and the Anthropological Discourse of Homosexuality." In *The Many Faces of Homosexuality,* edited by Evelyn Blackwood, 1–17. New York: Harrington Park Press.

Boellstorff, Tom. 1999. "The Perfect Path: Gay Men, Marriage, Indonesia." *GLQ—A Journal of Lesbian and Gay Studies* 5, no. 4: 475–509.

Bolton, Ralph. 1992. "Mapping Terra Incognita—Sex Research for AIDS Prevention, An Urgent Agenda for the 1990s." In *The Time of AIDS: Social Analysis, Theory, and Method,* edited by Gilbert Herdt and Shirley Lindenbaum, 124–58. Newbury Park, Calif.: Sage Publications.

Bourdieu, Pierre. 1994. "Structures, Habitus, Power: Basis for a Theory of Symbolic Power." In *Culture/Power/History: A Reader in Contemporary Social Theory,* edited by Nicholas B. Dirks, Geoff Eley, and Sherry B. Ortner, 155–99. Princeton: Princeton University Press. Originally published in Pierre Bourdieu, *Outline of a Theory of Practice* (Cambridge: Cambridge University Press, 1977).

Bourdieu, Pierre, and Loïc Wacquant, 1992. *An Invitation to Reflexive Sociology.* Chicago: University of Chicago Press.

Broughton, Simon, et al., eds. 1994. *World Music: The Rough Guide.* London: Rough Guides.

Brown, Richard, and Glen Elgin Margo. 1978. "Health Education: Can the Reformers Be Reformed?" *International Journal of Health Services* 8, no. 1:3–26.

Buffington, Rob. 1997. *"Los Jotos:* Contested Visions of Homosexuality in Modern Mexico." In *Sex and Sexuality in Latin America,* edited by Daniel Balderston and Donna J. Guy, 118–32. New York: New York University Press.

Burawoy, Michael, et al. 1991. *Ethnography Unbound.* Berkeley and Los Angeles: University of California Press.

Cáceres, Carlos F., and Ana M. Rosasco. 1997. "The Correlates of Safer Behavior among Homosexually Active Men in Lima." *AIDS* 11, Suppl. 1:S53–S59.

Cáceres, Carlos F., et al. 1991. "Sexual Behavior and Frequency of Antibodies to Type 1 Human Immunodeficiency Virus (HIV-1) in a Group of Peruvian Male Homosexuals." *Bulletin of PAHO* 25, no. 4:306–19.

Cáceres, Carlos F., et al. 1994. "Evaluating a School-Based Intervention for STD/AIDS Prevention in Peru." *Journal of Adolescent Health* 15:582–91.

Cáceres, Carlos F., et al. 1997. "Young People and the Structure of Sexual Risks in Lima." *AIDS* 11, Suppl. 1:S67–S77.

Cáceres, Carlos F., Barbara Vanoss Marín, and E. Sid Hudes. 2000. "Sexual Coercion among Youth and Young Adults in Lima, Peru." *Journal of Adolescent Health* 27, no. 5: 361–67.

Campenhoudt, Luc Van, and Mitchell Cohen. 1997. "Interaction and Risk-Related Behaviour: Theoretical and Heuristic Landmarks." In *Sexual Interactions and*

HIV Risk, edited by Luc Van Campenhoudt et al., 59–74. London: Taylor and Francis.

Campenhoudt, Luc Van, et al. 1997. *Sexual Interactions and HIV Risk.* London: Taylor and Francis.

Carballo-Diéguez, Alex. 1989. "Hispanic Culture, Gay Male Culture, and AIDS." *Journal of Counseling and Development* 68 : 26–30.

Cárdenas, Lourdes. 1988. "Dramatismo, esperanza y frustración: Dos enfermos de SIDA, entrevistas." In *El SIDA en México: Los efectos sociales,* edited by Francisco Galván Díaz, 173–79. México, D.F.: Universidad Autónoma Metropolitana.

Carrier, Joseph M. 1972. "Urban Mexican Male Encounters: An Analysis of Participants and Coping Strategies." Ph.D. diss., University of California, Irvine.

———. 1976. "Family Attitudes and Mexican Male Homosexuality." *Urban Life* 5 : 359–75.

———. 1985. "Mexican Male Bisexuality." In *Bisexualities: Theory and Research,* edited by Fritz Klein and Timothy J. Wolf, 75–85. New York: Haworth Press.

———. 1989a. "Gay Liberation and Coming Out in Mexico." *Journal of Homosexuality* 17, nos. 3–4 : 225–52.

———. 1989b. "Sexual Behavior and Spread of AIDS in Mexico." *Medical Anthropology* 10, nos. 2–3 : 129–42.

———. 1995. *De Los Otros: Intimacy and Homosexuality among Mexican Men.* New York: Columbia University Press.

Carrier, Joseph M., and Raúl Magaña. 1991. "Use of Ethnosexual Data on Men of Mexican Origin for HIV/AIDS Prevention Programs." *Journal of Sex Research* 28, no. 2 : 189–202.

Carrillo, Héctor. 1993–94. "Another Crack in the Mirror: The Politics of AIDS Prevention in Mexico." *International Quarterly of Community Health Education* 14, no. 2 : 129–52.

———. 1999. "Cultural Change, Hybridity, and Male Homosexuality in Mexico." *Culture, Health, and Sexuality* 1, no. 3 : 223–38.

Carrillo, Héctor, et al. 1992. *AIDS Hotline Training Manual.* San Francisco: San Francisco AIDS Foundation.

Carrillo-Rosado, Héctor. 1995. "Lifting the Veil of Silence: Sexuality, Social Influence, and the Practice of AIDS Prevention in Modern Mexico." Dr.P.H. diss., University of California, Berkeley.

Carrillo Rosado, María Elvira. 1997. "La implementación de un servicio de información y orientación sobre el SIDA vía telefónica basado en la terapia breve." Tesis de licenciatura, Universidad Nacional Autónoma de México.

Cass, Vivienne. 1983–84. "Homosexual Identity: A Concept in Need of Definition." *Journal of Homosexuality* 9, no. 2/3 (winter/spring): 105–26.

Castro, Roberto. 1989. "La educación como estrategia prioritaria contra el SIDA: Retos y dilemas." In *Ciencia y Sociedad en México,* edited by Jaime Sepúlveda Amor et al., 413–33. México, D.F.: Fondo de Cultura Económica.

Cedillo Nolasco, Rosa, and Aurora Morales Delgadillo. 1990. "Chicas de hoy: Un muestreo." In *El nuevo arte de amar,* edited by Sergio Bellinghausen, 47–51. México, D.F.: Cal y Arena.

Chauncey, George. 1982–83. "Female Deviance." *Salmagundi,* nos. 58–59: 3114–46.

———. 1994. *Gay New York: Gender, Urban Culture, and the Making of the Gay Male World, 1890–1940.* New York: Basic Books.

Clifford, James. 1986. *Writing Culture: The Poetics and Politics of Ethnography,* edited by James Clifford and George Marcus. Berkeley and Los Angeles: University of California Press.

Cohen, Mitchell, and Michel Hubert. 1997. "The Place of Time in Understanding Sexual Behaviour and Designing HIV/AIDS Prevention Programs." In *Sexual Interactions and HIV Risk,* edited by Luc Van Campenhoudt et al., 196–22. London: Taylor and Francis.

CONASIDA. 1995. "Indicadores y noticias de salud: Consejo Nacional de Prevención y Control del SIDA (CONASIDA)," Informe de Actividades, 1988–1994. *Salud Pública de México* 37, no. 6:669–76.

Connell, Robert W., and Gary W. Dowsett, eds. 1992. *Rethinking Sex: Social Theory and Sexuality Research.* Carlton, Vic.: Melbourne University Press.

Cornwall, Andrea, and Nancy Lindisfarne, eds. 1994. *Dislocating Masculinity: Comparative Ethnographies.* London: Routledge.

Cortés Guardado, Marco Antonio. 1997. *Integración y conflicto social en Jalisco.* Guadalajara: Universidad de Guadalajara.

Daniel, Herbert, and Richard Parker. 1993. "The Third Epidemic: An Exercise in Solidarity." In *Sexuality, Politics and AIDS in Brazil,* edited by Herbert Daniel and Richard Parker, 49–61. London: Falmer Press.

Davies, Peter, and Peter Weatherburn. 1991. "Towards a General Model of Sexual Negotiation." In *AIDS: Responses, Interventions and Care,* edited by Peter Aggleton, Graham Hart, and Peter Davies, 111–25. London: Falmer Press.

Dehesa, Germán. 1998. Prologue to *Mirada de mujer* by Bernardo Romero and Mónica Agudelo. México, D.F.: Plaza y Janés Editores.

De La Cancela, Victor. 1989. "Minority AIDS Prevention: Moving beyond Cultural Perspectives towards Sociopolitical Empowerment." *AIDS Education and Prevention* 1, no. 2:141–53.

Díaz, Rafael M. 1998. *Latino Gay Men and HIV.* New York: Routledge.

———. 1999. "Trips to Fantasy Island: Contexts of Risky Sex for San Francisco Gay Men." *Sexualities* 2, no. 1:89–112.

———. 2000. "Cultural Regulation, Self-Regulation, and Sexuality: A Psychocultural Model of HIV Risk in Latino Gay Men." In *Framing the Sexual Subject,* edited by Richard Parker, Regina Maria Barbosa, and Peter Aggleton, 191–215. Berkeley and Los Angeles: University of California Press.

Díaz Betancourt, Arturo. 1991. "De la lucha contra el SIDA: Ser y quehacer de las ONGs en México." *Sociedad y SIDA,* no. 6 (March): 5.

Döring, M. Teresa. 1990. *El mexicano ante la sexualidad.* México, D.F.: Ediciones y Distribuciones Hispánicas.

Dowsett, Gary W. 1996. *Practicing Desire: Homosexual Sex in the Era of AIDS.* Stanford: Stanford University Press.

Epstein, Steven. 1987. "Gay Politics, Ethnic Identity: The Limits of Social Constructionism." *Socialist Review* 17:9–51.

———. 1994. "A Queer Encounter: Sociology and the Study of Sexuality." *Sociological Theory* 12, no. 2: 188–202.

Escobar, Arturo, and Sonia E. Alvarez, eds. 1992. *The Making of Social Movements in Latin America.* Boulder: Westview Press.

Escoffier, Jeffrey. 1985. The Politics of Gay Identity. *Socialist Review* 82/83:119–53.

Ferrand, Alexis, and Tom A. B. Snijders. 1997. "Social Networks and Normative Tensions." In *Sexual Interactions and HIV Risk,* edited by Luc Van Campenhoudt et al., 6–21. London: Taylor and Francis.

Fishbein, Martin. 1967. "Attitude and the Prediction of Behavior." In *Readings in Attitude Theory and Measurement.* New York: Wiley.

———. 1993. Introduction to *The Theory of Reasoned Action: Its Applications to AIDS-Preventive Behaviour,* edited by Deborah J. Terry, Cynthia Gallois, and Malcolm McCamish, xv–xxv. Oxford: Pergamon Press.

Fishbein, Martin, and Susan E. Middlestadt. 1987. "Using the Theory of Reasoned Action to Develop Educational Interventions: Application to Illicit Drug Use." *Health Education Research* 2, no. 4:361–71.

Fisher, Jeffrey D., and William A. Fisher. 1992. "Changing AIDS-Risk Behavior." *Psychological Bulletin* 111, no. 3:455–74.

Forrest, Katherine A., et al. 1993. "Exploring Norms and Beliefs Related to AIDS Prevention among California Hispanic Men." *Family Planning Perspectives* 25, no. 3:111–17.

Foucault, Michel. 1980. *History of Sexuality.* Vol. 1, *An Introduction.* New York: Vintage.

Frankenberg, Ronald. 1963. "Participant Observers." *New Society* 23:22–23.

Freedman, Estelle B., and John D'Emilio. 1988. *Intimate Matters: A History of Sexuality in America.* New York: Harper and Row.

Freire, Paulo. 1988. *Pedagogía del oprimido.* México, D.F.: Siglo Veintiuno Editores.

Freudenberg, Nicholas. 1990. "AIDS Prevention in the United States: Lessons from the First Decade." *International Journal of Health Services* 20, no. 4:589–99.

Fry, Peter. 1985. "Male Homosexuality and Spirit Possession in Brazil." *Journal of Homosexuality* 11, no. 3/4:137–53.

Gagnon, John H. 1986. "Sexual Scripts: Permanence and Change." *Archives of Sexual Behavior* 15, no. 2:97–120.

Gagnon, John H., and William Simon. 1973. *Sexual Conduct: The Social Sources of Human Sexuality.* Chicago: Aldine Publishing Co.

Galván Díaz, Francisco. 1988. *El SIDA en México: Los efectos sociales.* México, D.F.: Universidad Autónoma Metropolitana.

Galván Díaz, Francisco, and Federico Luna Millán. 1992. "Walter vs. PEMEX ¿Prevalecerá el derecho?" *Sociedad y SIDA,* no. 24 (September): 1.

García, Brígida, and Orlandina de Oliveira. 1992. "El nuevo perfil del mercado de trabajo femenino: 1976–1987." In *La voluntad de ser: Mujeres en los noventa,* edited by María Luisa Tarrés, 157–71. México, D.F.: El Colegio de México, 1992.

García Canclini, Néstor. 1995. *Hybrid Cultures: Strategies for Entering and Leaving Modernity.* Trans. Christopher L. Chiappary and Silvia L. López. Minneapolis: University of Minnesota Press. Originally published as *Culturas Híbridas: Estrategias para Entrar y Salir de la Modernidad* (México, D.F.: Grijalbo, 1989).

Geertz, Clifford. 1973. *The Interpretation of Cultures.* New York: Basic Books.

Giddens, Anthony. 1990. *The Consequences of Modernity.* Stanford: Stanford University Press.

———. 1991. *Modernity and Self-Identity.* Stanford: Stanford University Press.

———. 1992. *The Transformation of Intimacy.* Stanford: Stanford University Press.

Glaser, Barney, and Anselm Strauss. 1992. *The Discovery of Grounded Theory.* Chicago: Aldine, 1973.

Gogna, Mónica, and Silvina Ramos. 2000. "Gender Stereotypes and Power Relations: Unacknowledged Risks for STDs in Argentina." In *Framing the Sexual Subject,* edited by Richard Parker, Regina Maria Barbosa, and Peter Aggleton, 117–40. Berkeley and Los Angeles: University of California Press.

Gold, Ron S. 1993. "On the Need to Mind the Gap: On-line versus Off-line Cognitions Underlying Sexual Risk Taking." In *The Theory of Reasoned Action: Its Applications to AIDS-Preventive Behaviour,* edited by Deborah J. Terry, Cynthia Gallois, and Malcolm McCamish, 227–52. Oxford: Pergamon Press.

Goldenberg, Sheldon. 1992. *Thinking Methodologically.* New York: HarperCollins.

Gómezjara, Francisco, and Estanislao Barrera. 1982. *Sociología de la prostitución.* México, D.F.: Fontamara.

González de la Rocha, Mercedes. 1989. "Crisis, economía doméstica y trabajo femenino en Guadalajara." In *Trabajo, Poder y Sexualidad,* edited by Orlandina de Oliveira, 159–85. México, D.F.: El Colegio de México.

González Rodríguez, Sergio. 1990. *Los bajos fondos: El antro, la bohemia y el café.* México, D.F.: Cal y Arena.

González Ruiz, Edgar. 1994. *Cómo propagar el SIDA: Conservadurismo y sexualidad.* México, D.F.: Rayuela Editores.

González Villarreal, Roberto. 1991. "Protesis y profilaxis: Nueva moral sexual." *Sociedad y SIDA,* no. 12 (September): 1.

Gortmaker, Steven L., and José Antonio Izazola. 1993. "El papel de la investigación cuantitativa de la conducta en la prevención del SIDA." In *SIDA, su prevención a través de la educación: Una perspectiva mundial,* edited by Jaime Sepúlveda, Harvey Fineberg, and Jonathan Mann, 25–47. México, D.F.: Editorial el Manual Moderno.

Gramsci, Antonio. 1987. *Selections from the Prison Notebooks of Antonio Gramsci.*

Edited and translated by Quintin Hoare and Geoffrey Nowell Smith. London: Lawrence and Wishart, 1971. Reprint, New York: International Publishers.

Green, James N. 1999. *Beyond Carnival: Male Homosexuality in Twentieth-Century Brazil.* Chicago: University of Chicago Press.

Green, Lawrence W. 1970. "Should Health Education Abandon Attitude Change Strategies? Perspectives from Recent Research." *Health Education Monographs* 1, no. 30:25–48.

———. 1985. "Health Education Models." In *Behavioral Health: A Handbook of Health Enhancement and Disease Prevention,* 181–98. New York: John Wiley.

Guizzardi, Gustavo, Renato Stella, and Jean Remy. 1997. "Rationality and Preventive Measures: The Ambivalence of the Social Discourse on AIDS." In *Sexual Interactions and HIV Risk,* edited by Luc Van Campenhoudt et al., 159–80. London: Taylor and Francis.

Gutmann, Matthew C. 1996. *The Meanings of Macho: Being a Man in Mexico City.* Berkeley and Los Angeles: University of California Press.

Hammersley, Martyn. 1992. *What's Wrong with Ethnography.* New York: Routledge.

Hart, Graham. 1993. "Safer Sex: A Paradigm Revisited." In *AIDS: Facing the Second Decade,* edited by Peter Aggleton, Peter Davies, and Graham Hart, 73–81. London: Falmer Press.

Hellman, Judith Adler. 1994. *Mexican Lives.* New York: New Press.

Herdt, Gilbert. 1981. *Guardians of the Flutes: Idioms of Masculinity.* New York: McGraw Hill.

Herdt, Gilbert, and Andrew M. Boxer. 1991. "Ethnographic Issues in the Study of AIDS." *Journal of Sex Research* 28, no. 2:171–87.

———. 1995. "Bisexuality: Toward a Comparative Theory of Identities and Culture." In *Conceiving Sexuality: Approaches to Sex Research in a Postmodern World,* edited by Richard G. Parker and John H. Gagnon, 69–96. New York: Routledge.

Herdt, Gilbert, and Shirley Lindenbaum, eds. 1992. *The Time of AIDS: Social Analysis, Theory, and Method.* Newbury Park, Calif.: Sage Publications.

Herdt, Gilbert, and Robert J. Stoller. 1990. *Intimate Communications: Erotics and the Study of Culture.* New York: Columbia University Press.

INDRE (Instituto Nacional de Diagnóstico y Referencia Epidemiológicos). 1994. *Boletín Mensual SIDA/ETS* 8, no. 11 (November).

Ingham, Roger, and Gertjan van Zessen. 1997. "From Individual Properties to Interactional Processes." In *Sexual Interactions and HIV Risk,* edited by Luc Van Campenhoudt et al. 83–99. London: Taylor and Francis.

Izazola, José Antonio, et al. 1989. "Conocimientos, actitudes y prácticas relacionadas con el SIDA: Bases para el diseño de programas educativos." In *SIDA, Ciencia y Sociedad en México,* edited by Jaime Sepúlveda Amor et al., 297–336. México, D.F.: Fondo de Cultura Económica.

Izazola-Licea, José Antonio, et al. 1991. "HIV-1 Seropositivity and Behavioral and Sociological Risks among Homosexual and Bisexual Men in Six Mexican Cities." *Journal of Acquired Immune Deficiency Syndromes* 4, no. 6:614–22.

Jackson, Peter A. 1989. *Male Homosexuality in Thailand.* New York: Global Academic Publishers.

———. 1997. "An Explosion of Thai Identities, 1960–1985: The Cultural Limits of Foucaldian History of Sexuality and Globalization Theory." Paper presented at the First International Conference, Beyond Boundaries, Sexuality across Cultures, July 29–August 1, Amsterdam.

Janz, Nancy K., and Marshall H. Becker. 1984. "The Health Belief Model: A Decade Later." *Health Education Quarterly* 11, no. 1 (spring): 1–47.

Kendall, Carl. 1995. "The Construction of Risk in AIDS Control Programs." In *Conceiving Sexuality: Approaches to Sex Research in a Postmodern World,* edited by Richard G. Parker and John H. Gagnon, 249–58. New York: Routledge.

Kippax, Susan, and June Crawford. 1993. "Flaws in the Theory of Reasoned Action." In *The Theory of Reasoned Action: Its Applications to AIDS-Preventive Behaviour,* edited by Deborah J. Terry, Cynthia Gallois, and Malcolm McCamish, 253–76. Oxford: Pergamon Press.

Kline, Anna, and Mark Van Landingham. 1994. "HIV-Infected Women and Sexual Risk Reduction: The Relevance of Existing Models of Behavior Change." *AIDS Education and Prevention* 6, no. 5:390–402.

Kulick, Don. 1998. *Travesti: Sex, Gender, and Culture among Brazilian Transgendered Prostitutes.* Chicago: University of Chicago Press.

Lamas, Marta. 1990. "Freud y las muchachas." In *El nuevo arte de amar,* edited by Sergio Bellinghausen, 67–75. México, D.F.: Cal y Arena.

Lancaster, Roger. 1992. *Life Is Hard: Machismo, Danger, and the Intimacy of Power in Nicaragua.* Berkeley and Los Angeles: University of California Press.

Larvie, Sean Patrick. 1999. "Queerness and the Specter of Brazilian National Ruin." *GLQ—A Journal of Lesbian and Gay Studies* 5, no. 4: 525–57.

Laumann, Edward O., et al. 1994. *The Social Organization of Sexuality: Sexual Practices in the United States.* Chicago: University of Chicago Press.

Lear, Dana. 1995. "Sexual Communication in the Age of AIDS: The Construction of Risk and Trust among Young Adults." *Social Science and Medicine* 41, no. 9: 1311–23.

Levine, Martin P. 1992. "The Implications of Constructionist Theory for Social Research on the AIDS Epidemic among Gay Men." In *The Time of AIDS: Social Analysis, Theory, and Method,* edited by Gilbert Herdt and Shirley Lindenbaum, 185–98. Newbury Park, Calif.: Sage Publications.

LeVine, Sarah. 1993. *Dolor y Alegría: Women and Social Change in Urban Mexico.* Madison: University of Wisconsin Press.

Liguori Ana Luisa, Miguel González Block, and Peter Aggleton. 1996. "Bisexuality and HIV/AIDS in Mexico." In *Bisexualities and AIDS: International Perspectives*, edited by Peter Aggleton, 76–98. London: Taylor and Francis.

Lorde, Audre. 1984. "Uses of the Erotic: The Erotic as Power." In *Sister Outsider: Essays and Speeches*, 53–59. Trumansburg, NY: Crossing Press.

Lumsden, Ian. 1991. *Homosexualidad, sociedad y estado en México*. México, D.F.: Solediciones.

———. 1996. *Machos, Maricones, and Gays: Cuba and Homosexuality*. Philadelphia: Temple University Press.

Magaña, J. R., and Carrier, J. M. 1991. "Mexican and Mexican American Male Sexual Behavior and Spread of AIDS in California." *Journal of Sex Research* 28, no. 3:425–41.

Magis Rodríguez, Carlos, et al. 1998. "La situación del SIDA en México a finales de 1998." *Enfermedades Infecciosas y Microbiológicas* 18, no. 6: 236–44. Full text posted at the SSA website, www.ssa.gob.mx/conasida/arts/eim/sida98.htm, accessed on 3/29/00.

Mane, Purmina, and Peter Aggleton. 2000. "Cross-national Perspectives on Gender and Power." In *Framing the Sexual Subject,* edited by Richard Parker, Regina Maria Barbosa, and Peter Aggleton, 104–16. Berkeley and Los Angeles: University of California Press.

Marcus, George, and Michael Fischer. 1986. *Anthropology as Cultural Critique: An Experimental Moment in the Human Sciences*. Chicago: University of Chicago Press.

Marin, Barbara VanOss, and Gerardo Marin. 1990. "Hispanics and AIDS: Introduction." *Hispanic Journal of Behavioral Sciences* 12, no. 2:107–9.

———. 1992. "Predictors of Condom Accessibility among Hispanics in San Francisco." *American Journal of Public Health* 82, no. 4:592–95.

Martínez López, Juana. 1998. "'Capacitación sobre SIDA': Un modelo aplicado dentro del área educativa del Comité Humanitario de Esfuerzo Compartido contra el SIDA, A.C. (CHECCOS, A.C.), en la ciudad de Guadalajara, Jal." B.A. thesis, National Autonomous University of Mexico.

McIntosh, Mary. 1981. "The Homosexual Role." In *The Making of the Modern Homosexual*, edited by Kenneth Plummer, 30–49. London: Hutchinson.

Medina, Antonio. 1999. "Reforma al código penal del D.F.: Un avance democrático." *Letra S*, monthly suppl. of *La Jornada*, no. 39 (October). Full text posted at the *Jornada* website, www.jornada.unam.mx.

Mejía, Max. 1988. "SIDA: Historias extraordinarias del siglo XX." In *El SIDA en México: Los efectos sociales*, edited by Francisco Galván Díaz, 17–57. México, D.F.: Universidad Autónoma Metropolitana.

Minkler, Meredith. 1997. "Community Organizing among the Elderly Poor in San Francisco's Tenderloin District." In *Community Organizing and Community Building for Health*, edited by Meredith Minkler, 244–58. New Brunswick: Rutgers University Press.

Minton, Henry, and Gary McDonald. 1983–84. "Homosexual Identity Formation as Developmental Process." *Journal of Homosexuality* 9, no. 2/3 (winter/spring): 91–104.

Mitchell, Stephen A. 1988. *Relational Concepts in Psychoanalysis: An Integration.* Cambridge: Harvard University Press.

Monsiváis, Carlos. 1990. "Paisaje de la batalla entre condones: Saldos de la revolución sexual." In *El nuevo arte de amar,* edited by Sergio Bellinghausen, 167–79. México, D.F.: Cal y Arena.

———. 1993. "¿Tantos millones de hombres no hablaremos inglés? (La cultura norteamericana en México)." In *Simbiosis de culturas: Los inmigrantes y su cultura en México,* edited by Guillermo Bonfil Batalla, 455–516. México, D.F.: Fondo de Cultura Económica.

———. 1998. "El mundo soslayado." Prologue to *La Estatua de Sal,* by Salvador Novo. México, D.F.: Consejo Nacional para la Cultura y las Artes.

Moreno, Hortencia. 1990. "Desde la más absoluta virginidad." In *El nuevo arte de amar,* edited by Sergio Bellinghausen, 39–43. México, D.F.: Cal y Arena.

Moriá, José María. 1994. *Breve historia de Jalisco.* México, D.F.: El Colegio de México.

Murray, Stephen O. 1987. "The Family as an Obstacle to the Growth of a Gay Subculture in Mesoamerica." In *Male Homosexuality in Central and South America,* edited by Stephen O. Murray, 118–29. Gai Saber Monograph 5. San Francisco: Instituto Obregón.

———. 1991. "Homosexual Occupation in Mesoamerica?" *Journal of Homosexuality* 21, no. 4: 57–65.

———. 1995. *Latin American Male Homosexualities.* Albuquerque: University of New Mexico Press.

Murray, Stephen O., and Manuel Arboleda. 1987. "Stigma Transformation and Relexification: 'Gay' in Latin America." In *Male Homosexuality in Central and South America,* edited by Stephen O. Murray, 130–138. GAI Saber Monograph 5. San Francisco: Instituto Obregón.

Murray, Stephen O., and Murray R. Dynes. 1995. "Hispanic Homosexuals: A Spanish Lexicon." In *Latin American Male Homosexualities,* edited by Stephen O. Murray, 180–92. Albuquerque: University of New Mexico Press.

Nelson, Steven D. 1994. "Wear Your Hat: Representational Resistance in Safer Sex Discourse." *Journal of Homosexuality* 27, no. 1/2: 285–304.

Novo, Salvador. 1979. "Memoir." In *Now the Volcano: An Anthology of Latin American Gay Literature,* edited by Winston Leyland, 11–47. San Francisco: Gay Sunshine Press.

O'Leary, Ann. 1985. "Self-efficacy and Health." *Behavioral Research Theory* 24, no. 4: 437–51.

Ortner, Sherry, and Whitehead, Harriet, eds. 1981. *Sexual Meanings: The Cultural Construction of Gender and Sexuality.* Cambridge: Cambridge University Press.

Paiva, Vera. 2000. "Gendered Scripts and the Sexual Scene: Promoting Sexual Subjects among Brazilian Teenagers." In *Framing the Sexual Subject,* edited by Richard Parker, Regina Maria Barbosa, and Peter Aggleton, 216–39. Berkeley and Los Angeles: University of California Press.

Parker, Richard G. 1991. *Bodies, Pleasures, and Passions: Sexual Culture in Contemporary Brazil.* Boston: Beacon Press.

———. 1993a. "After AIDS: Changes in (Homo)sexual Behaviour." In *Sexuality, Politics and AIDS in Brazil,* edited by Herbert Daniel and Richard Parker, 97–114. London: Falmer Press.

———. 1993b. "'Within Four Walls': Brazilian Sexual Culture and HIV/AIDS." In *Sexuality, Politics and AIDS in Brazil,* edited by Herbert Daniel and Richard Parker, 65–84. London: Falmer Press.

———. 1996a. "Behaviour in Latin American Men: Implications for HIV/AIDS Interventions." *International Journal of STD and AIDS* 7, Suppl. 2:62–65.

———. 1996b. "Empowerment, Community Mobilization, and Social Change in the Face of HIV/AIDS." *AIDS* 10, Suppl. 3:S27–S31.

———. 1999. *Beneath the Equator: Cultures of Desire, Male Homosexuality, and Emerging Gay Communities in Brazil.* New York: Routledge.

Parker, Richard G., Regina Maria Barbosa, and Peter Aggleton, eds. 2000. *Framing the Sexual Subject: The Politics of Gender, Sexuality and Power.* Berkeley and Los Angeles: University of California Press.

Parker, Richard G., and Manuel Carballo. 1990. "Qualitative Research on Homosexual and Bisexual Behavior Relevant to HIV/AIDS." *Journal of Sex Research* 27, no. 4:487–525.

Parker, Richard G., Delia Easton, and Charles H. Klein. 2000. "Structural Barriers and Facilitators in HIV Prevention: A Review of International Research." *AIDS* 14, Suppl. 1:S22–S32.

Parker, Richard G., Gilbert Herdt, and Manuel Carballo. 1991. "Sexual Culture, HIV Transmission, and AIDS Research." *Journal of Sex Research* 28, no. 1:77–98.

Patton, Cindy. 1989. "Resistance and the Erotic." In *AIDS: Social Representations and Social Practices,* edited by Peter Aggleton, Graham Hart, and Peter Davies, 237–51. New York: Falmer Press.

———. 1990. "What Science Knows: Formation of AIDS Knowledges." In *AIDS: Individual, Cultural and Policy Dimensions,* edited by Peter Aggleton, Peter Davies, and Graham Hart, 1–17. London: Falmer Press.

Paz, Octavio. 1985. *The Labyrinth of Solitude, The Other Mexico, Return to the Labyrinth of Solitude, Mexico and the United States, The Philanthropic Ogre.* Translated by Lysander Kemp, Yara Milos, and Rachel Phillips Belash. New York: Grove Press.

———. 1993. *La llama doble: Amor y erotismo.* México, D.F.: Editorial Seix Barral.

Pereyra, Guadalupe. 1992. "Caso PEMEX: SIDA y derechos humanos." *Sociedad y SIDA,* no. 27 (December): 1.

Pérez Franco, Lilia. 1988. "El Centro Nacional de Información de CONASIDA:

Entrevista con Gloria Ornelas." In *El SIDA en México: Los efectos sociales*, edited by Francisco Galván Díaz, 309–25. México, D.F.: Universidad Autónoma Metropolitana.

Plummer, Kenneth. 1981. "Homosexual Categories: Some Research Problems in the Labelling Perspective of Homosexuality." In *The Making of the Modern Homosexual*, edited by Kenneth Plummer, 53–75. London: Hutchinson.

———. 1982. "Symbolic Interactionism and Sexual Conduct." In *Human Sexual Relations*, edited by Mike Brake. New York: Pantheon.

Ponce, Dolores, Ana Irene Solórzano, and Antonio Alonso. 1990. "Lentas olas de sensualidad." In *El nuevo arte de amar*, edited by Sergio Bellinghausen, 13–35. México, D.F.: Cal y Arena.

Povinelli, Elizabeth A., and George Chauncey. 1999. "Thinking Sexuality Transnationally: An Introduction." *GLQ—A Journal of Lesbian and Gay Studies* 5, no. 4: 439–49.

Pratt, Marie Louise. 1986. "Fieldwork in Common Places." In *Writing Culture: The Poetics and Politics of Ethnography*, edited by James Clifford and George Marcus, 27–50. Berkeley and Los Angeles: University of California Press.

Preciado, Pedro. 1991. "ONG's contra el SIDA a debate." *Sociedad y SIDA*, no. 4 (January): 7.

Prieur, Annick. 1998. *Mema's House, Mexico City: On Transvestites, Queens, and Machos*. Chicago: University of Chicago Press.

Prieur, Annick, et al. 1990. "Gay Men: Reasons for Continued Practice of Unsafe Sex." Paper presented at the First European Conference on HIV and Homosexuality, Copenhagen. 1991: 13.

Ramírez, Jesus, et al. 1994. "AIDS Knowledge and Sexual Behavior among Mexican Gay and Bisexual Men." *AIDS Education and Prevention* 6, no. 2: 3163–74.

Ramos, Juanita, ed. 1987. *Compañeras: Latina Lesbians*. New York: Latina Lesbian History Project.

Ratcliffe, John, and Lawrence Wallack. 1985–86. "Primary Prevention in Public Health: An Analysis of Basic Assumptions." *International Quarterly of Community Health Education* 6, no. 3: 215–39.

Reyes, Alicia Yolanda. 1993. "EL VIH en Jalisco: ONG's y COESIDA." *Sociedad y SIDA*, no. 29 (February): 1.

Rhodes, Tim. 1994. "Outreach, Community Change and Community Empowerment: Contradiction for Public Health and Health Promotion." In *AIDS: Foundations for the Future*, edited by Peter Aggleton, Peter Davies, and Graham Hart, 48–64. London: Taylor and Francis.

Richardson, Diane. 1983–84. "The Dilemma of Essentiality in Homosexual Theory." *Journal of Homosexuality* 9, no. 2/3 (winter/spring): 79–90.

Rico, Blanca, Mario Bronfman, and Carlos del Río-Chiriboga. 1995. "Las Campañas contra el SIDA en México: ¿Los sonidos del silencio o puente sobre aguas turbulentas?" *Salud Pública de México* 37, no. 6: 643–53.

Riding, Alan. 1986. *Distant Neighbors: A Portrait of the Mexicans.* New York: Vintage Books.

Robledo Valencia, Luz Adriana. 1988. "Para mí fue un poco morir, casi el fin: Testimonio." In *El SIDA en México: Los efectos sociales,* edited by Francisco Galván Díaz, 183–90. México, D.F.: Universidad Autónoma Metropolitana.

Rofel, Lisa. 1999. "Qualities of Desire: Imagining Gay Identities in China." *GLQ— A Journal of Lesbian and Gay Studies* 5, no. 4: 451–74.

Rosas, Francisco. 1992. "Lecciones de trabajo comunitario." *Sociedad y SIDA,* no. 27 (December): 10.

Rosas, Francisco, and Juan Jacobo Hernández. 1992. "El SIDA y nuestra comunidad." *Sociedad y SIDA,* no. 24 (September): 6.

Rosenstock, Irwin M. 1974a. "Historical Origins of the Health Belief Model." *Health Education Monographs* 2, no. 4:328–35.

———. 1974b. "The Health Belief Model and Preventive Health Behavior." *Health Education Monographs* 2, no. 4:354–85.

Rosenstock, Irwin M., Victor J. Strecher, and Marshall H. Becker. 1988. "Social Learning Theory and the Health Belief Model." *Health Education Quarterly* 15, no. 2: 175–82.

Rubin, Gayle. 1984. "Thinking Sex: Notes for a Radical Theory of the Politics of Sexuality." In *Pleasure and Danger: Exploring Female Sexuality,* edited by Carole S. Vance, 267–319. Boston: Routledge and Kegan-Paul.

Schifter, Jacobo. 1989. *La formación de una contracultura: Homosexualismo y SIDA en Costa Rica.* San José: Ediciones Guaycán.

———. 1998. *Lila's House: Male Prostitution in Latin America.* New York: Harrington Park Press.

Sedgwick, Eve Kosofsky. 1990. *Epistemology of the Closet.* Berkeley and Los Angeles: University of California Press.

Sepúlveda, Jaime. 1993. "Prevención a través de la información y la educación: Experiencia en México." In *SIDA, su prevención a través de la educación: Una perspectiva mundial,* edited by Jaime Sepúlveda, Harvey Fineberg, and Jonathan Mann, 125–46. México, D.F.: Editorial el Manual Moderno.

Simon, William. 1973. "The Social, the Erotic, and the Sensual: The Complexities of Erotic Scripts." Paper presented at Nebraska Symposium on Motivation.

———. 1989. "Commentary on the Status of Sex Research: The Postmodernization of Sex." *Journal of Psychology and Human Sexuality* 2, no. 1:9–37.

———. 1996. *Postmodern Sexualities.* New York: Routledge.

Simon, William, and John Gagnon. 1986. "Sexual Scripts: Permanence and Change." *Archives of Sexual Behavior* 15, no. 2:97–120.

Sobo, Elisa J. 1995. *Choosing Unsafe Sex: AIDS-Risk Denial among Disadvantaged Women.* Philadelphia: University of Pennsylvania Press.

Sociedad y SIDA. 1991. "Policia de Zapopan: Luchar Contra el SIDA es Atentar a la Moral." *Sociedad y SIDA,* no. 4 (January): 15.

Stein, Arlene. 1989. "Three Models of Sexuality: Drives, Identities, and Practices." *Sociological Theory* 7, no. 1 : 1–13.

Strecher, Victor J., et al. 1986. "The Role of Self-efficacy in Achieving Health Behavior Change." *Health Education Quarterly* 13, no. 1 (spring): 73–92.

Taylor, Clark L. 1978. *"El Ambiente:* Male Homosexual Social Life in Mexico City." Ph.D. diss., University of California at Berkeley.

———. 1986. "Mexican Male Interaction in Public Context." In *The Many Faces of Homosexuality,* edited by Evelyn Blackwood, 117–36. New York: Harrington Park Press.

Terto, Jr., Veriano. 2000. "Male Homosexuality and Seropositivity: The Construction of Sexual Identities in Brazil." In *Framing the Sexual Subject,* edited by Richard Parker, Ana Maria Barbosa, and Peter Aggleton, 60–78. Berkeley and Los Angeles: University of California Press.

Tesh, Sylvia.1990. *Hidden Arguments: Politics, Ideology, and Disease Prevention Policy.* New Brunswick: Rutgers University Press.

Treichler, Paula. 1992. "AIDS, HIV, and the Cultural Construction of Reality." In *The Time of AIDS: Social Analysis, Theory, and Method,* edited by Gilbert Herdt and Shirley Lindenbaum, 65–98. Newbury Park, Calif.: Sage Publications.

UNAIDS/WHO. 1998. "Epidemiological Fact Sheet (June).

Universidad de Guadalajara." 1995. *Taller sobre estrategias para la prevención y control del VIH/SIDA: Informe final.* Typescript.

Uribe Zúñiga, Patricia, Carlos Magis Rodríguez, and Enrique Bravo García. 1998. "AIDS in Mexico." *Journal of the International Association of Physicians in AIDS Care,* (November). Full text posted at the IAPAC website, www.thebody.com/iapac/mexico/mexico.html, accessed on 3/29/00.

Valdespino Gómez, José Luis, and María de Lourdes García. 1991. "Epidemiología del SIDA en México: Logros y nuevos retos." *Sociedad y SIDA,* no. 14 (November): 8.

Watney, Simon. 1990. "Safer Sex as Community Practice." In *AIDS: Individual, Cultural and Policy Dimensions,* edited by Peter Aggleton, Peter Davies, and Graham Hart, 19–33. London: Falmer Press.

———. 1991. "AIDS, The Second Decade: Risk, Research and Modernity." In *AIDS: Responses, Interventions and Care,* edited by Peter Aggleton, Graham Hart, and Peter Davies, 1–18. London: Falmer Press.

———. 1993. "Emergent Sexual Identities and HIV/AIDS." In *AIDS: Facing the Second Decade,* edited by Peter Aggleton, Peter Davies, and Graham Hart, 13–27. London: Falmer Press.

Watts, Albert C., and Charles L. Breindel. 1981. "Health Education: Structural vs. Behavioral Perspectives." *Health Policy and Education* 2 : 47–57.

Weeks, Jeffrey. 1985. *Sexuality and Its Discontents.* London: Routledge and Kegan-Paul.

———. 1995. "History, Desire, and Identities." In *Conceiving Sexuality: Approaches to Sex Research in a Postmodern World,* edited by Richard G. Parker and John H. Gagnon, 33–50. New York: Routledge.

Wilson, Carter. 1995. *Hidden in the Blood: Personal Investigation of AIDS in the Yucatan.* New York: Columbia University Press.

Wohlfeiler, Dan. 1997. "Community Organizing and Community Building among Gay and Bisexual Men: The Stop AIDS Project." In *Community Organizing and Community Building for Health,* edited by Meredith Minkler, 230–43. New Brunswick: Rutgers University Press.

Index

Bastarde, Benoît, 341n.15
Bautista, Juan Carlos, 120, 124, 293
Beatriz (pseud.), 312; on masturbation,
    172; moderate sexual attitudes, 174; on
    sexual communication, 200; on sexual
    initiation, 187; on sexual passion, 194;
    on transition into sex, 187
Bell, Daniel, 177–78
Bellinghausen, Sergio, 8, 28, 293
Bisexuality: absence in gender-based catego-
    ries of sexual identity, 39; as a chosen
    sexual identity, 68–72
Bisexuals *(bisexuales)*, 39; attitudes toward,
    77; in contrast with heterosexuals with
    same-sex attraction, 85–90; identifica-
    tion of to avoid stigma of homosex-
    uality, 68; in object choice model of
    sexual classification, 62–63
Bodily communication. *See* Nonverbal
    sexual communication; Sexual
    communication
Bolton, Ralph, 341n.13
El Botanero, 117–18
Bourdieu, Pierre, 6, 34, 130, 170
Brazil, 17, 28, 333n.11, 337n.23
Brigadistas contra el SIDA (Rescue Workers
    against AIDS), 217
Bronfman, Mario, 9, 223, 224, 226
Brown, Richard, 336n.17
Buenas costumbres, 22
Buffington, Rob, 9, 60–61, 330n.18
Buga, 41–42, 328n.5
Buñuel, Luis, 150

Cable television, 157
Cáceres, Carlos F., 9
Candlelight marches, 222
Carballo, Manuel, 328n.4
Carballo-Diéguez, Alex, 9
Carmen (pseud.), 312; on barriers to safe
    sex, 257–58, 259; bisexuality, 66, 86–87,
    89; HIV/AIDS knowledge, 238; on sex
    education, 132; on sexual initiation, 191,
    192
Carrier, Joseph M., 8, 293, 302; on associa-
    tion between homosexuality and a re-
    ceptive style, 327n.3; concept of *interna-*

cional, 59, 330n.20; concepts of *activos/
    pasivos,* 39; on effects of gay liberation in
    Guadalajara, 123–24; on sexual silence,
    143–44; study of male homosexuality
    in Mexico, 24, 111; taxonomy of classi-
    fication of men with same-sex prefer-
    ences, 37
Carrillo, Héctor, 8
Casual sexual encounters, seeking of inti-
    macy within, 273–75. *See also* Sexual
    intimacy
Catholic church: effect on personal sexual
    ideologies, 165; limited effect on practi-
    cal decisions, 167; opposition to abor-
    tion and contraception, 166–71; opposi-
    tion to condoms, 241; opposition to
    adolescent masturbation, 171; opposi-
    tion to safe-sex campaigns, 218; position
    about sexuality, 166
Cedillo Nolasco, Rosa, 334n.1
Censorship, 165, 219
Chacalón, 264
Chancleras (sandal tappers), 53, 63
Chauncey, George, 64, 79–80, 125, 330n.1
CHECCOS (Humanitarian Committee of
    Shared Efforts against AIDS), 217, 230–
    33, 319
Chiapas, 170
Child development, modernizing discourse
    about, 172
Claudia (pseud.), 133, 168, 189, 312
Collectivist orientation, 285–86, 306
Communication: exception to rules of
    within families, 136–38; lack of within
    family about sexual matters, 132–33,
    304; and parental prohibitions, 138–39.
    See also Nonverbal sexual communica-
    tion; Sexual communication; Verbal
    communication
Community mobilization, 285
Community organizing, 285
Condoms: attitudes toward, 240–43,
    339n.4; black market in, 244; conserva-
    tive opposition to campaigns promoting,
    220; and loss of sexual satisfaction, 243;
    obtaining, 244–45; prevention of *en-
    trega,* 198; promotion of by HIV preven-

tion groups, 218; use of as information regarding state of relationship, 340n.9; verbal communication and, 340n.2. *See also* Safe sex

Confidentiality, 321

Consciousness raising, 285

Consejo Estatal del SIDA (COESIDA), State AIDS Council, 216–17, 220, 279, 297, 336n.16; free condoms, 244; self-censorship, 221, 222

Consejo Nacional de Prevención y Control del SIDA (CONASIDA), the National AIDS Council, 216–18, 338n.24; educational services, 221; evolution of messages, 223–24, 226–28; media campaign, 219, 221; national AIDS hotline, 221

Contraception, 102; attitudes toward, 166–67; impact of state on attitudes toward, 170–71, 301

Cornwell, Andrea, 329n.12

Cortés, Hernán, 21

Cortés Guardado, Marco Antonio, 156, 157, 167, 326n.7, 333n.5

Crawford, June, 206, 341n.14

Criollo, 21, 326n.8

Cristero War, 22

Cultural change: accelerated pace of some aspects, 298–300; and cultural hybridity, 292–95; hindering by internalized norms and values, 291–92; lack of in regard to abortion rights, 300–302; lack of in regard to sexual intimacy, 304–6; lack of questioning in some areas, 302–4; need for, 289–92; need for balancing in HIV/AIDS prevention work, 284–85, 308; and politics, 296–98; and public opinion, 295–96

Cultural hybridity, 15, 26–29, 80; and change, 292–95; and formation of Mexican sexual identities, 128; and sexual silence, 146

Cultural leaps, 299–300

Cultural scripts: concept of, 5–6, 334n.2; role in sexual partners' interpretations, 256; and trust, sex, and HIV prevention, 266, 268

Dalia (pseud.), 39, 166, 174, 312

Las Damas de Blanco (The Ladies in White), 220

"Dance of the 41 Faggots" ("El baile de los 41 maricones"), 17, 18, 326n.4

Daniel, Herbert, 9

Danzón, 100

Davies, Peter, 205, 340n.10

Dehesa, Germán, 158, 162

De La Cancela, Victor, 9

De la Torre, Ignacio, 18

Del Rio-Chiriboga, Carlos, 9, 223, 224, 226

Deviance (abnormality): notion of based on demeanor, 38, 39, 40, 53, 57–58; notion of based on sexual attraction, 61, 75, 85

DIATIB (Diagnosis, Treatment, and Biomedical Research Group), 217

Díaz, Porfirio, 18

Díaz, Rafael M., 9, 147–48, 149, 258, 339n.8

Discos gay (gay dance clubs), 111, 114–19, 297

Discussion groups, 317

Doble moral (double standards), 42,102, 108

Döring, M. Teresa, 8, 328n.7, 332n.2

Double lives: and disclosure of bisexuality, 71, 77; and disclosure of homosexuality, 67, 77, 84, 120, 123, 124–28, 292

Dowsett, Gary W., 32–33, 207, 332n.6

Ecstasy, 194–95, 206, 207–8

Eduardo (pseud.), 88–89, 195, 201, 312

Elena (pseud.), 103–4, 152, 195, 200–204, 312

Elisa (pseud.), 195, 197, 312

Ema (pseud.), 49–51, 92–93, 105–6, 310, 312, 329n.12

Enlace, 219, 224

Enrique (pseud.), 312; changes in personal situation, 298, 310; distinction between passionate sex and safe sex, 198–99; gay identity, 120–21; trust and love issues and safe sex, 271–72

Entrega, 193–94, 198

Epstein, Steven, 31, 33

Ernesto (pseud.), 64, 76, 187–88, 313

Homosexuality: and HIV/AIDS, 110, 213, 215, 227; in the media, 157, 159, 161, 299–300, 333 n.4; normalization of, 125, 298–300; personal theories of the etiology of, 74–78, 81; and rapid cultural change, 298–300

Homosexual life in Guadalajara, 110–28; constraints on disclosure for middle-class gays, 124–28; crafting individual gay identities, 120–23; emulation of U.S. styles, 115–16; encompassing of male diversity, 114–15; gay communities and identity politics, 123–28; generational shifts, 118–19; "more Mexican" drinking spaces, 117–18; and organization of urban space, 111–20

Homosexual Pride Liberation Group (GHOL), 13–15, 123, 217

Homosexuals: adjectives used to describe, 76; advantages of being, 65–68; gender-based classification of, 56–59; gender roles, sexual, 52–56; object choice classification of, 61–65; opposition to organized efforts to confront *homofobia*, 292; organizing efforts to combat HIV/AIDS, 217; as *pasivo*, 80–82; self-identification, 64; use of term, 325 n.1

Identity: bisexual, 68–72; formation, 32–33; gay, 67; heterosexual, 64–65; homosexual, 65–68; lesbian, 66–67; normal, 39–42

Identity politics, 123–28

Ignacio (pseud.), 126, 135, 152, 313

Inculcation, 138–39

Los inestables (Alberto Teruel), 18–19

Internacional (international), 59, 63, 64, 262

International Lesbian and Gay Association (ILGA), 13–15, 331 n.3

Internet, 294

Interpersonal scripting, 206

Interview participants, description of, 311–16. *See also specific pseudonyms*

Interviews, 8, 317, 318–19

Intimacy. *See* Sexual intimacy

Intrapsychic scripting, 206

Isabel (pseud.), 64–65, 201, 313

Islas Marías, 20

Ismael (pseud.), 202, 241, 314

Ivette (pseud.), 169, 175, 177, 201, 314

Izazola, José Antonio, 8

Jackson, Peter A., 342 n.5

Jalador, 57

Jalisco, 22, 157, 215, 296–97, 335 n.7

Javier (pseud.), 314; on gender and sexual roles, 44–45, 51; HIV/AIDS knowledge, 237; on masturbation, 172–73; on sexual communication, 202; on sexual initiation, 185; on sexual passion, 194; on transition into sex, 188, 189

Jotos/Jotitos, 18, 57, 63, 83, 326 n.6, 329 n.13, 330 n.2, 342 n.2

Juan (pseud.), 53–56, 64, 83, 270–71, 314

Judith (pseud.), 122–23, 145, 198, 314

Julio (pseud.), 145–46, 166, 278–79, 314

Kahlo, Frida, 21

Kendall, Carl, 341 n.14

"Killing the moment," 198, 199, 260

Kippax, Susan, 206, 341 n.14

Kulick, Don, 9

The Labyrinth of Solitude (Octavio Paz), 23, 24, 25, 42

Lancaster, Roger, 9, 28

Lesbians, 15, 62, 63, 66, 67, 111; negative attitudes about organizing, 127; organizing, 86; socializing, 19, 111, 112, 116

LeVine, Sarah, 8; on machismo, 23, 25; study of women and social change, 99–100, 293–94, 332 n.3, 342 n.1

Ligue, 111, 112

Liguori, Ana Luisa, 9

Lindisfarne, Nancy, 329 n.12

Locas, 64, 84

Lola (pseud.), 101–3, 314; on abortion, 169; on gender and sexual roles, 48; on safe sex vs. other relational needs, 277–78; on sex education, 135; on sexual initiation, 186; on transition into sex, 187, 189

Loquita, 52, 56

Lorde, Audre, 196, 334 n.4

Love: as justification for sex, 187; "real,"

266; socially determined, 266–67; and trust, 266–72

Low ends (*"Los bajos fondos"*), 25, 26

Ludwig, Dominique, 260

Lugar gay, 115

Lumsden, Ian, 8

Machismo: culture of, 10, 19–20; legacy of, 23–25; rejection of by younger married men, 98–99; and separation between high and low worlds, 25; union with *mexicanidad*, 23; view of women, 24; women's complicity in reproduction of, 99–100

*Machorra*s (tomboys), 24, 38, 39, 53

Magis Rodríguez, Carlos, 215, 335 n.3, 336 n.10, 336 n.11

Male strip shows, 295

Mandilón, 99, 100, 342 n.1

Manflora, 63, 331 n.3

Marcela (pseud.), 314; bisexuality, 87–88, 89; on sexual communication, 203, 204; on sexual passion, 196

Margo, Glen Elgin, 336 n.17

Mariachi, 10, 22, 244–45

Maria (pseud.), 39–40, 314

Maricones, 19, 25, 38, 57, 327 n.3, 329 n.13, 342 n.2

Mario (pseud.), 65–66, 121–22, 134–35, 315

Martha (pseud.), 315; on abortion, 168; effect of gender role expectations on behavior, 264–65, 304; HIV/AIDS knowledge, 236–37; self-sacrifice, 268–69; on sexual initiation, 185–86; on sexual silence, 144–45; on transition into sex, 189

Martínez López, Juana, 231, 232

Masturbation: adolescent, 135, 136, 171–72; adult, 172–73, 236

Matacuras, 22

Mayates, 57, 90, 331 n.4, 342 n.2

Media. *See* Radio; Television

El medio, 67. See also *El ambiente*

Men: according to Mexican machismo, 23; *bisexuales*, 62, 68–72; contemporary gay identities, 120–22; contemporary heterosexual identities, 106–10; effeminate,

38; in Gutmann's study, 98–99; *heterosexuales*, 62; *homosexuales/gays*, 62, 63–64; hybrid identities of, 80–84, 85, 88–90, 90–96; inequality of with women, 42–52; initiating sex between, 190–92; in the media, 160–63, 298–300; normal, 38, 56–59. *See also* Machismo

Mendoza, Vicente, 23

Mestizo, 21, 22, 326 n.9

Methodology, 317–24; data recording and analysis, 321–22; discussion groups, 320–21; generating data, 317–18; individual interviews, 318–19; limitations, 323–24; participant observation, 317, 319–20; reliance on narratives about the past, 322–23

Mexican Altiplano, 9

Mexicanidad (Mexicanness), 10; postrevolutionary notions of, 20–23; tensions with modernity, 26–29, 309; union with machismo, 23

Mexican Revolution, sexualization of the country, 19–20

Mexican sexual culture. *See* Sexual culture

Mexico City, 9, 215, 297, 310

Mexico City earthquake, 217

Miguel (pseud.), 94–95, 315

Millán, Alfonso, 60

Mirada de mujer, 158–62, 295, 298

Miriam (pseud.), 91–92, 104–6, 315

Mitchell, Stephen A., 183, 279, 280, 328 n.8

Modern, use of term in Mexico, 15–16

Modernity: and intimacy in the Mexican context, 305–6; and need for sense of identity, 32; and reflexivity, 293; and reinterpretation of tradition, 96, 292

Mónica's, 114–15

Monsiváis, Carlos, 57; on effect of Mexican Revolution on sexuality, 19–20; on emergence of homosexual subculture, 17–18; on influence of Europe on Mexico, 16; on influence of modern values, 27–28; on lifestyles associated with being a *maricón* or *joto*, 329 n.13; on rigid classifications of homosexuals, 58; on union of machismo and *mexicanidad*, 23; on U.S. influence on Mexico, 20

Morales Delgadillo, Aurora, 334n.1
Moreno, Hortencia, 24, 138, 332n.4
Movimiento feminista, 170, 291–92
Mujeres, but also gay, 83–84
Mujeres heterosexuales, 62
Mujeres/mujeres normales, 38, 88
Murray, Stephen O., 37, 323

Nationalism: based on original cultures, 21; based on preservation of traditions, 21–22; new forms of, 20–21
Negotiated risk, 246
NGO Abrazo, 229
Nicaragua, 28
Noche de faldas (skirts night), 115–16
Nongovernmental AIDS organizations, 217–18, 221, 336n.16; free condoms, 244; Guadalajara, 222; Jalisco, 297; Mexico City, 221
Nonverbal sexual communication, 194, 199–201, 250, 273, 304; in HIV prevention work, 256, 284
Normal *(normales):* but also heterosexual, 84–85; as a contemporary sexual identity, 39–42; in object-choice model of sexual identity, 63, 65; passing as, 56–59; in sex/gender model of sexual identity, 37–39
Novaro, María, 100
Novo, Salvador, 16–17, 18

Obvio (Obvias), 84, 249
Ojos tapatíos, 10, 325n.3
Olga (pseud.), 315; flexible sexual attitudes, 177; on homosexuality, 76–77; on masturbation, 172–73; on rationality during sex, 197
Los olvidados, 150
Ornelas, Gloria, 226
Osvaldo (pseud.), 67–68, 260–66, 273, 315

Pablo (pseud.), 315; on casual sexual encounters, 273; on communion with sexual partner, 207; effect of sexual role on risky behavior, 263–65; intuitive risk assessment, 251–52; on obtaining con-

doms, 244; on tension between sexual passion and safe sex, 258–59
Paiva, Vera, 9, 285–86
Panamerican Health Organization (PAHO), 216
Parker, Richard G., 9, 17, 28, 286, 328n.4, 333n.11
Parte blanca, 21
Participant observation, 8, 317, 319–20
Partido Acción Nacional (PAN), 219, 296–98
Partido Revolucionario Institucional (PRI), 158, 296–98
Pasivos, 24, 39, 55, 64, 327n.3; but also gay, 83–84; homosexuals as, 80–82
Patlatonalli, 127, 217
Paz, Octavio: classification of identities and sexual roles in Mexico, 37; on double role of sexual passion in Mexican culture, 195; *The Labyrinth of Solitude,* 23, 24, 25, 42; poetic language in describing erotic, 182; reference to *albures,* 151
Pedro (pseud.), 315; on abortion, 169; on normality, 41; on sex education, 135; on sexual passion, 193
PEMEX, 335n.1
Piapid, 220, 241
Piropos, 53
La Pitaya Yeye, 162–65
Planificar la familia, 166
Plaza del Sol, 10
Plummer, Kenneth, 32, 33
Poetic language, and description of erotic, 182
Politics, and cultural change, 296–98
Ponse, Barbara, 32
Porfirian era, 16, 21
Posada, José Guadalupe, 18
Positivism, 17
Postmodernism, 294
Power: arbitrary, 23; differential between sexual partners, 304–5; differential between sexual partners and HIV risk, 265–66; inequalities of in male-female relations, 48–56, 184, 304–5
Preciado, Pedro, 113, 297, 331n.3
Pre-Columbian history, 21

Prieur, Annick, 8, 83; on functions of *piropos*, 53; interviews with *mayates*, 330 n.17, 342 n.2; on machismo, 25; on social change, 294
Proscriptive messages, 138–39, 153
Prostitution, 19
ProVida (Prolife), 171, 219
Public health. *See* HIV/AIDS prevention work
Public opinion, and cultural change, 295–96
Puerto Vallarta, AIDS cases in 1994, 215

Radio: impact on cultural attitudes, 333 n.2; impact on sexual attitudes, 156–57; *La Pitaya Yeye*, 162–65
Radio Universidad, 162
Rafael (pseud.), 93–94
Ramírez, Jesus, 8
Ramiro (pseud.), 315; attitudes toward condoms, 243; on contraception, 166–67; HIV/AIDS knowledge, 237; on normality, 40; on sexual communication, 200
Ramos, Juanita, 9
Rationality versus spontaneity: in AIDS prevention messages, 198–99, 205, 281; in sexual scripting, 197–99
Raúl (pseud.), 52–56, 83, 315
"Real" love, 266
Reflection, and HIV prevention, 308. *See also* Self-reflection
Relational: issues and struggles, 279; needs competing with HIV prevention measures, 277–79
Remigio (pseud.), 184–85, 200, 315
Renata (pseud.), 189, 315
René (pseud.), 135, 234–36, 315
Rico, Blanca, 9, 223, 224, 226
Riding, Alan, 327 n.13, 333 n.1, 333 n.2
Risk, modern concept of, 341 n.14
Risk assessment, intuitive, 245–53, 273
Risk taking, association with sexual pleasure, 279–81
Rivera, Diego, 21
Rodrigo (pseud.), 90, 316
Role, effect of perceptions of on HIV risky behavior, 260–66

Rosaldo, Renato, 326 n.3
Rosario (pseud.), 186, 316
Rosasco, Ana M., 9
Rubén (pseud.), 190, 316
Rubin, Gayle, 326 n.2
Rules of the game, 6, 206
Ruth (pseud.), 316; on abortion, 168; on sexual communication, 202; on sexual initiation, 192; on sexual passion, 194; on sexual silence, 140–44

Safe sex: barriers against, 257–58, 259; distinction between passionate sex and, 198–99, 258–59; docility toward in sexual encounters, 276–77; effect of role perceptions on behavior, 260–63; trust and love issues and, 271–72; vs. other relational needs, 277, 281. *See also* Condoms
Sandoval Iñiguez, Juan, 241
San Francisco AIDS Foundation, 245, 341 n.16
Schifter, Jacobo, 9
Seduction, 181
Self-efficacy, 230, 285, 336 n.18
Self-empowerment, 230, 285
Self-reflection: collective, 285–86; promoting, 283–84, 285. *See also* Reflection
Self-sacrifice, and trust and love issues, 267, 268–70
Sepúlveda, Jaime, 219, 226
Serenatas (serenades), 244–45
Ser Humano-Guadalajara, 217, 218, 338 n.27
Sex: as altered state, 183, 194, 204–8; casual, seeking of intimacy within, 273–75; defined, 325 n.2; inability to talk frankly about, 332 n.1, 332 n.2; intimacy, nature of, 304–6; as refuge, 306; relational functions of, 277–81; transition into, 187–90. *See also* Sexual moment; Sexual passion
Sex education, 132–39, 152, 153; and HIV prevention education, 224, 254, 286
Sexual attitudes: flexibility and, 176–79; impact of radio and television on, 156–65; moderate, 173–76

Sexual communication: assumptions about in HIV prevention work, 152–53, 204, 246–47, 253, 267; effect of sexual silence on, 148–49; fragility of, 260; in HIV prevention programs, 286; and HIV risk assessment, 246–47; nonverbal, bodily, 199–201, 304, 305; outside the sexual space, 203–4; verbal communication as enhancer, 201–2; verbal communication as means for refusal, 202–3, 252. See also *Los albures* (sexual joking)

Sexual culture: changes in perceptions of manhood and womanhood, 98–101; dominance by traditional values, 293, 309; evolution of during 20th century, 15; external influences on, 16–21; future of, 308–10; history of homosexual subculture, 17–20; need for change, 289–92; use of as HIV prevention tool, 284–85

Sexual discomfort, 149

Sexual identities: amalgams and convolutions, 79–96; concept of, 31–33; defined by perceptions of family and belonging, 124–28; gender-based model of, 37–39, 63, 65, 84–85; labels, 33–35, 39, 95; *normal* as a contemporary identity, 39–42; object-choice model of, 62–65, 85; self-reflection about, 96

Sexual initiation, 183–92; between man and woman, 184–87; between men, 190–92

Sexual intimacy: instant, 273–75; permanence of, 304–6

Sexuality, defined, 325 n.2

Sexual joking *(los albures)*, 150–53, 164

Sexual molestation, of children, 135–36

Sexual moment: explaining in words, 182–83, 204; staging of, 206–7; two contrasting views of, 255–57

Sexual passion, 193–97; as inhibitor of rationality, 197–99; safe sex vs., 198–99, 258–59; and spontaneity, 257–60; suffering as price of, 195–96

Sexual positions, and perceptions of "common" women, 44–45

Sexual roles: classification of, 37; effect of

perceptions of, on risky behavior, 260–66; lack of change in inequality of, 304–6; traditional, 42–48

Sexual scripting, 130, 192–204, 206; rationality versus spontaneity, 197–99; sexual passion and, 193–97; theory of, 95

Sexual silence, 132, 139–50, 151, 153; and cultural hybridity, 146; effect on communication with sexual partners, 148–49; family perspective, 140–44; as foundation of traditional management of sexuality in Mexico, 139–40; and HIV prevention work, 284; individual's perspective, 144–47; price of, 147–50; as stigma management, 140–44

Sexual socialization, 2, 5, 129–30, 131–32, 184, 332 n.6; gender-based differences in, 192; parental prohibitions, 138–39; sex education, 132–39, 152, 153; sexual joking *(los albures)* and, 150–53, 164; sexual silence and, 132, 139–50

Sexual spontaneity, 197–99. *See also* Spontaneity

Shame, 149

Shared meanings, 206

Show travesti, 82, 114, 115, 116–17

Simon, William, 5; on cultural scenarios, 334 n.2; on experience of sexual self, 334 n.4; on poetry of sex, 182; on sexual communion, 207; on the sexual moment, 183; on sexual scripts, 130, 206

Single motherhood, 19

Soap operas, 158–62, 333 n.3. See also *Telenovelas*

Sobo, Elisa J., 340 n.7

Social cognitive theory, 225, 230

Social life, secularization of, 20

Socially determined love, 266–67

Social marketing techniques, 222–24

Social modeling, 337 n.19

S.O.S., 116–17

Spontaneity: in flow of sex, 197–99, 255, 304, 306, 307; in friendships and relationships, 306; sexual passion and, 207, 257–60

Stages of change model, 225

State, impact on attitudes toward contraception and abortion, 170–71

STOP AIDS Project, 341 n.16

Strategies, 6, 34

Suffering, as price of sexual passion, 195–96

Sumisas (submissive), 101

Talk radio, 162–65

El Taller, 115–16

Tapatíos, 10, 325 n.3

Taylor, Clark L., 8, 18, 19; classification of men with same-sex interest, 37; concept of *activos/pasivos,* 39; concept of *internacional,* 59; on social collusion regarding homosexuality, 142; on undesirability of separate homosexual society, 124

Telenovelas, 158–62, 295, 298, 301, 303–4, 333 n.4, 342 n.6. *See also* Soap operas

Televisa, 157, 158

Television: impact on cultural attitudes, 333 n.1; impact on sexual attitudes, 155–65, 295–96; *Mirada de Mujer,* 158–62, 295, 298; *La vida en el espejo,* 37, 298–300, 303–4, 333 n.4

Televisión Azteca, 157, 158, 299

TelSIDA, 221

Terto, Veriano, Jr., 9, 265

Teruel, Alberto: *Los inestables,* 18–19

Thailand, 342 n.5

Theory of reasoned action, 225

Tortilleras (tortilla patters), 24, 53, 84

Traditional, use of term in Mexico, 15–16

Trust, 266–76; and affronts to fidelity, 272; and instant intimacy, 273–75; and safe sex, 266; trust-love connection, 266–72

Universal, 19

Usabiaga, Luis, 163–65

Verbal communication: assumptions about in HIV/AIDS prevention work, 228, 233, 252, 340 n.2; HIV risk assessment and, 246–47; as means for refusal, 202–3, 252; as sexual enhancer, 201–2

La vida en el espejo, 37, 298–300, 303–4, 333 n.4

Virginity, 45, 133

Watney, Simon, 183

Weatherburn, Peter, 205, 340 n.10

Weeks, Jeffrey, 32, 33

Wilde, Oscar, 17

Wilson, Carter, 9

Women: according to Mexican machismo, 24; *bisexuales,* 62; complicity in reproduction of machismo, 99–100; contemporary gay identities, 122–23; contemporary heterosexual identities, 101–6; "giving in," 189; *heterosexuales,* 62; hybrid identities of, 85–88, 89–90; inequality of in Mexico, 48–56; *lesbianas,* 62, 63; in LeVine's study, 99–100; managed and controlled sexuality, 185; masculine, 38; in the media, 158–162; normal, 38; reputations, 186; sexual socialization, 138–39; in the workforce, 328 n.10

World AIDS Day, 222

World Health Organization, 216